Sonic Flux

SONIC FLUX

SOUND, ART, AND METAPHYSICS

Christoph Cox

THE UNIVERSITY OF CHICAGO PRESS
CHICAGO AND LONDON

The University of Chicago Press, Chicago 60637
The University of Chicago Press, Ltd., London

For more information, contact the University of Chicago Press, 1427 E. 60th St., Chicago, IL 60637.
Published 2018
Printed in the United States of America

27 26 25 24 23 22 21 20 19 18 1 2 3 4 5

ISBN-13: 978-0-226-54303-1 (cloth)
ISBN-13: 978-0-226-54317-8 (paper)
ISBN-13: 978-0-226-54320-8 (e-book)
DOI: https://doi.org/10.7208/chicago/9780226543208.001.0001

LIBRARY OF CONGRESS CATALOGING-IN-PUBLICATION DATA

Names: Cox, Christoph, 1965– author.
Title: Sonic flux : sound, art, and metaphysics / Christoph Cox.
Description: Chicago ; London : The University of Chicago Press, 2018. | Includes bibliographical references and index.
Identifiers: LCCN 2018015041 | ISBN 9780226543031 (cloth : alk. paper) | ISBN 9780226543178 (pbk. : alk. paper) | ISBN 9780226543208 (e-book)
Subjects: LCSH: Music—Philosophy and aesthetics. | Soundscapes (Music)—Philosophy and aesthetics. | Sound (Philosophy) | Sound installations (Art) | Metaphysics.
Classification: LCC ML3877.C77 2018 | DDC 534—dc23
LC record available at https://lccn.loc.gov/2018015041

⊗ This paper meets the requirements of ANSI/NISO Z39.48–1992 (Permanence of Paper).

FOR MY PARENTS

Christa Begemann Cox

AND

James D. Cox

CONTENTS

ACKNOWLEDGMENTS

Written over many years, *Sonic Flux* was made possible through the generosity, wisdom, camaraderie, and support of a great many people. The book took shape through a series of talks at academic and art spaces throughout the United States and Europe. I thank the audiences at those events and especially my hosts at the Museum of Contemporary Photography, Chicago (Natasha Hollins Egan); the University of California, San Diego (Ben Piekut, Jerry Balzano); Wesleyan University (Ron Kuivila); the Henry Art Gallery, Seattle (Sara Krajewski, Fionn Meade); the University of South Florida Contemporary Art Museum (Preston Poe, Robert Lawrence, Alexa Favata); Bryn Mawr College (Michael Krausz); the University of Copenhagen (Erik Granly, Søren Møller Sørenson, Torben Sangild, Brandon LaBelle); Yale University (Seth Kim-Cohen); the University of Amsterdam (Tereza Havelková); the MATA Festival (Christopher McIntyre, Missy Mazzoli); Aarhus University (Ansa Lønstrup); the Academy of Fine Arts Vienna (Diedrich Diederichsen, Constanze Ruhm); Kill Your Timid Notion Festival, Dundee (Barry Esson, Bryony McIntyre); Project Arts Centre, Dublin (Jennifer Walshe); Rensselaer Polytechnic Institute (Michael Century, Mary Anne Staniszewski); Amherst College (Jason Robinson); The Public School, New York City (Jeanne Dreskin, Alexander Provan); ISSUE Project Room (Lawrence Kumpf); New York University (Nina Katchadourian); Notam, Oslo (Notto Thelle, Jøran Rudi); the School of the Art Institute of Chicago (Lou Mallozzi); the Swiss Institute, New York (Piper Marshall); Dia:Beacon (Kelly Kivland); the Whitney Museum of American Art (Margie Weinstein, Christian Marclay); City University of New York (Claire Bishop, Meredith Mowder); the Art & Law Program (Sergio Muñoz Sarmiento); Goethe-Universität, Frankfurt (Bernd Herzogenrath); Tuned City Brussels (Raviv Ganchrow, Julia Eckhardt); the Museum of Modern Art, New York (Barbara London, Leora Morinis); the Center for Experimental Lectures (Gordon Hall); the New Museum of Contemporary Art (Alicia Ritson, Johanna Burton, Lauren Cornell); the

California College of the Arts (Leigh Markopoulos, Brian Conley); the Vera List Center for Art and Politics (Anne Barlow, Kristen Chappa, Lindsey Berfond); Brown University (Nathan Lee, Tony Cokes); Barnes Foundation (Katherine Skovira, Robert Whalen); the University of California, Berkeley (Jessica Ruffin, Paul Joseph Hoehn); and the Subtropics Festival, Miami (Gustavo Matamoros, Natalia Zuluaga).

Conversations and exchanges with friends, colleagues, scholars, and artists have been tremendously valuable in shaping my ideas and arguments. Special thanks to Seth Kim-Cohen for years of spirited discussion. Ed Dimendberg offered wise counsel and steadfast encouragement. Dan Smith provided expert elucidation of central Deleuzian concepts and arguments. Risha Lee at the Rubin Museum guided me through important aspects of South Asian sonic metaphysics. Cindy Keefer at the Center for Visual Music clarified aspects of Oskar Fischinger's work. Hauke Harder suggested alternative readings of several pieces by Alvin Lucier. John Gunther at Hampshire College provided extraordinary media support. Many others contributed helpful ideas and encouragement, among them Keith Ansell-Pearson, Johanna Burton, Ann Butler, Seth Cluett, Nic Collins, Tony Cokes, Brian Conley, Kira de Coudres, Charles Eppley, Luke Fowler, Jennie Gottschalk, David Grubbs, Jenny Jaskey, Branden Joseph, Galen Joseph-Hunter, Doug Kahn, Brian Kane, Nina Katchadourian, Matt Krefting, Chris Kubick, Christina Kubisch, Sanford Kwinter, Brandon LaBelle, Francisco López, Suhail Malik, Leigh Markopoulos, Gustavo Matamoros, Fionn Meade, Julie Beth Napolin, Paul O'Neill, Jenny Perlin, Ben Piekut, Monique Roelofs, Marina Rosenfeld, Aura Satz, Carsten Seiffarth, Mary Simpson, Åsa Stjerna, Jeannine Tang, David Toop, Stephen Vitiello, Salomé Voegelin, Jeff Wallen, Jennifer Walshe, Gregory Whitehead, and Neil Young.

Sincere thanks to Susan Bielstein and James Toftness, my editors at the University of Chicago Press, for their enthusiastic support of this project and expert guidance. I also thank the anonymous reviewers for the press whose careful reading and wise suggestions made this a better book, and Barbara Norton, who meticulously copyedited the manuscript.

I have learned much from students in my "Audio Culture," "Sonic Philosophy," and "Sonic Turn" courses at Hampshire College and the Center for Curatorial Studies, Bard College, and from my colleague Dan Warner, with whom I have taught "Audio Culture" for years.

For inviting me to guest-curate sound-based exhibitions, I thank Debra Singer and Matthew Lyons at The Kitchen; Toby Kamps at the Museum of

Contemporary Arts Houston; Sandra Percival at New Langton Arts; Regine Basha at No Longer Empty; Annie Gawlak at G Fine Art; Bradley McCallum at the Brick + Mortar International Video Art Festival; and Julian Navarro at CONTEXT Art Miami. I also thank the many artists who generously shared their work with me, among them Olivia Block, Manon de Boer, Jens Brand, Maria Chavez, Mike Dunford, Richard Garet, Andy Graydon, Florian Hecker, Ernst Karel, Seth Kim-Cohen, Jacob Kirkegaard, Anne Walsh, Annea Lockwood, Alvin Lucier, Christian Marclay, Mattin, Jake Meginsky, Angel Nevarez and Valerie Tevere, Carsten Nicolai, Pauline Oliveros, Lee Patterson, Michael Pisaro, Mathias Poledna, Éliane Radigue, Lis Rhodes, Billy Roisz, Steve Roden, Julian Rosefeldt, Stefan Rummel, Robert Sember, Wadada Leo Smith, Jan-Peter E. R. Sonntag, and Jana Winderen.

I am also grateful to Hampshire College deans Norm Holland, Jeff Wallen, Sura Levine, and Eva Rueschemann for granting faculty development funding to support my research. Of the many people who facilitated my image research, I offer special thanks to Bill Dietz at the Maryanne Amacher Archive; Silvia Neuhaus at the Estate of Max Neuhaus; Ernst Karel and Kendra McLaughlin at the Sensory Ethnography Lab; Annea Lockwood and Mimi Johnson; Carl Testa and Kyoko Kitamura at the Tri-Centric Foundation; Gisela Gronemeyer at MusikTexte; Rebekah Morin at the Milwaukee Art Museum; and Jonathan Hiam at the New York Public Library.

Earlier drafts, portions, and fragments of chapters were published along the way. I thank their publishers for allowing me to incorporate this material into *Sonic Flux*: "Lost in Translation: Sound in the Discourse of Synaesthesia," *Artforum* (October 2005); "Nietzsche, Dionysus, and the Ontology of Music," in *A Companion to Nietzsche*, ed. Keith Ansell-Pearson (Malden, MA: Blackwell, 2005); "Von Musik zum Klang: Sein als Zeit in der Klangkunst," in *Sonambiente Berlin 2006: Klang Kunst Sound Art*, ed. Helga de la Motte-Haber, Matthias Osterwold, and Georg Weckwerth (Heidelberg: Kehrer Verlag, 2006); "Every Sound You Can Imagine," in *Every Sound You Can Imagine* [exhibition catalog], Contemporary Arts Museum Houston, October 3–December 7, 2008; "Sound Art and the Sonic Unconscious," *Organised Sound* 14, no. 1 (April 2009); "Installing Duration: Time in the Sound Works of Max Neuhaus," in *Max Neuhaus*, ed. Lynne Cooke (New York: Dia Art Foundation, 2009); "The Breaks," *Christian Marclay: Festival* 3 (New York: Whitney Museum of American Art, 2010); "Beyond Representation and Signification: Toward a Sonic Materialism," *Journal of Visual Culture* 10, no. 2 (August 2011); "The Alien Voice: Alvin Lucier's

North American Time Capsule 1967," in *Mainframe Experimentalism: Early Computing and the Foundations of the Digital Arts*, ed. Hannah B. Higgins and Douglas Kahn (Berkeley and Los Angeles: University of California Press, 2012); "Music, Noise, and Abstraction," in *Inventing Abstraction 1910–1925*, ed. Leah Dickerman (New York: Museum of Modern Art, 2012); "Sonic Philosophy," *Artpulse* 16 (2013); and "Seeing Is Not Hearing: Synaesthesia, Anaesthesia, and the Audio/Visual," in *Art or Sound*, ed. Germano Celant (Venice: Fondazione Prada/Ca' Corner della Regina, 2014).

Finally, I express my deepest gratitude to my family for their unfailing support, generosity, humor, and patience: to my parents, Christa and Jim, and stepparents, Stan and Ritsuko; my sister, Lara, and brother-in-law, Matt; my lovely, ever-amazing, and sonically adventurous kids Lukas, Tristan, Livia, and Aengus; and, above all, my partner in all things, Molly, whose vitality, intelligence, and creativity sustain me.

INTRODUCTION

In the summer of 1979 New York City's experimental arts center The Kitchen mounted a festival titled "New Music, New York." The weeklong program presented performances by Philip Glass, Meredith Monk, Tony Conrad, George Lewis, and Laurie Anderson, among others, and marked the coming-of-age of minimalist and experimental music. In the spring of 2004, The Kitchen and a host of other New York arts institutions celebrated the twenty-fifth anniversary of that event with a festival titled "New Sound, New York," billed as "a citywide festival of performances, installations and public dialogues featuring new works by sound artists who are exploring fresh connections across music, architecture and the visual arts."[1] The shift in title—from "Music" to "Sound"—is emblematic, for, over the past several decades, "music" has lost its monopoly on the field of sonic art, becoming a subcategory within the broader field of "sound," the subject of increasing cultural fascination. Not only has "sound art" emerged as a prominent form of art making and exhibition embraced by galleries and museums across the globe, but the academy has also witnessed the rapid rise of "sound studies" within and across disciplines in the humanities and social sciences.[2] In the field of music itself, composers, producers, and improvisers have become increasingly attracted to those sonic domains against which music has always defined itself: noise, silence, and nonmusical sound.

This book aims to come to terms with this sonic turn in the arts and culture and, more specifically, to conceptualize sound art as a practice situated between and beyond music and the visual arts. Though historical considerations play an important role, my project is primarily philosophical, an effort to think conceptually about sound, noise, and silence in the sonic arts—and in the so-called visual arts as well. I want not only to think philosophically about sound, but also to ask how sound can alter or inflect philosophy. What concepts and forms of thought does sound affirm, provoke, or generate? How does sonic thinking challenge the ontologies and epistemologies that prevail in our ordinary and philosophical thinking? And how does sound unsettle the established purviews of art-historical and curatorial consideration? These are some of the questions that resonate in the chapters that follow.

Central to the book is the concept of the *sonic flux*, that is, the notion of sound as an immemorial material flow to which human expressions contribute but that precedes and exceeds those expressions. This concept is gleaned from key philosophical and theoretical texts from the late nineteenth century on and resonates throughout the history of experimental sonic practices in the twentieth and twenty-first centuries. With the invention of the phonograph in 1877, Thomas Edison unwittingly disclosed, and submitted to aesthetic attention, a world of sound beyond music and speech, for this mechanical contraption registered with equal facility and made ontologically equivalent not only the articulate sounds phonographers aimed to record, but also the noises of the environment, and the hum, hiss, and crackle of the apparatus itself. The impact of this discovery is evident in the noise studies of Luigi Russolo, Edgard Varèse, and Pierre Schaeffer in the first half of the twentieth century; in John Cage's landmark composition *4′33″* from 1952; in the "gradual processes" of minimalist composition and the drone installations of La Monte Young, Éliane Radigue, Max Neuhaus, Alvin Lucier, and Maryanne Amacher in the 1960s, '70s, and beyond; in R. Murray Schafer's notion of the soundscape and the practices of field recording it inspired; in the emergence of ambient and noise musics during the 1970s and '80s; in the pulverization of meaning and the affirmation of linguistic materiality pursued by sound poets from the Futurists and Dadaists through the Lettrists, Henri Chopin, Bernard Heidsieck, Steve McCaffery, and Christian Bök; and in the varied practices of prominent contemporary sound artists such as Christina Kubisch, Francisco López, Jacob Kirkegaard, Jana Winderen, and Toshiya Tsunoda. The tremendous heterogeneity of their sonic output notwithstanding, all these figures affirm and explore the sonic substratrum in its material flow, and, in the process, contribute to the development of the sonic flux as a philosophical concept.

The sonic flux revealed by these inventors and artists joins the profusion of flows catalogued by Manuel DeLanda in his remarkable book *A Thousand*

Years of Nonlinear History, which conceives all of nature and culture as a collection of flows—of lava, minerals, biomass, genes, bodies, food, language, money, information, and so on—that are congealed and dissolved, captured and released through immanent historical processes that are isomorphic across these various domains.[3] Yet, as Arthur Schopenhauer and Friedrich Nietzsche point out, the sonic flux is not just one flow among many. It deserves special status insofar as it elegantly and forcefully manifests and models the myriad fluxes that constitute the natural world.

The philosophical position I develop here is, like DeLanda's, a materialist and realist one that not only affirms the general revival of realism and materialism in contemporary philosophy, but also aims to spur the development of a new materialist aesthetics that challenges the prevailing orthodoxy in aesthetic theory. Developed in relationship to textuality and visuality, the theories that have dominated cultural discourse since the 1970s (notably psychoanalysis, poststructuralism, and deconstruction) are confounded by the sonic, which eludes analysis in terms of representation and signification. Theorists such as Seth Kim-Cohen have criticized both the progenitors and the current practitioners of sound art for their philosophical naiveté, for failing to make the textualist and conceptualist turn made by literature, visual art, and architecture in the 1960s and '70s.[4] I push in the opposite direction, arguing that sonic art reveals the idealism inherent in the prevailing theoretical programs and calls for an alternative, realist account not only of sound but of the arts in general. I take up Friedrich Kittler's contention that sound recording (which provided the key technological condition of possibility for sound art) opened an ontological domain foreclosed by theories of visual and linguistic representation. In Kittler's heterodox Lacanian idiom, recorded sound bypasses "the imaginary" and "the symbolic" to give access to "the real": the perceptible plenitude of matter that underlies all representation, a material core that is not a fundament but a primordial flux out of which all signals and signs emerge and into which they inevitably recede.[5] Implicitly Kantian—or what Quentin Meillassoux calls "correlationist"—presuppositions have lead theories of representation and signification to dismiss this domain as noumenal, inaccessible to discourse and culture or a product of them.[6] Yet, in the work of philosophers such as Schopenhauer, Nietzsche, Henri Bergson, Gilles Deleuze, DeLanda, and others, I discern an alternative realist and materialist metaphysics that dismantles these presuppositions and accounts for the ways that sound art provides access to the auditory "real."

Structuralism and poststructuralism prided themselves on decentering the human subject—on what Michel Foucault, Jacques Derrida, and Louis Althusser variously called the "death of man," the "end of man," or the critique of humanism.[7] Yet, as in the work of their predecessor, Martin Heidegger, this decentering generally took the form of a recentering on discourse and language that, at its core, remained deeply humanist. As Meillassoux has so incisively argued, these philosophical programs never questioned the Kantian insistence that the world is only ever the world *for-us*, the world as mediated or constituted by discourse.[8] Sonic materialism promises to complete the antihumanist project—as Nietzsche puts it, "to translate humanity back into nature."[9] Pursuing this project, *Sonic Flux* challenges the pervasive phenomenological and poststructuralist accounts of sound and sound art that begin and end with the human subject as the receiver and interpreter of auditory signals. Instead, I argue that sound art is best understood by way of a philosophical naturalism and materialism that rejects the ontological and epistemological oppositions between subject and object, mind and matter, culture and nature. Just as sound forms a continuous, anonymous flux that includes but exceeds human contributions, I understand listening as a way of contracting or capturing a portion of this flow through biological or mechanical means. I take sound art to grasp the essence of phonography, which shifts aesthetic attention from the rarefied domain of music to what John Cage called "the entire field of sound," and to investigate what Cage called "sounds in themselves" "rather than vehicles for man-made theories or expressions of human sentiments."[10] This concern with the materiality and independent reality of sound, I argue, is evident throughout the history of sound art.

"Sound art" is a thorny label, one rejected by prominent artists, critics, and curators, yet adopted opportunistically by others.[11] Like any label, it is clumsy and inexact, lumping together heterogeneous art works and practices, ignoring their differences and particularities and obscuring their connections and allegiances to other artistic fields and categories. Nonetheless, here and in what follows I readily employ the term, which I find useful in a number of ways. In a basic sense, "sound art" registers the fact that "music" is no longer coextensive with the field of sonic art, that there exist artistic practices in which sound is paramount—field recording, sound installation, and soundwalks, for example—that stretch or fall outside the conventions of music, musical performance, and musical recording. Cage responded to this proliferation of sonic practices by extending the term "music" over the entire field of sound (intentional or nonintentional, human-made or otherwise), thereby filling the category until it burst. The emergence of the label "sound art" in the 1980s and its widespread use since the late 1990s provided an alternative and, I think, more helpful strategy, expanding the field of sonic arts beyond music.[12] The categories "music" and "sound art" surely overlap. Yet the latter label allows the critic, theorist, or artist to redraw the boundaries in revealing ways, to demonstrate material and conceptual connections among disparate practices and media. In this sense, then, "sound art" does not name a natural kind or genre but serves as a conceptual device that enables one to point to commonalities among disparate practices and projects—to grasp, for example, the ways that George Brecht's text score *Drip Music (Drip Event)* (1959–62), Alvin Lucier's performance/recording *I Am Sitting in a Room* (1970), Annea Lockwood's installation *A Sound Map of the Hudson River* (1982), Christian Marclay's photograph *The Sound of Silence* (1988), Christina Kubisch's *Electrical Walks* (2003–), and Luke Fowler's film trilogy *A Grammar for Listening* (2009) resonate with one another. Finally, and more philosophically, I argue that "sound art" aptly names projects within and beyond music that reveal what, following Deleuze and DeLanda, I call the "intensive" dimension of sound.

My analysis of sound art and the sonic flux is thus metaphysical or ontological insofar as it attempts to give a philosophical account of what sound is and how it comes to be individuated, of the sonic flux and the works of art that manifest it. For much of the twentieth century, metaphysics was rejected by leading analytic and continental philosophers who conceived it as claiming to investigate entities that transcend either nature or knowledge and are thus either nonexistent or inaccessible. The first line of criticism stems from Nietzsche, who took the term "meta-physics" literally, as an attempt to describe "super-natural" entities that exist prior to and apart from the world of nature. A staunch naturalist, he could not abide such entities and thus dismissed metaphysics altogether. The second line of criticism stems from Kant, for whom metaphysics occupies a domain that exceeds knowledge and experience and thus cannot be the subject of theoretical inquiry. In the twentieth century, these two senses were conjoined in Martin Heidegger's rejection of "ontotheology" and Jacques Derrida's deconstruction of "the metaphysics of presence." Likewise, leading philosophers in the analytic tradition sought what Hilary Putnam called "a moratorium on the kind of ontological speculation that seeks to describe the Furniture of the Universe and to tell us what is Really There and what is Only a Human

Projection."[13] For Putnam and other analytic antirealists, ontology was conceived not as an account simply of what there is, but rather as an account of what there is according to a conceptual scheme and its set of ontological commitments. Ontology was thus rendered radically epistemic, relative to human access and systems of determination.

Yet the philosophers that guide my thinking about sound share a very different assessment of metaphysics, rejecting declarations of the "end of metaphysics" and instead affirming an "immanent metaphysics" that accepts only entities generated by the material and energetic processes that constitute nature.[14] This immanent metaphysics is both realist and materialist. It is realist in maintaining that reality is mind-independent, that the flows of matter and energy that fundamentally constitute the world are autonomous from the human mind and indifferent to our beliefs, desires, and descriptions of it. This is not the commonsense or direct realism according to which the world is more or less as it ordinarily appears to us to be, but rather a transcendental realism for which the objects of empirical experience are the ongoing products of virtual structures and intensive processes that are immanent to matter but ordinarily hidden in its results (though capable of being disclosed through science and art). Although realism is a position that recent (especially continental) philosophers and cultural theorists have been wary of embracing,[15] materialism is pervasive in philosophical and theoretical discourse today, covering distinct and often competing variants (dialectical materialism, eliminative materialism, speculative materialism, vital materialism, radical atheist materialism, transcendental materialism, etc.) that are sometimes confused with one another, casually conflated with explicitly nonmaterialist positions such as object-oriented ontology and actor-network theory,[16] or linked with antirealist positions.[17] The materialism I endorse maintains that matter (or, more precisely, patterned matter-energy) is all there is, and that all entities and events in the universe are the products of immanent and contingent material and energetic processes. This materialism thus acknowledges the basic asymmetry between thought and matter: thought depends on matter, but matter does not depend on thought, language, or conceptualization, which materialism understands as contingent evolutionary endowments of beings that are material through and through. Though focused on sound, *Sonic Flux* aims to make a modest contribution to this broader philosophical project.

The book also contributes to the burgeoning field of sound studies, which arose in the late 1990s concurrent with the widespread acceptance of sound art as a viable field of practice and exhibition in the arts.[18] Yet my ontological approach and philosophical orientation diverge from the main currents of research within sound studies, which—under the banner "sound culture studies" or "auditory culture"—tends to center on the role of sound, listening, and recording technologies in specific cultural and historical contexts, and to track the circulation of meaning and power within them. One critic has suggested that my approach is not only different from but sharply opposed to these tendencies within sound studies, that the ontological turn I pursue "directly challenges the relevance of research into auditory culture, audile techniques, and the technological mediation of sound."[19] This is not at all the case. While my philosophical realism is at odds with the antirealism prevalent in cultural studies, I maintain that sonic ontology and auditory culture are complementary rather than opposed, operating at different levels of scale. As I show in chapter 2, sonic ontology requires not only an account of the sonic flux in general, but also more regional analyses of its capture and coding by various nonhuman forces and assemblages, and by human communities and social formations. Though I focus on the sonic flux more broadly and on the general mechanisms of its capture, cultural studies of sound can serve as vital extensions of this project, examining the articulation of sound in specific cultural and historical configurations. I only challenge auditory cultural studies to acknowledge the sonic flux (and flows of matter-energy-information in general) as real and primary, preceding any particular social coding and always disrupting, decoding, and overflowing such human interventions.

CHAPTER 1 POINTS TO THE LIMITATIONS OF THE PREVAILING AESthetic theories and argues that the sonic arts require an alternative, materialist theory. Drawing from the sonic metaphysics of Schopenhauer and Nietzsche, and developing this metaphysics via the notion of intensity developed by Deleuze and DeLanda, I sketch such an alternative theory and introduce the notion of the sonic flux. I show how sonic materialism undermines an ontology of objects and substitutes an ontology of flows, events, and effects—features central to the work of sound artists such as Maryanne Amacher as well as Chris Kubick and Anne Walsh, whose work I examine. I go on to argue that this materialist account is not only relevant to the sonic arts, but also provides an alternative model for understanding artistic production and reception in general.

Chapter 2 develops this notion of the sonic flux and charts the various ways it has been captured by living beings, humans in particular. Through a critical reading of historical accounts by Jacques Attali and Chris Cutler, I examine the mechanisms by which noise is transformed into meaningful sound, and sound is captured by various systems of recording (biological, symbolic, mechanical, etc.). I pay special attention to the crisis of musical notation in the 1950s and the subsequent emergence of sonic art forms attentive to the perennial flux of sound and its (only ever partial and local) capture. The chapter includes an extended reading of Christian Marclay's oeuvre, in which this history of sonic flux and capture is explicitly engaged. I conclude the chapter with speculations about the circulation of sound in the age of MP3 and digital streaming.

Chapter 3 extends the analysis of the previous chapter, focusing on the ways that phonography challenges humanist and idealist conceptions of sonic production, meaning, and listening. Developing Friedrich Kittler's argument that sound recording provides access to "the real," I counter Roland Barthes's canonical semiotic account of listening with a materialist philosophical and biological argument that naturalizes the human production and reception of sound, placing it on par with mechanical production and recording. I explore this argument through an analysis of key works by Alvin Lucier, whom I consider to be a deeply materialist, realist, and naturalist composer and sound artist.

Chapter 4 develops an ontology of sound and argues that sound art plays a crucial role in manifesting this ontology. Drawing from G. W. Leibniz, Michel Serres, and Gilles Deleuze, and examining work by the sonic artists Éliane Radigue, Jacob Kirkegaard, Francisco López, Annea Lockwood, Joan La Barbara, and others, I argue that sonic flux has two dimensions: an intensive dimension that I term "noise" and an actual dimension in which this intensive continuum is articulated (for example, by speech and music). The richest works of sound art, I suggest, are unique among audible phenomena in that they disclose the intensive dimension of sound and its processes of actualization.

Chapter 5 argues that sound art marks a radical shift in the concept of temporality, a shift from time to duration. I examine John Cage's important distinction between time-objects and purposeless processes, and its connection with Bergsonian and Deleuzian philosophies of temporality. I show how this distinction fueled the debate between Michael Fried, on the one hand, and Robert Morris and Robert Smithson, on the other, and has animated sound-art practice ever since. The chapter examines the oeuvre of the sound-installation pioneer Max Neuhaus and concludes with a critical analysis of a recent collaboration between the sound artist Florian Hecker and the philosopher Quentin Meillassoux, who aim to show, both sonically and conceptually, that the world is not a becoming or a flux, but a "hyper-chaos."

The final chapter challenges the paradigm of "synaesthesia," the banner under which sound so often appears in visual-art contexts today. I argue that the aesthetic discourse of synaesthesia is predominantly conservative and recuperative, ultimately supporting the dominance of the visual and resisting the incursion of sound into the space of the gallery and museum. Exploring the tensions between the assimilation and the segregation of sound and image in the history of modern visual art and film, the chapter shows how contemporary artists such as Mathias Poledna, Manon DeBoer, Julian Rosefeldt, Luke Fowler, and the Sensory Ethnography Lab propose counterstrategies that reject the fantasy of sensorial fusion and instead affirm a productive difference and tension between seeing and hearing.

PART I

The Sonic Flux and Sonic Materialism

1 TOWARD A SONIC MATERIALISM

In April 1992 the composer and sound artist Maryanne Amacher mounted a site-specific installation in four adjoining spaces of a cultural complex in the southern Japanese city of Tokushima. Titled *Synaptic Island: A Psybertonal Topology*, the piece was one in a series of works in which Amacher explored "structure-borne sound," the acoustic effects generated when sound travels through the material infrastructure of buildings and is shaped by their walls, floors, and corridors. Amacher's interest in what she called "aural architecture" extended to the architecture of the human body, particularly the anatomical structure of the inner ear, which not only passively receives sound but, when stimulated by closely spaced pure tones, mechanically generates sounds of its own—combination tones and otoacoustic emissions—that transform the ears into miniature synthesizers and amplifiers. Prior to the weeklong run of the installation, Amacher spent a month researching on-site, experimenting with electronic frequencies and textures, and precisely configuring loudspeakers in an effort to articulate crisply tactile "soundshapes" or "sound characters" felt as sculptural forms large and small in distinct regions of the space, some perceived as though miles away and others as extreme close-ups. Amacher hoped to allow visitors to apprehend sound as a physical event, "to experience what is inside the sounds—what they are as energy."[1]

By all accounts, Amacher's installations are extraordinarily intense—waves and shards of sonic pressure coursing through the space and the body, throbbing the walls, vibrating the viscera, and swirling around the head in patterns of vertiginous complexity.[2] Recorded excerpts from *Synaptic Island* confirm

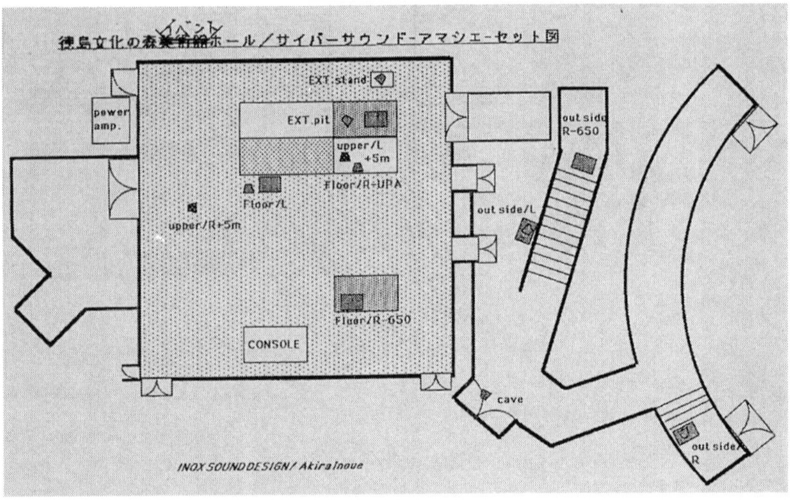

Fig. 1.1 Installation diagram for Maryanne Amacher's multimedia work *Synaptic Island: A Psybertonal Topology*, Tokushima 21st Century Cultural Information Center, Tokushima, Japan, 1992. Courtesy of the Maryanne Amacher Archive.

these reports, revealing dense choral swarms, thunderous blasts, sweeps of granulated distortion, and passages of hallucinatory pulsation. Yet, however rich and engaging, these recordings remain mere "artifacts"—as Amacher put it, "like hearing a movie or theater script read aloud, WITHOUT ACTORS OR IMAGES"—the piece itself truly existing only as a site-specific event, bound to the material and technological conditions of its installation in Tokushima, 1992 (fig. 1.1).[3]

How does one talk about such work, which has no fixed duration, is site-specific and sculptural, and is fundamentally concerned with sound as a physical, intensive force? Though unique, Amacher's work is emblematic of a wide range of sonic practices that elude the formal analyses of traditional musicology and the primarily visual focus of art history. Moreover—and this is central to my project here—such practices are poorly served by the critical orthodoxy that has reigned in cultural theory since the "linguistic turn." The theories of textuality, discourse, and visuality at the heart of cultural theory remain largely unresponsive to the sonic, failing to confront the powerful, asignifying materiality that characterizes so much experimental work with sound.[4] In this chapter I propose an alternative theoretical framework, a materialist account that is attentive to the ontology of sound and thus is better suited to analysis of the sonic arts. I suggest, moreover, that this materialist account can provide a model for rethinking artistic production in general and for avoiding the conceptual pitfalls encountered by the prevailing theories of representation and signification.

Signification, Discourse, and Materialism

Since the late-1960s aesthetic theory has been dominated by a set of antirealist critical approaches—notably semiotics, psychoanalysis, poststructuralism, and deconstruction—that have come to constitute a kind of orthodoxy. Epistemologically, these theoretical programs reject naive conceptions of representation and signification that construe images and signs as picturing or designating a pre-given world. Ontologically, they reject essentialism, which construes the world as a set of conceptual or material essences to which images and signs refer. In contrast with the fixity and inflexibility of essentialism, the critical orthodoxy affirms the contingency of meaning and the multiplicity of interpretation. Culture is construed as a field or system of signs that operate within intricate relations of referral to other signs and to subjects and objects considered as effects of signification. Cultural criticism then is conceived as an interpretive enterprise that consists in tracking signs or representations (images, texts, symptoms, etc.) through the associative networks that give them meaning—networks that are always in flux, ensuring that meaning is never secure or stable.

Rejecting realism, which claims access to extradiscursive reality, the dominant modalities of cultural theory maintain that experience and perception are always mediated by the symbolic field. Indeed, all the theoretical approaches that constitute this orthodoxy share a deep suspicion of the extrasymbolic, extratextual, or extradiscursive, insisting on the absence, infinite deferral, or fiction of what Jacques Derrida has called the "transcendental signified," that is, a fundamental reality that could arrest or ground the proliferation of discourse, signification, and interpretation.[5] Thus, for example, Ferdinand de Saussure banishes from semiotics the physical stuff of sound. Jacques Lacan casts aside culture's material substrate, which "resists all symbolization absolutely," declaring that "there's no such thing as a prediscursive reality" because "every reality is founded and defined by a discourse," and, even more sharply, that "it is the world of words that creates the world of things." Derrida's notorious claim that "there is nothing outside of the text" offers another expression of this idea, as does Roland Barthes's remark that, apropos the domain of discourse, "there is nothing beneath," and Stuart Hall's assertion that "nothing meaningful exists outside of discourse." Finally, Slavoj Žižek, the most prominent current exemplar of this tradition, concludes that "the pre-synthetic Real . . . is, *stricto sensu*, impossible: a level that must be retroactively presupposed, but can never actually be *encountered*."[6]

These theories are philosophically rich and have proven to be powerful tools for cultural analysis. They rightly reject essentialism and insist on the contingency and indeterminacy of meaning and being. Yet the price of antirealism has been an epistemological and ontological insularity that the philosopher Quentin Meillassoux has aptly termed "correlationism": the position according to which "the real" is inextricably correlated with our mode of apprehending it, such that what exists can only ever be what exists for thought or discourse.[7] For the correlationist, nature is either cast aside as "in-significant" or deemed a social construction. Moreover, despite its avowed antihumanism, orthodox cultural theory often falls prey to a provincial and chauvinistic anthropocentrism, treating symbolic interaction as evidence of human uniqueness and superiority. It thus accords with the deep-seated metaphysical and theological tradition it claims to challenge, a tradition according to which, by virtue of some special endowment (soul, spirit, mind, reason, language, etc.), human beings occupy a privileged ontological position elevated above the natural world. The Kantian or "correlationist" epistemology and ontology of cultural theory is apparent in its dualistic division of the world into two domains, a phenomenal domain of symbolic discourse that marks the limits of the knowable, and a noumenal domain of nature and materiality that excludes knowledge and intelligibility.[8]

These presuppositions and conclusions are evident in one of the most sustained theoretical examinations of sound art and kindred musical forms, Seth Kim-Cohen's *In the Blink of an Ear*.[9] Kim-Cohen attributes the absence of a rich theoretical discourse on the sonic arts to the tendency of composers such as John Cage and Pierre Schaeffer, and sound artists such as Francisco López and Christina Kubisch, to treat sound as a material substance external to signification and discursivity. In an effort to raise the level of discourse on sound art to that on the visual arts and literature, Kim-Cohen adopts the textualist, correlationist paradigm of those fields. On his account, realist claims concerning the materiality of sound can only be essentialist, since they posit a domain outside discourse and a substance the existence and nature of which is not determined by the field of signification. Such a substance and domain, Kim-Cohen concludes, is meaningless at best and nonexistent at worst. "Since being human is a state inexorably tied to language," he remarks, "linguisticity is the order that obtains."

> The suggestion of an unadulterated, untainted purity of experience prior to linguistic capture seeks a return to a never-present, Romanticized, pre-Enlightenment darkness. . . . If some stimuli actually convey an experiential effect that precedes linguistic processing, what are we to do with such experiences? . . . If there is such a strata [*sic*] of experience, we must accept it mutely. It finds no voice in thought or discourse. Since there is nothing we can do with it, it seems wise to put it aside and concern ourselves with that of which we can speak.[10]

Drawing the sonic arts within the purview of orthodox cultural theory, Kim-Cohen accepts the presuppositions of textualism and discursivity, affirming a distinction between phenomena and noumena rendered as the distinctions between language and the extralinguistic, culture and nature, text and matter. The limits of discourse are the limits of meaning and being. If the sonic arts are to be meaningfully examined, Kim-Cohen concludes, we will need to conceive them within the realm of representation and signification.

The musicologist Benjamin Piekut goes further. Drawing from Bruno Latour and Donna Haraway, Piekut criticizes Cage for endorsing the characteristically "modern" division between culture and nature and then attempting, as far as possible, to shake off the constraints of culture so as to compose in accordance with nature.[11] Such a strategy, argues Piekut, is nonsensical, both because culture, subjectivity, and politics can never be subtracted from the epistemological frame, and because "nature" is a cultural construction. Piekut's correlationist alternative is to eliminate the opposition between nature and culture by subsuming the former under the latter. "There has never been a separate, non-political realm of nature," he writes, endorsing the actor-network theorist Annemarie Mol's assertion that "reality does not precede the mundane practices in which we interact with it."[12]

And yet surely reality, nature, and sound far precede our arrival and cultural production, we latecomers in the history of the universe; and surely human history and culture are a part of that natural history rather than miraculous exceptions to it. The dominant strains of cultural theory have either ignored this fact or maintained, in strict correlationist fashion, that all history is human history, that any account of what precedes human culture is itself a cultural construction or projection.[13] Such accounts create an untenable divide between the claims of cultural theory and those of natural science, prompting the need for an alternative to the orthodox position. The materialist theory I propose here maintains that the prevailing critiques of representation and humanism are not thoroughgoing enough. A rigorous critique of representation would altogether eliminate the dual planes of culture/nature, human/nonhuman, sign/world, text/matter—not in the manner of Hegel, toward an idealism that would construe all existence as mental or spiritual, but in the manner of Nietzsche and Deleuze, toward a rigorous materialism that construes human symbolic life as a particular instance of transformative processes evident throughout the natural world—from the chemical reactions of inorganic matter to the rarefied domain of textual interpretation—processes Nietzsche called by various names, among them "becoming," "interpretation," and "will to power."[14]

Representation and the Sonic Arts

Undoubtedly, musical composition and sound installation are historically situated and socially embedded practices that are culturally meaningful. Yet music has long been acknowledged to stand apart from the mimetic or representational arts, and not to refer to the world in the manner of images or signs.[15] That music eludes analysis in terms of representation and signification has led a prominent tradition in the philosophy of music to conceive it as purely formal, abstract, and autonomous—"self-contained and in no need of content from outside itself," to quote Eduard Hanslick, who inaugurated this tradition in the mid-nineteenth century.[16] However, the most significant sound-art work of the past half century—for example, the work of Max Neuhaus, Maryanne Amacher, Alvin Lucier, Christina Kubisch, Carsten Nicolai, Francisco López, and Toshiya Tsunoda—has explored the materiality of sound: its texture and temporal flow, its palpable effect on and affection by the materials through and against which it is transmitted. What these works reveal, I think, is that the sonic arts are not more abstract than the visual, but rather more concrete, and that they require not a formalist analysis, but a materialist one.

Historically, music's nonrepresentational status has led it to be construed in two opposing ways. The composer and theorist R. Murray Schafer traces these to the two Greek myths concerning the origin of music.[17] Pindar's twelfth Pythian Ode, writes Schafer, locates the origin of music in Athena's invention of aulos playing to honor the wailing sisters of the beheaded Medusa. An alternative account is evident in the Homeric hymn to Hermes, which traces music's origins to Hermes' discovery that a tortoise shell could be used to form the resonant chamber for a lyre. The first myth celebrates music as the subjective expression of raw emotion, while the second describes it as revealing the objective sonic properties of the universe. Music is thus conceived to be either subrepresentational, a primitive eruption of desire and emotion (hence its suppression by moral conservatives from Plato to the mullahs of radical Islam), or superrepresentational, pure mathematics. This is how Descartes could write of music that "its aim is to please and to arouse various emotions in us," while Leibniz could claim that the beauty of music "consists only in the harmonies of numbers and in a calculation that we are not aware of, but which the soul nevertheless carries out."[18]

Schopenhauer: Below Representation

Two important nineteenth-century theories of art—those of Schopenhauer and Nietzsche—richly combine these two poles in ways that are helpful for building a materialist theory of the sonic arts. Schopenhauer's metaphysics is explicitly Kantian; and, just as Kant distinguishes between phenomena and noumena, appearance and the thing in itself, so Schopenhauer distinguishes between the world as "representation" and the world as "will."[19] At bottom, he argues, the world is will: an undifferentiated, propulsive energy or force. Yet, for the most part, this absolute is manifested and experienced only indirectly, mediated through the representations that pervade the familiar world of appearance, which consists of discrete entities that inhabit time and space and are subject to natural laws. Distinct from these appearances or representations, the thing in itself is, for Kant, a purely theoretical posit, a necessary supposition of his epistemological and moral system. Schopenhauer, however, argues that each of us has a direct internal experience of the thing in itself, namely, as will: the force of desire and action that animates us and distinguishes our inner experience of ourselves from our outer experience of other human beings, who, for each of us, remain objects among objects, representations among representations. Whereas Kant remains a transcendental idealist or correlationist, Schopenhauer's theory breaks through the realm of appearance, making the realist claim that we do in fact have access to the world in itself. For Schopenhauer, this absolute is not primarily something we know but something we are, and this ontological access to the thing in itself reveals our fundamental connection with everything else in the world, with the will as it surges through and beyond all appearances or representations.[20] Scientific study of these representations allows us to understand (though not feel) such internal forces at work throughout the natural world, from gravity, electricity, and magnetism to organic growth, animal desire, and human knowing and willing—all of which Schopenhauer calls (by analogy with our own intimate experience) "will."[21]

Awareness of the fact that the natural world is pervaded and driven by a blind, irrational force is, for Schopenhauer, cause for despair, vitiating any specifically human or individual meaning, purpose, or project. Art, however, offers temporary relief from this despair, since it presents us with what Schopenhauer calls "Platonic Ideas," pure formal types disconnected from the practical concerns of everyday life. Contemplation of such aesthetic Ideas allows us, momentarily, to transcend the life of desire and struggle so as to become, in Schopenhauer's famous phrase, "*pure*, will-less, painless, timeless *subject[s] of knowledge*."[22]

Schopenhauer notably distinguishes music from the visual and literary arts (painting, sculpture, architecture, and poetry) and accords it a special status. For Schopenhauer, music has nothing to do with the world of representation or with the presentation of Platonic Ideas. In an astonishing passage, he writes that music is "quite independent of the apparent world, positively ignores it, and to a certain extent, could still exist even if there were no world at all, which cannot be said of the other arts."[23] This would seem to be the most hyperbolic declaration of musical autonomy. But it is precisely the opposite. Schopenhauer liberates music from the world of appearance, the world of representation, only to plunge it into the world of things in themselves, the world of will. For music, he argues, is a direct expression of the will:

> Music differs from all the other arts by the fact that it is not a copy of appearance, or, more exactly, of the will's adequate objectivity, but is directly a copy of the will itself, and therefore expresses the metaphysical to everything physical in the world, the thing in itself to every appearance. Accordingly, we could just as well call the world embodied music as embodied will.[24]

For Schopenhauer, then, music is still in some sense a copy. What it renders, however, is not the world of objects and things that make up the apparent world, but the primary forces of which those objects and things are composed. That is, it offers an audible expression of nature in all its dynamic power.

Schopenhauer's theory of music is constrained by the Kantian language of representation, appearance, and thing in itself. Yet it offers an important start toward the construction of a materialist philosophy of sound and music. Schopenhauer acknowledges the nonrepresentational character of music and accommodates both its Pindaric connection to emotion and desire and its Homeric grasp of fundamental truths about nature.[25] His rejection of musical representation is not a claim to the autonomy or super-representational status of music, but an argument for the groundedness of music in the patterns of becoming immanent to nature.

Nietzsche: The Naturalization of Art

Nietzsche takes us much further toward a materialist theory of music and sound. His first book, *The Birth of Tragedy out of the Spirit of Music*, draws on Schopenhauer's account while divesting it of its Kantian baggage. Ostensibly, the book is a philological investigation into the origins of tragic drama and the profound importance accorded to that art form by the ancient Greeks. Yet Nietzsche gives the book a much broader significance, construing *The Birth of Tragedy* as a critique of late nineteenth-century culture and an account of art and music in general. The Greeks, argues Nietzsche, distinguished between the visual or plastic arts, on the one hand, and music, on the other—the discrete forms and serene composure of visual art honoring the god Apollo, the wild fluidity of music honoring Dionysus. Nietzsche aims to show that Attic tragedy represents the truce between, and union of, Dionysus and Apollo, and that it also resolves an assortment of other oppositions in Greek theology, art, culture, psychology, and metaphysics that can be tied to the Dionysian/Apollonian opposition: Titans/Olympians, lyric poetry/epic poetry, the Asiatic-barbarian/the Hellenic, music/sculpture, intoxication/dreams, excess/measure, unity/individuation, pain/pleasure, and so on.

This fondness for oppositions and their dialectical resolutions prompted Nietzsche to remark retrospectively that *The Birth of Tragedy* "smells offensively Hegelian."[26] Yet, Nietzsche's own assessment notwithstanding, the central opposition between Dionysus and Apollo is certainly not properly dialectical. Were it so, the Dionysian would be sublated in a higher form.

But tragedy does no such thing. Rather, it thoroughly affirms the Dionysian, which is made sensible through Apollonian figures and forms. "We must understand Greek tragedy," Nietzsche writes, "as the Dionysian chorus which ever anew discharges itself in an Apollonian world of images. . . . Thus the drama is the Apollonian embodiment of Dionysian insights and effects."[27] "In the total effect of tragedy," he writes later in the text, "the Dionysian predominates" (§21). Moreover, the overarching argument of *The Birth of Tragedy* is that, despite its historical eclipse, tragic pessimism is fundamentally superior to the optimism and progressivism of Socratic dialectics, of which the Hegelian dialectic is clearly a late flowering.

Dionysus and Apollo, then, ought not to be figured as a Hegelian thesis and antithesis.[28] Nor ought they to be figured as Kantian noumenon and phenomenon or thing in itself and appearance. Of course, Nietzsche explicitly adopts this Kantian terminology in his presentation of the Dionysian/Apollonian pair. But we should take heed of his remark, in the 1886 preface to *The Birth of Tragedy*, that that book "tried laboriously to express by means of Schopenhauerian and Kantian formulas strange and new valuations which were basically at odds with Kant's and Schopenhauer's spirit and taste" ("Attempt at a Self-Criticism," §6). Derived from Schopenhauer, Nietzsche's use of the dichotomy between appearance and the thing in itself is twice removed from Kant's. Indeed, as we have seen, Schopenhauer's own adoption of the dichotomy is peculiarly un-Kantian. Kant's distinction draws the line between nature and reason, between what can be empirically experienced and what, beyond nature and experience, can be rationally thought. Schopenhauer's thing in itself, however, is not an item (or domain) of thought or reason but one of direct visceral experience. "Thus it happens to everyone," writes Schopenhauer, "that the thing in itself is known immediately in so far as it appears as his own body, and only mediately in so far as it is objectified in the other objects of perception."[29] In place of Kant's distinction between experience and thought, Schopenhauer marks a difference between two different kinds of experience or knowledge: the experience of the object and the experience of the subject, knowledge of the outside and knowledge from the inside, extensity and intensity. Kant's aim is ultimately to argue for the existence of a moral and theological realm that is supernatural, apart from the realm of nature and experience—"to deny *knowledge*, in order to make room for *faith*," as he famously put it.[30] Schopenhauer has no such moral or theological motives and, indeed, openly scoffs at Kant's ethics and theology.[31]

Schopenhauer, then, goes some way toward naturalizing Kant's distinction between appearance and the thing in itself. Yet, in Schopenhauer's hands, this distinction remains curiously and problematically transcendent insofar as he accepts Kant's description of the thing in itself as outside space and time. This last vestige of transcendent dualism disappears from Nietzsche's account. According to Nietzsche, the Apollonian and the Dionysian (which play, respectively, the roles of appearance and the thing in itself in *The Birth of Tragedy*) are thoroughly immanent to nature. Indeed, before they are figures that describe human artifacts such as music, sculpture, and drama, the Apollonian and the Dionysian are natural forces, "artistic energies which burst forth from nature herself, *without the mediation of the human artist*—energies in which nature's art impulses are satisfied in the most immediate and direct way" (§2; my italics; cf. §§4, 5, 6, and 8).[32] For Nietzsche, then, nature itself is an artist who forms individuals and dissolves them in turn; and art consists in the "imitation of nature" not insofar as it offers realistic representations of natural entities, but insofar as it reiterates these "*art impulses of nature*" (§2; italics mine).[33] In affirming art and nature in the same breath, Nietzsche radically departs from Schopenhauer, for in Schopenhauer's aesthetics (which, in many respects, follows Kant's) the role of art is to offer a temporary respite from the natural, phenomenal world, enabling a "contemplation without interest" that disengages the will. On Nietzsche's account, however, art exists as a thorough affirmation of nature and its power—of what Spinoza calls *natura naturans*. Nietzsche's celebration of art is, then, a celebration of nature and an affirmation of existence.[34]

To be sure, the Kantian-Schopenhauerian language Nietzsche often employs in *The Birth of Tragedy* can be read as endorsing these transcendent dualisms: ontological distinctions between a "true" and an "apparent" world or epistemological distinctions between an unknowable absolute and empirical experience or knowledge. Yet this does not sit well with Nietzsche's insistence that the Dionysian and the Apollonian are "forces of nature." Nor does it square with his later assessment of *The Birth of Tragedy* as, ultimately, anti-Schopenhauerian and anti-Kantian, or with his claim that, in this text, "there is only one world," and "the antithesis of a real and an apparent world is lacking."[35] I suggest, then, that we read the Dionysian/Apollonian opposition as prefiguring a thoroughly naturalist opposition that plays a central role in Nietzsche's later writing: namely, the opposition between becoming and being.

We know that the Dionysian and the Apollonian are "*art impulses of nature*," "artistic energies which burst forth from nature herself" (§2). But what are the characteristics of these natural impulses (*Triebe*) and energies (*Mächte*)? The Apollonian affirms the *principium individuationis*, "the delimiting of the boundaries of the individual, *measure* in the Hellenic sense" (§4). The Dionysian, by contrast, affirms "the mysterious primordial unity" (§1 and passim), "the shattering of the individual and his fusion with primal being" (§8). The Apollonian is associated with "moderation" and "restraint," the Dionysian with "excess" (§§4 and 21). The Apollonian is concerned with pleasure and the production of beautiful semblance, while the Dionysian is fraught with "*terror*," "blissful ecstasy," and "pain and contradiction" (§§1, 5, and passim). The Apollonian celebrates the human artist and hero, while the Dionysian celebrates the individual artist's dissolution into nature, which Nietzsche calls the "Ur-artist of the world" (§5; cf. §§1 and 8). The Apollonian is a gallery of "appearances," "images," and "illusions," while the Dionysian consists in the perpetual creation and destruction of appearances. "In Dionysian art and its tragic symbolism," Nietzsche concludes, "nature cries to us with its true, undissembled voice: 'Be as I am! Amid the ceaseless flux of appearances, I am the eternally creative primordial mother, eternally impelling to existence, eternally finding satisfaction in this change of appearances!'" (§16).[36]

What Nietzsche is offering in these poetic descriptions is an ontology—an account of what there is, of the genesis of individuals from pre-individual forces and materials. This account is strikingly similar to accounts in his later work, where Nietzsche contrasts becoming with being(s) and explains the genesis of the latter from the former.[37] *Twilight of the Idols*, for instance, insists on the reality of "alteration," "change," and "becoming," noting that only a "prejudice of reason forces us to posit unity,[38] identity, permanence, substance, cause, thinghood [and] being."[39] A few pages earlier Nietzsche calls unity, thinghood, substance, and permanence "lies," lauding Heraclitus "for his assertion that being is an empty fiction," and praising the senses for telling the truth by showing "becoming, passing away, and change."[40] Indeed, assessing *The Birth of Tragedy* in *Ecce Homo*, Nietzsche explicitly connects the Dionysian with Heraclitean becoming, commenting that, in Heraclitus, one finds an "affirmation of passing away *and destroying*, which is the decisive feature of a Dionysian philosophy; saying Yes to opposition and war; *becoming*, along with a repudiation of the very concept of *being*."[41]

The Birth of Tragedy, then, presents a deeply naturalistic theory of art.

Art is not some unique achievement of human beings that defines a province of "culture" distinct from, and elevated above, "nature." On the contrary, Nietzsche's "nature" is itself artistic, creative, and productive; and we human beings "have our highest dignity in our significance as [one of nature's] works of art." Human beings themselves are artists, Nietzsche concludes, only insofar as they "coalesce" with nature as the "Ur-artist of the world" (§5, translation modified).

It's not difficult to see that nature is extravagantly creative, endlessly generating an immense variety of inorganic and organic forms: from crystals and canyons to biological species of the most astonishing variety, no two individuals of which are identical—a vast proliferation of material difference. Yet we are likely to take Nietzsche's rhapsodic celebration of nature's creative powers as rhetorical, for we generally understand art and creativity as requiring conscious agency. Nietzsche's assertion of nature as artist, then, will be read as metaphorical at best and theological at worst, since "the creativity of nature" seems to imply a divine creator.

Nietzsche, however, operates in the wake of the "death of God" and commits himself to tracking down and eliminating all the vestiges of theological thought.[42] Among these is the ancient and venerable hylomorphic model, according to which the genesis of entities requires the external imposition of form upon inert matter. Such is the account of formation in the Judeo-Christian tradition, in Plato, and in Aristotle, an account that continues to grip the scientific and aesthetic imagination today. Nietzsche, however, anticipates contemporary scientific and philosophical materialists—among them Gilbert Simondon, Ilya Prigogine and Isabelle Stengers, Gilles Deleuze and Félix Guattari, and Manuel DeLanda—in rejecting hylomorphism, opting instead for a theory of self-organization.[43] For Nietzsche, matter itself is creative and transformative without external agency, a ceaseless becoming and overcoming that temporarily congeals into forms and beings, only to dissolve them back into the natural flux. Nietzsche's name for this flux is the "will to power," which describes a theory of natural causality and effectivity internal to matter and proceeding without any external agency. For Nietzsche, "there is no 'being' behind doing, effecting, becoming; the 'doer' is only a fiction added to the deed—the deed is everything";[44] and there exist only "dynamic quanta in a relationship of tension with all other dynamic quanta, whose essence consists in their relation to all other quanta."[45] Natural change, then, is the result of intensive forces that generate new configurations and assemblages. As a thoroughgoing naturalist and materialist, Nietzsche draws no fundamental distinctions between inorganic and organic nature, or between nature and culture. The operations of the will to power are as evident in the processes of chemical reaction and bonding as they are in organic growth and competition, artistic creation and interpretation. (Indeed, Nietzsche often polemically extends the term "interpretation" to cover all natural processes.)[46]

Dionysus, or the Intensive

The will to power, then, names the pre-individual, a-subjective forces and processes that drive natural change.[47] Insofar as it dissolves the boundaries between individuals and the distinction between subjects and objects, this domain of becoming is described by the early Nietzsche as a "primordial unity." Yet this language is misleading, for it suggests a kind of undifferentiated mass or immobile pool—a description that does not adequately characterize either the Dionysian or becoming. For the early Nietzsche, the Dionysian is "the eternal and original artistic power" (§25), "dissonance" (§§17 and 24–25), "struggle" (§16), "the contradiction at the heart of the world" (§9), a force associated with "excess" (§4), creation and destruction (§§16, 8, and passim), "extravagant sexual licentiousness," and "savage natural instincts" (§2). Clearly, the Dionysian is a dynamic field composed of forces, energies, and drives in tension with one another. The later Nietzsche qualifies the notion of "unity," describing the Dionysian in terms of difference, tension, force, energy, and power. "This world," he writes in a note from 1885, is "a monster of force, without beginning, without end," "a play of forces and force-waves simultaneously one and 'many.'" "This, my *Dionysian* world of eternal self-creating, of eternal self-destroying—do you want a *name* for this world?," Nietzsche asks, and then responds: "*This world is the will to power—and nothing besides!* And you yourselves too are this will to power—and nothing besides!"[48]

The Dionysus of *The Birth of Tragedy* is indeed a precursor to the later Nietzsche's most important ontological doctrines: becoming, will to power, and eternal recurrence. In *Beyond Good and Evil*, he more soberly develops the notion of the will to power in a way that helpfully reveals the connections between Dionysus/Apollo and becoming/being. All natural change, he proposes, is the result of an intensive domain of "drives" and "affects," "a kind of instinctive life [*Triebleben*]" or "*pre-form* of life" that "lies contained in a powerful unity before it undergoes ramifications and developments in the organic process." Calling this field of forces the "will to power," he again concludes that "the world viewed from inside" "is 'will to power' and nothing besides."[49] Here, too, Nietzsche expresses his basic ontology in terms of a "powerful unity." But this "unity" is now expressly a dynamic play of drives, affects, passions, and forces.[50] Nietzsche is trying to construct an ontology in which forces, powers, movements, tensions, affects, and events precede the individual subjects and objects to which they are ordinarily attributed. In *The Birth of Tragedy*, he describes Apollonian individuals as temporary emissions ("image sparks" [*Bilderfunken*]) from the Dionysian ferment. The later Nietzsche offers a similar account, describing subjects and objects as condensations and concretizations of forces and affects, particular instances and trajectories of the will to power.

With the oppositions between Dionysus/Apollo and becoming/being, Nietzsche is clearly searching for a way to account for the genesis and dissolution of forms, and the manifestation of these processes in both nature and art. This line of thinking is most fully and richly developed in Deleuze's distinction between the transcendental and the empirical. This distinction, of course, derives from Kant, who argued that ordinary empirical experience is made possible by a set of a priori conditions he termed "transcendental."[51] Deleuze follows Kant in distinguishing between the empirical and the transcendental but naturalizes the distinction and shifts it from an epistemological to an ontological register. While Kant's "transcendental idealism" aims to discover the *conceptual* and *cognitive* conditions for *all possible experience*, Deleuze's "transcendental empiricism" aims to describe the *genetic* conditions of *the real*, that is, the material conditions that drive the production of empirical or "actual" entities.[52] The transcendental field theorized by Deleuze is itself comprised of two complementary aspects: "the virtual" and "the intensive." The former is a modal concept intended to replace the notion of "the possible," which, Deleuze maintains, presumes an ontology of representation that prevents the emergence of the new. ("Possible worlds" theories, for example, conceive the possible as preexisting the real that resembles it except for the addition of existence or reality.) In contrast with "the possible," "the virtual," for Deleuze, names the set of entirely real tendencies, capacities, and thresholds (boiling or melting points, for example) that inhere or subsist in matter but may or may not be actualized in any particular entity or event. The actualization of these virtual tendencies involves divergence or difference such that actual entities and events do not resemble the virtual structures they incarnate. "The intensive," then, names the engine that actualizes the virtual, the set of forces, powers, and differences that produce empirical beings.[53] Whereas Kant sharply divides the transcendental from the empirical as form from content, Deleuze maintains that the virtual, the intensive, and the actual present a continuum, allowing that certain experiences (notably aesthetic ones) enable the virtual and the intensive to be apprehended via the senses.[54]

Discussing this distinction between the intensive and the actual, Deleuze writes:

> Difference is not diversity. Diversity is given, but difference is that by which the given is given, that by which the given is given as diverse. Difference is not phenomenon but the noumenon closest to the phenomenon. . . . Every phenomenon refers to an inequality by which it is conditioned. Every diversity and every change refers to a difference which is its sufficient reason. Everything which happens and everything which appears is correlated with orders of differences: differences of level, temperature, pressure, tension, potential, *difference of intensity*. . . . Disparity—in other words, difference or intensity (difference of intensity)—is the sufficient reason of all phenomena, the condition of that which appears.[55]

Deleuze uses Kantian language here to express a thoroughly non-Kantian point. It is true, Deleuze argues, that an important distinction must be drawn between what appears and the conditions for the possibility of this appearance; but those conditions of possibility are not conceptual or cognitive, as they are for Kant; rather, they are thoroughly material, immanent in nature itself. The passage above concludes: "The reason of the sensible, the condition of that which appears, is not space and time [as Kant maintained] but the Unequal in itself, *disparateness* as it is determined and comprised of difference of intensity, in intensity as difference."[56] What appears (the diversity of the actual, empirical individuals that populate the world of our experience) is the product or manifestation of material intensive "differences" that operate at the micro level of physical, chemical, and biological matter but ordinarily remain hidden at the level of actual, extensive things. This emphasis on the constitutive nature of difference has allowed Deleuze to be linked with theorists of difference such as Saussure, Derrida, Lacan, Irigaray, and Levinas. Yet Deleuze's differences are not linguistic, conceptual, or cultural in origin. Operating below the level of representation and signification, these differences subsist in matter itself.

Below representation and signification, the sonic arts manifest this field of intensity, which both Deleuze and Nietzsche term "Dionysian."[57] "This primordial phenomenon of Dionysian art is difficult to grasp," writes Nietzsche, "and there is only one direct way to make it intelligible and grasp it immediately: through the wonderful significance of *musical dissonance*" (§24). Music—and, particularly, sonic difference or discord—makes audible the dynamic flux of becoming that precedes and exceeds empirical individuals and the *principium individuationis*. Representing and symbolizing nothing, it presents a play of sonic forces and intensities. "This [Dionysian] world [of music] has a coloring, a causality, and a velocity quite different from those of the world of the plastic artist and the epic poet," Nietzsche writes (§5). Yet it is also the condition of possibility for empirical individuals and the stable forms of the visual and textual arts. Thus the relationship between the Dionysian and the Apollonian, on the one hand, and music and the visual and textual arts, on the other, is one not of opposition but of transcendental conditioning—and not of conceptual conditioning, as in Kant, but of material conditioning, the genesis of forms through intensive forces, vectors, thresholds, and gradients. Just as the intensive world of the will to power or difference is manifested in actual entities, so too does the "inchoate," "intangible" world of music, for Nietzsche, "discharge itself in images," "emit image sparks," and manifest itself "as a specific symbol or example" (§§5 and 6).

Sound as an Immemorial Flux

On Nietzsche's account, Greek tragedy is born "out of the spirit of music."[58] Its essence lies in the tragic insight that the flux of becoming forms empirical individuals—dramatic poems, the figure of the hero on stage, the stage itself, us spectators—and dissolves them back into the maelstrom of forces and intensities. Beyond the book's analysis of classical drama, *The Birth of Tragedy* offers an ontology of music and art in general. Nietzsche asks us to forgo talk of representation and signification in favor of an account of art premised on the flux of becoming and the capture and presentation of forces immanent to the materials and media with which it operates.

For Nietzsche, this flow of forces is most clearly evident in music, which has a special relationship to natural becoming. Music does not *represent* this becoming as a sign of something absent or other. Rather, it "coalesces" with natural becoming, capturing or enveloping a region of it, exploring its possibilities, and presenting it for aesthetic and metaphysical apprehension. Music has the capacity to "render nonsonorous forces sonorous," as Deleuze frequently puts it.[59] That is, it makes audible the general flux of forces and movements that constitute natural becoming: duration, pressure, tension and relaxation, attraction and repulsion, consistency and dissolution, and so on—pure tendencies, intensities, and events presented independently of the world of bodies and objects that constitutes the domain of representation and figuration.

Nietzsche calls this Dionysian flux of forces a "primordial unity." But, as we have seen, becoming is not some undifferentiated abyss. The flux of matter and energy is expressed in different ways and articulated into various layers or strata, each composed of different substances and forms, constituting a particular stream with its own consistency and degree of autonomy. Deleuze and Guattari distinguish three such strata—the physicochemical, the organic, and the anthropomorphic or alloplastic—and, within these, various intrastratic layers or flows.[60] Manuel DeLanda has further developed Deleuze and Guattari's account, offering a rich history and ontology that charts the relative speeds and transformations of the various flows constituting the material world: flows of lava, magma, and minerals; flows of genes, bodies, food, viruses, and diseases; and flows of goods, money, language, information, memes, and norms.[61]

To these one could add myriad other natural and cultural flows: flows of air, wind, water, oil, electricity, traffic, images, and so on.[62] Both Nietzsche and Deleuze invite us to think of music not simply as the rendering audible of inaudible forces in general, but also as participating in a particular natural flux: a properly *sonic* flux. In a brief but suggestive passage, Deleuze presents just such an idea: "One can . . . conceive of a continuous acoustic flow . . . that traverses the world and that even encompasses silence," he writes. "A musician is someone who samples [*prélève*] something from this flow."[63] Just as Nietzsche conceives artists or musicians as immersing themselves in a field of forces and drawing something from it, so Deleuze suggests that we think of sound as a continuous, anonymous flux to which human beings contribute but which precedes and exceeds them—an ever-changing and variegated sonic domain of incalculable size and infinite temporal dimension to which new material is added every moment. Just as evolutionary biology examines genetic flows independently of the organic entities through which they pass, and evolutionary linguistics studies linguistic flows independently of the individuals and communities who speak them, Nietzsche and Deleuze suggest that a materialist theory of sound and music must conceive the sonic not as originating from punctual entities, but as a primary flux that precedes such entities and to which they contribute. Structuralism, psychoanalysis, and Marxism accustomed us to thinking of language, textuality, desire, and ideology as general structures that circulate through subjects, constituting them rather than being constituted by them. Yet these theoretical programs remained at the level of the human. Nietzsche, Deleuze, and DeLanda naturalize these insights, subsuming the human within the general field of fluxes that constitute the natural world.

In the final essay published before his death, Deleuze describes this purely immanent, a-subjective, impersonal transcendental field as "*a* life": that is, life as a continuous flux distinguished from the qualified bodies through which it flows and in which it is expressed. Such a conception of life is what the ancient Greeks called *zoë* and distinguished from *bios*. In his study of the Dionysus myth, the philologist Carl Kerényi clarifies that, in Greek thought, *bios* designates "the characteristic traits of a specified life, the outlines that distinguish one living thing from another"—in other words, this or that specific individual, who lives and dies. By contrast, *zoë* designates "life in general, without further characterization . . . and experienced without limitations": the life that passes through individuals but is irreducible to them, "the thread upon which every individual *bios* is strung like a bead, and, which, in contrast to *bios*, can be conceived of only as *endless*."[64] The Greeks associated *zoë*, this impersonal and pre-individual life, with the god Dionysus, whom Nietzsche associates not only with fluid becoming, but with music, conceiving music as revealing and contributing to an anonymous sonic flux. In this conception, then, the sonic arts render audible the primary becoming that precedes and exceeds individuals, subjects, and objects, an intense flux driven by differential material forces, thresholds, and gradients. At the same time, they constitute a distinct stratum within this becoming: a *sonic* flux. We will see that this sonic flux is not simply a philosophical posit but a sensuous reality discovered, investigated, and made manifest by experimental composers and sound artists throughout the twentieth and twenty-first centuries.

Sonic Events and Sound Effects

One might object to this notion of an immemorial sonic flux on the grounds that sound is entirely relative to (human or animal) hearing and thus can have no autonomous existence. On this view, sound would be purely phenomenal or mental. Such has been the prevailing philosophical conception of sound. Yet this orthodoxy is undermined by a set of arguments sharply presented by the philosopher Casey O'Callaghan, who endorses a sonic realism.[65] Philosophical accounts of perception, O'Callaghan notes, have typically treated vision as the primary sense and objects of vision as the paradigmatic objects of sensory perception. From Descartes and Locke on, it has been customary to distinguish between primary and secondary qualities, the former (for example, size and shape) taken to be qualities objects have independent of observers, the latter (for example, color and taste) qualities that objects have only relative to observers and their perceptual capacities. As invisible, intangible, and ephemeral entities, sounds have little in common with ordinary visual objects and substances. Hence, philosophers have been inclined to regard them as secondary qualities of the objects we see: the sound *of* a bird, the sound *of* an air conditioner, by analogy with the color *of* a door or the smell *of* a flower. On this view, then, sounds are denied independence in two ways: they are bound to objects as their qualities; and these qualities exist only relative to their apprehension by a mind.

Such is the idealist, phenomenalist conception of sound that has prevailed in philosophy. But once we stop taking vision as paradigmatic and investigate sound itself, a different ontological conception emerges. Visual objects persist through time and survive the alteration of their qualities. (The door, for example, remains when it is painted a different color.) By contrast, qualities don't survive in this way. (The redness of the door does not survive its repainting.) In this respect, sounds appear to be much more akin to independently existing objects, since they survive changes to their properties. A sound that begins as a low rumble may become a high-pitched whine, while remaining a single sonic stream. In such an occurrence, the object that produces it (a car, for example) does not lose one sound and gain another. The sound is continuous, though its sensible qualities change. Sounds have sources, of course, and these are often relatively durable objects. Yet we can identify distinct sonic streams that come from a common source. We can also (and generally do) experience sounds without experiencing their sources; and we can experience those sources without any sounds. So while sources generate or cause sounds, sounds are not bound to their sources as qualities. Rather, they are distinct individuals or particulars like objects.

This is precisely what—albeit in the idealist language of phenomenology—

Pierre Schaeffer, the father of musique concrète, aimed to show in his analysis of the *objet sonore*: the sonorous object considered independently of its source, an entity to which audio recording draws particular attention but which ordinary experience also routinely encounters.[66] ("There are many sounds in the forest," writes the Schaefferian entomologist and sound artist Francisco López, "but one rarely has the opportunity to see the sources of most of these sounds.")[67] For Schaeffer, the sonorous object has a peculiar existence distinct from the instrument that produces it, the medium in or on which it exists, and the mind of the listener. Sounds are not qualities of objects or subjects; rather, they are ontological particulars and individuals. ("As soon the call is in the air," writes López, "it no longer belongs to the frog that produced it.")[68] And this is why works of musique concrète are not representations—of objects in the world or of worldly sounds—but presentations of sonorous objects.

Yet Schaeffer's language of the "sonorous object" misses the mark, for sounds are peculiarly temporal and durational, tied to the qualities they exhibit over time.[69] This temporal character is not incidental but definitive, distinguishing, for example, the song of the American robin from that of the scarlet tanager, or the spoken words "protect" and "protean." If sounds are particulars or individuals, then they are so not as static *objects* but as temporal *events.*[70] The hegemony of the visual (and the ontology of objects it privileges) regards sounds as anomalous entities that it exiles to the domain of mind-dependent qualities. If we begin with sound, however, a different ontological conception emerges, for sounds support an ontology of events and becomings of a sort developed by Deleuze.[71] Inspired by the Stoics, Deleuze distinguishes between two kinds of entities. In the first place, there exist bodies that have various qualities, that act and are acted upon, and that inhabit various states of affairs in the world. Yet, in addition to bodies, there exist incorporeal events or effects that are caused by bodies but differ in nature from them. Deleuze asks us to think of the ontology of the verb (events) as distinct from that of the noun (bodies) and adjective (qualities). Moreover, instead of construing the verb as a predicate attributed to a prior subject, Deleuze, like Nietzsche ("the 'doer' is only a fiction added to the deed—the deed is everything") and Bergson ("*there are changes, but there are underneath the change no things which change: change has no need of a support*"),[72] attempts to think the verb as a pure becoming independent of a subject. Such becomings are best captured by verbs in the infinitive ("to cut," "to eat," "to redden," etc.), which are bound to no subject or particular context.[73] They simply describe powers of alteration in the world, powers of becoming that are variously instantiated.

As continuously varying fluxes that are separable from their causes and maintain their own independent existence, sounds exemplify this ontology of events and becomings, and they do so in two senses. In the first place, sounds are not punctual or static objects but temporal, durational flows. They thus accord with an empirical account of events and becomings as processes and alterations. Beyond this empirical sense, a Deleuzian account proposes that sounds are also events and becomings in another sense, a "pure," "incorporeal," or "ideal" sense. We saw that sounds are not only events but effects, results of bodily causes that are nonetheless distinct from those causes and have an independent existence of their own. Sounds are effects not only in the sense that they are the results of causes (the sound *of* a violin) but also in the sense in which scientists speak of the "Kelvin effect," the "Doppler effect," or the "Zeeman effect."[74] Such descriptions refer to recurrent patterns of possibility—diffuse multiplicities that nevertheless have a coherence or consistency. The isolation or individuation of such effects is very different from that of a thing, substance, subject, or person. Deleuze calls them "haecceities," which names the mode of individuation of events: a wind (the mistral or sirocco, for example), a river, a climate, an hour of the day, a mood (such as jealousy), and the like.[75] Effects of this sort are demarcated historically (hence their frequent attribution to the scientist who isolated them), but they are recurrent, forming relative invariants that are not reducible to their empirical instantiations.

This notion of "effect," independent of cause, has a broad and important set of usages in the world of audio. Musicians use the term to refer to the distinctive timbral and textural modulations (reverb, fuzz, echo, flange, distortion, etc.) produced by electronic signal processing devices known as "effects units." Sound researchers Jean-François Augoyard and Henry Torgue have adopted this list of "effects" and expanded it beyond the domain of music to generate a catalog of eighty-two sonic effects (*effets sonores*) that they use to characterize everyday urban soundscapes: attraction, blurring, chain, dilation, fade, and so on. Though inspired by Schaeffer, Augoyard and Torgue abandon Schaeffer's "object" in favor of Deleuze's "effect" in an effort to describe the soundscape not as field of discrete entities, but as a flux of haecceities, recurrent but transitory auditory modalities and intensities.[76] An even more extravagant expansion of the notion and number of auditory effects can be found in the voluminous archives of "sound effects" that have been key features of the radio and film industries since the 1920s. Ontologically and aesthetically, the sound effect is a peculiar entity. Generally anonymous, unattributed to an author or composer, these sounds are produced for incorporation into radio plays, films, television shows, or video games. Yet they float free of these concrete instances, constituting a general reserve capable of deployment in very different productions and contexts. In films, they get attached to particular objects and situations in the image track to provide a convincing auditory complement; but they are very often generated from sources and events that are wildly different from the visual objects they are made to accompany (sheets of metal produce the sound of thunder; frozen romaine lettuce generates the sound of broken bones). Moreover, heterogeneous sound effects are often combined to generate new sound effects that further diverge from their components and sources.[77]

These ontological and aesthetic peculiarities of sound effects have been explored by a number of artists.[78] Working with commercial sound effects libraries, the duo Chris Kubick and Anne Walsh present these effects in their virtual state, as detached sound files indexed by titles that are at once singular and generic ("Amphibian Morph 4 From Rock to Flesh," "Metal Squeal Huge 2.R," "Power Buzz, invisible .R"). The sounds themselves likewise manifest this combination of the singular and the generic. Though generated by particular sources and causes, they are capable of signifying and functioning more broadly. Kubick and Walsh's *Full Metal Jackets* (2005), for example, is a sound sculpture composed of thirty-two small speaker drivers scattered down a thirty-foot wall (fig. 1.2). A computer draws randomly from an archive of five hundred sound files documenting falling bullet shell casings and sends them to the speakers via eight different channels. At the base of the wall and facing it, a monitor lists (in real time) the file names, which carefully detail the type of casing and the material surface on which the shell fell. Yet, sonically, the installation is remarkably tranquil and nonviolent, like a spare, aleatory percussion composition or a cascade of rain. One's attention is drawn to the timbral and textural differences between the sounds rather than to their real-world or cinematic causal referents.[79] Kubick and Walsh's sculpture *To Make the Sound of Fire* (2007) similarly highlights the disjunction between source, sound, and function. Consisting of a Plexiglas box containing a few sheets of crumpled wax paper (used by Foley artists to generate the sound of fire), the silent piece invites viewers to imagine the sound such a material might make and to compare it with their silent mental conjurings of "the sound of fire." The infinitive title highlights

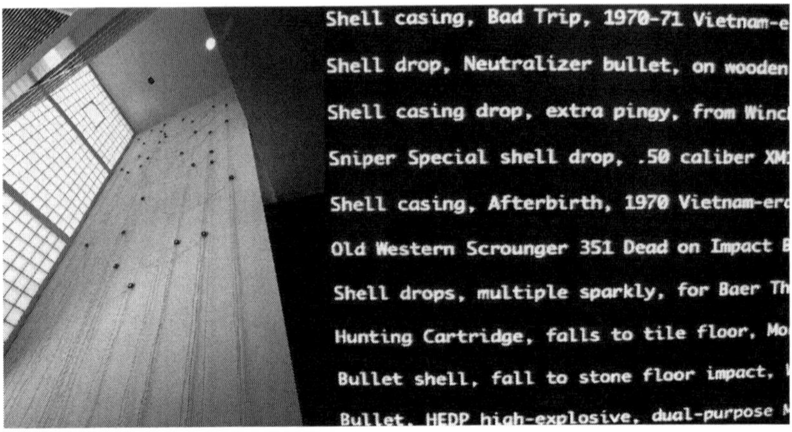

Fig. 1.2 Chris Kubick and Anne Walsh, *Full Metal Jackets II*, 2005, multichannel, generative sound and text installation. Yerba Buena Center for the Arts, San Francisco, CA, 2005. Courtesy of the artists.

the role of this and all sound effects as haecceities or singularities, elements or processes to be drawn into proximity with others in the incarnation of actual cinematic entities and events.

Kubick's *Hum -Human* (or *Hum Minus Human*) (2012) elegantly encapsulates several features of the sonic ontology I've been describing.[80] A single-channel video, the project presents a nearly randomized subcatalog of drones collected by searching through a commercial sound effects archive using the keyword "hum" and then subtracting the set of results labeled "human." The file names of these effects flash onscreen over a pulsing monochrome ground accompanied by a volatile mix of buzzing, sputtering, and crackling noises, at times frenetic and at other times calm (fig. 1.3). The piece freely combines the sounds of nature, culture, and industry—arc welders and cicadas, electric guitar amplifiers and bumblebees (the etymological source of the word "drone" in English)—that form the sonic backdrop of our lives. In one sense, the "minus human" in the title simply describes the search function. But it has a broader significance as well, attuning us to that Schopenhauerian, Nietzschean, and Deleuzian sonic flux that precedes and exceeds human being.

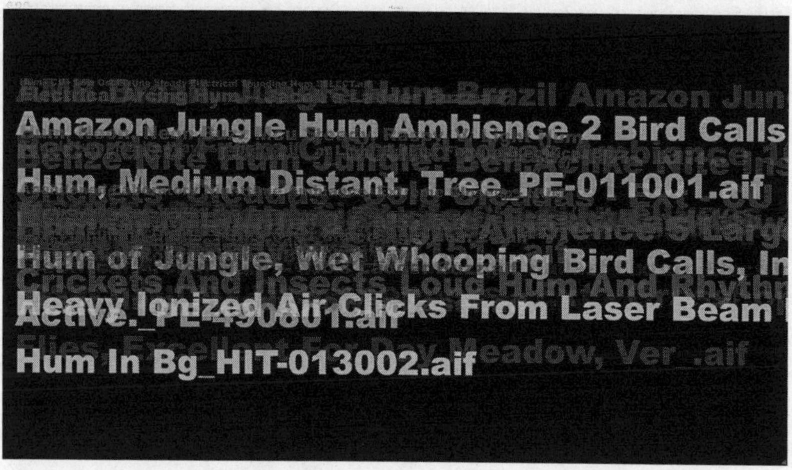

Fig. 1.3 Chris Kubick, *Hum -Human*, 2012, video, 13 minutes, color, sound. Courtesy of the artist.

A Materialist Aesthetics

This materialist theory of sound as an anonymous sonic flux suggests a way of rethinking the arts in general. Sound is not a world apart, a unique and autonomous domain of nonsignification and nonrepresentation. Rather, sound and the sonic arts are firmly embedded in the material world and in the powers, forces, intensities, and becomings that compose that world. If we proceed from sound, we will be less inclined to think in terms of representation and signification and to draw distinctions between culture and nature, human and nonhuman, mind and matter, the symbolic and the real, the textual and the physical, the meaningful and the meaningless. Instead, we might begin to treat artistic productions not as complexes of signs or representations, but as complexes of force with various degrees of consistency and distinctness.

Deleuze conceives the work of art and artistic production along these lines. In his view, works of art are never representations and never signify.[81] They *present* rather than *represent*. And what they present are blocs of sensations extracted from the flux of becoming. Deleuze endows the work of art with a fundamental independence from the world of subjects, objects, and states of affairs. As a sensual compound with its own consistency or composition, the work of art is independent of its creator, whom it often outlives and in the absence of whom it is able to circulate in the world and produce effects. For the same reason, it is also independent of any determinate viewer or listener and operates anew on each audience that encounters it. Finally, the work of art is independent of its model. A painted still life is not a vase of flowers; a photograph is not a city street. Rather, both are independent beings, "beings of sensation," as Deleuze and Guattari put it: "The work of art is a being of sensation and nothing else: it exists in itself."[82]

The work of art does not present the qualities *of* an object or the perceptions, moods, or feelings *of* a subject. Rather, it presents those sensations themselves, what Deleuze calls "percepts" and "affects," forces independent of those who have or undergo them: "packets of sensations and relations that outlive those who experience them."[83] "We attain to the percept and the affect," Deleuze and Guattari write, "only as to autonomous and self-sufficient beings that no longer owe anything to those who experience or have experienced them: Combray like it never was, is, or will be lived."[84] A novel, film, painting, or sculpture, for example, does not represent actual objects, persons, or states of affairs, nor does it render the qualities of actual objects or portray the emotions of actual persons. Rather, it is a mechanism for contracting forces and preserving them in this contracted state. It detaches sensations from objects and subjects, presenting them as pure intensive forces that inhere in things but are not reducible to them, having the power to act and affect as sensations independently of the subjects and objects who might bear or undergo them. Deleuze gives the example of a scene from G. W. Pabst's 1929 film *Pandora's Box*, in which, amorously gazing into Lulu's eyes (fig. 1.4), Jack the Ripper suddenly spots a knife and is gripped with fear before finally succumbing to the desire to kill her. On Deleuze's account, what the scene fundamentally presents is not "people who are assumed to be real with individual characters and social roles, objects with uses, real connections between these objects and these people"; rather, it presents a series of pure potentialities extracted from these people and objects: the intensity of the light on the knife; the capacity of the knife to cut or kill; the affects of compassion, terror, resignation considered as "pure 'possibles'" irreducible to any of their instances or attached to this or that object or subject.[85] If these affects and percepts weren't detachable from the particular characters, figures, or objects that express them, if they didn't present forces and potentialities that exceed these actual entities, then works of art would not affect us. They would be mere documents, flat

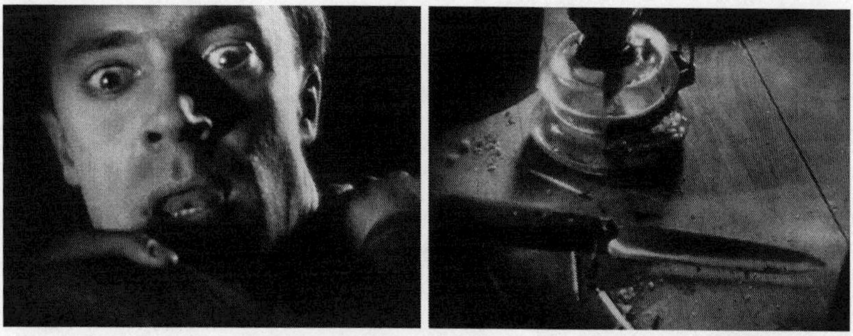

Fig. 1.4 *Pandora's Box*, dir. G. W. Pabst, 1929, 35mm film, 133 minutes, b&w, silent.

descriptions of states of affairs and properties stuck to particular empirical things and individuals toward which we would be indifferent.

Deleuze's insistence on the autonomy of sensation and of the work of art in general invites comparison to quintessentially modernist aesthetic theories such as those of Roger Fry and Clive Bell. Fry, too, rejects the notion that art is fundamentally imitative or representational, arguing instead that it gives access to a domain ("the imaginative life," he calls it) that doubles "actual life" it without resembling it.[86] For both Fry and Deleuze, art suspends the tendency to responsive action characteristic of actual life, allowing us to be, in Fry's words, "focused upon the perceptive and emotional aspects of the experience" "regarded as ends-in-themselves."[87] Yet, though Fry grants that the "emotional elements of design" have a deep connection to physical forces such as "the sensations which accompany muscular activity" and "all the infinite adaptations to the force of gravity which we are forced to make,"[88] the domain of art is, for Fry, ultimately the domain of pure form, freedom, and disinterested contemplation.

Here again we see the post-Kantian decision faced by Schopenhauer and Nietzsche and encountered again within artistic modernism, both early and late: the move away from ordinary empirical objects toward either the transcendence of form or the immanence of self-organizing matter. As we have seen, Schopenhauer, Nietzsche, and Deleuze take the latter route. In Deleuze, the vector of abstraction characteristic of affects, percepts, and the work of art in general is not away from materiality but toward it. Art is not a vehicle for the transcendence of life, nature, and matter. On the contrary, it plunges us into those domains. Or rather, below the level of lived bodies, qualified objects, and states of affairs, it plunges us into *a* life, *zoë*, the intensive continuum of becoming, for "affects" and "percepts" are synonymous with the prepersonal, pre-individual singularities, capacities, and tendencies that constitute material becoming. Art provides an opening onto the impersonal and prepersonal transcendental field that Deleuze variously calls the "plane of immanence" or the "body without organs," which always exists below or alongside formed bodies and individuals. The intensities and affects that populate this field, plane, or flux precede and exceed the human. Indeed, all art, for Deleuze, involves "man's nonhuman becoming," which is not a matter of imitation or resemblance but rather the exploration of intensities that bring us into contact with entities of very different orders.[89]

All art, then, is tragic or Dionysian, involving a dissolution of the *principium individuationis*, a desubjectivation, that reaches what Nietzsche calls "primal being" and Deleuze the "plane of immanence," the "plane of consistency," or the "body without organs." Complete dissolution would, of course, mean death. And so both Nietzsche and Deleuze recommend that one hold on to the minimum of subjectivity, identity, and organism necessary to explore a multiplicity of nonhuman becomings while warding off complete annihilation.[90] In Nietzsche's aesthetics, this is the role of the Apollonian, which provides that minimum of individuation necessary to peer into the Dionysian abyss.

Art is the privileged domain of this cautious but rigorous experimentation with nonhuman becomings and the intensive flux. For both Nietzsche and Deleuze, it plays a central ontological role. The conception of art they propose challenges the Kantian "transcendental aesthetic" considered as a theory of the sensible describing the conditions of possible experience and instead charges the work of art with discovering the conditions of real experience: "the being of the sensible reveals itself in the work of art, while at the same time the work of art appears as experimentation."[91] This experimentation has nothing to do with representation, signification, or interpretation. The work of art is not a secondary surface derived from an actual world that it would represent or to which it would refer; nor is it an ideal entity that refers only to itself and things of its kind—signs to other signs, images to other images. Rather, the work of art is itself a piece of the real, and art making is an experimental practice that plunges into material becoming, capturing and revealing the conditions that make possible the domain of subjects and objects populating the world of ordinary empirical actuality. On this account, sound and music don't inhabit some anomalous domain of nonrepresentation and nonsignification. Rather, their peculiarity lies solely in their ability to go below representation and signification so as to reveal the experimentation with forces, intensities, sensations, and affects that characterizes all artistic production.

I asked earlier how one might talk about Maryanne Amacher's sound installations, which frustrate analysis in terms of representation and signification. The artist herself tended to describe them formally in cinematic, televisual, or theatrical terms, as "episodes" that staged dramatic events among various "sound characters": "'What happens to *Wave #4* when it's set up to meet *The Fright*?' or '*Deep and Deepest Tone* disappears. Was it really shot down by the *High Beat Force*? Will it re-appear? When it does two weeks later it's supporting *The Coast*, who we all know has fallen in love with *God's Big Noise*.'"[92] While surely summoning the conventions of science-fiction movies, detective stories, and superhero comics, Amacher suggests a way to reconceive these audiovisual and textual media. After all, her characters are entirely invisible and sonic, composed of frequencies, intensities, and forces that impose and superimpose themselves on one another. Indeed, these sound characters are both *events* in Deleuze's sense and *effects* in the sense of Kubick and Walsh, Augoyard and Torgue. That is, they are subsistent, durational sonic consistencies identifiable by their characteristic timbres, textures, speeds, and trajectories, capable of being deployed in different situations or contexts that partially shape and transform them. Amacher's sound installations, then, suggest that film, television, and comics be read not as representations or signifying forms, but as blocs of sensations and configurations of affects, energies that impinge upon the body of the viewer, reader, and auditor and render it an active element in a field of forces.[93]

For theories of signification and representation, the view I am presenting and defending here—the proposal of a realist and materialist conception of sound as an asignifying material flux—will prompt the charge of essentialism.[94] But the charge is misplaced, for essentialism requires the existence of fixed and unchangeable forms or types that underlie or transcend natural variety and material change. On the materialist account I've outlined here, sound is thoroughly immanent, differential, and ever in flux, and the forces and intensities it presents are themselves the results of contingent historical processes. Instead of denying difference and contingency, thinking about sound in the way that I propose leads us to understand difference beyond the domain of "culture," signification, and representation—that is, to see these cultural processes as particular manifestations of a broader differential field: the field of nature and matter.[95] Such a materialist and realist account of the sonic arts will enable us to conceive of sound as both irreducible to culture and also shaped by it. It enjoins us to suspend the idealist and humanist language of representation and signification that has characterized cultural theory over the past half century, and to reconceive aesthetic production and reception via a materialist model of flow, force, and capture.

2 A BRIEF HISTORY OF THE SONIC FLUX

So far I have presented the sonic flux in general terms as a nonlinear flow of matter and energy on par with other natural flows. But the sonic flux is inseparable from its concretization, actualization, and coding—the various ways it has been seized, slowed, and organized into more or less discrete forms, structures, and entities.[1] We need, then, to consider sound not only from the perspective of the Dionysian profusion of forces that constitute its transcendental or virtual face, but also from the point of view of the mechanisms, codes, and systems that capture these forces and through which they pass.

From the start, we should avoid construing this capture or actualization of the sonic as the imposition of form on raw material. Sound is not a neutral substratum that is given form from without. Rather, it is replete with capacities and tendencies of its own with which any appropriation of the sonic must contend. The intensive properties of pressure, density, speed, viscosity, elasticity, and temperature play decisive roles in the sonic field. As vibration, sound is difference or variation—specifically, a variation in the intensive parameter of pressure. It is also repetition—vibrational difference that recurs, endures, and is extended in time. This duration is itself variation, for sound comes into being, alters, and dies or dissipates. Moreover, sonic becoming is not only temporal but spatial. Sound waves have size and travel through space at speeds determined by the mediums and temperature gradients through which they pass. As any squirrel, whale, or architect knows, sound is spatially affective, interacting uniquely with the materials, shapes, and configurations of the space in and through which it moves.

The relationship between the human voice and the structure of the Greek amphitheater, or Gregorian chant and the Romanesque cathedral, or chamber music and the private salon is one of the mutual affective conditioning of one material by another, not simply the containment of musical matter by solid form.

Sound is also marked by tendencies and capacities of other sorts. A vibrating string or column of air manifests a set of singularities, particular nodal points that mark its fundamental frequency and series of overtones. When one set of vibrations encounters another, the two enter into affective relations of covibration—relations of reinforcement, canceling, interference, phasing, beating, and so on, that are deemed "consonant" or "dissonant" and, depending on the cultural context, are grasped as stable or unstable, exhibiting tendencies toward rest or movement. Systems of temperament and tonality exert selection pressures on the sonic flux, determining sets of relevant pitches and establishing the relations between them. In tonal music, the tonic is a pitch attractor that forms a center around which other pitches are organized and toward which they tend. More broadly, the history of music is replete with singularities, moments of phase transition—Arnold Schoenberg's atonal revolution, for example, or Ornette Coleman's free jazz—in which new organizations of sound suddenly become possible and new sonic attractors are revealed.

We can conceive a *longue durée* history of sound akin to the history of fluid plasmas, biomass, genes, and information described by Manuel DeLanda in his wonderfully synthetic book *A Thousand Years of Nonlinear History*. Such an account of sound would be at once historical and ontological. It would keep one ear turned to particular manifestations of music and sound (performances, compositions, recordings, soundscapes, installations, spoken language, etc.), while keeping the other on the overall movement of this sonic flux, which ceaselessly volatilizes any particular instance and submits it to a universal cacophony. Salient manifestations would be treated less as masterworks than as sonic singularities, moments of inflection or bifurcation that reroute the flow of sound. Thus, while this sonic flux would be semiautonomous relative to other flows, these singular points would reveal the overdetermining effects of biological, political, economic, technological, and cultural forces on it.

A history of this sort would be tremendously detailed and complex, taking into account an enormous number of variables and operations and mapping several different subflows. It would draw resources from myriad fields of knowledge: scientific, anthropological, literary, musicological, and art-historical descriptions of global and local soundscapes and their transformations over time; the evolution of inorganic, organic, and technological entities capable of registering and emitting sonic vibrations; the analysis of natural and social rhythms of sonic production and audition; a mapping of the physical, biological, cultural, social, political, and religious forces that shape and constrain the sonic flux; the history of language considered as the extraction of phonemes from the sonorous continuum; the history of music considered from the perspective not of great composers or musicians but of sonic trajectories and singularities; the history of architecture considered as a history of sonic management and containment; and so forth.[2]

This monumental project would draw from the studies in sonic history, sonic anthropology, soundscape ecology, and sound art that have proliferated over the past two decades, and also from earlier studies stretching back to Chladni, Helmholtz, Edison, Marconi, and Bell. My project in this chapter is more modest and preparatory. I want to begin to sketch a history of the sonic flux by examining some of the mechanisms of territorialization and deterritorialization, actualization and counteractualization, that mark the history of music. In doing so, I hope to give an account of the turn from *music* to a broader notion of *sound* that grounds the emergence of sound art and the discourses on sound that provide resources from which a more comprehensive history of the sonic flux could be generated.

Noise, Deterritorialization, and Self-Organization

Jacques Attali and Chris Cutler give us a start on this project, offering grand synthetic accounts that provide helpful frameworks for sketching a history of sound and its capture. Historiographically, each of these accounts draws from Marxist and McLuhanist theories, describing modes of production and their formation and overcoming through immanent processes. Yet both accounts can be read in more Nietzschean and Deleuzian terms, as accounts of the territorialization and deterritorialization, the coding and decoding of sonic flows.[3] Ontologically, Attali begins from a conception of sound as a fluid and intensive power, a fundamentally unruly and threatening force that undermines (or threatens to undermine) all stable forms and social arrangements. Attali's name for this sonic force is "noise"; and "*noise*," he writes, "*is violence*: it disturbs. To make noise is to interrupt a transmission, to disconnect, to kill."[4] Here Attali combines two conceptions of noise: one sonic, the other more general and drawn from information theory, for which "noise is the term for a signal that interferes with the reception of a message, even if the interfering signal itself has meaning for that receiver" (27)—static on the line, interference in the channel, sound through the walls, dirt on the image, dysphonia, cacophony. Noise is nonsense: the absence of sense, interference with sense, or the proliferation of sense beyond the point of intelligibility. In any case, it is a domain of (relatively, as we will see) unstructured differences: "destruction, disorder, dirt, pollution, an aggression against code-structuring messages" (27). Sonically, it is a source of aesthetic displeasure, psychological annoyance or confusion, and a potential source of pain, damage, and destruction. "In its biological reality," Attali notes, "noise is a source of pain. Beyond a certain limit, it becomes an immaterial weapon of death. . . . Diminished intellectual capacity, accelerated respiration and heartbeat, hypertension, slowed digestion, neurosis, altered diction: these are the consequences of excessive sound in the environment" (27). From ancient accounts on, these various conceptions of noise—the physical, the psychological, the social, and the aesthetic—have been combined in the notions of "discord" and "disharmony," which signify displeasure, disintegration, and social disruption.

Attali sometimes lapses into a hylomorphic description of noise as a primordial substance or flow that is given form by music. Yet, for the most part, his conception of noise is more sophisticated and precise. His merging of the sonic and the information-theoretical conceptions of noise is crucial, revealing that noise is not undifferentiated or neutral matter but self-organizing matter in which differences are only relatively unstructured. Noise is not simply negative, an entropic force of destruction, disorder, and so on; it is positive and productive as well. In Attali's sense, "noise" expresses the tendency of any system toward deterritorialization and decoding, opening it up to the reservoir of possibilities that overflows any given form. Attali writes:

> A network can be destroyed by noises that attack and transform it, if the codes in place are unable to normalize and repress them. Although the new order is not contained in the structure of the old, it is nonetheless not a product of chance. It is created by the substitution of new differences for the old differences. Noise is the source of these mutations in the structuring codes. For despite the death it contains, noise carries order within itself; it carries new information.[5] This may seem strange. But noise does in fact create meaning: first, because the interruption of a message signifies the

> interdiction of the transmitted meaning, signifies censorship and rarity; and second, because the very absence of meaning in pure noise or in the meaningless repetition of a message, by unchanneling auditory sensations, frees the listener's imagination. The absence of meaning is in this case the presence of all meanings, absolute ambiguity, a construction outside meaning. The presence of noise makes sense, makes meaning. It makes possible the creation of a new order on another level of organization, of a new code in another network. . . . But this *order by noise* is not born without crisis. Noise only produces order if it can concentrate a new sacrificial crisis at a singular point, in a *catastrophe*, in order to transcend the old violence and recreate a system of differences on another level of organization. . . . In other words, catastrophe is inscribed in order, just as crisis is inscribed in development. There is no order that does not contain disorder within itself, and undoubtedly there is no disorder incapable of creating order. (33–34)

It's not that noise is *too little*, lacking form, sense, order, differentiation, and the like; rather, it's that it is *too much*, overwhelming the system with energy, information, and potentiality. In Deleuze's terms, noise is undifferen*c*iated but not undifferen*t*iated.[6] That is, noise is no longer or not yet organized (differen*c*iated, actualized into a distinct form) by music; but it is nonetheless differential, "*an ideal continuum* . . . defined not at all by homogeneity but by the coexistence of all the variations of differential relations, and of the distributions of singularities that correspond to them":[7] noise as the coexistence of all signals—wideband, background sound. It is replete with differences, tendencies, attractors, singularities and potential bifurcations—what Attali calls "catastrophes."[8]

Attali's history of noise is a history of these catastrophes or bifurcations and the singularities or basins of attraction into which they drive the sonic flux. He rejects the Hegelian and Marxist notion of history as a necessarily progressive unfolding and instead adopts Deleuze and Guattari's conception of history as a virtual coexistence marked by tendencies and capacities that are or are not actualized.[9] "In codes and in value," Attali writes,

> the domination of one of the networks [that is, musical codes or attractors] no longer excludes the existence of the others, as flotsam from the past or fragments of the future. There is no longer any sudden rupture, but instead the successive dominance of certain codes and networks over others still present. . . . It is senseless to classify musicians by school, identify periods,

discern stylistic breaks, or read music as a direct translation of the sufferings of a class. Music, like cartography, records the simultaneity of conflicting orders, from which a fluid structure arises, never resolved, never pure. (43–44, 45)[10]

On Attali's account, the deterritorialization/reterritorialization and decoding/recoding of sonic flows are driven by both internal and external pressures. "Each network pushes its organization to the extreme, to the point where it creates the *internal* conditions for its own rupture, its own noises," he writes (35). As an example, Attali cites the expansion of tonality and heightened chromaticism of late Romantic music that led to the sudden breakdown of the tonal system and the emergence of expressionist atonality (34). "But a noise that is *external* to the existing code can also cause its mutation," he continues, summoning a biological conception of noise as an engine of difference and variety. New technologies such as printed reproduction, for example, were intended to extend the reach of oral communication and the culture of Latin. Yet, as we will see in more detail later, the printed score simultaneously deterritorialized musical performance and reterritorialized this musical flow onto a form that fixed and hardened it: the score. The deterritorialization of the spoken word enabled by print also led to the proliferation of vernacular languages and, with them, the consolidation of territorial nationalities (35). Musical instruments such as Beethoven's piano and Jimi Hendrix's electric guitar are also able to inaugurate such musical mutations, "mak[ing] possible a new system of combination, creating an open field for a whole new exploration of the possible expressions of musical usage" (35).

Systems of Sonic Capture

Following his elaboration of this ontology and historical methodology, Attali's book offers an account of three broad musical codes or forms of sonic organization and the bifurcations that propel each into the next: a premodern, ritual, and oral code that he terms "sacrifice"; the code of musical literacy that he names "representation"; and the code of electronic recording that he calls "repetition." In the book's conclusion, Attali sketches what he takes to be an emergent fourth mode: "composition."

Though schematic, Attali's broad historical account is rich, compelling, and generative. Yet his normative critique of modern and contemporary musical culture is problematic and unconvincing. Attali's prime target is audio recording, which, he argues, made possible the total commodification of music, fostering an alienated musical culture in which human beings relate to one another solely through the passive consumption of musical commodities and no longer through any form of communal activity. Though recorded music saturates everyday life, he maintains, it is no longer genuinely social. Rather, it consists in a proliferation of simulacra, copies without an original, identical consumer products that are individually stockpiled. Acquisition replaces any form of real listening, and the din of background music silences genuine musical production and creativity.

THE SONG: BIOLOGICAL AND SOCIAL CAPTURE

Instead of outlining Attali's presentation of these four modes of sonic organization, I want to turn to and develop another account that, though broadly similar, offers a more nuanced and compelling assessment of audio recording and the musical practices of the past hundred years or so. In a series of essays written since the early 1980s, the theorist, improviser, and composer Chris Cutler offers an expansive account of sonic territorialization, deterritorialization, and reterritorialization that divides along much the same historical lines as Attali's but with a different trajectory.[11] What Attali terms "codes" Cutler calls "memory systems," basic forms of sonic capture or recording. The first of these is biological and social, registered in the individual human body and the social body of the cultural community. For most of human (and animal) history, this form of memory was the only available mechanism of sonic capture, a form characterized by multiple mechanisms of selection and recording. In human beings, sound is seized by the ear (with its particular structure and range of hearing, the products of long evolutionary selection); registered by the brain according to schema of relevance that are both biological and social; consolidated through repetition in the physical and mental habits of the individual and the collective habits of the social group; reproduced by the mouth and hand; and transmitted through a social field that encompasses multiple generations, thus ensuring its survival as tradition. These repetitions and rhythms are marked in the auditory material itself, which is structured by recurring patterns, formulas, epithets and other mnemonic devices that aid the memory of performers and auditors alike.[12]

Though historically primary, this form of recording persists alongside subsequent systems. It characterizes not only, for example, the archaic

Greek oral tradition that produced the *Iliad* and the *Odyssey*, but also the orally and aurally transmitted ceremonial songs of, for example, the Navajo or Maori and the folk musics prevalent across the globe today.[13] While fundamentally traditional, aimed at the preservation of ancestral culture, folk forms of transmission inevitably involve variant repetition and alterations that are amplified and passed on, ensuring that the song has no fixed or singular identity but is always in flux. As such, the biological memory system operates according to the same principle as biological reproduction, which combines repetition and difference, preserving genetic material without exact replication, and thus constantly generating variety and genetic drift.[14] Likewise, traditional songs and poems are passed down from generation to generation, repeated by bards or performers but always with a difference (due to inspired invention, adaptation to the local situation, forgetfulness, accident, etc.) that causes the song to diverge. These variations are vetted by the community, which consolidates the song according to its tastes, needs, and hierarchies in a manner analogous to natural selection.[15] The biological system of memory, then, constricts and selects from the sonic flux while also affirming the essential transience and fluidity of sound. The auditory flow it produces is essentially anonymous, authored not by a creative individual but by the entire community and its lineage, a fact marked, for example, by the epic poem's invocation to the muse or by the attribution "traditional" characteristic of folk music. The performer is thus not a creator but a node through which the sonic flux passes.

Like any system of capture, biological and social memory involves both territorialization and deterritorialization—or what, following Deleuze, Pierre Lévy calls "actualization" and "virtualization."[16] Virtualization is a process that involves detachment from the present (the here and now) and movement toward a general problematic field from which new actual entities are generated as solutions. Take the example of language. On the one hand, language involves territorialization or actualization: the extraction of phonemes from a sonic flux replete with virtual potentials. On the other hand, however, language deterritorializes or virtualizes sound. The *presence* of the prelinguistic vocal utterance or cry is routed through a virtual field or structure consisting of standard elements and rules that govern the generation of new utterances. These grammatical rules do not *exist* (as present entities) but rather *subsist* or *persist* (in the manner of the past or future).[17] They are actualized in speech but remain virtual potentials, the inventive powers of which are not exhausted by their actualization and do not resemble those actualizations. Lévy calls this virtualization of language "grammatization," suggesting that—given the virtual, iterative structure of language that exceeds any given instantiation or context—speech is preceded conceptually by what Jacques Derrida calls "arche-writing": the structuring of every spoken utterance by a differential transcendental field of elements and rules that is nonpresent, real but not actual.[18]

This virtualization precedes language, for every system of memory virtualizes its contents. The genes of any living individual store information that precedes and exceeds their particular expression, information transmitted by ancestors to descendants. This is equally true of the instincts or habits that are manifested in the individual organism: the extraction of water and mineral nutrients from the soil, the capturing of sunlight, the cellular respiration of oxygen, the metabolic harvest of energy from food, the circulation of blood, and so on. Every entity is formed by syntheses that compose it, hold it together, and forestall its dissolution. And each of these is a form of unconscious memory that persists or subsists across a series of actual individuals.[19]

The biological memory system described by Cutler is an instance of this more general natural system of territorialization and deterritorialization, actualization and virtualization. Biological and social forms of memory territorialize sound, segmenting it into pitches and systems of pitch, carving it into rhythms and forms, structuring it via repetitions and expectations. At the same time, they deterritorialize or virtualize the song, which is no longer an utterance attached to a particular body in a particular time and place but now flows through many bodies and generations, retaining the past while serving as a reservoir for ever new instantiations. Alongside the variant and fluid passage of the song through individuals, communities, and generations, Cutler notes, the song persists as a virtual "matrix" or "field."[20] As Cutler puts it: "This mode centers around the *ear* and can only exist in two forms: as sound and memory of sound."[21]

THE SCORE: WRITING AS SONIC CAPTURE

A second mode of sonic capture and recording—written musical notation—emerged in Europe in the Middle Ages. Initially, notation was intended merely as a supplement to biological and communal memory, an aide-mémoire for accomplished musicians.[22] Yet centuries later, under the pressure of economic and political forces, the score emerged as a formidable system of musical memory. The transition from feudalism to capitalism meant the collapse of the courtly patronage system that had supported musicians for centuries. Musicians and composers were thrust onto the open market, which demanded exchangeable objects or commodities. A hitherto ancillary resource was enlisted as a solution to the problem of how to commodify the inherently transitory nature of sound and the fluid matter of music.

The institution of the score gave music the form of fixed, exchangeable objects: musical "works."[23] The contemporaneous institution of copyright allowed music (in the form of the notated score) to become the legally protected private property of a particular creative individual. These conditions served to fix music in the form of stable, finished products, bounded entities no longer subject to revision. Written memory thus arrested the variation and drift characteristic of biological capture. The institution of the score also firmly established musical authorship and a hierarchical division of labor between the composer (the creator of musical works) and the performer (whose role became the faithful execution of the composer's instructions). With creativity restricted to the private act of composition and public performance beholden to a notated score, a firm line was drawn not only between composition and performance, but also between composition and improvisation, which waned among performers of art music.

The objecthood of the score shifted musical attention from the ear to the eye, as music became something to see and read before it was something to hear. Indeed, the emergence of "musical works" under capitalism is an exemplary instance of what Karl Marx calls "the fetishism of commodities" and what Georg Lukács calls "reification": the process by which the products of human, social activity take on a life of their own and confront their producers as autonomous objects with a "phantom objectivity."[24] What began as a mere supplement to musical performance became an autonomous entity that governed performances and to which they were held accountable.[25] The score thus came to perform the metaphysical sleight of hand that fascinated both Nietzsche and Wittgenstein: the pre-post-erous inversion by which the concept "leaf" was taken to be the cause of actual, particular leaves; or, in the musical case, a symbolic, inaudible entity—the score—became the cause of and the standard of judgment for actual musical performances.[26]

Indeed, these features of musical notation have led a prominent tradition in musical aesthetics to assert that musical works are Platonic essences: ideal (and, for some theorists, eternal) structures that exist independently of their physical, sonorous manifestations.[27] For the musical Platonist, music is fundamentally constituted by *ideal musical works* that are physically (and multiply) embodied in visible *scores* and audibly realized (always imperfectly) in series of *performances*. Thus, the musical Platonist transmutes contingency into necessity and accords the virtuality of the musical code a transcendent rather than transcendental status. Elevating the musical "work" (a product of particular historical and cultural forces) to the status of a transhistorical and transcultural necessity, the Platonist ignores the fact that most musical production across the globe proceeds and has always proceeded without works or scores. By hypostatizing the "work," musical Platonism reverses the true order of genesis: the audible sonic flux is captured by the score, from which the very notion of the musical "work" is derivative. Moreover, the musical "work" imagined by musical Platonism—the perfect and eternal type embodied in a score—is utterly contradictory: an inaudible audible, an eternal temporal. Such a conception of the "work," purely mental and soundless, could only ever be an idealized performance, derivative rather than originary.[28]

The "work" and the score are no more eternal or ideal than are genes or languages. They are contingent historical and cultural products, forms of sonic capture that arise as responses to conjunctions of physical, biological, and social forces. As a collection of written pages, the score is surely distinct from the audible actualizations that it governs; and yet the sonic flux precedes the score that captures it and derives from it. A virtual entity, the score (a visual, static, inaudible set of marks on paper) does not resemble its actualizations or performances (invisible, dynamic, and audible events or processes), but serves only as a set of instructions for the actualization of music—a necessarily incomplete set of instructions ensuring that each actualization will be unique, divergent from all others.

Of course, this divergent actualization proceeds differently in the written system of memory than in the biological system of sonic capture; and the two systems manifest different processes of territorialization and deterritorialization or virtualization. On the one hand, as we've seen, the score is a powerful agent of territorialization. It binds and regulates the flow of sound much more fully and tightly than does biological memory. In the written system, the flow of sound no longer simply passes through a series of bodies, which can only measure the fidelity of current versions against those no longer present. It now passes through a persistent template fixed in writing and law. This template provides a readily available standard against which to judge performances, thus restricting their variation and drift. On the other hand, the score manifests new processes of deterritorialization and virtualization. We saw that the oral transmission of language and music already involves a break with presence: recourse to a virtual structure (the structure of language or of the song) that precedes and exceeds any present individual and utterance. Like any form of writing, the score intensifies this break with presence. An exteriorization of memory, it detaches the musical piece from every particular body, time, place, and cultural-historical context, allowing it to circulate in the absence of its composer and any determinate performer or audience.[29]

Biological memory requires continuity, a continuous chain of bodies and generations through which the song can pass. A break in that chain would mean musical extinction, for, in the absence of a form of recording supplemental to biological and communal memory, the song would die. Musical notation extends this chain and can prevent such extinction; but it does so at the price of a fundamental discontinuity. Written memory produces a vast archive of music, allowing works from very different periods and contexts to sit side by side, enabling random access to all of written history. By severing the musical work from the context of its creation, written memory also allows it to be reinstantiated elsewhere. This is precisely the fear expressed in the *Phaedrus* by Plato's Socrates: that written memory allows meaning to circulate in the absence of the intention and context that animates it, thus opening itself to improper instantiation, misapprehension, and misunderstanding.[30] In its very structure, written memory thus entails "the absence of the sender, the addressor, from the marks that he abandons, which are cut off from him and continue to produce effects beyond his presence and beyond the present actuality of his meaning, that is, beyond his life itself." "To write," concludes Derrida,

> is to produce a mark that will constitute a kind of machine that is in turn productive, that my future disappearance in principle will not prevent from functioning and from yielding, and yielding itself to, reading and rewriting. . . . For the written to be the written, it must continue to "act" and to be legible even if what is called the author of the writing no longer answers for what he has written, for what he seems to have signed, whether he is provisionally absent, or if he is dead, or if in general he does not support, with his absolutely current and present intention or attention, the plenitude of his meaning, of that very thing that seems to be written "in his name" . . . . This essential drifting, due to writing as an iterative structure cut off from all absolute responsibility, from *consciousness* as the authority of the last

analysis, writing orphaned, and separated at birth from the assistance of his father, is indeed what Plato condemned in the *Phaedrus*.[31]

Writing, then, is a sort of prosthesis: an externalization of memory that attaches to and extends orality and the capabilities of the human body but is also fundamentally uncanny and alien to them. It is, as Derrida puts it, a machine that produces effects in the absence of an animating consciousness and intention.

AUDIO RECORDING: ELECTRONIC CAPTURE

These features of writing are intensified by the third system of sonic memory, which emerged at the end of the nineteenth century: audio recording or phonography. Via various technologies (initially wax cylinders and phonograph records; later magnetic wire and tape, digital audio recorders, compact discs, MP3s, and audio streams), audio recording literalizes the machinic nature of written memory, its status as an external, unconscious, mechanical prosthesis. Recording intensifies the uncanniness of written memory, for the phonographic apparatus detaches sound from its source of production and allows the voices of the dead to return like ghosts. A score might allow a group of living musicians to produce a new performance of *The Rite of Spring*; a recording allows us to hear the dead Stravinsky himself. The score may virtualize sound, but it is never blamed for disembodying it. Moreover, whereas the musical score was restricted to the symbolic registration of discrete pitches in a limited range, the phonograph can record and play back the entire audible universe. The voice of Elvis, the call of the extinct Kauaʻi ʻōʻō bird, the horns and whistles of Vancouver harbor in 1973[32]—all the world's sound can be filed in this virtual archive to be endlessly reanimated or actualized.

Audio recording thus intensifies the territorialization and deterritorialization characteristic of written memory and engages new forms of territorialization and deterritorialization as well. It captures sound itself in an exchangeable container, thus perfecting the reification and commodification of music made possible by the written score. Audio recording increases the circulation of the musical object, allowing it to be actualized even by those who lack the skill of musical literacy. The phonograph record thus collapses the distance between the visual score and its auditory performance. Whereas the score provided only a blueprint allowing skilled musicians to realize a musical work, the phonograph record can deliver actual performances and requires not a skilled performer but only a common machine. Short-circuiting the literate culture of the score, the phonograph record registers performances of all sorts: operas and symphonies, but also folk songs, Tin Pan Alley numbers, speeches, and idle chatter. Indeed, beyond the strictly musical, it captures any audible phenomena, thus vastly extending the range of sonic capture.

Audio recording also allows for spatial and temporal deterritorializations and virtualizations that amplify and outstrip those of written memory. Like written memory, it produces a discontinuous archive. Yet this archive is now no longer a collection of symbolic representations, but a library of sound itself.[33] As Cutler puts it, "recording throws the life of music production back onto the ear. As with [the biological system of memory], the first matter is again Sound. Recording *is* memory of sound."[34] Prior to Edison, sound was bound to presence, to the here and now of the voice, the musical instrument, or the sounding world. After all, sound waves are by nature temporal, evanescent, or, as Edison liked to call them, "fugitive."[35] Audio recording, however, gives sound another, virtual existence that overturns the ordinary logic of time and space. It allows the "here" to be transported elsewhere—for soundscapes from a Costa Rican rainforest to be heard in a car traveling on a Tokyo freeway—and the elsewhere to be brought here—for Senegalese pop, Indian classical music, Los Angeles punk rock, and the calls of Antarctic seals to exist side by side on the radio dial or the shelves of a public library. Indeed, audio recording involves an ontological flattening of its source material. Every recording has the same ontological status: the registration of vibrations on a surface. "The fact is," Cutler writes, "that, considered as raw material, a recorded sound is technically indiscriminate of source. All recorded sound, as recorded sound, is information of the same quality. A recording of a recording is just a recording, no more, no less."[36]

Recording also withdraws sound from its determinate moment in chronological and historical time, transporting it into what Deleuze calls the virtual time of "Aion," a floating, indefinite time.[37] Recitations of folk songs and performances of scores can only ever be present. But audio recordings fundamentally elude the present moment. They are always at once past and to come, registering bygone sonic moments and casting them into an indefinite future that is never exhausted by playback in the present. To some extent, this is true of all virtual structures (biological memory and the song, written memory and the score), which, by definition, deterritorialize the here and now. But the peculiar uncanniness of audio recording (the voice of a dead friend, recordings of the wind from 1935)[38] testifies to a difference: audio recording extracts a sonorous surface from a segment of the past and gives it an untimely existence. It rends that surface from the lived present of bodies and states of affairs, maintaining it as a pure reserve that can be actualized in the present but does not belong to it. The recorded past is no longer the past as it was lived or experienced, but a past in general; and the future to which it is given is no longer a particular but an indefinite future. The recorded past is the virtual past described by Henri Bergson: not the empirical past that follows the present (the past that is present no more), but the transcendental past-in-general that is contemporaneous with the present (the past generated alongside the present as its virtual counterpart).[39] Recording can also produce purely virtual events that have no foothold in a particular past. Since the experiments of Les Paul in the late 1940s, multitrack recording, overdubbing, and effects processing have generated sonic streams that have no existence independent of their recorded manifestation, no reference to a singular event in the chronological past. This nonreference to an empirical past confirms the basic temporal character of sound recording: its untimeliness, its unmooring from any particular past, present, or future.

This characterization of the temporal structure of audio recording suggests a challenge to Attali's account and provides the impetus for Cutler's divergence from it. Echoing Theodor Adorno and Max Horkheimer's critique of the culture industry, Guy Debord's account of the society of the spectacle, and Jean Baudrillard's theory of symbolic exchange, Attali attributes to audio recording a relentless repetition, a stockpiling of the past that is creative only in its generation of surplus value. For Attali, recordings are simply dead labor, past creativity congealed in the form of objects for commodity exchange. Recording is "the murder of creativity," he writes, "the blasphemous herald of the death of a society in which reality is only ever a normalized, liquidating artifice. . . . Repetition today does indeed seem to be succeeding in trapping death in the object, and accumulating its recording. . . . [It] makes death exchangeable, in other words, represents it, puts it on stage, and sells it as a spectacle."[40] Yet the fundamental untimeliness of audio recording—its relationship not only to a past in general but also to an indefinite future—suggests otherwise. And so does the history of recording, from musique concrète through dub reggae, hip-hop sampling and turntablism, plunderphonics, remix culture, mashups, and beyond.[41] *Contra* Attali, an audio recording is not simply a dead object that stockpiles the past. It is also a particular form of virtualization that has a futural trajectory as well. No less than the traditional song or the written score, an audio recording is a volatile, virtual entity capable of divergent actualization. Indeed, as detachable chunks of sound produced in large quantity, circulating widely, requiring no specialist literacy to actualize them, and regulated by no canons of fidelity to a tradition or template, audio recordings are more citable and manipulable than previous forms of sonic capture. As Cutler puts it, "recording makes possible the manipulation or assembly of sound, or of actual performances, in an empirical way; that is to say, through listening and subsequent decision making."[42] This is just what the celebrated pianist Glenn Gould had in mind when, in 1964, he gave up live performance in favor of recording, through which he attempted to generate ideal performances consisting of multiple takes and myriad spliced segments. For Gould, recording was a glorious mechanism of deterritorialization, capable of withdrawing music from the particularities and vicissitudes of live performance and historical time. Yet Gould was no Platonist. The ideal musical work, he insisted, is not a mental entity that becomes physically manifest in live performance; it is a technological product assembled empirically in the studio from multiple fragments.[43]

Writing soon after his retreat into the recording studio, Gould foresaw "a new kind of listener—a listener more participant in the musical experience," one who, equipped with basic music technology, could edit and splice bits of sound to produce new sonic events and works.[44] Such empirical manipulation of audio recordings was already imagined in the 1920s by the artist and polymath László Moholy-Nagy in a pair of articles proposing novel uses for the phonograph.[45] In its nearly half century of existence, Moholy-Nagy noted, the phonograph had thus far been used only as an apparatus of reproduction, a machine to play recorded music and speech. Yet it could readily be transformed into an apparatus of production, an instrument for making music, or what Moholy-Nagy more broadly termed "sound effects." The surface of the record, he suggested, could be hand cut to generate "hitherto unknown sounds and tonal relations." Graphic designs might be laid into wax to create what he called a "groove-manuscript score." Such innovations, Moholy-Nagy thought, would allow the composer to avoid the detour of musical notation and its subsequent interpretation by musicians, and would instead reestablish a direct, amateur experimentation with sound. In short, then, Moholy-Nagy grasped that "repetition" was replete with all the potentials of "composition."

The phonograph and phonograph record could also become instruments for musical composition and improvisation. In the 1920s and '30s, composers such as Stefan Wolpe, Paul Hindemith, Ernst Toch, and John Cage experimented with phonograph recordings in compositions and performances.[46] But the use of recorded sound did not become a prominent tool for creation and composition until 1948, when the French radio engineer Pierre Schaeffer broadcast a set of "noise studies" built entirely from recordings—not only of musical instruments but of worldly sources such as pots, pans, and railroad trains. In the wake of Schaeffer's experiments—and particularly after the widespread availability of magnetic tape, which could be easily manipulated—classically trained composers such as James Tenney began altering and manipulating pop songs; Terry Riley, Steve Reich, Pauline Oliveros, and Brian Eno built tape delay systems as tools for sonic capture and composition; and the Beatles, Frank Zappa, Miles Davis, and Lee "Scratch" Perry adopted strategies of tape collage and musique concrète.[47] In the decades that followed, sampling, remixing, and the manipulation of recorded sound became standard practices that transformed the reified musical object into fluid, open-ended auditory material. Endlessly iterated and generations removed from its source, such material becomes effectively anonymous, and the technology to capture, alter, and release it is so readily available that its proliferation is staggering. As Gould foresaw in the mid-1960s, the boundaries between the roles of "composer," "performer," and "recording engineer" have become increasingly blurred. Contemporary electronic music acknowledges this blur by applying the generic term "producer" to anyone who grabs the sonic flux and alters it. Forgoing the notions of authorship and work characteristic of the written system of sonic capture, such producers tend to see themselves as curators rather than creators. "Neither the artist nor the remixer are 'creators' in the traditional sense," notes the producer Kevin Martin. "It's more the case that both the artist and the remixer act as 'filters' for a sort of cultural flow."[48] Martin's assessment is echoed by the producer Brian Eno, who notes that "an artist is now much more seen as a connector of things, a person who scans the enormous field of possible places for artistic attention, and says, What I am going to do is draw your attention to *this* sequence of things."[49]

Such technologies and practices, then, not only return music to the ear but also reinvigorate improvisation. The twentieth century saw a tremendous revitalization of musical improvisation in the West, a movement led largely by jazz. Jazz has many characteristics of a folk music: it is a primarily an oral-aural form (the jazz score is merely a chart, a sketch), and it frequently relies on the institution of "standards," familiar tunes that provide springboards for creative transformation. Yet the history of jazz is so intimately bound up with the history of recording that many scholars and critics take jazz to have been essentially created by recording, which served as its primary means of dissemination and education.[50] Recording thus supplemented and extended oral transmission, enabling a dispersed and dehierarchized model of apprenticeship that substituted the recorded multiple for the singular presence of the living master.

This conjunction of jazz and recording technology had profound effects on European art music. It's no coincidence that, during the postwar period, in the wake of jazz's golden age and the widespread availability of magnetic tape, the classical musical score was subjected to deconstruction and dissolution, as indeterminate compositions, graphic scores, and experimental compositions dismantled the fixity of the musical object and encouraged real-time invention and improvisation. The score for Karlheinz Stockhausen's *Klavierstück XI* (1956), for example, consists of a large sheet of paper displaying nineteen musical passages among which the performer is invited to move at random. Similarly, the first section of Pierre Boulez's *Third Sonata for Piano* (1958) is a collection of ten pages that can be arranged in any order. Morton Feldman's *Intersections* and *Projections* (both 1950–53) specify only relative pitch (high, middle, or low) and number of pitches, leaving the rest of the decisions to the performer. More radical still is the score for Earle Brown's "graphic score" *December 1952* (1952), a white page sparsely sprinkled with an array of black bars of various lengths and widths (fig. 2.1).[51] The performance instructions are simple and deliberately vague: "for one or more instruments and/or sound-producing media," they read. "The composition may be performed in any direction from any point in the defined space for any length of time and may be performed from any of the four rotational positions in any sequence."[52]

A jazz enthusiast, Brown turned to indeterminate notational strategies as a way to jump-start the improvisatory impulse that had waned under the regime of the notated score. "I couldn't understand why classical musicians couldn't improvise, and why so many looked down on improvisation," noted Brown. "The whole series [of open-form pieces] *October*, *November*, and *December* [*1952*] was progressively trying to get them free of having every bit of information before they had confidence enough to play."[53] From the other side, composers emerging out of the "free jazz" explosion of the 1960s

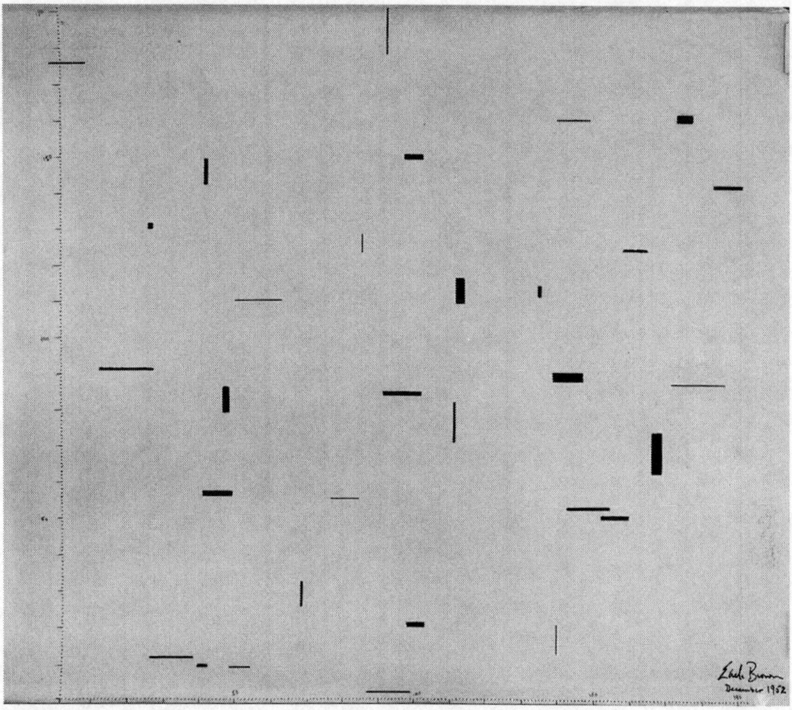

Fig. 2.1 Earle Brown, *December 1952*, excerpt from *FOLIO (1952/53) and 4 SYSTEMS (1954)*, $11^{15}/_{16} \times 16^{3}/_{4}$ inches. © 1961 by Associated Music Publishers. Print courtesy of The Earle Brown Music Foundation.

came to see experimental notation as a way of reterritorializing what had become a chaotic flux. Hence, Anthony Braxton, Wadada Leo Smith, and others began to use novel notational schemes to create a common point of reference so that improvisation could be genuinely collective rather than individualistic and competitive (fig. 2.2).[54] John Zorn modeled musical performance on various games (baseball, lacrosse, hockey, cricket, etc.), specifying a set of virtual parameters that initiated rule-governed, but nonetheless indeterminate, musical actions.[55]

Whether used to facilitate or to rein in improvisation, the turn toward experimental notational schemes often had political underpinnings. Brown's prodding of performers to become co-creators of his pieces sprang in part from a rejection of the hierarchy in classical music that made performers subservient to the composer and the score, a hierarchy that many experimental composers felt to be unsavory. "When you get right down to it," remarked Brown's mentor, John Cage, "a composer is simply someone who

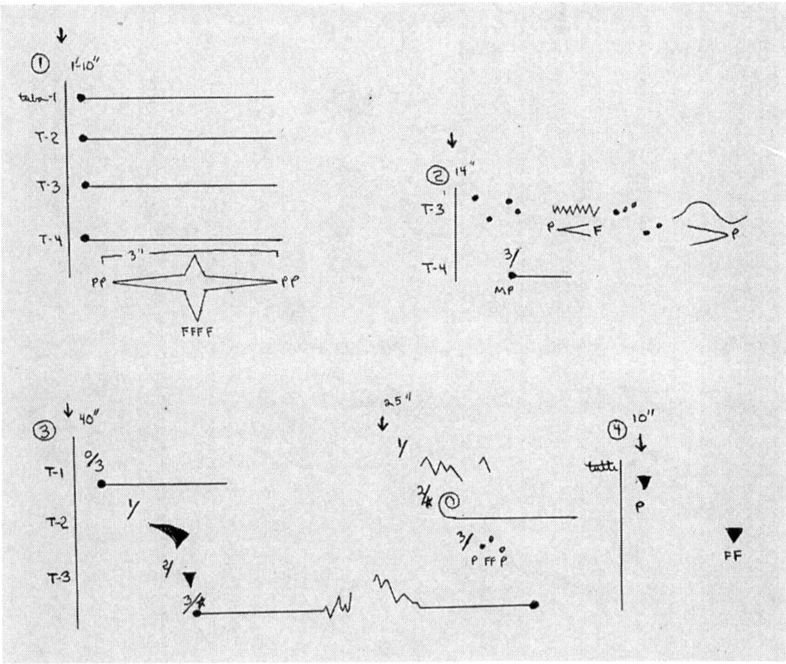

Fig. 2.2 Anthony Braxton, page 1 of *Composition #15* (1970), three pages of regulated symbolic notation for any four instruments. Courtesy of Anthony Braxton and the Tri-Centric Foundation.

tells other people what to do. I find this an unattractive way of getting things done. I'd like our activities to be more social and anarchically so."[56] Deeply political composers such as Cornelius Cardew shared Cage's aim and construed musical composition and performance as utopian activities that could foster experiments in radical democracy. Cardew thus envisioned his classic graphic score *Treatise* (1963–67) as a prompt for a group of musicians (or even nonmusicians) to engage in a discussion about how to perform the piece, arrive at a consensus about how to do so, and then, in a collective performance, follow the rules they had set themselves.

Such projects rigorously challenge the basic features of the classical musical score. Shattering the temporal logic of the traditional score, graphic scores are no longer virtual containers of sound that preserve, register, or record a sonic form or event that precedes them or prescribe a determinate performance that follows from them. Their orientation is entirely futural. Graphic scores are prompts or provocations for the production of new sonic events without a prior model. The divergent actualization that characterizes

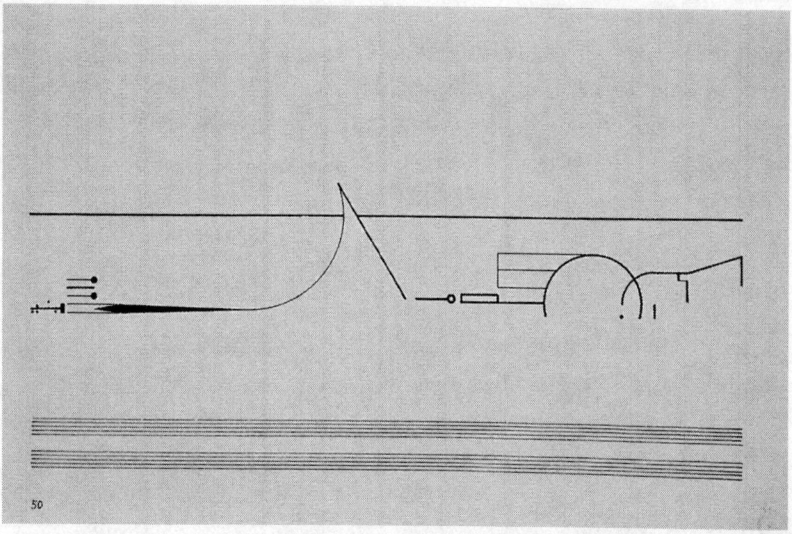

Fig. 2.3 Cornelius Cardew, *Treatise*, page 50, 1963–67. © 1970 by Hinrichsen Edition, Ltd. Used by permission of C. F. Peters Corporation.

performances of the classical score (and, indeed, of the traditional song) is taken to the limit. Where the classical score aims at a one-to-one correspondence between visual symbols and musical tones, the graphic score denies such correspondence. Thus, faithful performances of a given graphic score might bear no audible similarity to one another. In this way, graphic scores also undermine classical notions of the musical "work" and musical "authorship." The composer is the author of the visual score but not truly of its actualizations, which he or she may not even recognize as such. With the graphic score, then, the visual and audible content of music diverge, becoming two parallel streams. No longer truly functional, the visual score becomes an element in its own right and approaches the condition of visual art.

December 1952 still vaguely resembles a classical score, but one that has been largely erased (fig. 2.1). It thus anticipates the *Erased De Kooning Drawing* produced by Brown's friend Robert Rauschenberg the following year. Yet it also resembles the modernist drawings and paintings of Piet Mondrian and Paul Klee. These correspondences between visual art and the musical score were celebrated by the Polish-born composer Roman Haubenstock-Ramati, who suggested that any abstract picture could be treated as a musical score.[57] It was Haubenstock-Ramati who famously praised the pianist David Tudor for his astonishing facility with experimental scores, quipping that Tudor "could play the raisins in a slice of fruitcake."[58] The comment was made in jest; but it proved prescient, as Fluxus artists and other experimental composers began to treat all sorts of objects and events as provocations for sonic production. The last vestige of the classical score—its status as writing—thus disappeared. The score had been dispersed into the world of things, and the world of things had become ripe for sonification.

Interlude—Christian Marclay: Repetition and Difference

Christian Marclay's work over the past several decades presents a rich and helpful résumé of these developments and ingenious extensions of them. His work in the sonic and visual arts investigates the deconstruction and dispersal of the classical score, the generative potential of recording, and productive disjunctions between ear and eye. Marclay's first move was to volatilize the turntable and the record. In the late 1970s—working parallel to, but largely unaware of, hip-hop DJs such as Kool Herc, Grandmaster Flash, and Grand Wizard Theodore—Marclay put Moholy-Nagy's proposals into practice, transforming the turntable into a musical instrument and treating the record not as a finished product to be passively consumed, but as raw material for creative manipulation.[59] The aim was to make difference of repetition, to extract unrealized potential and new performances from the embalmed content of the musical commodity. Working entirely with found objects—thrift-store albums and record players discarded by elementary schools—Marclay composed and improvised sound collages and montages, sometimes literally cutting up records and pasting them together in new configurations. His routines and improvisations employed as many as eight turntables, on which he layered and mixed segments of records prepared with stickers, tape, objects attached with glue, and newly cut center holes. Marclay foregrounded the material properties of the record, the often damaged grooves cut into its flexible vinyl surface, the spiral channel that a nick or scratch could transform into a relentless stutter. From the hodgepodge of the thrift-store record bin, Marclay understood that the temporal structure of the recorded archive is discontinuous, nonlinear, and untimely. His turntablist practice followed suit, ignoring the historical and contextual peculiarities of his sources and building collages based solely on the sonic potential of the material. "To my ears they were only sounds, very abstract and detached from their original sources," Marclay noted. "They lost their identity and became fragments to be mixed—a loop, a texture, a transition, a beat, an intro, a word."[60]

Live performance gave Marclay a way to animate the inert musical object and set it against others in a productive tension.[61] But he also wanted to reveal that the recorded object has a life of its own. In 1985 he released a set of his own turntable performances on a commercial LP under the title *Record without a Cover* with an instruction engraved in one of its sides: "Do not store in a protective package." Without such protection, the records would inevitably accumulate scratches and attract dust and debris. What began as all-but-identical mass-produced objects would slowly diverge from one another, becoming unique works of art via the accumulated traces of their singular and contingent trajectories. The project alluded to the tradition of "experimental music," which only specifies a set of initial conditions from which sound then ramifies and diverges, initiating what John Cage called "an act the outcome of which is not foreseen."[62] (A particularly direct example can be heard in Steve Reich's early tape works *It's Gonna Rain* [1965] and *Come Out* [1966], in which two tape recorders playing the same vocal fragment gradually go out of phase, generating interlocking patterns of vertiginous complexity.) Marclay engages with this tradition but routes it through commercial culture, submitting the prefab world of Andy Warhol's Campbell's soup cans to Reich's tape-phase procedure, thus allowing time, chance, and the vicissitudes of commodity circulation to "improvise," generating new sonic material and producing results that he could not have foreseen in advance.[63]

A pair of photographic projects from 1988 tracks another sort of divergence. In *The Sound of Silence* (fig. 2.4), a photo of Simon & Garfunkel's 1964 single "The Sounds of Silence," Marclay exploits the record's paradoxical title to offer a reflection on the differences between photography and phonography and the disjunctions between image, text, object, and sound. As visual phenomena, the photograph, the record object, and its text all refer to a sonic flux that they capture in various ways but cannot themselves release. Yet by the same token, these mute media adequately capture the silence that the song itself precludes. A visual representation of the spoken word, text bears a close relationship to sound. But this relationship nonetheless remains symbolic and, ultimately, arbitrary. Photography and phonography share a common history, emerging in the nineteenth century as systems for the mechanical registration of sensory information. Yet the two remain

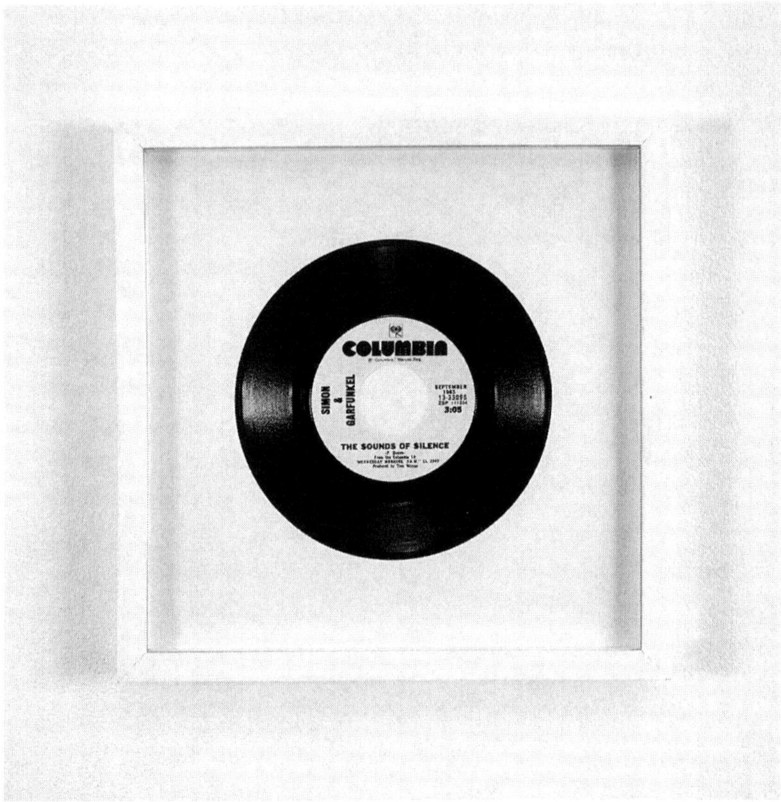

Fig. 2.4 Christian Marclay, *The Sound of Silence*, 1988, b&w photograph, 10¾ × 10¾ inches; framed: 12 × 12 inches. © Christian Marclay. Courtesy Paula Cooper Gallery, New York.

incommensurable, separated by the chasm that divides the sensory modalities. Another project from the same year, *Chorus II*, highlights and amplifies this chasm. An array of photographs depicts a collection of open mouths (fig. 2.5). Whether they are singing or speaking, yelling or laughing, we will never know, for the image is powerless to convey this. The title of the piece suggests togetherness and concert; but the images are clearly of heterogeneous provenance, and their individual frames set them apart.

A later project, *Mixed Reviews* (1999–2010), intensifies these disjunctions. Vivid and bombastic sentences pulled from music reviews—efforts to translate musical experience into language—are strung together to form a horizontal wall text that cuts across the exhibition space. Each installation of the piece translates the text into the local language, increasing the

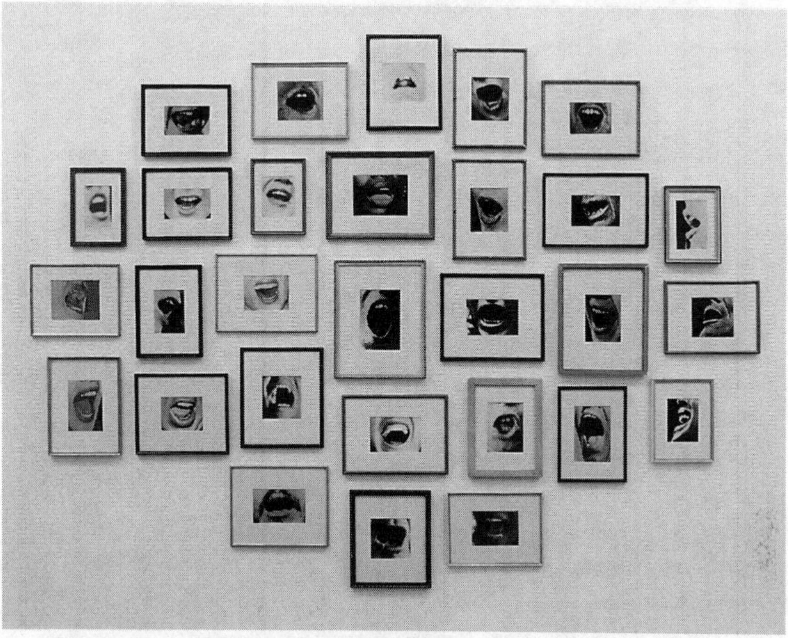

Fig. 2.5 Christian Marclay, *Chorus II*, 1988, b&w photograph, framed, 29 parts: various dimensions. Overall: 56 × 74 inches. © Christian Marclay. Courtesy Paula Cooper Gallery, New York.

distance between musical referent and linguistic sign. In a video version, *Mixed Reviews (American Sign Language)* (2001), a deaf actor renders the text as a flow of wildly expressive bodily gestures. The circuitous course of translation—from sound to texts in multiple languages to gestural signs on video—operates like the game of telephone, ensuring that the output will diverge substantially from the input. Even so, the text fires the aural imagination, provoking a silent experience that is nonetheless intensely musical. The video is likewise silent, but the actor's hands, arms, and face powerfully capture the physicality of sound, the waves and forces it releases and the social trajectories it engages.

These projects are not evidence of some nostalgia for lost unity, nor are they commentaries on the incapacities or disabilities of various media. Rather, they are testaments to the generative powers of difference and translation. Forestalling the stultifying collapse of the senses and media into identity or unity, and the conformist fantasy of perfect correspondence, they celebrate ingenious leaps between sensory modalities and media that produce genuine novelty. Perfect replication, we know from biology, would be a recipe for death and extinction. Life and creativity thrive on mutation, variation, and divergence.

Such leaps and divergences are actively cultivated by the series of photographic and video scores Marclay has produced since the mid-1990s. For the first of these, *Graffiti Composition* (1996), Marclay pasted thousands of poster-sized sheets of blank score paper on walls, billboards, and kiosks around the city of Berlin, inviting the public to contribute musical ideas. He periodically photographed the results, selected 150 of these, and then printed them on a set of cards to be used as incitements to musical performance (fig. 2.6). The piece certainly pays homage to pioneering works of indeterminate and graphic notation. Yet it also embraces earlier moments in the history of musical recording. Its five-line staves solicited, and often received, conventional musical notation—along with spray-painted tags, doodles, text fragments, dirt, and other residues of urban street life. At the same time, the collective, anonymous process of composition recalls the musical modality of oral-aural cultures that preceded the emergence of the musical score. Marclay himself describes the piece using a biological metaphor that aptly captures the fluidity and open-endedness of the rhapsodic song and graphic score alike. Introducing a performance of the piece in 2006, he rejected the label of "composer," preferring instead the role of the gardener: "I just planted a seed in Berlin in 1996 and a few times watered it, made sure it was growing o.k. But that's where my role stops. And I'm able tonight to sit back with you and look at it—or *listen* to it—grow."[64]

A later piece, *Shuffle* (2007), also consists of a deck of photographs to be used as a musical score. This time, however, the images document the fragments of conventional musical notation that pervade contemporary culture, printed on street signs, clothing, awnings, umbrellas, tattoos, and bric-a-brac of all sorts. They may be intended as mere decoration, signifiers of "music" in general; but Marclay takes these found objects seriously. The collection as a whole combines the Duchampian readymade (and perhaps also the "Green Box") with Stockhausen's *Klavierstück XI* to create a musical score of endless permutation. As in *Graffiti Composition*, anonymity plays a key role here, too, though in *Shuffle* it's the anonymity of a vast cadre of designers who go unnamed and uncredited in the visual culture of modern life. Marclay's photographs, then, are a form of sampling—not of musical sound, oddly, but of its visual representation. Photography and phonography approach one another and generate sparks across the divide.

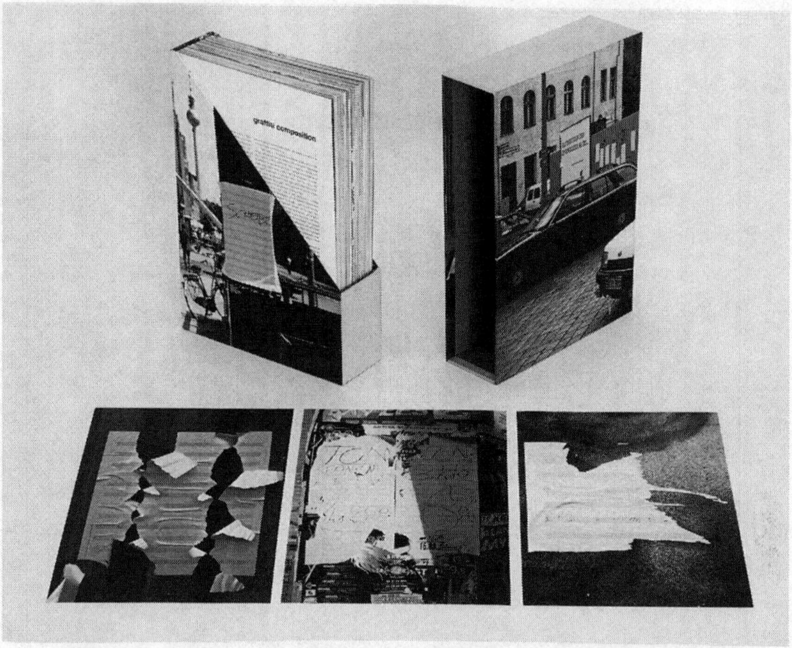

Fig. 2.6 Christian Marclay, *Graffiti Composition*, 2002, portfolio of 150 images, Indigo prints on Cougar stock, 14 × 9 inches, edition of 25, published by Paula Cooper Gallery. © Christian Marclay. Courtesy Paula Cooper Gallery, New York.

Closely linked with these projects are two others, *Zoom Zoom* (2008) and *Manga Scroll* (2010), both of which employ onomatopoeia, that curious effort of language to coin words that imitate the sounds to which they refer. Onomatopoeia attempts to circumvent the semantic content (the signified) that generally stands between the signifier and its referent—an effort by the word not just to *represent* the referent but to *be* it. Yet onomatopoeias turn out to be conventional signs, not natural ones, and, moreover, signs that are culturally specific. (The American says "chirp," the Spaniard "pio." The English "cock-a-doodle-do" is the Italian "chicchirichi.") What's more, Marclay's onomatopoeias are textual and visual, not spoken or sonic: *Zoom Zoom* is a photographic compendium of onomatopoeias found on banners, trucks, champagne bottles, candy wrappers, and elsewhere; *Manga Scroll* is a string of onomatopoeias lifted from English-language versions of Japanese comic books. Performers, then, are asked to undertake a roundabout translation: not to imitate sounds but to use their musical instruments to resonify graphisms that vainly attempt to imitate the noises of the world.

This proliferation of translations and leaps across various domains becomes dizzying when we consider that *Manga Score* pays tribute to the composer and vocalist Cathy Berberian's *Stripsody* (1966), which itself alludes to *Blam* (1962), *Whaam!* (1963), and other early paintings by Roy Lichtenstein—making Marclay's piece a deferred and circuitous response to Haubenstock-Ramati's suggestion that any painting might be treated as a graphic score.

Beginning with his early turntable compositions and improvisations, Marclay's work has always followed the logic of sampling and the remix, generating new material from old, insisting that every work is a remix that is itself perpetually open to remixing. His visual scores intensify this trajectory. In the case of these works, remixing takes place not merely within a single medium—from records to records, films to films—but across media—from photographs and films to musical performances. Furthermore, like any graphic score, they are structurally incomplete. As Umberto Eco put it in an early essay on musical indeterminacy, such scores "are quite literally 'unfinished': the author seems to hand them on to the performer more or less like components of a construction kit"—a matrix for divergent actualization.[65]

Screen Play (2005) provides a rich example. A thirty-minute montage of short clips from black-and-white films (home movies, adventure films, westerns, documentaries, educational films, etc.) periodically overlaid with simple graphic elements (colored lines, dots, staves, and wipes; fig. 2.7), *Screen Play* begins with the basic instruction: "To be interpreted by a small group of musicians." But how to interpret the score? The intermittent overlay of musical staves and visual metonymies suggests that the video might be read purely formally, the placement and movement of objects on the screen taken as indications of pitch, duration, or rhythm. Yet the abundant visual cues of sonic events (crashing waves, footsteps, fireworks, and the like) seem to direct performers to become Foley artists whose aim is to supply the missing audio. More loosely, performers might simply compose or improvise a soundtrack, following the general movement and mood of the visual flow. Any or all of these strategies is possible; and, in order to amplify differences among them, Marclay generally programs three different ensembles to play the score on any given occasion. Each time the film is given a different soundtrack, which, in turn, produces a different film.[66]

All these elements and interests come together in Marclay's masterpiece *The Bell and the Glass* (2003). At once a stand-alone work of art and a visual score, this double-screen video projection is premised on the unlikely conjunction of two famous objects on permanent display in Philadelphia: the

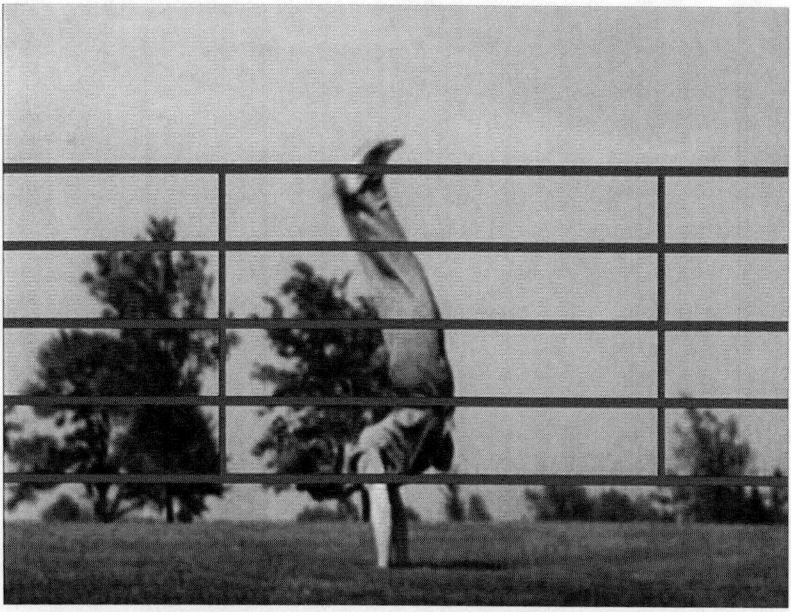

Fig. 2.7 Christian Marclay, *Screen Play*, 2005, DVD, 29 minutes, 40 seconds, produced by Performa. © Christian Marclay. Courtesy Paula Cooper Gallery, New York.

Liberty Bell and Marcel Duchamp's *Large Glass (The Bride Stripped Bare by Her Bachelors, Even)*. The two screens function like the turntablist's two decks, mechanisms through which fragments of all sorts are drawn into a mix. Discs, spirals, rotating drums, pulsing dots, and phonographs appear on both screens throughout the video, referring no doubt to the rotating objects and devices in the lower ("bachelor's") section of *The Large Glass*, but also serving as visual allusions to Marclay's turntablist practice, which he launched in the late 1970s in a band with a Duchampian name: the Bachelors, Even.

Arranged vertically, the two screens in *The Bell and the Glass* also operate as the symmetrical staves of the traditional musical score: the lower ("bachelor's") half functioning as the bass clef, and the upper ("bride's") half as the treble. Instances of musical notation (three interviews with Duchamp that Marclay transcribed into staff notation; Duchamp's chance composition *Erratum Musical*; and a collection of songs celebrating the Liberty Bell) appear throughout the video in the manner of *Shuffle*, as found musical material to be read by musicians. Indeed, the entire video is conceived as a graphic score, all its visual elements (images, texts, score fragments, etc.)

aimed at provoking musical accompaniment to the video's existing sonic elements (Duchamp's voice, the ringing of souvenir Liberty Bells, overlaid string passages, etc.).

In two interview fragments that recur throughout the video, Duchamp gleefully refers to "the breaks" in *The Large Glass*, the cracks caused in 1926 when the work was damaged during transport. Marclay homes in on this phrase, which becomes an organizing figure of his video, referring not only to the *Glass*, but also to the crack in the Liberty Bell that rendered it at once iconic and mute. More broadly, "the breaks" signifies the connection and disconnection between these two objects, the conjunction and disjunction between the visual and the sonic, and, by extension, between the visual cuts of cinematic montage and the auditory cuts of the turntablist's art, which—from disco, dub, and hip-hop through drum 'n' bass and dubstep—has consisted largely in isolating and extending what DJs call "the breaks" or "breakbeats," those sections of funk and rock songs during which the melody instruments drop out and the bass and drums come to the fore.

"The break," then, is the cut, line, or bar that both conjoins and disjoins the two terms of an opposition: bride and bachelor, bell and glass, sound and image, phonography and photography, mass culture and high art, staff notation and graphic score. It is also, for Duchamp and Marclay alike, the caesura between past and future, between what the artist puts into the work and its indeterminate destiny. Reflecting on the accidental cracks in the *Glass*, Duchamp remarks: "I like the breaks. . . . There's almost an intention there . . . , a curious intention that I'm not responsible for, a readymade intention, in other words, that I respect and love." It is his principle, Duchamp says elsewhere in the video, "to accept any *malheur* as it comes." This openness to chance, to accident, to any eventuality whatsoever defines the work of Duchamp and Cage, a lineage that Marclay makes his own. From his turntablist practice through his graphic scores, Marclay takes the ready-made object as raw material for the generation of new work and affirms this fate of his own work as well, acknowledging that nothing remains fixed, that the future will always diverge from the past, and that, well, those are the breaks.

Digitality, Decommodification, and Deterritorialization

Marclay challenges the supposed fixity of the musical score and the record object, revealing them to be virtual structures capable of wildly divergent actualizations. However, in its trajectory of deterritorialization, audio recording today has all but outstripped the object. The predominant mode of sonic capture and circulation is no longer the record or tape, or even their digital offspring, the compact disc, but data encoding formats such as MP3 and streaming audio. The easy and perfect copyability of digital data deals the final blow in the assault of recorded media on the original, removing the last vestiges of aura and object fetishism that still clung to the LP and, to a lesser extent, the CD. The world is now flooded with identical copies, which data compression technologies such as MP3 enable to circulate almost instantaneously around the globe via email and internet downloads or streams.[67] Moreover, as digital data, recorded sound is more easily manipulated and altered than ever before through digital audio workstations that are standard issue on most computers or available as freeware.

Despite careless claims about its "immateriality" or "dematerialization," digital data is still surely physical and material.[68] Yet its miniaturization and status as code readily transferable across platforms (CD, internet, portable media player, mobile phone, etc.) mean that it no longer truly qualifies as an object. Of course, the sonic flux has never been identical with the object, its material support and vehicle, its form of capture. And ever since Edison, the sonic flux has skipped across a series of material supports: tin and wax cylinders, electromagnetic waves, shellac and vinyl discs, magnetic wire and tape, CD, MP3, and so on. Yet, with digitalization, the physical support has nearly attained the fluidity of the flux it carries. This nonobjecthood and perfect copyability mean that, for the most part, recorded music is no longer even a commodity and has little economic value. As the media historian Jonathan Sterne puts it:

> Compared to the number of MP3s freely given and received through file-sharing, few meet the basic definition of exchange value: they are not paid for and do not require as much labor (in exchange for a wage or salary) to procure. Further, the exchange itself does not deprive the original owner of the file's use. . . . Epochal proclamations are tempting when confronted with this state of affairs: one could say that if recording shifted music from use-value to exchange-value, then digitization in the form of the MP3 liberated recorded music from the economics of value by enabling its free, easy, and large-scale exchange.[69]

This is not to suggest, as some have, that digital file sharing heralds a post-capitalist economy founded on the gift and potlatch.[70] The commodity value of the musical object has been transferred elsewhere—onto digital hardware, internet and telecommunications services, data mining, and the electrical infrastructure that makes the flow of data possible in the first place. The proliferation of identical recorded multiples without exchange value has also reinvested value in the uniqueness, presence, and aura of real-time live performance, the release of recorded works as originals or limited editions, and the revival of the LP and cassette as auratic objects.[71]

But my aim here is not to offer a description and assessment of commodity relations within contemporary capitalism. Rather, it's simply to point out that the digital capture of sound intensifies the virtualizing and deterritorializing tendencies of biological and written memory, allowing the sonic flux to spill beyond the confines of the cultural community, the rarified sphere of the concert hall, and the commodity object. Like previous forms of audio recording, digital capture dissolves the distinctions between "high" and "low," "here" and "there," "now" and "then," "music" and "noise," but greatly miniaturizes the vehicle, perfects the mechanism of replication, and vastly increases the speed of circulation. To paraphrase Marx, all that's sacred is profaned, all that's solid melts into the digital network. Indeed, digital recording is a consummate manifestation of the deterritorialization characteristic of capitalism, which liquefies all social relations and decodes all flows, approaching an absolute threshold against which it recoils and initiates a recuperation.[72] This tendency toward deterritorialization goes hand in hand with the seemingly opposed tendency noted earlier: the tendency toward reification, the reterritorialization and capture of flows onto the detachable, transportable commodity, the value of which is measured according to a universal form of equivalence—money. Digital data is likewise a universal form of equivalence capable of translating qualitatively different entities and flows (textual, sonic, visual, financial, etc.) into the strings of ones and zeros that constitute information. Yet, in the case of audio recording, the deterritorialization of digital data surpasses the limit of commodification.

The *song* captures the sonic flux via the physiology of the body and the conservative traditions of the cultural community, while generating variation through imperfect replication. The *score* arrests this variation and improvisation by fixing the song in writing as a bounded physical object that, however, allows it to float freely, untethered to any particular historical or cultural context. The *record* transforms sound itself into an exchangeable object, while intensifying the temporal and spatial deterritorializations initiated by the score and dissolving the distinction between musical and nonmusical sound. And the *MP3* accelerates the circulation and replication of audio recording, dereifying it, rendering it as pure information that confounds the logic of scarcity on which commodification depends. All these modes mark out various ways in which the sonic flux is interrupted, cut, sampled, captured, and diverted. Taken together, they form a nonlinear history of that flux, revealing the ways that it is inflected by biological, social, technological, political, and economic forces that work to territorialize and deterritorialize its relentlessly fluid and protean materiality.

3 THE SYMBOLIC AND THE REAL

PHONOGRAPHY FROM MUSIC TO SOUND

In the second half of the twentieth century, audio recording contributed to the dismantling of the classical score, spurred the revaluation of improvisation, and initiated new practices of sampling, mixing, and remixing. Indeed, the DJ culture of "cut 'n' mix" elegantly models the operations of the sonic flux: a continuous material flow of sound is interrupted, captured, segmented, filtered, relayed, and released back into the din in altered form. Yet the musical and ontological significance of the phonograph and its successors goes even deeper than this. Phonography discloses the sonic flux as such, the primary noise from which music is derived, and it provokes a materialist account of listening and the voice that cuts through the domain of the symbolic and plunges us into the real.

Hearing Things

MACHINIC SPEECH

The two inventors of the phonograph, Thomas Edison and Charles Cros, thought of their devices primarily as enabling the capture and extension of the human voice. For Cros, the phonograph (which he called the "paleophone") was a machine for preserving "beloved voices" and "the musical Dream of the too short hour."[1] Edison, too, conceived the phonograph as primarily a tool for the duplication of speech. In his list of ten uses for the machine, only two—namely, "4. Reproduction of music" and "6. Music boxes and toys"—concern anything other than vocal utterance.[2]

Yet these audio recording apparatuses fundamentally challenged idealist conceptions of the voice and language. At least since Plato, a prominent philosophical tradition has conceived speech as intimately tied to being and presence—specifically, to one's *own* being and *self*-presence. Our speech announces and affirms our living, physical existence and our conscious, mental intentions. Emanating from our very bodies as breath and vibration, speech is the ex-pression of our interiority—the discourse of the soul, as Plato called it.[3] And yet the words we speak are never our own. Every word we utter is borrowed—sampled—from a language: the virtual reservoir that Saussure called *langue* and the empirical stream of vocal actualizations he termed *parole.* As a form of sampling, even speech, then, is a technology, a prosthesis. Writing is even more evidently so. As Jacques Derrida famously noted in a passage considered in the previous chapter, writing "constitute[s] a kind of *machine* that is in turn productive, that my future disappearance in principle will not prevent from functioning."[4] Cast adrift from us, our written signs are able to signify even in our absence or after our deaths. (Indeed they *must* be able to do this. This machinic functioning is the very definition of writing.) Owing to this structural alienation from our bodily presence and animating intentions, the written sign can be understood in ways we never intended and drawn into contexts we never imagined or sanctioned. Writing operates in our stead, survives us, and continues to function without us.

This is no less true of audio recording or phonography (literally, "voice-" or "sound-writing"). As part of the archive of recorded sound, the recorded voice is submitted to the possibility of endless sampling, splicing, editing, and all manner of sonic modification. While it promises a return to the presence of the voice, audio recording does so at the price of an uncanny alienation of the voice from the body and mind that are said to have animated it. Recorded sound is often termed "disembodied," but that's not quite right. Rather, audio recording exchanges one body for another: a fleshy substrate for a mechanical one consisting of rotating plates, spinning discs, styluses, lasers, wheels, vibrating membranes and the like. With evident glee, Edison described this mechanical body to a newspaper reporter in 1878:

> This tongueless, toothless instrument, without larynx or pharynx, dumb, voiceless matter, nevertheless mimics your tones, speaks with your voice, utters your words, and centuries after you have crumbled into dust will repeat again and again, to a generation that could never know you, every idle thought, every fond fancy, every vain word that you choose to whisper against this thin iron diaphragm.[5]

The recorded voice reveals the technological character of vocalization in general, the production of sound as a physical rather than a spiritual fact. Like the voice, which has generally been endowed with an essential spirituality, music has, for millennia, enjoyed the reputation of being the most ethereal and metaphysical of the arts. Transient and intangible, it was said to offer an aesthetic experience that altogether eluded physicality. Allied variously with reason and spirit, music seemed to elevate human beings above the rest of the material universe. The phonograph shattered these fond illusions and gave credence to a new materialism.[6] When Edison sang "Mary Had a Little Lamb" into the phonograph's mouthpiece, a vibrating membrane drove a stylus that carved grooves into a strip of paraffin paper. Running the process backwards, the phonograph repeated Edison's song, revealing sound and music to be nothing other than the vibrations and tracings of material objects. At the same time, it provided further evidence that the human being is nothing but a complex fleshy machine.

HEARING AND LISTENING

Yet before the phonograph "speaks," it hears. Before the phonograph's horn is a mouth, it is an ear. Alexander Graham Bell made this gruesomely clear when, in 1874, he employed an amputated human ear as a sound transducer in the construction of his "ear phonautograph," an important precursor to the phonograph.[7] Both Bell's experiment and Edison's invention were instances of what Jonathan Sterne calls a "tympanic" turn in nineteenth-century science: a turn from "models of sound reproduction based on imitations of the mouth to models based on imitations of the ear," "from machines modeled on the production of sound through speech or music to machines based on the production of sound at the perceptual end—the middle ear's transduction of vibrations into perceptible sound," "from imitations of the causes of sound to imitations of sound as an effect."[8] Bell and Edison aimed to show not only that *speaking* is a mechanical process, but that *hearing* is as well.

This claim is likely to be taken metaphorically, for surely no machine can truly be said to hear. It may register, perhaps, but hearing is something different and something more. Just as speech requires an animating intention, hearing requires conscious apprehension and understanding. We should investigate these seemingly obvious claims. To do this, I want to turn to Roland Barthes's classic 1976 essay "Listening," which will allow us to examine a set of platitudes about listening and to reveal their inadequacy.[9]

Barthes's essay distinguishes three types of listening and the various domains to which they apply. The categorical scheme that organizes these types is an odd mixture: an Aristotelian essentialist taxonomy to which a specifically historical account is attached, the sum of which is glossed by a Peircian typology of signs. Barthes proceeds like Aristotle, laying out the phenomena, reflecting on them, and sorting them into plausible types. Not even considering the possibility of inorganic or mechanical audition, he immediately ties hearing to life, to the "living being." But even that's not quite right, for Barthes doesn't consider the possibility of a vegetal audition either. Instead, he climbs further up the *scala naturae* to animals. The first type of listening is mere "hearing," "a physiological phenomenon" that can be described "by recourse to acoustics and to the physiology of the ear." It is passive and receptive, characterized by the sonic "index" or "alert" that "either reveals danger or promises the satisfaction of a need." Though it survives in human beings as an evolutionary vestige, this type of listening is properly animal.[10]

Only the second type of audition is truly human. Distinguishing it from mere "hearing," Barthes initially calls it "listening" and later "deciphering." This modality is no longer merely physical, involving a physical organ (the ear) and a passive or automatic nervous system; rather, it is "psychological," engaging the brain, mind, or soul in all its activity, interiority, and creativity.[11] This second mode is hermeneutic and semiotic, a matter of "deciphering," interpreting a meaning that is not on the surface but "hidden," "obscure," "secret."[12] What one decodes or interprets are "signs"; and what one hears falls within the structure of signification. With this type of audition, we have moved from nature to culture. "Here, no doubt, begins the human," Barthes writes. "I listen the way I read, i.e., according to certain codes."[13]

To distinguish these first two types of listening, Barthes deploys a set of binary oppositions that have sustained philosophical idealism from Plato and Judeo-Christian thought through Kant, Hegel, and beyond: animal/human, nature/culture, passive/active, body/mind, exterior/interior, and so on. Such oppositions have for millennia served a metaphysical program aimed at distinguishing human beings from animals—indeed, from nature in general—by insisting that human beings are endowed with some immaterial attribute that elevates them above the rest of nature. We should be skeptical of this program. Before proceeding to discuss Barthes's third mode of listening, then, I'd like to pause to ask: Is human listening truly distinguishable from animal hearing? Is listening the active capacity Barthes takes it to be? Is it even characteristic of living beings?

MATERIALISM AND SENSATION: A PHILOSOPHICAL GENEALOGY

Barthes accepts the traditional view that listening requires something more than auditory stimulation and a physical organ that registers it—that a subject, self, or soul is necessary in order to apprehend, grasp, synthesize, and interpret what is passively received by the body. This orthodox view is challenged by a materialist philosophical tradition that presents a very different conception of sensation and perception. David Hume, for example, argues that the self is not the presupposition of perception but the result of it. Everything begins with perceptions, for Hume; and the self or subject, he writes, is "nothing but a bundle or collection of different perceptions, which succeed each other with an inconceivable rapidity, and are in a perpetual flux and movement."[14] The self or the I, Hume concludes, is a retroactive fiction inscribed in the structure of our grammar and thus difficult to dislodge.[15]

Friedrich Nietzsche fully concurs. For Nietzsche, it is "only owing to the seduction of language" that we posit a subject as the foundation of experience, perception, and action.[16] "The 'subject' is not something given but a fiction added on, tucked behind," he declares. "Is it even necessary to posit an interpreter behind the interpretation?" he asks, and then responds: "Even that is fiction."[17] For Nietzsche, this fiction of the subject is theological, for it posits as the origin of all activity some thing or substance that transcends the actions and passions—the becomings—that constitute the world of experience and nature. "I am afraid we are not rid of God," he concludes, "because we still have faith in grammar."[18]

The theology inscribed in grammar corresponds to that ancient desire of human beings to give themselves a special origin and status in the world. What happens when we let go of this idea of a transcendent subject that stands behind perception, sensation, action, and becoming in general? For Hume, doing so means admitting that there is a "great analogy betwixt" "the identity of a self or person" and "that identity which we attribute to plants and animals."[19] Nietzsche goes further. He repeatedly argues that allegedly "higher" human functions such as our capacities for logic, language, and textual interpretation are simply species-specific variations on the natural functions of assimilation and organization characteristic of even the "lowest" living creatures: the amoeba and protoplasm.[20] In Nietzsche's polemical language, "all events in the organic world are a subduing, a *becoming master*, and all subduing and becoming master involves a fresh interpretation."

"Interpretation," he tells us in the same passage, means "forcing, adjusting, abbreviating, padding, inventing, falsifying," and other such activities of assimilation and transformation.[21] What Nietzsche here calls "interpretation" he elsewhere calls "will to power," which he maintains is the basic principle of change evident throughout nature, from the chemical reactions and energetic forces of inanimate matter to the nutritive and reproductive operations of animals and plants, the formative activity of human labor, the textual interpretation of scholars, and the creativity of artists.

Whereas idealist accounts of perception consider mind, soul, or conscious, deliberative thought to be the active, transcendent force that animates the passive body, Nietzsche insists that "the soul" is an emergent property, a product of the struggle for dominance that takes place among the myriad drives, affects, and instincts of which the human subject is composed.[22] For Nietzsche, "a 'thing' is a sum of its effects, synthetically bound together by a concept";[23] and a subject is the sum of its affects, its capacities to be affected and to affect. Intelligence, understanding, knowledge, and consciousness are latecomers, weak and superficial capacities in comparison with the vast and powerful swarm of unconscious affects and drives that compose us. Consciousness, on his account, emerged solely to enable language as a means of communication among human beings. Hardly evidence of human superiority, consciousness and language are evolutionary compensations for the physical weakness of human beings compared with animals and the rest of nature.[24]

This line of thought was developed more fully by Nietzsche's contemporary, the great and undervalued late nineteenth-century empiricist philosopher, novelist, and evolutionary theorist Samuel Butler. Butler insists that nature—from rocks and plants through animals and humans to machines—is a unity that operates according to a basic set of evolutionary principles. Hence, Butler cannot tolerate the idea that consciousness or intelligence somehow sets human beings apart from and above the rest of nature. On the contrary, he insists that consciousness is secondary to "habit," the basic process of life. Indeed, for Butler, one is conscious only of what one has not yet mastered, what has not yet become unconscious memory and habit. To say of animals and plants that their activity is not conscious is to say that they perform such activities with perfect mastery. Far from elevating human beings, then, consciousness is evidence of human inexperience and frailty.[25]

Gilles Deleuze and Félix Guattari take up this tradition and bring us back to the question of sensation and perception. Everything in nature, for Deleuze and Guattari, composes itself via what they variously call "habits" (a term they draw from Hume, Butler, William James, and Félix Ravaisson), "contemplations" (a nod to Plotinus), or "contractions" (in homage to Henri Bergson).[26] It is not that the thing or the subject *has* habits; rather, it *is* these habits. It is formed as an entity through habit. A habit is acquired by "contraction," that is, by the binding of various natural flows (for example, of sunlight, water, or air) into a provisional unity or composition (for example, a flower). Such contraction or synthesis is passive in the sense that it does not require a preexisting subject that performs this synthesis; for, as we have seen, Deleuze and Guattari reject as theological the hylomorphic model of natural genesis according to which form must be imposed on matter from without. Rather, for them, nature is self-organizing, and entities and identities are emergent properties with inherent tendencies and capacities.[27] This is true even of inorganic matter. Pushed past critical thresholds by increased heat or pressure, chemical solutions shift from turbulent and chaotic behavior to regular oscillations, coherent convections, and the like. Such "dissipative structures" have been richly explored by the physical chemist and Nobel laureate Ilya Prigogine, who concludes that "in equilibrium, matter is 'blind,' but in far-from-equilibrium conditions it begins to be able to perceive, to 'take into account,' in its way of functioning, differences in the external world."[28] This notion of perception as "taking account" derives from Alfred North Whitehead, an inspiration for both Prigogine and Deleuze. Whitehead describes all of nature as "perceptive" in the sense in which every entity "takes account" of its surroundings.[29] In a discussion of Whitehead, Brian Massumi explains that an electron, for example,

> "takes account" of the electromagnetic field of the nucleus of the atom in the dynamic form of its orbit and in its quantum character (the unity of the dynamic form expressed as its orbit and energy level). The electron registers the "importance" of its fellow creatures of the nucleus, and expresses it in the dynamic unity of its own pathmaking. The trees along the river take account of the surrounding mountains in how they are able to take in the rain washing down from them, negotiating with their shadows for their growth, or availing themselves of the mountain's protection from the wind.[30]

Matter is sensitive, and every entity is what Deleuze calls a "primary sensibility." "Every organism, in its receptive and perceptual elements, but also in its viscera," he writes, "is a sum of contractions, of retentions and expectations."[31] And this is true for both the living organism and for inanimate matter: for "rocks," "physical causalities," and "chemical affinities."[32] That is, a thing or a body is a set of materials and forces that hold together, a composition that maintains itself in existence for some period of time until it eventually succumbs to forces of dissolution. Such syntheses are passive, but they are also creative insofar as they bring something new into the world: retentions and expectations that compose an entity and that hold disparate things together. What's more, these habits and contractions operate at every level and scale. They are not only personal but super- and subpersonal. In living beings, for example, they operate at the macro level of the species via the hereditary memory of inheritance and instinct. But every entity, every self or soul, is also composed of microhabits that Deleuze calls "little selves" or "larval selves."[33] "A soul must be attributed to the heart, to the muscles, nerves and cells," he writes, "but a contemplative soul whose entire function is to contract a habit."[34]

Aware that this might sound like rhapsodic panpsychism, Deleuze immediately qualifies his remark. "This is no mystical or barbarous hypothesis," he declares. "On the contrary, habit here manifests its full generality: it concerns not only the sensory-motor habits that we *have* (psychologically), but also, before these, the primary habits that we *are*, the thousands of passive syntheses of which we are organically composed."[35] Deleuze (and Guattari) propose not mysticism or panpsychism, but an account of nature and of natural entities that can do without transcendent minds, gods, or souls. The "souls" and "selves" that enter their account of habit are not primary but secondary, the result of natural processes of passive syntheses and self-organization: not "subjects" but "superjects," "injects," or "ejects."[36] Like Nietzsche, Deleuze and Guattari maintain that all of nature—rocks, plants, animals, human beings, and so on—is habitual, contractive, contemplative. Deleuze describes this position as a sort of vitalism and has been criticized on these grounds.[37] Yet his vitalism does not consist in the attribution of life, mind, or subjectivity to inanimate matter. On the contrary, consistent with his critique of hylomorphism, Deleuze rejects both sides of the opposition between "life" and "inert matter." Consistent with Darwinism, he shows that life originates immanently in mindless, mechanical repetition and contraction.[38] Conversely, he undermines the other side of the opposition, revealing that matter is not inert material waiting to be formed from without, but rather is self-organizing—precisely through immanent mechanical repetition and contraction. His "vitalism," then (if it still makes sense to call it that) dispenses with the scientifically objectionable features of traditional vitalisms: the mysterious, transcendent forces that are said to animate nature from without. Indeed, Deleuze challenges the notion that anything is necessary to animate nature other than the passive syntheses of nature itself, whose entities are emergent and contingent rather than pre-given and essentialist. Moreover, Deleuze and Guattari's peculiar vitalism is conjoined with vitalism's traditional opponent, mechanism, though their mechanism, too, is of an unusual sort. They famously describe all the component "habits" and "contractions" of entities as "machines"—"desiring-machines," to be exact—and call the self-organizing structures of matter the "machinic phylum."[39] The term "machine," here, is not metaphorical, they repeatedly insist.[40] Rather, a "machine" is "any system that interrupts flows"; and what we ordinarily call a machine is simply a particular instance of this broader conception.[41] For Deleuze and Guattari, nature (which is all there is) is the total set of flows (of water, air, genes, petroleum, language, binary code, etc.) and the total interlocking set of machines that cut into these flows, extract something from them, alter them, and generate new entities as a result.[42]

A MATERIALIST THEORY OF LISTENING

With this, we are almost back to where I left off before the philosophical detour: the question of phonographic hearing and a critique of the common distinction between listening and hearing as theorized by Roland Barthes. (We will have to wait a bit longer to get to Barthes's third form of listening). The materialist tradition I have surveyed challenges all the oppositions Barthes marshals in defense of his distinction. It levels the ontological field, placing the perceptive and interpretive capacities of human beings on par with those of animals, plants, rocks, and machines. The distinction between human activity, on the one hand, and animal (and vegetable and mineral) passivity, on the other, is undermined by the account of passive synthesis according to which the human subject is the result of countless presubjective, spontaneous contractions that are nonetheless creative—"interpretive," in Nietzsche's extended sense. And with this, the distinction between the psychological and physiological, mind and matter, is undermined as well. Nature is shown to be creatively productive without the direction of an animating, transcendent mind or spirit; and minds are shown simply to be emergent results of various contracting machines.

Recall that, for Deleuze, we *are* a "primary sensibility." We are made of contracting machines; but we also perceive or sense in the more ordinary meanings of those terms. Even at this more macro level, however, the operation is the same. To sense is to extract something from a flow, to retain or preserve a series of vibrations.[43] When we hear, for example, the eardrum vibrates along with a series of air pressure changes that are contracted together to produce the experience of a single sound.[44] To hear a melody is not to hear a succession of discrete notes or chords, but to contract these together into a unity of retention and anticipation.[45] Such contractions are not different in kind from what Hume calls "habit" and from the more primordial syntheses described by Deleuze, Nietzsche, and Butler. Indeed, Deleuze and Guattari refer to the body as a recording surface and suggest that nature itself is a synthesizer. All this, then, provides an answer to the old conundrum: "If a tree falls in the forest and there is no one to hear it, does it make a sound?" The answer is: of course it does; and only the most unreconstructed idealist could claim otherwise. For nature is replete with recording surfaces that contract vibrations. So, too, is it full of recording machines fabricated by human beings (whom Butler conceives as the external reproductive system for "the mechanical kingdom" by analogy with plants, which employ insects as their means of reproduction).[46]

This point is nicely driven home by Mungo Thomson's delightfully simple and surprisingly dramatic film installation *Silent Film of a Tree Falling in the Forest* (2005–6). The installation is devoid of human beings, but full of machines. A mechanical device (Thomson's camera) has recorded a set of events (trees falling in forests) by generating a chemical reaction caused by crystals of light-sensitive silver compounds exposed to light. A projector displays the film in a gallery alongside a large color photograph of a chainsaw mounted on a camera tripod. In all but one of the six one-minute sequences that compose the film, trees fall mysteriously without any evident cause, human or nonhuman. In the final sequence, a tractor with no visible operator drives in from the right, pulls a tree out of the ground with a large mechanical claw, drops it on the ground, and then retreats out of the frame. Played back in a gallery, the silent film seems to confirm the idealist response to the conundrum: that, indeed, without a subject to hear the event, a falling tree makes no sound. Yet the viewer watching the film actually perceives the soundless event, which undercuts the idealist response and our ordinary audiovisual experience. Moreover, the film's silence draws attention to the fact that a sync-sound film surely could reveal the sonic event that accompanies the visual one. This is underscored by the fact that, while the film is silent, the installation is not. The insistent clatter of the projector draws attention to itself as a mechanical surrogate for human perception. Shown as a loop, the viewer is also made aware that the projector will continue to present the same events in his or her absence and even in the absence of any viewers whatsoever, and, perhaps, that the walls and floors will continue to register the sound and light of the projector as well.

It is not absurd, then, to conceive of the phonograph and its mechanical kin as auditors on par with human listeners. A phonograph record or magnetic tape is a sensitive surface that contracts and preserves vibrations. Yet the phonograph hears differently than does the human ear, whose habits of "listening" have attuned it to articulate sound—speech, music, and the like. As Friedrich Kittler notes in his philosophical genealogy of modern media: "The phonograph does not hear as do ears that have been trained immediately to filter voices, words, and sounds out of noise; it registers *acoustic events as such*."[47] That is, it discloses what John Cage called "the entire field of sound."[48] The crackling of embers, the sputter of a motorboat, the reverberations of a room[49]—audio recording registers all this with the same facility that it captures a Bach cantata, a presidential address, or a child's first words. "The earliest phonographers," notes the sound artist Paul DeMarinis,

> discovered that when they recorded a sound, upon playback three sounds were heard. The first sound they heard was of course the sound they intended to record.... The second set of sounds heard coming from the horn of the phonograph were the inadvertent sounds of the environment, which rode along unnoticed during the recording process.... But a third sound was heard as well—the sound of the recording apparatus itself.... The rumblings of the mechanism, too, register upon the wax, and the texture and grain of the wax has its own raspy voice, a voice that sang along with every diva and accompanied every chance sound passing by the microphone. Surface noise, channel noise, the song of long ago and far away, presented a gift in disguise to the recordist and artist alike. This noise is the audible indication that information is being sent. In effect, this "noise floor" is the sound of silence of any given channel.[50]

"Articulateness," concludes Kittler, "becomes a second-order exception in a spectrum of noise."[51]

Indeed, as Jonathan Sterne shows, phonography "marks a shift in understandings of sound and practices of sound reproduction." Earlier attempts at the mechanical capture of sound (the construction of automata, for example) were oriented to the *source* of sound, attempting to imitate the processes of sound's production. Moreover, such attempts privileged particular sources, namely, the human mouth as the source of articulate speech, or musical instruments as the source of musical sound. By contrast, the phonograph and its kin were concerned with sound not as emanating from a particular entity or subject but "as a kind of *effect* in the world." Cut loose from its source, articulate sound became one sound effect among many. "Sound itself, irrespective of its source, became the general category or object for acoustics and the study of hearing," writes Sterne. "Speech, music, and other human sounds were reduced to special categories of noises that could be studied by the sciences of sound. In acoustics, frequencies and waves took precedence over any particular meaning that they might have in human life."[52]

The phonograph listens, too; but the scope of its contraction is broader or less discriminate than ours, taking in the whole of what we sometimes call "background noise." Refusing to distinguish between foreground and background, it reveals noise as the very source and destination of articulate sound. The phonograph reveals this background noise as a perennial sonic flux, a portion of which its recording contracts. And it vastly expands the resources of aesthetic attention, contemplation, and creation. Kittler gets at this via a heterodox materialist and technological reading of Jacques Lacan. A domain of articulate sound governed by formal rules, music (like speech) belongs to what Lacan calls "the symbolic order." Both consist of selected sets of tones and utterances produced and received according to established cultural rules and norms. The musical score and alphabetic writing further reduce this sound world to a small collection of visual symbols: twelve notes, twenty-six letters, and a modest array of qualifying signs. But phonography reveals something different, disclosing what undergirds the symbolic order but is disavowed by it: what Lacan calls "the real," the perceptible plenitude of matter and nature. With audio recording, chords and ratios give way to frequencies and vibrations, logic to physics, and musical meter to physical time. "The real takes the place of the symbolic," Kittler concludes; the phonograph "subverts both literature and music (because it reproduces the unimaginable real they are both based on)."[53]

WILLIAM S. BURROUGHS: THE TAPE RECORDER AND THE SOFT MACHINE

In his examination of perception and memory, Freud famously likened the mind—or the "psychic apparatus" (*psychischer Apparat*), as he was fond of calling it—to a recording device: the *Wunderblock* or "mystic writing pad," a child's toy composed of a waxed board overlaid with a thin sheet of waxed paper and a thicker sheet of celluloid. Words or marks made on the celluloid with a stylus would be registered on the waxed paper but could easily be erased by lifting the two sheets attached to the underlying board, which would nonetheless retain faint impressions. This little machine, writes Freud, "shows a remarkable agreement with my hypothetical structure of our perceptual apparatus," which combines fleeting perceptions with lasting memory traces.[54]

Of course, unlike our memory, Freud notes, the mystic writing pad cannot generate new texts by itself. "It is true," he writes, "that, once the writing has been erased, the Mystic Pad cannot 'reproduce' it from within; it would be a mystic pad indeed if, like our memory, it could accomplish that."[55] Here Freud falls back on a set of traditional philosophical oppositions—organism/machine, activity/passivity, life/death, interior/exterior, and so on—that his own equation of the psychic apparatus with a recording apparatus called into question.[56] Indeed, Freud's notion of the unconscious (figured as the very base of the mystic writing pad) undermines just these oppositions, insofar as it reveals conscious life (in all its spontaneity and presence) to be driven by a mechanism of desires and repressed traces that it does not and cannot govern or control.

In a collection of remarkable theoretical essays, literary texts, and audio recordings from the 1960s and '70s, William S. Burroughs radicalizes Freud's suggestion, asserting without reservation that the mind is a recording machine and pushing this thesis to its limit.[57] Burroughs inverts the traditional oppositions, associating the human mind and body ("the soft machine," in Burroughs's parlance) with passivity and external control, and the mechanical tape recorder with activity, spontaneity, and novelty. For Burroughs, consciousness and speech are by no means spontaneous, original, or self-present. On the contrary, they are passive playback apparatuses for an impersonal system of recording that precedes them. "You are a programmed tape recorder set to record and play back," he writes, insisting that this is not a metaphorical or analogical formulation but a literal description of the psychic apparatus.[58] The mind is a repository of "prerecordings," an archive of received opinion, prejudice, ideology, gossip, instinct, physical habits, conceptual furrows cut by grammar and logic, and mental patterns of association—all of it recorded by the nervous system through genetic or linguistic means, and manifested in everyday speech and action.[59]

Language, Burroughs repeatedly declares, is a virus; and this too is no metaphor. Quoting from a textbook on viral infection, Burroughs notes that viruses are characterized by (1) parasitic attachment to a host, (2) replication, and (3) passage to another host—a description that nicely captures the macro-scale transmission of language through human subjects, who are not so much its creators as its hosts.[60] Biochemically, viruses unsettle the opposition between life and death.[61] They are self-reproducing entities but lack metabolic autonomy and thus require a living host to provide the energy and materials necessary for their continued existence and propagation. For Samuel Butler, a parasitic relationship of this sort accounts for the evolution of machines, which reproduce and propagate themselves through human "agency."[62] And, of course, the biological conception of the virus has been extended (again, without metaphor) not only to the mechanical world—to the computer viruses that John von Neumann famously called "self-replicating automata"—but also to what Richard Dawkins first called "memes," self-replicating units of cultural transmission.[63]

Reel-to-reel and cassette tape recorders provided Burroughs with the means of counteracting the "word virus" and subverting the prerecordings that infect the human nervous system. Audio recording externalizes patterns of speech and behavior, enabling a careful analysis that reveals their functioning. "Get it out of your head and into the machines," Burroughs writes in an experimental text,

> a tape recorder is an externalized section of the human nervous system you can find out more about the nervous system and gain more control over your reactions by using the tape recorder than you could find out sitting twenty years in the lotus posture or wasting your time on the analytic couch listen to your present time tapes and you will begin to see who you are and what you are doing here. . . . study your associational patterns and find out what cases in what prerecordings for playback.[64]

But the tape recorder is not just a device for analysis. It is also a tool for intervention and invention. Working with Ian Sommerville and Brion Gysin, Burroughs devised a set of procedures to manipulate and alter audio recordings as a way to scramble the viral code, "isolate and cut association lines of the control machine," and generate new juxtapositions, texts, sounds, and ideas.[65] In "Silver Smoke of Dreams," Burroughs and Sommerville recited passages from Burroughs's cut-up novel *The Ticket That Exploded,* randomly rewinding or fast-forwarding as they recorded. The resulting piece is a somber sound poem composed of stuttered word fragments all but emptied of semantic content. Two other experiments, "Sound Piece" and "Inching, Is This Machine Recording?," were produced by manually rubbing the tape back and forth across the recording head, a process that distends words and eliminates their contours, transforming them into repetitive squeals and belches, and anticipating the turntablist practice of "scratching" vinyl records. Other pieces such as "Present Time Exercises," "K-9 Was in Combat with the Alien Mind-Screens," and "The Saints Go Marching through All the Popular Tunes" splice and overlay Burroughs's voice with snippets of radio news reports, television dramas, shortwave static, and accelerated music.[66]

These techniques might be seen as attempts to assert personal agency over the impersonal viral flow of linguistic and cognitive "prerecording." Yet this is not quite right, for the agent is neither truly human nor personal. Burroughs's techniques are largely aleatoric, allowing novelty to arise by chance rather than decision. The author's role is more akin to that of a spectator or a judge than a creator. Moreover, these experiments rely on and celebrate the agency of the machine rather than that of its operator. "Take any text speed it up slow it down run it backwards," Burroughs writes,

> and you will hear words that were not in the original recording new words made by the machine . . . words which were not in the original tape but which are in many cases relevant to the original text as if the words themselves had been interrogated and forced to reveal their hidden meanings it is interesting to record these words made literally by the machine itself.[67]

Tape recordings can also influence events or generate new ones, Burroughs insists, producing new memes, provoking new associations, and acting as a force in the world with palpable effects.[68]

Like Kittler and Sterne, Burroughs notes that the tape recorder has a wider range of perception than we do. Paraphrasing an essay on memory and perception from *New Scientist,* Burroughs remarks that "our sensory input is in effect recorded on an endless time loop, providing some seven seconds of delay for scanning before erasure. In this time the brain edits, makes sense of, and selects for storage key features."[69] Whereas human perception and short-term memory edit and erase portions of the tape, the tape recorder registers indiscriminately and thus reveals a world of sensory information that escaped our perceptual grasp. Our sensory memory, then, is a massively redacted version of the broader memory field registered by the tape recorder, a memory field that, without the agency of the machine, remains for us largely unconscious.[70] The experience of déjà vu, Burroughs notes, reveals this recording and editing operation in action, constituting a "brief erasure failure, so that we encounter stored memory data coming round again."[71] Such experiences highlight the peculiar temporal structure of the recorded memory field. Tape recordings can, of course, dislocate time, "activating a past time . . . yesterday voices phantom car holes in time accidents of past time played back in present time."[72] But Burroughs insists that they also have a predictive power: "When you make cut-ups you do not get simply random juxtapositions of words, . . . they mean something, and often . . . these meanings refer to some future event. . . . Perhaps events are pre-written and pre-recorded and when you cut word lines the future leaks out."[73]

PHONOGRAPHY, *SIGNIFIANCE*, AND SONIC MATTER

We can now return to Barthes's typology of listening. I noted earlier that it's an odd mixture. The first two types (animal hearing, human listening) are essentialist and ahistorical, capacities given in the very nature of the organism. The third type of listening is suddenly historical and specifically "modern." Barthes introduces it via a "brief detour into the realm of psychoanalysis."[74] This detour is instructive and ought to be read symptomatically. As a practice of listening and interpretation, psychoanalysis emerged in the late nineteenth century alongside the birth of modern auditory technologies—telephone, radio, and phonograph—that greatly intrigued Freud. Implicitly acknowledging this fact, Barthes immediately quotes a passage in which Freud advises that the analyst

> must turn his own unconscious like a receptive organ towards the transmitting unconscious of the patient. He must adjust himself to the patient as a telephone receiver is adjusted to the transmitting microphone. Just as the receiver converts back into sound-waves the electric oscillations in the telephone line which were set up by sound-waves, so the doctor's unconscious is able, from the derivatives of the unconscious which are communicated to

> him, to reconstruct that unconscious, which has determined the patient's free associations.[75]

In order to forestall his own selection and censorship, the analyst must try to suspend his deliberative, conscious attention, "not directing [his] notice to anything in particular, and . . . maintaining the same 'evenly-suspended attention' . . . in the face of all that [he] hears."[76] The analyst must, in other words, transform himself into a recording machine.

Yet Freud's choice of technology is puzzling. Instead of the phonograph (a recording apparatus), he chooses the telephone (an apparatus of electronically mediated speech, but not a storage medium). Kittler reads this passage as suggesting that Freud has a vexed relationship to the phonograph—that psychoanalysis and phonography are, indeed, competitors.[77] Contrary to Barthes's contention that psychoanalysis inaugurates a properly modern form of listening, Kittler suggests that Freud's mode of listening is, in fact, conservative, aimed at forestalling the modernity that phonography inaugurates. While Freud and Barthes still want to insist that, in Lacan's phrase, "the unconscious is structured like a *language*," phonography reveals, on the contrary, that the unconscious is *noise*.[78]

His psychoanalytic framework notwithstanding, Barthes shows some awareness of this tension. While psychoanalysis remains wedded to the signified and the depth of interpretation, Barthes maintains that listening since Freud (or, more accurately, since the phonograph) gives access to something beyond the "content" of the interlocutor's voice: to what Barthes famously calls its "grain," "the materiality of the body emerging from the throat."[79] Barthes conceives this as a shift from the signified to the signifier, from *signification* to *signifiance*. But here again Barthes, like Freud, retreats, wishing to constrain within language and the symbolic order what contests it from without: the auditory real, the very materiality of sound that Saussure banished from language and semiology. ("It is impossible that sound, as a material element, should in itself be part of the language," writes Saussure. "Sound is merely something ancillary, a material the language uses. . . . Linguistic signals are not in essence phonetic. They are not physical in any way. They are constituted solely by differences which distinguish one such sound pattern from another.")[80]

This materiality of sound is abundantly explored in the tradition of sound poetry, which, not coincidentally, begins at the dawn of the phonographic era with the work of Paul Scheerbart and Christian Morgenstern, the Russian

Futurists, and the German Dadaists. In a helpful critical survey of this tradition, the poet and theorist Steve McCaffery shows how early sound poetry shifted attention from *the sentence* to *the word*, renouncing syntactical and semantic meaning in favor of an exploration of the nonsemantic, material aspects of language. (As one of its inventors, Hugo Ball, put it, the sound poem "tries to elucidate the fact that man is swallowed up in the mechanistic process. In a typically compressed way the poem shows the conflict of the *vox humana* with a world that threatens, ensnares, and destroys it, a world whose rhythm and noise are ineluctable.")[81] The advent of the tape recorder in the late 1940s allowed sound poets such as Henri Chopin, Bernard Heidsieck, and Bob Cobbing to go further, abandoning *the word* in favor of *sound*—a shift "from phonic to sonic," as McCaffery puts it.[82]

At the end of his essay, Barthes briefly invokes the music of John Cage as engaging this third type of listening, no longer a deciphering or decoding of signifieds but a "dispersion" or "*shimmering* of signifiers."[83] Here, too, Barthes strikes close but misses the mark: Cage's music is never about the signifier but always about the sonic real, sonic materiality itself. Cage is interested not in language and chatter but in silence, which he identifies with noise, conceived as an anonymous sonic flux that precedes and exceeds human sounds and signals.

Alvin Lucier: From Signification to Noise

To explore these ideas more fully, I want to turn to the work of one of Cage's successors, Alvin Lucier, whose key works involve just this dispersal of the human subject into noise and a movement from the symbolic to the real. I will focus on Lucier's first mature works and, in particular, an important piece that has received little attention, *North American Time Capsule* (*NATC*), composed in 1967.[84]

NATC occupies an intriguing and curious place both in Lucier's oeuvre and in the generational shift from the classic electronic music of the 1950s to the experimental electronics of the 1960s and '70s. Classic electronic music was wedded to a vast corporate and institutional infrastructure that relied on immense, immobile equipment housed in universities and research laboratories. The resulting compositions came to exist on tape as fixed and final products with no possibility for live performance (save live playback) and no opportunity for improvisatory intervention. Despite their use of a novel medium, early electronic composers such as Herbert Eimert,

Milton Babbitt, and Karlheinz Stockhausen tended to pursue the aims of the classical avant-garde and, in particular, to extend the theory and practice of serialism. In opposition to this establishment, Lucier and his compatriots (among them David Behrman, Gordon Mumma, Frederic Rzewski, and Pauline Oliveros) constituted a sort of musical counterculture. Following the lead of David Tudor, they favored cheap (or homemade), portable electronic gadgets and put them in the service of open-ended or process-based compositions intended for live performance. Unconcerned with traditional conceptions of musical form or with elaborately calculated logics of pitch, rhythm, and timbre, the experimentalists reveled in the volatile unpredictability of the electronic signal, empirically exploring the life of sounds and the nature of auditory perception.[85]

NATC shares some of the institutional and technological features of classic electronic music. Its one and only version was recorded at Sylvania Applied Research Laboratories on a bulky assemblage of mainframe equipment—a vocoder prototype—that required the assistance of a professional engineer. Yet for all this, *NATC* bears the hallmarks of experimental composition, characterized by John Cage as initiating "an act the outcome of which is unknown."[86] Lucier approached the piece without a written score (musical or technical), instead offering performers only the whimsical instruction "prepare a plan of activity using speech, singing, musical instruments, or any other sound producing means that might describe—to beings very far from the earth's environment either in space or in time—the physical, social, spiritual, or any other situation in which we find ourselves at the present time."[87] The technical execution of the piece was handled by Lucier, who approached the vocoder and its components as a novice eager to discover what the machine could do. "I did what David Tudor would do with an organ," recalls Lucier, "you know, pull out all the stops and stuff. Tudor would have a table of electronics in which one thing was plugged into something else, so complex that he didn't know, when he turned a dial, what was going to happen. I had this extraordinarily complex machine still in its stages of completion, and [*NATC*] was just an opportunity for me to use it as an enormously wonderful and interesting piece of electronic equipment."[88]

This experimental attitude toward existing electronic equipment connects *NATC* with other key works in Lucier's oeuvre—for example, *Music for Solo Performer* (1965), in which a performer fitted with EEG electrodes excites percussion instruments via the electrical impulses of his or her brain (fig. 3.1), and *Vespers* (1968), which makes creative use of echoloca-

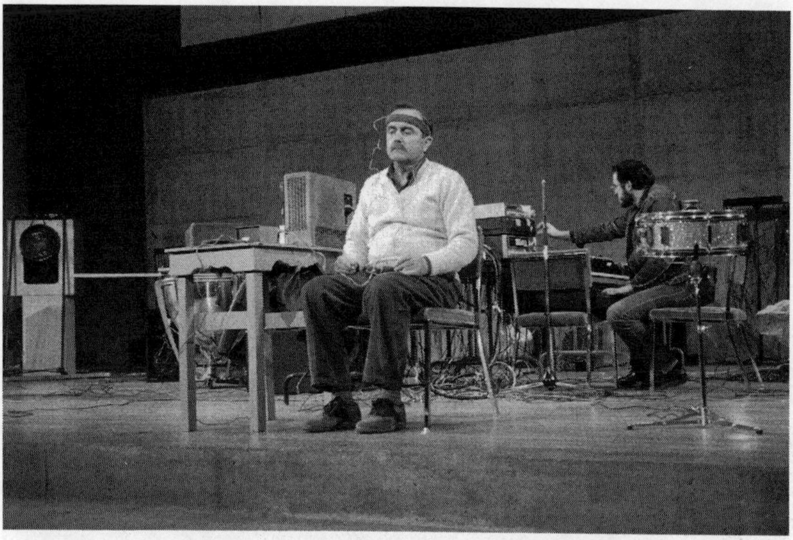

Fig. 3.1 Alvin Lucier, *Music for Solo Performer*, 1965, performance at the Cage Symposium, Wesleyan University, Middletown, Connecticut, 1988. Photo © Gisela Gronemeyer.

tion devices built to aid the blind. *NATC* is also the first in an important series of pieces composed by Lucier between 1967 and 1970 that explore the transformation and materiality of the human voice. Even more profoundly, the piece provides a key to Lucier's worldview—musical and otherwise—and highlights his rigorous naturalism.

A BRIEF HISTORY OF THE VOCODER

NATC is among the first musical applications of the vocoder. But in 1967 the device already had a rich scientific and musical history.[89] Indeed, the vocoder played a key role in the founding of digital technology and the inauguration of electronic and computer music. In 1928 Homer Dudley, a telephone engineer at Bell Labs, began to work on solving a major problem in long-distance telecommunication: how to compress broadband speech signals (with a frequency range exceeding 3000 Hz) for transport across the very narrow (200 Hz) bandwidth of transatlantic telegraph cables. Dudley was unconcerned with the semantic content of speech; he was interested solely in its material structure, which, he discovered, could be separated into two basic components: a sound source (produced by the vibrating vocal chords) and its modulation (by the nose, throat, tongue, and lips). He surmised that the solution to the problem would involve not compressing speech itself, but transmitting an adequate description of the voice's two components and then using that description to reconstruct a version of it at the other end. He initially attempted to describe and transmit information about the movements of the speaker's vocal apparatus, but this proved to be far too difficult.[90] Dudley eventually hit on a purely electronic solution. Using a bank of narrow-band filters, he sampled the energy levels of the speech signal at ten different frequency ranges (an eleventh sample registered the fundamental pitch of the voice), encoded these as a series of numbers, and then transmitted this coded description. At the receiving end, a synthesizer read the code and reconstructed the sound using an oscillator to recreate the fundamental frequency and a corresponding set of filters to shape it. Patented in 1935, Dudley named his device the Vocoder, a contraction of "VOice-CODER" or "Voice Operated reCOrDER."

In 1948 Dudley brought a version of his Vocoder to Germany, where he visited Werner Meyer-Eppler, director of the Institute for Phonetics and Communication Research at Bonn University. Impressed by the device, Meyer-Eppler used it during a lecture at the music academy in Detmold. Among the attendees was Robert Beyer, a sound engineer from Cologne's Nord-Westdeutscher Rundfunk (North-West German Radio) who had long been interested in the possibility of electronic musical instruments. Beyer introduced himself to Meyer-Eppler, and the two began a collaboration to advance the cause of electronic music. Together they delivered lectures at the 1950 International Summer School for New Music in Darmstadt, where they met the composer Herbert Eimert, who joined them in the project of founding an electronic music studio. A year later, at the newly renamed Westdeutscher Rundfunk (West German Radio), they began to build the first facility for purely electronic composition.[91]

A half decade later, back at Bell Labs, the vocoder found its way into the earliest experiments with computer music. Engineers in the acoustic research division were working with Dudley's technology to convert analog voice signals into digital data. In an effort to send several conversations down a single telephone line, they enlisted the aid of the computer. One evening two Bell engineers, Max Matthews and John Pierce, attended a concert of piano music at nearby Drew University. Unimpressed by the performance, one whispered to the other, "The computer can do better than this." Taking up the challenge, Matthews began to experiment using the computer as a music synthesizer and a year later launched MUSIC 1, the first computer program dedicated to sound synthesis.[92]

All of a sudden a group of engineers and scientists had become composers. The linguist and psychoacoustician Newman Guttman produced the first piece of computer music in 1957, a seventeen-second demonstration titled "The Silver Scale." Pierce, head of Bell Labs' communication sciences division, responded in 1959 with the cheery anthem "Stochatta." Matthews himself composed a series of longer and more innovative pieces in which the computer was made to approximate the sound of a singing voice. Then, in 1961, with the Bell physicist John Larry Kelly, he recorded a computer version of the 1892 pop song "Daisy Bell (Bicycle Built for Two)." Using vocoder technology, Kelly programmed the IBM 704 to sing the famous song over Matthews's calliope-like electronic accompaniment.[93] The novelist Arthur C. Clarke, who happened to be visiting his friend Pierce, overheard the demonstration and incorporated it into his screenplay for *2001: A Space Odyssey*, in which, at the film's climax, the dying computer HAL 9000 offers "Daisy" as its swan song.

At the 1964 World's Fair in New York, Bell Labs exhibited a new and improved vocoder. It was there that Wendy (then Walter) Carlos, a student at the Columbia-Princeton Electronic Music Center, first encountered the device and became enthralled. After graduating from Columbia, she met Robert Moog, who became a close collaborator. Carlos's enormously successful 1968 LP *Switched-On Bach* was something of an extended advertisement for Moog's synthesizer, and the two went on to build a custom vocoder intended specifically for musical use. In 1971 Carlos featured the vocoder in her soundtrack for Stanley Kubrick's adaptation of *A Clockwork Orange*.

Within a few years the vocoder had become a staple of electronic music and of popular culture more broadly. Musical instrument manufacturers such as Korg, Bode, and Synton began producing portable versions that were eagerly deployed by Kraftwerk, Pink Floyd, Herbie Hancock, Zapp, Laurie Anderson, Neil Young, and countless other musicians. *Doctor Who*'s Daleks and Stephen Hawking brought the signature vocoder sound—a squelched, tinny, and overly enunciated monotone—into the culture at large, where it heralded a cyborg future.

LUCIER AT SYLVANIA

Little of this history was known to Lucier when he first encountered the device. In 1962, Lucier returned from a Fulbright in Rome, where he had befriended Rzewski and encountered the work of Cage, Tudor, and La Monte Young, composers who challenged Lucier's classical training and suggested an alternative path. Back in the United States Lucier accepted a position at Brandeis University as director of its Chamber Chorus. A 1963 Chorus performance at New York City's Town Hall brought Lucier into contact with Robert Ashley and Gordon Mumma, emerging composers of electronic music and organizers of the ONCE Festival, a multimedia extravaganza held annually in Ann Arbor. Ashley and Mumma invited the Chorus to the 1964 ONCE Festival, and in 1966 Lucier reciprocated by bringing Ashley, Mumma, and their friend Behrman to Brandeis for a concert of works by the four composers. The concert was a success, and so, calling itself the Sonic Arts Group (later the Sonic Arts Union), the quartet launched a tour of the United States and Europe.[94]

The next February, at Boston's annual Winterfest, the Sonic Arts Group performed a concert sponsored by Sylvania Electronic Systems, a lighting, consumer electronics, and telecommunications firm located near Brandeis in the Boston suburb of Waltham. Lucier's piece on the program, *Music for Solo Performer*, delighted Sylvania representatives, who commissioned him to compose a new work for a vocoder under development by engineer Calvin Howard.

Sylvania's vocoder consisted of an array of components: a *telephone receiver* that registered vocal input; a *spectrum analyzer* able to sort and filter sonic frequencies; a *pitch detector* that determined the basic pitch of the auditory input; a *voiced/unvoiced detector* that distinguished (voiced, pitched) sounds produced by the vibrating vocal chords from (unvoiced, "noise") sounds produced solely by the mouth, lips, and tongue; a *digital encoder* that translated this information into binary pulses; a *digital decoder* that translated the code back into auditory information; and a *spectrum synthesizer* that used this information to recreate the original input. Armed with an array of vocal material, musical instruments, and electrical appliances, Brandeis students spoke, sung, read, and played into the vocoder receiver while Lucier and Howard flipped switches and twisted knobs to manipulate the various elements of speech and transform them into nonsemantic sound (fig. 3.2). Over the course of two days, Lucier recorded eight tracks of material that he later mixed down to produce the existing stereo version of the piece—a wild cacophony full of zipping pulses, sirenlike whines, grating gurgles, metallic hisses, sibilant whispers, jarring screeches, and bursts of white noise.

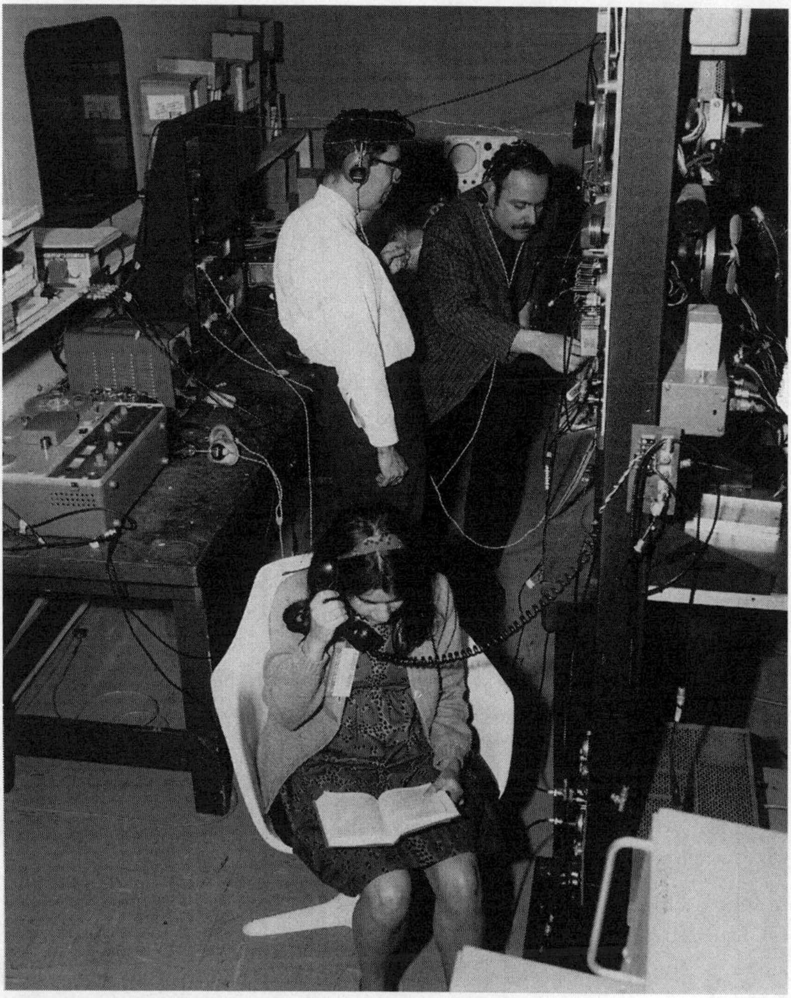

Fig. 3.2 Alvin Lucier (standing, right) recording *North American Time Capsule*, for voices and vocoder, Sylvania Electronic Systems, Waltham, Massachusetts, April 1967. Courtesy of the New York Public Library.

ALIENATING THE VOICE

True to its origins in telephony, the vocoder has always been an instrument of communication, a teleological device aimed at the transmission of messages. However alien its means or sound, the vocoder is made to deliver intelligible speech. Dudley's vocoder and Kubrick's HAL humanized the machine by making it talk. Carlos and Kraftwerk moved in the opposite direction, using the vocoder to mechanize the human voice. Regardless, meaning and sense were to be preserved, and both machine and human were made to affirm their submission to the symbolic order.

Lucier's approach to the vocoder was entirely different and considerably more radical. The score for *NATC* tells us that the piece is aimed at communication with aliens. But Lucier admits that this is a red herring, "just a fanciful idea, a provocation for what the piece would be."[95] Even a cursory listen reveals the degree to which *NATC* undermines the aim of delivering intelligible speech. Instead of communication with aliens, *NATC* is concerned with alienating communication and with the alien nature of communication. Rather than concerning himself with the vocoder's intelligible output, Lucier placed himself (and the listener) in the middle of the process, where speech is transformed into electrical signals and code. While most telephonic and musical users have been fascinated with the vocoder's capacity for vocal synthesis, Lucier was interested in it as a tool for vocal analysis. But even this puts it too mildly, for in Lucier's hands the vocoder became a machine with which to liquidate speech and to abolish the identity of the speaking subject, shattering all syntax and pulverizing every symanteme, morpheme, and phoneme into fluid sonic matter.

Such a project connects Lucier to contemporaries such as Henri Chopin, who employed electronic equipment to shift the interest of poetry from language and meaning to sound. This shift is manifested in a series of vocal works composed by Lucier in the late 1960s and early 1970s that begin with spoken texts, which are then radically altered through electronic means. Lucier's 1969 composition *The Only Talking Machine of Its Kind in the World* is dedicated to "any stutterer, stammerer, lisper, person with faulty or halting speech, regional dialect or foreign accent or any other anxious speaker who believes in the healing power of sound." The piece invites a speaker to "talk to an audience through a public address system for a long enough time to reveal the peculiarities of [his or her] speech," then asks friends to build a tape-delay system that would "annihilate" these peculiarities and hence relieve the anxiety of public speaking.[96] As such, the piece shifts attention from meaning to the voice itself and treats electronic instruments as therapeutic prosthetics that heal by transforming vocal tics into loops of nonlinguistic sonic material. A related piece, *The Duke of York* (1971), calls on one performer to use electronic equipment "to alter the vocal identity" of another performer by electronically modifying the material characteristics of their voice.[97] In the recorded version, recitations of a Roman letter, an operatic aria, and a pop song are gradually and cumulatively tweaked, at first rather modestly through panning and filtering.[98] By the end of the piece, however, Lucier's voice has become a plaintive howl submerged in feedback and frenetic blasts of electronic noise. More radical still is *I Am Sitting in a Room* (1970), Lucier's most famous composition. In a wonderfully direct and recursive gesture, the prose score for the piece serves as its vocal content:

> I am sitting in a room different from the one you are in now. I am recording the sound of my speaking voice and I am going to play it back into the room again and again until the resonant frequencies of the room reinforce themselves so that any semblance of my speech, with perhaps the exception of rhythm, is destroyed. What you will hear, then, are the natural resonant frequencies of the room articulated by speech. I regard this activity not so much as a demonstration of a physical fact, but more as a way to smooth out any irregularities my speech might have.

The text is spoken into one tape recorder and then repeatedly played back into another—thirty-two times in the best-known recording, a 1980 version that features Lucier recording himself in the living room of his Middletown, Connecticut home.[99] Over the forty-five-minute duration of the performance, Lucier's voice—and particularly his characteristic stutter (fittingly manifested on the key words "rhythm" and "smooth")—is gradually engulfed by the space. After ten cycles speech has become a surging wash of metallic tones, like a slow, distorted steel-drum performance. After twenty cycles it has become a distant carillon dirge; after thirty, a nervous, squelchy drone.

Though *I Am Sitting in a Room* is often taken to be an exploration of sonic space akin to the earlier composition *Chambers* (1968), Lucier explicitly (and, of course, repeatedly) proposes a different understanding of the piece. More than the "demonstration of a physical fact"—the discovery and amplification of a room's resonant frequencies—the piece concerns the dissolution of speech and of the speaker into sound and space. What begins as first-person speech in a domestic setting gradually becomes anonymous sound that overwhelms and eradicates the performer's personality. Meaning and sense dissolve into rhythm; identity and self are absorbed into space.

Of the compositions in this vocal series, only *I Am Sitting in a Room* achieves the power and radicality of *NATC*. But *NATC* goes further, explicitly reflecting on (1) the alien nature of speech, language, and communication, (2) the status of language as a prosthesis—a "virus," as Burroughs put it—a virtual structure that precedes and exceeds the utterance of any given speaker, and (3) vocalization as the product of a machine subject to mechanical failures of all sorts: glitches, scratches, erasures, broken parts, power failures, and so on. *NATC* draws attention to this communicative alienation. Words intended to identify their speakers to alien others are uttered into the vocoder, a device built to transport them by electronic means to distant places and times. But the messages fail to reach their destinations, or, at least, fail to reach them intact, for along the way they are sampled, clipped, bent, layered, and otherwise mangled. More than a half century later (presuming we are among the temporal—if not extraterrestrial—aliens to which the piece is addressed), *NATC* presents itself to us not as a recording of North American inhabitants circa 1967 or even as glossolalia or Babelian babble, but as glorious electronic sound—no longer signal, but noise.

LUCIER'S REALISM

This undermining of the symbolic order (the domain of language, meaning, signification, and communication) is not gratuitous or nihilistic. It delights less in the destruction itself than in the discovery that follows. Lucier's project is aimed at uncovering what underlies the symbolic order but is disavowed by it: the real.

On Kittler's account, the vocoder played a significant role in this disclosure of the real,[100] for with the vocoder the human voice becomes a data stream like any other. Significant speech is described as frequencies and envelope curves that are transformed into noise and then back again into intelligible data. The vocoder takes any two acoustic streams regardless of their provenance and maps them onto each other. It subtracts sense, meaning, or signification and leaves only the material flow of vibration, frequency, and sound.[101] In so doing, it enacts the ultimate return of the repressed, for the symbolic order (like culture in general) is founded on a nature, materiality, and physicality that it relentlessly disavows. Banished from language, which wants to believe that it is "not physical in any way," this sonic materiality returns as the real, opened up by recording technologies from the phonograph to the vocoder, the tape recorder, and the computer.

If music belongs to the symbolic, then sound belongs to the real. And, indeed, along with pioneers such as John Cage and Pierre Schaeffer, Lucier's work marks an important transition from musical composition to the expanded field of sound art.[102] Sound art is the art of the auditory real. It is concerned not with the communication of musical values but with an exploration of what Cage called "the entire field of sound" and the nature, movement, and transmission of sound as a material, physical substance.[103]

Lucier is sometimes described as a "phenomenological composer," but this characterization is misleading.[104] It misconstrues his work as concerned with the *apprehension* of sound rather than with *sound itself*. The idealist sees no way to get from the one to the other; and so he or she either deems reality mental or rests content with the description of its appearances. Lucier's position, however, is much closer to that of phenomenology's historical nemesis: materialism or naturalism. His reliance on science and collaborations with natural scientists are well-known; and, by his own account, Lucier often "do[es] little more than frame [scientific experiments] in an artistic context."[105] For Lucier (and for the naturalist in general), there is no strict division between subject and object, self and world, perception and substance—and this not because (à la Berkeley or Hegel) everything is mind or discourse, but because everything is nature and matter. Human beings are *of* the world, not set apart from it as mental or spiritual spectators. In *Music for Solo Performer*, Lucier shows that the brain itself is an electrical generator and a musical instrument in its own right. *I Am Sitting in a Room* demonstrates the continuity between the human voice and its material surroundings. And *Music on a Long Thin Wire* (1977; fig. 3.3) allows those material surroundings—air currents, changes in air pressure or temperature, ambient vibrations, and so on—to perform the piece without human intervention.[106]

True to his naturalism, Lucier also draws no rigorous boundaries between the human, the animal, and the machine. Instead, his work consistently explores the continuum that stretches from one domain into the others. *Vespers* employs mechanical devices to endow performers with the sensory capacities of bats and dolphins. *Bird and Person Dyning* (1975) sets up a feedback system between a human performer and an electronic bird (itself an intriguing conjunction of the animal and the machine). Lucier's performances of *The Duke of York* present a personal and cultural history in which he successively channels the Roman emperor Augustus, the nineteenth-century French composer Hector Berlioz, and the mid-twentieth-century American pop singer Johnnie Ray. The piece ends with an extended series of electronically distorted whale calls that project a future union between human, animal, and machine.[107] *Quasimodo the Great Lover* (1970) adopts the long-distance communication of whales as a structural principle that is realized as a series of electronic relays. And *NATC* renders this interest

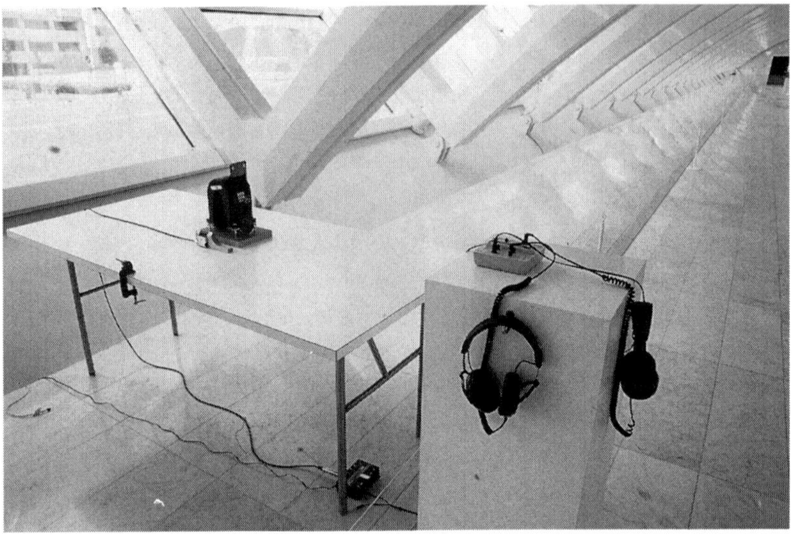

Fig. 3.3 Alvin Lucier, *Music on a Long Thin Wire*, 1977, installation at the Milwaukee Art Museum, 2006. © John R. Glembin and the Milwaukee Art Museum.

in long-distance communication as an alliance between the human, the machine, and some future alien interlocutors.

TIME CAPSULES

But *NATC* is not just a piece about the transmission of signals over vast expanses of space. As its title suggests, it is also engaged in a theorization of time. Indeed, I want to suggest that, along with the series of pieces that historically and conceptually follow it, *NATC* proposes a theory of time and memory that underscores Lucier's naturalism and that richly resonates with a tradition of philosophical naturalism that extends from Benedict de Spinoza through Henri Bergson and Gilles Deleuze.

Sonically, *NATC* comes off as garble, babble. Anyone who hears it will wonder what such babble could possibly communicate to future or alien beings. As we have seen, this garble is largely the result of Lucier's interest in vocal analysis, or the pulverization of the voice in the passage from meaning to sound. Yet the sonic chaos of the piece also has another source: a density due to aural simultaneity, the layering of eight separate tracks, each of which, presumably, registers a number of different voices. This interest in simultaneity and accumulation engages a conception of time and memory, as we can see through a comparison of *NATC* with several other pieces that historically surround it.

(Hartford) Memory Space, for example, calls on each member of an ensemble to travel to a designated place (Hartford, for example), to record (mentally, graphically, or electronically) the sounds of that space and then recreate those sounds in a concert situation by way of the voice or conventional musical instruments. In performance, each musician presents his or her recreation (or memory) simultaneously with all the others. As Lucier describes it:

> I wanted [the performers] to stick as closely as possible to their remembrance of the environment, so I isolated [them] from one another. It was as if each of them were on an island but the audience could see and hear all those islands. The islands could be parts of the town, or places in the streets, and the audience would see and hear a composite of which the individual players were only a part.[108]

True to its title, the piece thus conjoins time (memory) and space (geographical location). Indeed, it offers a spatial model of time and memory in the manner of Bergson's famous diagram of the inverted cone (fig. 3.4). Bergson figures the present as the apex of the cone (S), the base (AB) of which represents the totality of the past. Various horizontal slices or planes (A′B′, A″B″, etc.) represent regions of memory, each of which contains the totality of the past in more or less contracted or dilated form. Just as the present carries along with it the entirety of the past, each memory accesses this totality from a particular point or region. *(Hartford) Memory Space* operates in a similar fashion. Each performer presents a (remembered) part of the whole city, and the simultaneous performance of these parts offers an approximation of the total urban soundscape, which, however, remains virtual, out of earshot.

Fig. 3.4

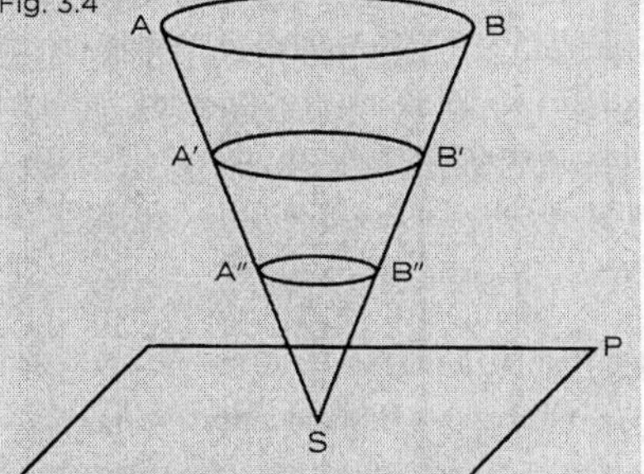

Operating by the slow layering and accumulation of sonic information, *The Duke of York* and *I Am Sitting in a Room* temporalize this simultaneity, and Lucier's remarks about these pieces amplify the conception of time and memory laid out in *(Hartford) Memory Space*. He suggests that the synthesizer (*Duke of York*) and the tape recorder (*I Am Sitting in a Room*) are models of memory. "It struck me that tape is now memory," he told Douglas Simon; "you can store information on tape just as you can store it in your brain, only it's more accessible. So tape for me was a substitute for using your brain to remember."[109] Similarly, reflecting on *The Duke of York*, Lucier remarked:

> I think the real reason I used [the synthesizer] is that it was called a *synthesizer*, probably from the old RCA synthesizer that was designed to imitate the sounds of musical instruments with a new technology. I had always hated that idea. It had seemed to me a waste of time to try to synthesize the sounds of perfectly good acoustical instruments with a new technology. But since *The Duke of York* has to do with the layering of one identity on another to make a composite image, I thought that the notion of synthesis was justified.[110]

Here Lucier reveals that the piece is not fundamentally about imitation, but about memory as a form of synthesis or accumulation. ("Memories, it had to do with memories," he told Thomas Moore.)[111] And, indeed, this notion of memory is not subjective or psychological, but what Deleuze calls "ontological," a kind of "Being-Memory" or "world memory."[112] The project began as a deeply personal project, an effort to tap into or to channel the musical memory of his wife, Mary.[113] But, like Bergson's widening cone, the project quickly expanded "to include not only popular songs but any vocal utterances taken from poems, plays, operas, or any real or fictitious written material."[114] From here, the piece became world historical and even cosmic. "Theoretically," Lucier continues, "you could imagine that you had something to do with all the vocal utterances that were ever made and that you might bring yourself back through time to when you were a small animal."[115] Finally, Lucier goes one step further:

> I also had in mind that there's a single source of life, the idea of a single-cell splitting into two and then four and then eight, geometrically. This piece, however, would work back the other way. If you could do it infinitely, everyone would process that sound according to every memory they ever had, thereby going back to where they had a connection; it's a grandiose idea.[116]

Exploration of the personal memory of a loved one quickly connects Lucier to all human beings, our distant animal past, and, finally, the entire history of life on Earth. The domain "my past" or "Mary's past" opens out onto the past in general. And for Lucier, all this is made possible by the synthesizer as an external model of memory and temporal synthesis.

Here again we see Lucier affirm a naturalism according to which nature forms a profound continuum, a field in which each entity and temporality enfolds every other. We find a model of memory that conceives it not as personal or psychological but as impersonal, pre-individual, ontological. And, challenging the traditional notion of time as centered on a present that passes into the unreality of the past, Lucier affirms a notion of the past as an immense totality that presses into the future.

It is this notion of time that *NATC* so richly exemplifies. If *The Duke of York* explores the virtuality of the past—its coexistence, through memory, with the present—*NATC* explores the virtuality of the future. Like *The Duke of York*, *(Hartford) Memory Space*, and *I Am Sitting in a Room*, *NATC* models memory and time as an intense accumulation and subsistence of sensory material. But, through the very notion of the time capsule, it projects this past into an unknown future. It collects elements from an infinite reservoir and offers it to imagined futural others for their own creative selection and transformation. As such, it highlights the model of time inherent in experimental music in general, which initiates "acts the outcomes of which are unknown." Opposed to the classical model of time (and the time of classical music) as the passage through a pre-given totality, *NATC* construes time as an open whole in which an infinite and accumulated past projects a future that is genuinely novel.

NATC, then, reveals Lucier's abiding interests and encapsulates his philosophical position. It inaugurates his project to dissolve the voice into sonic matter, announces his commitment to a thoroughgoing naturalism or materialism, and suggests a conception of time and memory that is consonant with this naturalism, according to which matter and temporality constitute a unitary whole that each entity, each moment, and each sound enfolds and expresses in unique and unforeseen ways.

PART II

Being and Time in the Sonic Arts

4 SIGNAL TO NOISE

AN ONTOLOGY OF SOUND ART

As both a term and a practice, "sound art" has become increasingly prominent since the late 1990s. The label has been embraced by many artists, curators, and critics, and the number of museum and gallery exhibitions dedicated to (or prominently featuring) sound art has grown exponentially in recent years.[1] Yet the meaning of the term remains contested, and prominent figures have dismissed the concept of "sound art" altogether. In a wall text introducing an exhibition of sonic art at MoMA PS1 in 2000, the sound-installation pioneer Max Neuhaus responded to the explosion of interest in sound art by questioning the nature and viability of the practice. So-called sound art, he wrote, is nothing but an "art fad." As a term and a category, he maintained, it does no useful work and does not helpfully supplement existing categories such as "music" and "sculpture."[2] Neuhaus's response captures a set of prevalent misgivings about sound art, in particular the suspicion that the label is merely a way to repackage music in response to a soaring art market and a floundering music industry.[3] It also resonates with the view of many contemporary artists that sound is not so much the medium of their art but simply one tool among many in an increasingly multimedia or postmedium tool kit.[4]

Neuhaus is a venerable figure whose assessment of the status of sound in contemporary art deserves to be taken seriously. Nevertheless, I want to defend the value of the term "sound art," which, though clumsy and inexact, has become established in the artistic lexicon and, more important, is distinguishable from "music" on both historical and philosophical grounds. Resisting both the "musicophobia" that Brian Kane diagnoses in recent discourses on sound art, and its inverse, the "musicomania" that would subsume all sonic art under the category of music, I contend that sound art constitutes a distinct field, one that partially overlaps with experimental music while also extending beyond music and disclosing something that music ordinarily does not.[5]

Noise

The history of experimental music in the early twentieth century evinces a recurrent desire by composers to carve out a domain of sonic art beyond music—an "art of noises" (Luigi Russolo), "organized sound" (Edgard Varèse, John Cage), musique concrète (Pierre Schaeffer and Pierre Henry), and so on. These efforts have largely been assimilated by music and retrospectively understood as part of its history. Yet, for many artists working toward the end of the twentieth and beginning of the twenty-first century, these early figures pointed to developments that are less easily brought under the banner of music. Alvin Lucier's *Vespers*, in which blindfolded performers explore a space using echolocation devices, would seem closer to science or performance art than to anything in the musical tradition. To take another example, the line that runs from Russolo, Varèse, Cage, and Schaeffer through the "soundscape compositions" of Luc Ferrari, Hildegard Westerkamp, and Annea Lockwood to the more recent "field recording" practices of Toshiya Tsunoda, Jana Winderen, and Jacob Kirkegaard increasingly diverges from the concerns of music and the purview of music history. Inspired by Cage, Schaeffer, Westerkamp, and others, the "militant sound investigation" of the art collective Ultra-red most often takes the form of community meetings that stage listening sessions organized around social questions such as "what is the sound of anti-racism?" or "what is the sound of the war on the poor?"[6] These and other such practices point to the need for, and relevance of, an extramusical category of sonic art for which "sound art" has emerged as the leading label.

But what defines "sound art" and distinguishes it from "music"? For some, the distinction lies in the contrast between exhibition and performance, and thus involves a difference in both venue and temporality. On this view, music is tied to the performance of compositions with a fixed duration on a stage or in a concert setting, while sound art typically takes the form of continuous or recurrent sound environments that don't involve performers and are presented in galleries and museums.[7] The role of space and site is emphasized by some, who insist that, unlike music, sound art is site specific and actively engages its architectural environment.[8] These standard definitions helpfully capture a range of sound-art practices; yet, as their proponents generally acknowledge, such characterizations fail to be exhaustive, and important works fall outside their grasp. Ultra-red's practice of social listening would fall outside these definitions, as would Winderen's recordings of ultrasound emissions and Francisco López's concert-style presentations of "environmental sound matter." While retaining the category of sound art, then, I'd like to make it both broader and more specific—broader in that it partially overlaps with music, and more specific in that it marks an ontological difference within sonic experience. Sound art, I propose, draws attention to a transcendental or intensive domain of sound that has gradually become manifest over the course of the twentieth century. In contrast with ordinary music, speech, and signal, I will call this domain *noise,* though we will see that the extension of this term far exceeds that of its ordinary usage.

We can begin to attune ourselves to this conception of noise by considering a set of passages from the philosopher Michel Serres's rich and poetic book *Genesis*—passages that, in what follows, I aim slowly to unpack. Early in the book, Serres writes:

> Background noise [*le bruit de fond*] is the ground of our perception, absolutely uninterrupted, it is our perennial sustenance, the element of the software of all our logic. It is the residue and cesspool of our messages. . . . It is to the logos what matter used to be to form. Noise is the background of information, the material of that form. . . . Background noise may well be the ground of our being. It may be that our being is not at rest. . . . The background noise never ceases; it is limitless, continuous, unending, unchanging. It has itself no background, no contradictory. . . . Noise cannot be made a phenomenon; every phenomenon is separated from it, a silhouette on a backdrop, like a beacon against the fog, as every message, every cry, every call, every signal must be separated from the hubbub that occupies silence, in order to be, to be perceived, to be known, to be exchanged. As soon as a phenomenon appears, it leaves the noise; as soon as a form looms up or pokes through, it reveals itself by veiling noise. So noise is not a matter of phenomenology, so it is a matter of being itself. . . . Yes, noise is metaphysical. It is the complement to physics, in the broadest sense. One hears its subliminal huffing and soughing on the high seas.[9]

We tend to think of noise as something secondary or derivative. It is disruptive, disturbing an initial state of calm. It interferes with communication and thought, making it difficult to hear, speak, understand, or concentrate. Noise, then, is a nuisance that we wish to eliminate and that we believe can, in principle, be eliminated. Information theory lends scientific support to this everyday supposition, taking noise to be what interferes with the transmission of messages and signals. For the information theorist, noise is the entropic force that drags the ordered signal toward randomness as it flows through a channel. As a practical science, information theory takes as its aim the elimination or suppression of this entropic force and, as far as possible, the restoration of messages and signals in all their original purity and clarity.[10]

The opposition between signal and noise (or music and noise) would thus seem to conform to the traditional metaphysical oppositions between substance/accident and essence/appearance, both of which pit something primary or fundamental against various imperfect and contingent manifestations. Yet from Hume and Nietzsche through Quine and Derrida, such oppositions have come under serious philosophical attack. Likewise, a rigorous philosophical consideration of sound should question the distinction between signal and noise.

One way of doing so is to show that the distinction is relative rather than absolute. Varèse, for example, asserts that it is simply a matter of perspective. "Subjectively," he quips, "*noise* is any sound one doesn't like."[11] The information theorist Abraham Moles concurs by way of a telling example. He notes that—though certainly musical—an orchestra tuning up is generally considered to be noise, while the clapping of an audience—a form of white noise—is taken to be meaningful and, hence, signal. "In short," Moles concludes, "there is *no* absolute structural difference between noise and signal. They are of the same nature. The only difference which can be logically established between them is based exclusively on the concept of *intent* on the part of the transmitter. *A noise is a signal that the sender does not want to transmit.*"[12]

This relativization would seem to put signal and noise on par with each other, allowing noise an ontological role of its own, one no longer subordinate to signal. Yet this relativism, too, privileges signal. It construes the distinction between signal and noise (or music and noise) solely from the perspective of communication and meaning, and thus of human intentions and values. Yet, before there were creatures to exchange signals, there was noise: the crackling of cosmic radiation, the rush of solar wind, the roar of the sea, and so on. And even now, every signal is issued against the backdrop of this noise. As Serres puts it, noise is the background hubbub of life, the ceaseless sonic flux: the hum of fluorescent lights, the rustling of leaves or fabric, the sound of traffic, radio static—indeed, all of these combined. It is from this background that any signal comes to the fore, temporarily drawing our attention to it and away from the background noise.

In this sense, noise is not an ordinary empirical phenomenon, not simply one sound among many. Rather, it is a transcendental phenomenon, the condition of possibility for signal and music. To get at this transcendental dimension, I want to turn to the great early modern philosopher Gottfried Wilhelm Leibniz, to whom Serres alludes at the end of the passage quoted above and throughout *Genesis*.[13] Two centuries before Freud, Leibniz presented a powerful theory of the unconscious that has particular relevance to auditory experience and, as we will see, to sound art.[14]

Leibniz and the Auditory Unconscious

Leibniz is often classified with René Descartes as an early modern European rationalist. But the two developed significantly different theories of knowledge, mind, and metaphysics. For Descartes, the mind is completely transparent to itself, and all thought is conscious thought. Clear and distinct ideas serve as the standard for truth and epistemic certainty; and Descartes insists that clear ideas are necessarily distinct, and vice versa. Leibniz objects that clear ideas always have an element of confusion or indistinctness about them and that conscious thought makes up only a small portion of mental content. To illustrate this claim, he routinely offers the example of a man who lives near a mill or a waterfall. Such a man, he notes, no longer distinctly hears the sounds made by the mill or waterfall even though they are ever-present. Now, Leibniz maintains that such a person does in fact register these sounds, but only unconsciously, as background, as something ordinary and not singular. And this is true of so-called white noise generally, of which Leibniz's favorite example is the sound of the sea. He writes:

> Each soul knows the infinite—knows all—but confusedly. It is like walking on the seashore and hearing the great noise of the sea: I hear the particular

> noises of each wave, of which the whole noise is composed, but without distinguishing them. But confused perceptions are the result of impressions that the whole universe makes upon us; it is the same for each monad.[15]

When I walk along the seashore, my perception of "the great noise of the sea" is clear; that is, it is fully and powerfully audible. But it is also confused, since I hear this sound as a mass and fail to distinguish its elements—the individual waves—which remain obscure. Nevertheless, I must in some sense hear the individual waves; otherwise I could not hear the aggregate. Hence the sound of each individual wave must be distinct for me, though in an unconscious, and hence obscure, sense. What is clear, then, is also confused; and what is distinct is also obscure.

The sounds of the mill, waterfall, and sea are cited by Leibniz as evidence for his theory of "minute perceptions" (*petites perceptions*), according to which each of our conscious perceptions is grounded in a vast swarm of elements that do not tend to reach conscious thought.[16] Such unconscious perceptions have what Leibniz calls a *virtual* existence.[17] They determine conscious perception but are generally not present to it. Leibniz notes that memory, too, has a virtual existence. Our present experience takes place against the backdrop of a vast reservoir of memory, which, for the most part, remains virtual. However, a photograph, a song, or a chance encounter can draw a portion of this reservoir into actuality, temporarily illuminating it and offering a glimpse of the totality.[18]

This virtual field has, for Leibniz, a truly cosmic significance. Each of the "minute perceptions" that unconsciously determine conscious perception is itself the effect of causes that ramify out to infinity. Each individual wave is the result of a multitude of forces: the speed and direction of the wind, air temperature and pressure, the temperature and viscosity of the water, and so on. As a result, each conscious perception is the local registration of the entire state of the universe at any given moment. The same is true of memory. The reservoir of memory contains not only particular memories or experiences—traces of all the past events I have experienced—but everything to which those experiences and memories are connected: in short, the entirety of the past.[19] This is not an extravagant idea if we acknowledge that, evolutionarily speaking, I am my entire past—my personal past as well as the past of my entire species and, indeed, of natural history in general. Such forces or tendencies are in me or are contained in (genetic and bodily) memory in a virtual state, an obscure state of indistinctness, latency, and dilation. When we manifest a particular tendency or remember an event or experience, we draw it from this reservoir, actualizing it or contracting it. Hence, in the passage cited above, Leibniz can conclude that each individual (or "monad") "knows the infinite," "knows all," albeit "confusedly"—that is, virtually.

To return to Leibniz's sonic examples, what we call white noise contains, in principle, all frequencies of sonic energy in a sort of dilated state such that no one element comes to the fore or draws our attention. In his book *Sound Ideas*, Aden Evens reminds us that

> vibrations do not disappear, but dissipate, echoing all the while, for energy is conserved. Every vibration, every sound, hangs in the air, in the room, in bodies. Sounds spread out, they become less and less contracted, they fuse, but they still remain, their energy of vibration moving the air and the walls in the room, making a noise that still tickles the strings of a violin playing weeks later. Every sound masks an entire history of sound, a cacophony of silence.[20]

If we accept Leibniz's argument, we hear each of these sound waves—past and present—but we hear them confusedly. Indeed, like the man who lives near a water mill, this sound remains background to us and constitutes what we call silence. Only the singularity of a signal—speech or music, for example—stands out against this background, contracts it, and renders sound clear and noticeable.

We saw that, for Leibniz, each individual "knows [and hears] the infinite—knows [and hears] all—but confusedly." He goes on to imagine God as one who knows and hears the totality. In the passage quoted in part above, Leibniz writes that "confused perceptions are the result of impressions that the whole universe makes upon us," concluding that "God alone has distinct knowledge of the whole."[21] This theological posit may seem quaint and outmoded; but, in a recent book on noise, the information scientist Bart Kosko comes to a strikingly similar conclusion. "Is the universe noise?" Kosko asks, and then continues:

> That question is not as strange as it sounds. Noise is an unwanted signal. A signal is anything that conveys information or ultimately anything that has energy. The universe consists of a great deal of energy. Indeed a working definition of the universe is all energy anywhere ever. . . . The noise-signal

duality lets a sincere pantheist counter that he loves or wants God and that God just is the entire universe but spelled with fewer letters. So to him the universe is not noise but one big wanted signal.[22]

Kosko and Leibniz thus seem to figure the distinction between signal and noise as the result of an epistemological limitation. What we limited human beings hear as noise—that is, as confused perception—would be perceived by a superior intellect as a clear signal. For God, there are no confused ideas, no noise. Leibniz and Kosko fall back on the idea that the distinction between noise and signal is merely a matter of perspective and that noise is ultimately a secondary, superfluous phenomenon, the result of a deficiency.

Yet Leibniz's theory of "minute perceptions" suggests an alternative understanding that relinquishes the theological posit.[23] Instead of construing the relationship of signal to noise as a distinction between part and whole (I clearly grasp this small zone or region, but the vast whole escapes me), Leibniz, the inventor of differential and integral calculus, construes the relationship as a differential threshold (or singularity) between conscious perception and an auditory unconscious. The sound of the sea, we saw, is derived from an infinity of small perceptions (the sound all the individual waves), which we unconsciously register but do not consciously perceive. What we do consciously perceive is the differential result of these minute perceptions that manifests itself as the ocean's roar. Leibniz's other prominent auditory example approaches this idea from the other side. For the man who lives near the water mill, it is not the parts but the entire sound that is—or has become—imperceptible. This sound has ceased to be remarkable and has become ordinary, unconscious, background. Leibniz thus makes it possible for us to grasp the distinction between signal and noise not as one between part and whole, between ignorance and knowledge but as one between the singular and the ordinary, perception and its conditions of genesis, the actual and the virtual—or what, following Deleuze, I have called the "intensive."

According to this reading, noise is not some linear accumulation of signals (which would still subordinate the former to the latter). Rather, noise is the set of intensive sonic forces that are capable of entering into differential relations with one another in such a way that they pass a threshold of audibility and become actualized as signal. (Leibniz notes that it is not a steady increase but "a tiny increase or addition" that brings this unconscious or intensive noise to conscious or actual awareness.)[24] The roar of the sea is not *composed of* the sound of the individual waves that are its *elements*.

Instead, the roar is *derived from* the waves, which are its *differentials*. Noise and signal, then, are not differences in degree or number but differences in kind, distinct domains. Noise is no longer merely one sound among many, a sound that we do not want to hear or cannot hear. Rather, it is the ceaseless and intense flow of sonic matter that is actualized in, but not exhausted by, speech, music, and articulate sound of all sorts. Recall that, in a seminar on Leibniz, Deleuze offers just such a suggestion. "One can . . . conceive of a continuous acoustic flow . . . that traverses the world and that even encompasses silence," he writes. "A musician is someone who samples something from this flow."[25] This is the idea I want to pursue here: noise as the ground, "the continuous acoustic flow" that provides the condition of possibility for every articulate sound, as that from which all speech, music, and signal emerge, and to which they return.

Sound Art and the Sonic Flux

If what we ordinarily call "music" actualizes this sonic flux, then what is the role of sound art? I suggested at the outset that sound art turns an ear toward the transcendental or intensive dimension of sound that Leibniz has helped us grasp. While this domain remains generally unconscious and inaudible, Leibniz notes that certain bodily and mental states—illness, dizziness, swooning, head injury, dreamless sleep, and so on—allow an influx of "minute perceptions" and an opening onto this intensive dimension.[26] Likewise, while Serres maintains that, generally speaking, "noise cannot be a phenomenon," he follows Leibniz in granting that "one hears its subliminal huffing and soughing on the high seas," that "we never hear what we call background noise so well as we do at the seaside."[27] Moreover, like Deleuze, Serres maintains that, for senses attuned to it, this noise, this transcendental intensity, can be revealed through art, as it is in Balzac's story "The Unknown Masterpiece," in which the painter Frenhofer produces a portrait of the courtesan Catherine Lescault (known as *la belle noiseuse*) as a sort of Aphrodite-in-process, the barest emergence of a figure from a riot of sensuous intensities (a "surge of differences") that remain merely chaotic and abstract to onlookers accustomed only to the canons of representation and phenomenal perception.[28] Leibniz has little to say about art, but it is clear that aesthetic forms can also provide access to this dimension insofar as they suspend our ordinary sensorimotor habits and the aim of practical activity in favor of an exploration of the very stuff of perception and sensation. In chapter 1, we saw that Nietzsche construes the formal organization of music as grounded in a chaotic flux of sonic forces, drives, and energies he terms "Dionysian."[29] Leibniz allows us to develop this idea and to reveal how sound art discloses this transcendental dimension of the sonic.

Leibniz pursued the auditory unconscious through ordinary experience. Yet sound recording amplified it and brought it to the fore. We saw earlier that, for Friedrich Kittler, Edison's and Cros's invention of the phonograph in 1877 was a watershed event in the history of sound, disclosing a sonic domain beyond music that Kittler, too, calls "noise."[30] Edison wished to capture the human voice in speech and song, but he could not help but also capture the reverberations of the room, the hum of electricity, the whir of the machine, and the countless incidental sounds that pervade the auditory field, for the phonograph is an indiscriminate register, and its machinic contraction is markedly nonhuman. As a cultural device, the phonograph performs a sort of *trompe l'oreille*. It draws the ear to attention, but instead of delivering articulate sound, it transmits "acoustic events as such," the vast "spectrum of noise."[31] For more than a century now, audio engineers have attempted to eliminate or reduce this field of noise, which, however, sound artists embrace as their very material.

Arnold Schoenberg is generally credited with inaugurating the first musical revolution of the twentieth century, abandoning tonality in favor of a free atonal music that explored the expressive potential of the entire chromatic scale. Yet, while Schoenberg's atonal revolution and subsequent invention of twelve-tone composition relinquished hierarchy of pitch, it retained much of the inherited apparatus of post-Renaissance European music, notably the division of the octave into twelve equal steps, the notation of pitch as discrete points on a staff, the instrumentation of the classical orchestra, and the distinction between musical and nonmusical sound. The Italian Futurist Luigi Russolo dispensed with all that, inaugurating an alternative lineage that led toward sound art. In the wake of Edison, he turned his ear toward the sonic flux of the world, treating all sounds as aesthetically engaging. Attuned to "the noises of trams, of automobile engines, of carriages and brawling crowds," Russolo maintained, the modern ear no longer finds sensuous satisfaction in the chromatic scale's restricted set of pitches or in the "anemic sounds" produced by the modern orchestra.[32] "Today," he wrote, "the machine has created such a variety and contention of noises that pure sound [that is, musical sound] in its slightness and monotony no longer provokes emotion."[33] Instead, Russolo maintained, modern life demanded an expanded conception of sonic art that would exceed music, encompassing all sound and requiring new instruments and new forms of notation. He dismissed the modernist notion that the art of music is pure and autonomous from nature. This idea of music as "a fantastic world superimposed on the real one, an inviolable and sacred world," Russolo claimed, must give way to an "art of noises" that would draw from "*the infinite variety of noise-sounds*" we encounter in life and nature.[34] In place of the purity of musical tones, Russolo celebrated the sonic messiness of the real, its cacophony, simultaneity, and multiplicity.

The critique of separation and the affirmation of continuity are central to Russolo's aesthetic position, as they were to Futurism generally.[35] Russolo's mentor, Filippo Tommaso Marinetti, perceived "deep analogies between the human, animal, vegetable, and mechanical worlds"; and the Futurist painter Carlo Carrà maintained the "continuity and simultaneity in the plastic transcendencies of the animal, mineral, vegetable, and mechanical kingdoms."[36] Likewise, Russolo understood sound as a continuum. The art of noises would encompass this entire domain, from "the rumbling of thunder, the whistling of the wind, [and] the roaring of a waterfall" to "the rustling of leaves," "all the noises made by wild and domestic animals," "the throbbing of valves, the bustle of pistons, [and] the shrieks of mechanical saws."[37] This affirmation of continuity extended beyond sound's sources and timbres. Decrying "the stupid walls of the artificial and monotonous semitone," Russolo also rejected any division of the sonic spectrum into discrete pitches, believing that "in nature and in life, sounds and noises are *all enharmonic*," composed of infinitely small microtonal gradations.[38] Whether in "the howling of the wind" or the whine of "dynamos and electric motors," nonmusical sounds rise and fall continuously, without division or leaps in pitch.[39] In its absurd limitations, he argued, the tempered harmonic system is analogous to a system of painting that would accept only the seven colors of the spectrum—red, orange, yellow, green, blue, indigo, and violet—and would abolish all the infinite gradations between them.[40] The art of noises, on the contrary, would follow painting in admitting the continuous spectrum of pitches and timbres encountered in the world. To that end, Russolo invented new noise instruments (*intonorumori*) that favored glissandi (continuous sweeping pitches) and designed an "enharmonic notation" consisting of continuous lines rather than discrete points (fig. 4.1).

Russolo explored the sonic world opened up by Edison and Cros. Yet, with recording technology still in its infancy, he lacked the practical means

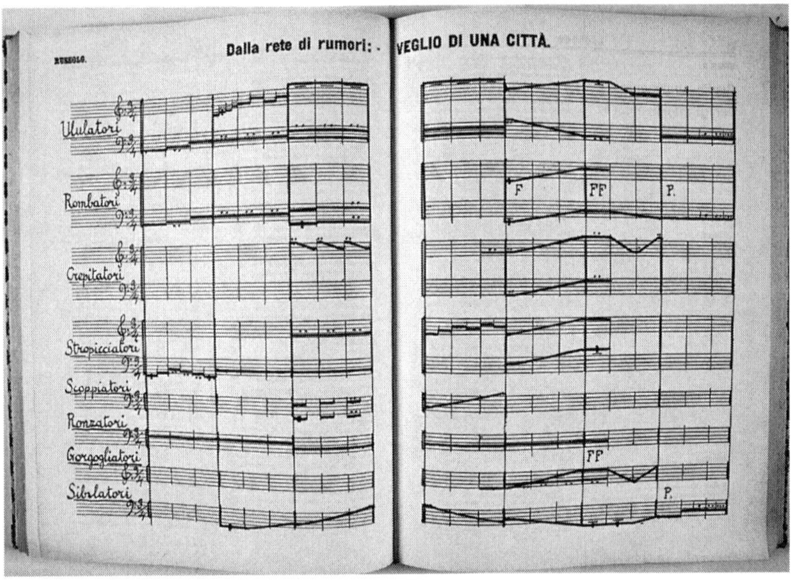

Fig. 4.1 Luigi Russolo, excerpt from *Risveglio di una città*, a score for *intonarumori* (noise intoners), *Lacerba*, March 1, 1914.

to capture worldly noise directly. His *intonorumori* were thus a sort of stopgap solution, a departure from conventional musical instruments but nonetheless a variant of the traditional orchestra. By the 1940s radio stations had become arsenals of the latest recording equipment, which, by the end of the decade, included magnetic tape. In the spring of 1948 Pierre Schaeffer, an engineer at Radiodiffusion Française, began working with phonograph turntables, a disc-cutting lathe, mixers, and filters to record and manipulate what he called "concrete" sounds, "sound fragments that exist in reality."[41] Abandoning "abstract music," which begins in the composer's head and passes through the detour of notation before finally becoming audible through performance, Schaeffer experimented directly and empirically with found sounds, attempting to dispense with musical drama and meaning in order to "isolate the in-itself-ness of the sound phenomenon" and subordinate musical form to sonic matter.[42] On October 5, 1948, the Parisian channel of French National Radio broadcast a "Concert of Noises" that premiered five of Schaeffer's "noise studies"—assemblages of train whistles, clattering saucepans, spinning tops, canal barges, and coughing—hoping that listeners would ignore the sources of these sounds and instead attend to the sounds themselves.[43]

As a radio engineer, Schaeffer was attuned to the virtual domain of sound, its transmission of an invisible and inaudible field of waves to be contracted or actualized by radio receivers and amplifiers at singular points within the broadcast range. The phonograph and tape recorder further deterritorialize sound, detaching it from its source and, indeed, from any determinate time and place, giving it a floating existence. Moreover, to Schaeffer's delight, phonography withdraws sound from its visual source and field of reference, calling attention to its sonic substance and autonomous fluid existence.[44] Indeed, in its very name and operation, Schaeffer's musique concrète occupied the borderline between the actual and the virtual, drawing exclusively from worldly sound while extracting its sonic core.

A decade prior to Schaeffer's experiments, John Cage called for a shift from music to background noise. "Wherever we are, what we hear is mostly noise," he wrote in 1937. "When we ignore it, it disturbs us. When we listen to it, we find it fascinating. The sound of a truck at fifty miles per hour. Static between the stations. Rain. We want to capture and control these sounds, to use them not as sound effects but as musical instruments."[45] In the decades that followed, Cage remained fascinated with noise but lost interest in controlling it or making music with it. His 1952 composition *4′33″* simply offers an auditory opening onto background noise, drawing attention to the sonic field ignored or concealed by everyday hearing. Like Luigi Russolo before him, Cage's attunement to noise was facilitated by the machinery of modern life, particularly by the "oscillators, turntables, generators, means for amplifying small sounds, film phonographs, etc." celebrated in his 1937 credo.[46] It's non-technological simplicity notwithstanding, *4′33″* owes its inspiration to technologies of sound reproduction and transmission. Under the title *Silent Prayer*, the piece was initially conceived in 1948 as a submission to the Muzak corporation, which piped a steady stream of recorded background music into department stores, restaurants, hotels, and factories.[47] The immediate predecessor to *4′33″* was *Imaginary Landscape #4*, scored for twelve radios. For Cage, the radio was a tool of indeterminacy, requiring that the composer and performers submit themselves to whatever happened to be floating through the airwaves at the time. Indeed, radio is a perfect model for acoustic flow: it is always there, a perpetual transmission, but we tap into it only periodically.[48] *4′33″* operates in precisely this radiophonic manner: for a brief window in time, it attunes us to the infinite and continuously unfolding domain of worldly sound. "Music is continuous; only listening is intermittent," Cage often remarked, extending the term "music" to the entire sonic flux in such a way as to undermine any notion of music as an intentional or human act.[49]

Against the ordinary conception of noise as loud and disruptive, Cage equated it with silence, at the same time rejecting the usual conception of silence as the absence of sound.[50] For Cage, "noise" meant precisely what I have been calling "background noise," the intensive murmur that fills every silence, or rather, that of which so-called silence is made. Indeed, Cage's conception of silence (and, by the same token, noise) operates on two different levels. On the empirical level, he takes silence to be *a sound*—namely, background noise, in the ordinary sense of the phrase. In this sense, Cage asks us to shift our auditory focus from foreground to background, from one field of sounds to another. Yet, for Cage, silence also operates on a transcendental level, as the mostly inaudible "ground of our perception" to which Serres attunes us: the perpetual sonic flux of the world that is the condition of possibility for the audibility of any sound whatsoever.[51] Cage thus recapitulates Leibniz's sonic figures. Silence is the sound of the mill or the waterfall, the perceptual background that we no longer hear. But it is also the sound of the seashore, whose roar registers the intensive forces that produce it, a transcendental flux that we grasp without distinctly hearing it.[52] *4′33″* presents an aural opening onto a region of this sound, which we perceive more or less clearly (the sounds of wind and rain, the shuffling of feet and the muttering of the audience Cage heard at the piece's premiere);[53] but this experience also draws our attention to what remains out of earshot: the limitless and perennial flow of noise, which we perceive only obscurely.

Inspired by Russolo, Schaeffer, Cage, and the growing ecology movement of the late 1960s, the Canadian composer R. Murray Schafer proposed in the early 1970s to treat the world as a "vast musical composition which is unfolding around us ceaselessly."[54] Schafer termed this "the world soundscape," describing it as a "macrocosmic" flow of sound composed of more limited "soundscapes" or acoustic environments. His aims were simultaneously artistic and ethical, conceiving the world soundscape and each more local soundscape as an ecosystem full of endangered, invasive, and predatory sounds. In this context, musical or sonic activity primarily took the form not of composing particular musical works but of altering the nature of the entire sonic flux (or a portion of it) to suit the aesthetic and physiological needs of living beings. Schafer termed this practice "acoustic design," which included

> the elimination and restriction of certain sounds (noise abatement), the testing of new sounds before they are released indiscriminately into the environment, but also the preservation of sounds (soundmarks), and above all the imaginative placement of sounds to create attractive and stimulating acoustic environments for the future.[55]

To pursue this project, Schafer and a band of like-minded colleagues at Simon Fraser University formed the World Soundscape Project (WSP), which set out to analyze existing soundscapes, design alternative acoustic environments, and make creative interventions in the form of discrete compositions and in situ projects. Though the WSP was attuned to the "world soundscape," the magnitude and transcendental nature of this flux always put it out of earshot; so, in practice, the group's analytical projects and interventions took place at specific sites, notably the acoustic environment of Vancouver, which the WSP examined in detail over the course of several decades.[56]

Campaigning against "noise pollution," the WSP promoted "hi-fi soundscapes," those "possessing a favorable signal to noise ratio," "in which discrete sounds can be heard clearly because of the low ambient noise level."[57] These ethical and ecological concerns led Schafer to value signal over noise, the hi-fi over the lo-fi, and thus to part ways with Russolo, Schaeffer, and Cage, who affirmed noise in all its variety. Nonetheless, the work of the WSP (and particularly the composer Hildegard Westerkamp) helped to foster the practice of "soundscape composition" or "field recording," which consists in composing with location recordings or simply presenting such documents for aesthetic appreciation. Though clearly indebted to the work of Pierre Schaeffer, soundscape composition (today a thriving field) remains both ontologically and aesthetically distinct from musique concrète.[58] Both practices explore the relationship between the transcendental and the empirical; but, whereas Schaefferian musique concrète withdraws sound from its geographical and temporal particularity in order to reveal sound-as-such in its virtual state, soundscape composition provokes the listener to shuttle between attention to the particularities of site and attention to the sonic substance that can be extracted from it. In practice, of course, these distinct positions are often conjoined, and the tensions between (and within) them have fueled sound artists for decades.

Whatever the characteristics of particular soundscapes, the broadband sound of the sonic flux—the totality of all sounds at any given moment—could only take the form of a drone. Drones have been central to the world's musics for millennia, intoned by the Highland bagpipe, the indigenous Australian didgeridoo, the European hurdy-gurdy, the Indian tambura, and the drone strings of the banjo, sitar, and sarod. Indian classical music in particular testifies to the aesthetic and ontological primacy of the drone. The Vedas and Upanishads declare the fundamental connection between sound and the absolute as embodied in the syllable *om*, which, chanted as a drone, expresses the totality of the universe.[59] The notion of a primordial sound or vibration that precedes all created beings was eventually developed by Indian musical scholars as the notion of *Nāda-Brahman*, which conflates the metaphysical absolute (*Brahman*) with sound (*nāda*). Moreover, the Sanskrit *nāda* does not designate pure tones but "droning, roaring, howling, screaming," and is etymologically connected to *nādi*, the rushing of a river or stream.[60] Here, too, we find a distinction between the empirical and the transcendental. The musical treatise *Sangīta-makaranda* distinguishes between two types of sound or vibration. *Āhata nāda* is what we call music, the sound produced when an object or instrument is struck or bowed. But this audible music is premised on a transcendental conception of sound, *anāhata nāda* or "unstruck sound," the ordinarily inaudible cosmic vibration that makes empirical sound possible. Through meditation and the intense contemplation of music, the Indian tradition teaches, one can ascend to this unstruck sound.[61] (Leibniz's rationalism led him to a similar distinction. He argued that the music we hear is made possible by mathematical differentials that, though not consciously perceived, exist virtually and are apprehended unconsciously. Thus "music," according to Leibniz, "consists only in the harmonies of numbers and in a calculation that we are not aware of, but which the soul nevertheless carries out, a calculation according to the beats or vibrations of sounding bodies, which are encountered at certain intervals.")[62]

What we know as sound art is founded on two different understandings of this transcendental sonic domain. A disciple of the Hindustani classical singer Pandit Pran Nath, La Monte Young adopted a mystical-rationalist conception of *anāhata nāda* as "an abstract mathematical concept in the mind of God," "the Pythagorean equivalent of the music of the spheres."[63] The drones or sustained tones that characterize his compositions and installations are calculated and notated with mathematical precision, continuing the efforts of Pythagoras, Boethius, and Johannes Kepler to discern the cosmic harmony and make it audible.[64] An alternative approach was offered by

Cage, who, we have seen, affirms a conception of the sonic transcendental that, while equally cosmic, is fully materialist. Cage does not search for the pure tone or attempt to calculate the underlying structure of the universe. On the contrary, for Cage, the transcendental font of all music is the eternal cacophony of noise; and the droning sonic flux is not a precise collection of mechanically generated sine tones, but the chaos of worldly sound, in all its irregularity, multiplicity, and relentless duration: not number but the forces of sonic matter.[65]

Room Tone

Since the late 1960s sound artists have pursued these various tendencies and interests—the pure tone and worldly noise; the mystical, the rationalist, and the materialist conceptions of the drone; the deactualization of music and sound toward the virtual, and the actualization of these virtual conditions—often in combination. Consider, for example, the series of sonic environments produced by Éliane Radigue in 1969 and 1970—among the earliest instances of sound installation.[66] In the 1950s Radigue studied with Pierre Schaeffer and served as an assistant to Pierre Henry, who loaned her a mixing board and a pair of Tolana phonogènes designed to record and play tape loops at variable speeds. After briefly experimenting with concrete sounds, Radigue became fascinated with the feedback effects generated between the two tape recorders, and between a microphone and a loudspeaker—effects produced by the machines themselves and modulated by the slightest gesture or barest touch of a potentiometer. Radigue recorded and layered these feedback flows onto tape loops of different lengths and played several loops simultaneously in gallery installations of open duration she called *propositions sonores* (sonic propositions), considering them something other than music.[67] *Omnht* (1970), for example, accompanied a nearly empty, starkly white exhibition by Tania Mouraud. Through speakers hidden in the walls, three asynchronous tape loops generated tense and undulating currents of seismic bass crossed by unstable squeals and prickly pulses that emerged and receded back into the flow.[68] Like Young, Radigue conceived these installations as eternal or endless, continuous and immersive fields of electrical and sonic vibration.[69] Yet, like Cage, she preferred noise to pure tones, relishing the threshold at which a feedback circuit abruptly shifts from equilibrium to nonequilibrium, exploring not the harmony of the spheres but the singular points beyond which order cascades into chaos.

These same tendencies and combinations have driven many other key works in the history of sound art. Max Neuhaus's *Times Square* (1977) places a series of pure tones within the cacophony of central Manhattan. Alvin Lucier's *Music on a Long Thin Wire* (1977) activates a Pythagorean monochord via the material pressure differentials present in the space. And Christina Kubisch's *Electrical Walks* (2003–) employ purpose-built headphones to render audible those regions of the electromagnetic flux in which we are constantly bathed but of which we are ordinarily unaware, fluxes that are made sensible as dense drones and crisp polyrhythmic pulses.

Following this trajectory, a spate of more recent projects investigates what sound technicians call "room tone," the low-level sonic murmur generated by the minute movements of air particles in enclosed spaces. Filmmakers record room tone to establish the soundtrack's foundation, a sonic baseline without which dialogue and diegetic sound would seem artificial and unmoored. On a technical level, then, film practice acknowledges background noise as the necessary condition for significant sound. Foregrounding this background, Chris Kubick and Anne Walsh's installation *Room Tone* (2007) catalogs hundreds of room-tone recordings, which are selected, fragmented, and combined by a generative audio program and sent through a four-channel speaker system that emits an ever-shifting collage of "silence" in its infinite variety. The differential juxtaposition of these recordings makes audible their unique characteristics, as do a series of text sketches that offer a playful taxonomy ("Off-Screen Room Tone," "Neo-Platonic Room Tone: Abbey Church of St. Denis, Fr."; "Room Tone 'La Vide'"; "Silence, Confession Booth Tone"; "Bassy Fox Hole Rumble"; etc.).[70] Walsh and Kubick's typology of silence, then, complements the acoustical engineer's division of white noise (the virtual, pure, or ideal enfolding of all frequencies at equal energy) into various actual kinds: pink noise, brown noise, gray noise, and so on.

The uniqueness of each room's "silence" is the starting point for Brandon LaBelle's *Room Tone (18 Sounds in 6 Models)* (2008). In Leibnizian fashion, this project takes room tone as a dense perceptual multiplicity that, in principle, registers all the complex materiality of a given space: its dimensions, the materials of its construction, the nature and placement of its contents, its geographical location, and so on. LaBelle made three different recordings of his Berlin apartment and sent them to six architects, each of whom was asked to use them as the sole basis from which to construct a three-dimensional rendering of the space. Not surprisingly, the infinite complexity of the sound sources—contractions of cosmic sound—made their full explication a practical impossibility, resulting in architectural models that diverge widely from one another.[71]

Andy Graydon's *Chora* series (*Chora in Three* and *Chora for*, both 2008) also works with the complex implications and foldings that constitute "silence." Both projects contrast the site and temporal specificity of room tone with the portability made possible by audio recording and the modulating or complicating effect of the new spaces and times into which such recordings can be played back. Graydon began with recordings of room tone that were then broadcast in the same space at a later time (*Chora in Three*) or in a different space (*Chora for*). They thus produce sonic folds of space and time that challenge audiences to unfold them or to recognize the impossibility of such a task.[72]

All these recent projects pay homage not only to Cage but also to Alvin Lucier's classic sound work *I Am Sitting in a Room* (1970), which, via sonic folding, explores the resonances between sound and architectural enclosure.[73] Recall that Lucier's piece begins with a brief spoken text that reflexively describes the procedure of its construction and outlines its aims. The Danish sound artist Jacob Kirkegaard's *4 Rooms* (2006) follows the same procedure but with different aims (fig. 4.2).[74] In each of four abandoned rooms in the heart of Chernobyl's "zone of exclusion," the artist recorded ten minutes of room tone. He then repeatedly played back the initial recording and rerecorded it, effectively amplifying this room tone and highlighting the room's acoustic signature, which emerged as a complex drone composed of a cluster of unstable harmonics. Lucier's piece moves from personal, human, and domestic speech to pure anonymous sound; Kirkegaard's project begins where Lucier's leaves off and aspires, in a sense, to reverse the process. The depopulated rooms recorded by Kirkegaard are profoundly overdetermined by the nuclear disaster that, twenty years earlier, forced their sudden evacuation. Thus, the drones that emerge from these rooms are presumably inflected by the radioactive particles and electromagnetic waves that still move invisibly within them. They are also haunted by the human beings that once inhabited these spaces. Like sound, radiation does not die but only dissipates, dilates, or loses energy. Kirkegaard's recordings, then, can be heard as an effort to amplify or contract these dissipated or dilated sounds, to rescue sonic emissions that outlive those who produced them. They disclose the immemorial background noise out of which human sounds emerge and into which they recede, pointing toward an elemental time the half-life of

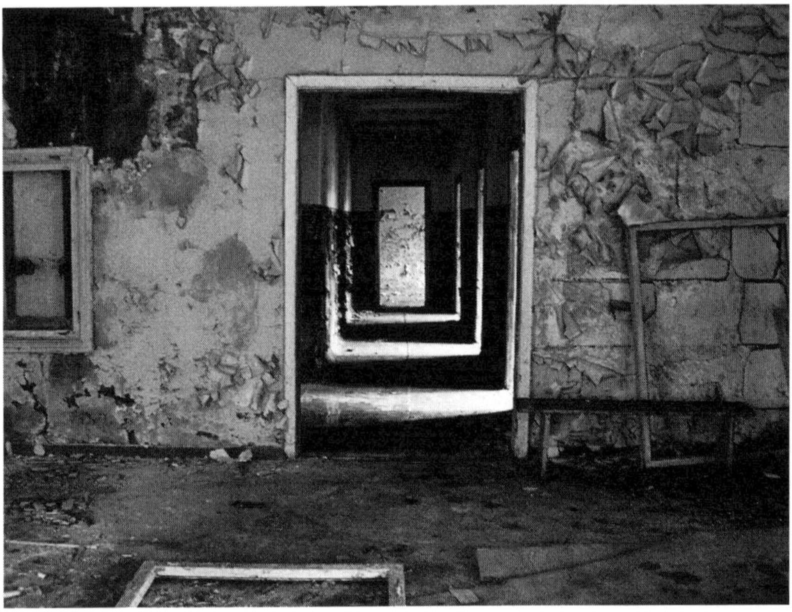

Fig. 4.2 Cover image of Jacob Kirkegaard's DVD, *AION*, 2011, an audiovisual companion to the audio recording *4 Rooms*. Courtesy of the artist.

which dwarfs human history—a fact underscored by the title of Kirkegaard's video companion piece: *AION* (2006).

Like Kirkegaard's *4 Rooms*, Francisco López's *Wind [Patagonia]* (2007) foregrounds the temporality and intensity of background noise.[75] On the face of it, the CD's content is simple and austere: an hourlong, unedited, and unprocessed recording of wind as it sweeps through the Argentine Patagonia.[76] Nonetheless, the recording is immersive, sensually complex, and conceptually revealing. It draws our attention to a host of auditory phenomena that ordinary hearing ignores or relegates to the background. Indeed, López's project works to explore the very nature of sound, hearing, and sound recording. As a whole, the piece focuses on the very medium of sonic transport—air—and amplifies the fact that sound is simply the result of pressure changes in that medium. Its subject matter—wind—is the most elemental and primeval sonic stuff. To focus on it is to transcend the limits of our ordinary ontology, composed as it is of relatively stable visible objects, for wind is invisible but intensely powerful: pure becoming, pure flow. It is immemorial but never the same. And it is nothing but the play of differential forces, differences in air pressure and temperature that generate immense currents, fronts, and bursts across the surface of the Earth—phenomena that are contracted by our ears (and by the microphone membrane) as sound. López's piece thus discloses not only empirical noise but also its inaudible conditions of possibility, the differential forces from which sound and hearing spring. More than any other work by López, *Wind [Patagonia]* reveals the artist's Schaefferian inspiration, using sound recording to deactualize sonic material and reveal its intensive conditions.[77]

Sound, Symbol, Sample

Lopez's piece, like Cage's *4′33″*, is a sort of sample of the sonic flux. It delimits a region of this flux for aesthetic attention and, in doing so, both discloses the intensive dimension of sound and points to the immemorial or "ancestral" flow from which the sample is drawn. Objecting to this position, Brian Kane contends that no artwork can disclose its ontological condition and that to claim otherwise is to commit a category mistake, confusing ontology with reference, embodiment with exemplification.[78] In Kane's view, an object necessarily embodies its ontology but cannot exemplify it. Ontology does not come in degrees: something either is or is not. However, exemplification (a form of reference) does come in degrees. While every swatch from a bolt of fabric is ontologically equal (each is equally a swatch), some exemplify the fabric's pattern better than others—relative to a symbol system that sorts and weights properties or predicates. Hence, for Kane, every work of sonic art is ontologically on par with every other; and a work of art can never disclose the sonic flux itself but can only exemplify or refer to properties embedded within systems of signification and representation. An ontology of sound, Kane concludes, can only ever be an "ontography." It can never describe sound as such, but only ever how it is construed within a particular auditory culture.

Kane's Quinean claim that "ontology does not come in degrees" is surely contentious. Much of the philosophical tradition opposes it, as do many contemporary non-Quinean ontologists. The distinctions between the Forms and material particulars, God and his creatures, substances and accidents, essences and appearances, minds and bodies, primary and secondary qualities, Dasein and ordinary things, the scientific and the manifest images, and so on all testify to the prominence of ontological hierarchy throughout the history of philosophy. Today ontological pluralists maintain that different entities (tables and numbers, for example) enjoy different kinds of existence and require different quantifiers; and grounding theorists argue that ontology concerns not merely what there is but what is more fundamental.[79] These caveats notwithstanding, I accept the claim that "ontology does not come in degrees" but endorse its Spinozist, Deleuzian, and DeLandian rather than its Quinean formulation. Ontology is flat (no entity differs from any other in ontological status); and being is univocal (said in one and the same sense of everything that exists). As DeLanda puts it, "reality is *a single matter-energy* undergoing phase transitions of various kinds. . . . Rocks and winds, germs and words are all different manifestations of this dynamic material reality, or, in other words, they all represent the different ways in which this single matter-energy *expresses itself*."[80] Though univocal and flat, this ontology nonetheless distinguishes the intensive processes of production from the actual empirical individuals we encounter, the dynamic material reality from its particular expressions. My claim is simply that works of art can reveal these production processes, and that some artworks do this more richly and profoundly than others.

In a broad sense, this idea is prevalent in twentieth-century art and aesthetics. The theatrical productions of Bertolt Brecht and the films of Jean-Luc Godard, for example, disclose the material, formal, and ideological conditions of production that are concealed by conventional theater and cinema. For Clement Greenberg, the modernist work of art is defined by its ability to foreground the material specificity of its medium and to avoid imitating the effects characteristic of other media. Structural filmmakers such as Paul Sharits and Hollis Frampton explore the material elements of cinema (celluloid, light, and projection) that are physically and conceptually prior to its ability to represent objects or to generate narrative. Structural film and modernist painting reveal the ontology of film as film, painting as painting. And Brecht and Godard are guided by a central tenet of the Marxist theoretical tradition: the resistance to reification, which dissimulates material and social processes as pre-given things, becomings as beings.[81]

Frampton's performance piece "A Lecture" proposes that every film is generated by modifying and subtracting from a perennial luminous flux. "Our rectangle of white light is eternal," he notes. "Only *we* come and go; we say: This is where I came in. The rectangle was here before we came, and it will be here after we have gone."[82] This claim parallels and resonates with Deleuze's and Cage's proposal of a continuous sonic flux from which sound artists and musicians extract or sample to produce particular works. Sound art, then, is not unique in its ability to disclose the various intensive fluxes that constitute the world; but, unburdened by the demands of representation, it has a special capacity to do so. A sound installation, then, can do more than merely reveal itself to be an entity among other entities. It can disclose the material forces that generate entities and can thus thwart the reification that would take such actual, empirical things as constituting the whole of ontology.

Kane's distinction between embodiment and exemplification is his own (or rather, Nelson Goodman's), not mine; and it misses the mark. A sound installation is not a symbol for anything; and reference is not a relationship among symbols but a causal connection to an extrasymbolic reality.[83] Nonetheless, as we have seen, sound installation is a sort of sample. Let's return to this idea, which will reveal the differences between my conception of sampling and Kane's. A geochemist collects samples from the Fraser River in British Columbia in order to develop a chemical profile of the river and its watershed.[84] Each sample is a time capsule that reveals the deep history and possible futures not only of western Canada but of the landscape and climate of the planet as a whole. Shed by rocks in the river's headwaters, strontium-87 (an isotope used in radiometric dating) provides a chemical signature that allows her to determine how much of the mineral material in the river water came from the older Rocky Mountains and how much came from the younger Coast Range. The concentrations of calcium, bicarbonate, and organic residue allow her to estimate how much carbon will be extracted from the atmosphere and eventually buried beneath the ocean floor. Of course each sample is selective: from a larger and ever-changing flow, the geochemist extracts a few small portions and searches them for particular elements and compounds relevant to her scientific interests. And certainly she frames her project and expresses her findings within the language and protocols of contemporary scientific research. Nonetheless, her statements refer not solely to a conceptual scheme or symbol system but to a mind- and discourse-independent reality—for example, to the real effects of carbon release or burial on the atmosphere, which affects human beings but is indifferent to their existence, thought, meanings, and values. Moreover, each sample is not merely a unique particular but a microcosmic portal—a sort of Leibnizian monad—that opens out onto a vast geological and biological history that it registers in highly contracted form.

The sonic sampling of rivers has been central to the composer and sound artist Annea Lockwood's practice since the late 1960s, resulting in a series of installations that manifest the tremendous aural richness and complexity of the world's waterways.[85] Her tools are microphones, hydrophones, and recorders rather than bottles, pumps, and filters, but Lockwood's aims and attitudes are in many ways similar to those of her scientific counterparts. The artist takes her recordings to reveal "the process of geological change in real time," the power of flowing water as it shaves minerals from rocky slopes, sculpts stones, and cuts furrows in the Earth in its incessant passage from mountains to sea.[86] "The energy flow of a river can be sensed very directly," notes Lockwood, "through the sounds created by the friction between current and riverbanks, current and riverbed."[87] Indeed, what her installations make audible are precisely the hydraulic forces that drive the river's flow and the qualitative changes produced by different regimes of flow: the churning turbulence of its vortices and eddies; the pulsed lapping at its banks; the changes of gradient that increase the river's speed; the pressure of its surge through rapids, riffles, sieves, and cascades; and so on.

Lockwood's *A Sound Map of the Hudson River* (1982; fig. 4.3) presents a vast and varied catalog of noise textures drawn from the entire length of the river, from its source in the high Adirondacks to its terminus in Lower New York Bay and the Atlantic Ocean.[88] Samples from the higher altitudes present sonic tumults of astonishing complexity—dizzying swarms of crackling pops and bassy gurgles against a background roar. Careful attention to the din reveals distinct layers, discrete particles, and aleatory movements that quickly exhaust efforts to track them. Auditory volume is linked to the volume and rate of the river's flow as it widens and accelerates downstream. The piece (and the river's course) ends in the thunderous pulse of surf as it crashes on the shore of Staten Island. Like the scientist's, Lockwood's samples are selective, recorded in specific locations at specific times with particular technological tools for a particular purpose. Nonetheless, Lockwood captures real vibratory disturbances of the soundscape that register real intensive differences (of level, pressure, temperature, speed) and real thresholds or singularities subsistent in fluid matter. Like Leibniz at the seashore or the waterfall, we hear the noise and, obscurely, some of the myriad, teeming sound particles of which it is composed. And these reveal to us not merely something spatially, temporally, or culturally local, but something of the broader sonic flux of which Lockwood's piece is a microcosm.

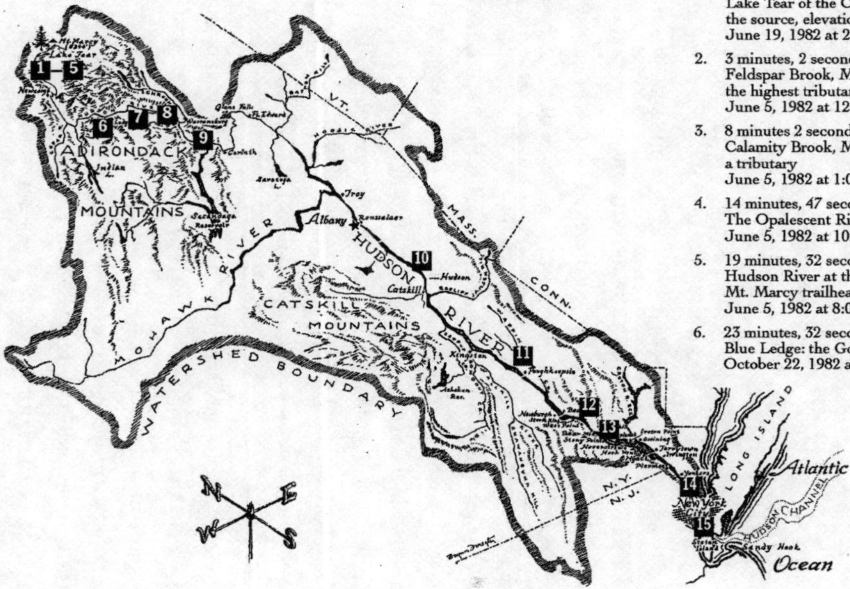

Recording Sites

1. 0 minutes, 2 seconds
   Lake Tear of the Clouds, Mt. Marcy — the source, elevation 4,322 feet
   June 19, 1982 at 2:00 PM
2. 3 minutes, 2 seconds
   Feldspar Brook, Mt. Marcy — the highest tributary
   June 5, 1982 at 12:00 noon
3. 8 minutes 2 seconds
   Calamity Brook, Mt. Marcy — a tributary
   June 5, 1982 at 1:00 PM
4. 14 minutes, 47 seconds
   The Opalescent River — a tributary
   June 5, 1982 at 10:30 AM
5. 19 minutes, 32 seconds
   Hudson River at the Mt. Marcy trailhead
   June 5, 1982 at 8:00 AM
6. 23 minutes, 32 seconds
   Blue Ledge: the Gorge
   October 22, 1982 at 5:00 PM
7. 26 minutes, 32 seconds
   The Glen
   May 2, 1982 at 12:00 noon
8. 30 minutes, 7 seconds
   Confluence of Patterson Brook and the Hudson River
   May 1, 1982 at 6:00 PM and May 2, 1982 at 6:00 AM
9. 35 minutes, 12 seconds
   Luzerne
   May 1, 1992 at 3:00 PM
10. 38 minutes, 29 seconds
    Stuyvesant (tugboat and train)
    May 23, 1982 at 6:00 AM
11. 45 minutes, 4 seconds
    Staatsburg
    (the marina at Norris Park)
    April 26, 1982 at 6:00 AM
12. 50 minutes, 29 seconds
    Garrison
    May 9, 1982 at 6:00 AM
    October 31, 1982 at 5:00 AM
13. 56 minutes, 28 seconds
    Iona Island and Marsh
    April 17, 1982 at 5:30 AM and September 12, 1982 at 7:30 AM
14. 62 minutes, 27 seconds
    Englewood Brook Falls, Palisades
    October 19, 1982 at 7:00 AM
15. 67 minutes, 32 seconds
    Great Kills Beach, Staten Island

Fig. 4.3 Recording sites for Annea Lockwood's audio composition *A Sound Map of the Hudson River*, 1982. Courtesy of the artist and Lovely Music.

But why should works such as those by Lockwood and López reveal their transcendental conditions any more than other entities and, specifically, more than conventionally musical works? After all, everything that exists is the product of intensive processes and the actualization of virtual tendencies and capacities. The Hudson River is no more a manifestation of the intensive and the virtual than the Adirondack Mountains, the ongoing product of a magma plume pressing billion-year-old anorthosite from Earth's mantle through its crust.[89] Nonetheless, while difference or intensity is the condition of all that exists and of all change, it tends to be canceled out, hidden, or covered over in its products, that is, the qualified, extended entities that constitute the domain of ordinary empirical experience. We see the Adirondacks, but not the pressure and temperature gradients that generate and maintain them; the chicken, but not its embryogenetic differentiation via chemical gradients, thresholds, and polarities.

Such actual entities form the basis of our ordinary ontology, which is centered around what J. L. Austin wryly calls "moderate-sized specimens of dry goods," the objects of our everyday experience: apples, chairs, trees, cars, and so on.[90] This ordinary ontology extends to include larger objects such as mountains or stars and can accept scientific objects such as subatomic particles, provided that they are taken to be tiny versions of ordinary things—stable, solid, and durable, though very small. Indeed, when we speak of matter, we tend to think solely of *solid* matter. (Few, I think, would take liquids, gases, or plasmas—water, air, or fire, for example—as paradigms of matter.) This ordinary ontology privileges the senses of sight and touch; or rather, the senses of sight and touch determine this everyday ontology. The invisible, intangible, and ephemeral objects (so to speak) of smell, taste, and hearing seem to have only a shadowy existence relative to the standard of the ordinary solid object, whose presence is guaranteed by eyes and fingers and enshrined in "common sense," which names an entrenched hierarchy of the senses rather than some common agreement among them.

The tendency of products to occlude processes, and the propensity of ordinary ontology to follow suit, are the sources of an objective illusion exposed throughout modern thought: Marx revealed the commodity to be, in reality, a nexus of social forces; Nietzsche showed that beings are merely becomings arrested by thought or language; Bergson uncovered the primary flux of duration that is obscured by spatial extensity and numerical multiplicity; Whitehead dissolved objects into events, occasions, and processes; Heidegger disclosed all things to be constituted by a network of relations and practical activities that ordinarily withdraw from view; and so on. Likewise, and with reference to several of these philosophical figures (e.g., Nietzsche, Bergson, Whitehead), scientists such as Ilya Prigogine showed that stable entities and states are the products of difference-driven processes, and that experiments can be designed to sustain systems far from equilibrium such that their intensive differences are not canceled and their virtual structure is made manifest.[91]

As we have seen, Schopenhauer and Nietzsche privileged music as giving perceptual access to the intensive domain that conditions and produces the world of representation. Music is an audible and palpable flux composed of manifest differences in tension, density, level, and pressure—a continuous variation that is invisible and intangible yet powerfully physical, thus disrupting the ordinary ontology that has always struggled to grasp it. Schopenhauer heard these intensities in the music of Beethoven, as did the early Nietzsche in Wagner. Nonetheless, music tends to tame and territorialize this flux. Distinguishing itself from unintentional or nonmusical sound, it segments the sonic continuum, rendering duration as meter, and frequency as intervals and chords. It routes the sonic flux through systems of tuning and symbolic coding and shapes it into repeatable patterns. As John Cage puts it, music generally functions by transforming the "purposeless process" of the sonic flux into a set of "time-objects."[92] Moreover, our ordinary relationship to music is one of unthinking familiarity—the apprehension and production of perceptual and affective clichés, ready-made forms, conventions, and cultural associations that prevent us from hearing it as anything else. In short, for the most part, music operates for us according to the model of recognition and does not provoke us to think or to ask "what is this sound?" and "what are its conditions of existence?" What I am calling "sound art" is what does provoke us to ask these questions, compelling us beyond the objects of recognition and representation toward the material forces that generate them. Rather than marking out a category or genre distinct from music, it names that which, *both within and beyond music*, discloses the intensive dimension of sound.

Take, for example, the early vocal experiments of the musician and composer Joan La Barbara. Trained in the European operatic repertoire, La Barbara abandoned that path in 1970 to join New York City's downtown experimental music and art scene.[93] By the middle of the decade she had developed an astonishing vocal technique evident in a series of "explorations" and "études" debuted in art galleries and performance spaces. In the earliest of these, "Voice Piece: One-Note Internal Resonance Investigation" (1974), La Barbara settles on a single pitch and explores its resonance in the chest, throat, mouth, nose, cheekbones, eye sockets, and top of the skull.[94] The effort of the lungs, the vibration of the vocal cords, the constriction of the throat, and the tension of the lips and tongue become palpable for performer and listener alike. Relatively pure tones prismatically divide into arrays of unstable harmonics and multiphonics or collapse into granulated noise, buzzing populations of scattering sound particles. "Des Accords pour Teeny" (1976) plunges more fully into this molecular sound world, while the more tonally and dynamically varied "Hear What I Feel" (1974) explores various vocal thresholds (the "crack" of the voice; the slight surge that pushes it over the edge away from silence; etc.) along with guttural expulsions and bestial wails that constitute a sort of nonhuman becoming. Drawing an analogy with science, the critic and composer Tom Johnson described these early works as "basic research," experiments of the sort that are only later developed into recognizably "musical products."[95] It's not that the intensive forces disclosed by La Barbara and others are absent from such musical products, but that they tend to be concealed, only occasionally arising like a kind of symptom or eruption of the sonic unconscious.

For millennia, the art of sound has been identified exclusively with music, or what the Greeks called *musiké*, which encompassed poetry and dance as well. If one accepts this identification, then "sound art" is a superfluous, redundant, and pretentious moniker. Yet, we have seen that, over the past century or so, a new domain of sound has opened up and a new experience of sound has emerged, a domain and experience heard faintly by Leibniz and amplified by Edison and his heirs. Exploration of this domain has marked the entire history of sonic experimentation in the twentieth century. In the 1950s, '60s, and '70s, sound art fully turned toward this intensive dimension of sound and has continued to make this dimension the subject of its inquiry. As such, it broadens the domain of the audible and discloses a genuine metaphysics of sound.

5 SOUND, TIME, AND DURATION

In 1968, at only twenty eight years old, the celebrated avant-garde percussionist Max Neuhaus abruptly ended his career as a musician. Neuhaus had become disenchanted with the temporal framework of musical composition and performance—the presentation, at specified times, of ephemeral works with beginnings, middles, and ends—and admired the very different temporality of visual art, which viewers could approach on their own temporal terms. Still committed to the sonic, he began to devote himself to what he was the first to call "sound installation," launching a set of projects that abandoned live performance in favor of electronic transmission, the concert hall in favor of public spaces and institutions, and metrical music in favor of meterless drones.

Neuhaus consistently articulated this career change as a turn from time to space, a shift of interest from the time of music to the space of sound. In a program note from 1974, he wrote:

> Traditionally composers have located the elements of a composition in time. One idea which I am interested in is locating them, instead, in space, and letting the listener place them in his own time. I am not interested in making music exclusively for musicians or musically initiated audiences. I am interested in making music for people.[1]

Two decades later, Neuhaus echoed this idea in the 1994 introduction to his collection of "Place Works":

> Communion with sound has always been bound by time. Meaning in speech and music appears only as their sound

events unfold word by word, phrase by phrase, from moment to moment. The works collected in this volume share a different fundamental idea—that of removing sound from time, and setting it, instead, in place.[2]

In 2002, reflecting on his "permanent" sound installations, Neuhaus told an interviewer: "The important idea about this kind of work is that it's not music. It doesn't exist in time. I've taken sound out of time and made it into an entity."[3]

This distinction of music from sound art as the distinction of time from space has been embraced by younger artists such as Stephen Vitiello and many critics aiming to define sound art.[4] Yet the distinction between time and space is a red herring, for the real distinction concerns different conceptions of time: music and sound art tend to inhabit and reveal fundamentally different temporalities. To see this, we need to situate sound art within the general shift in temporal thinking that took place during the 1950s and '60s, manifest in both the Cagean tradition in experimental music and postminimalism in the visual arts.

Beyond the Musical Object: From Being to Becoming, Time to Duration

John Cage's work of the 1950s launched an attack on the musical object that entailed a rethinking of musical time. Cage articulated this most clearly in a series of lectures delivered at Darmstadt in 1958 collectively titled "Composition as Process." The central formal aspect of European art music, he notes, is the production of "time-objects": "the presentation of a whole as an object in time having a beginning, a middle, and an ending, progressive rather than static in character, which is to say possessed of a climax or climaxes and in contrast a point or points of rest."[5] Such time-objects bind musical flow within definite temporal limits and tend to give it the narrative shape characteristic of linear conceptions of time and history. Against this notion, Cage sought a different conception of time, one that transcends human construction. "The world, the real," he noted, "is not an object. It is a process."[6] And "art," he was fond of saying, must "imitate nature in her manner of operation."[7] Hence, Cage endorsed a conception of music as "a process essentially purposeless," "a process the beginning and ending of which are irrelevant to its nature."[8] In place of the bounded, narrative conception of time characteristic of the classic musical work, Cage affirmed duration and simultaneity. He wanted his music to mirror and to become part of the open, ateleological flux of the world, and he affirmed that this flux is not singular but multiple, a conjunction of many different flows.

The two notions of time contrasted by Cage—that of the time-object and that of the purposeless process—match the terms of an opposition made by one of the twentieth century's greatest philosophers of time, Henri Bergson, who became an important influence on Cage in the early 1950s.[9] Bergson famously contrasted two different experiences of time. The first is exemplified by the figure of the clock, on which moments—discrete, present units—are laid out side by side in spatial succession. This is the conception of time that has dominated our thinking since at least the seventeenth century: time as an objective, quantitative measure of events, something that is not a part of events, movement, or change but that measures them from the outside. This conception of time is essentially quantitative or numerical; and number, Bergson argues, is inherently spatial insofar as it is discrete, discontinuous, and infinitely divisible. Thus, according to Bergson, the notion of time as a quantitative measure subordinates time to space.[10] Moreover, insofar as it considers time to be a matter of discrete moments, clock time is unable to account for the *passage* of time, the movement from one moment to another without which time is nothing at all. This key feature of passage points to a more fundamental experience of time that Bergson calls "duration": time as a qualitative process, a flow in which past, present, and future permeate one another to form a genuine continuum.[11]

Cage's compatriot Morton Feldman drew just this distinction, pitting his own position against that of Karlheinz Stockhausen, who, along with Pierre Boulez, was a consistent artistic opponent. Feldman objected to Stockhausen's idea that the composer could "reduce . . . [time] to so much a square foot," that "time was something he could handle and even parcel out, pretty much as he pleased." "Frankly this approach bores me," Feldman bluntly declared. Alluding to Bergson, he continued: "I am not a clockmaker. I am interested in getting to Time in its unstructured existence." "I feel that the idea is more to let Time be, than to treat it as a compositional element. No—even to construct with Time won't do. Time simply has to be left alone." Recalling Cage, he remarked that his interest was "not how to make an object, not how this object exists by way of Time, *in* Time, or *about* Time, but how this object exists *as* Time. Time regained, as Proust referred to his work."[12] This interest in time as duration, in making music that would not control time but would flow with it and as it, led Feldman, late in his career,

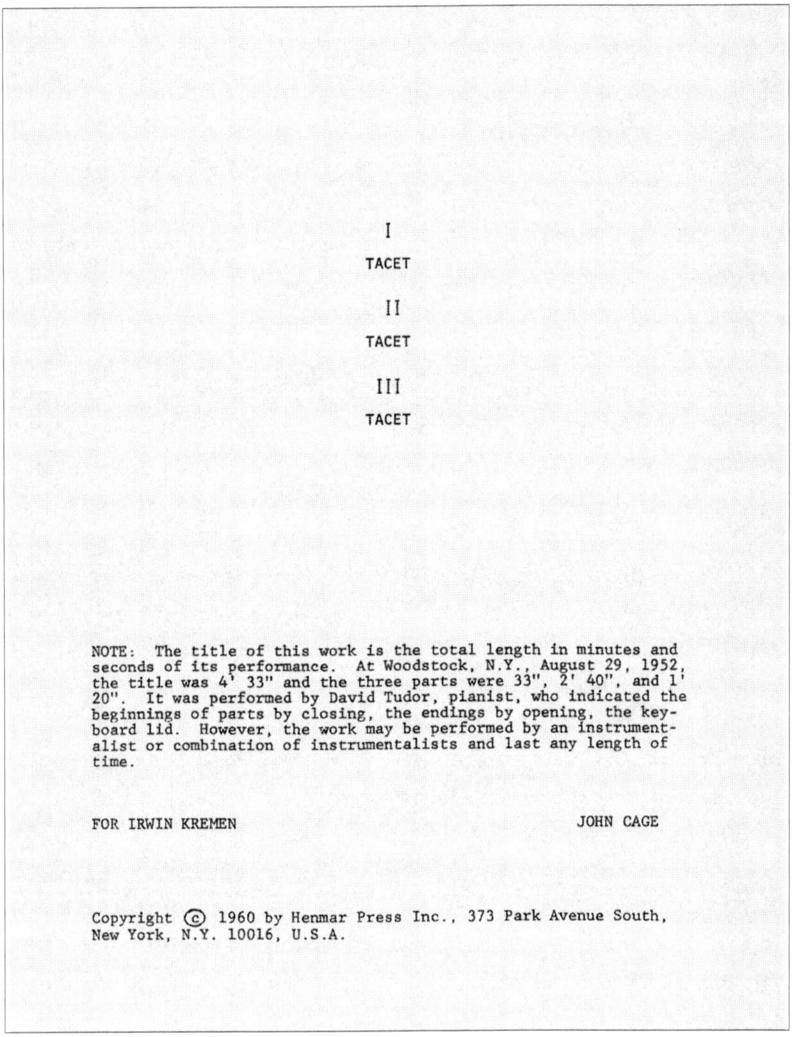

I

TACET

II

TACET

III

TACET

NOTE: The title of this work is the total length in minutes and seconds of its performance. At Woodstock, N.Y., August 29, 1952, the title was 4' 33" and the three parts were 33", 2' 40", and 1' 20". It was performed by David Tudor, pianist, who indicated the beginnings of parts by closing, the endings by opening, the keyboard lid. However, the work may be performed by an instrumentalist or combination of instrumentalists and last any length of time.

FOR IRWIN KREMEN JOHN CAGE

Copyright © 1960 by Henmar Press Inc., 373 Park Avenue South, New York, N.Y. 10016, U.S.A.

Fig. 5.1 John Cage, text score of *4′33″*, 1952. © 1960 by Henmar Press, Inc. Used by permission of C. F. Peters Corporation.

to compose works of extraordinary length, such as the four-hour *For Philip Guston* (1984) and the five-and-a-half-hour *String Quartet II* (1983). “Up to one hour you think about form,” Feldman wrote, “but after an hour it’s scale. Form is easy—just the division of things into parts. But scale is another matter. Before my pieces were like objects; now they’re like evolving things.”[13]

These two conceptions of time are also directly at issue in Cage’s most famous composition, *4′33″* (1952; fig. 5.1), which sets up a confrontation between measured time and limitless duration. The title of the piece refers explicitly to the spatialized time of the clock—a fact Cage underscores by noting that the title could also be read "four feet, thirty-three inches."[14] And, of course, the performance of the piece is regulated by a stopwatch. Yet the arbitrariness of this temporal frame (determined through chance procedures and infinitely elastic)[15] and the sonic experience it discloses indicate that *4′33″* aims to engage another experience of time—the time of duration, a time that does not parse out musical events but bears witness to the general acoustic flux of the world.

Cage's sequel, *0′00″ (4′33″ No. 2)* (1962; fig. 5.2), intensifies this argument about temporality. The piece calls for "nothing but the continuation of one's daily work, whatever it is, . . . done with contact microphones, without any notion of concert or theater or the public." "What the piece tries to say," remarked Cage, "is that everything we do is music, or can become music through the use of microphones; so that everything I'm doing, apart from what I'm saying, produces sound." Again, Cage includes the temporal marker, but this time reduces it to zero, putting it under erasure. "I'm trying to find a way to make music that does not depend on time," he said of the piece. "It is precisely this capacity for measurement that I want to be free of."[16]

The aim of *4′33″* and *0′00″*, then, is to open time to duration and to open musical experience to the domain of worldly sound. It is also to open human experience to something beyond it: the nonhuman, impersonal flow that precedes and exceeds it. "I think music should be free of the feelings and ideas of the composer," Cage famously remarked. "I have felt and hoped to have led other people to feel that the sounds of their environment constitute a music which is more interesting than the music which they would hear if they went into a concert hall." [17] To this end, Cage urges the composer to "give up the desire to control sound, clear his mind of music, and set about discovering means to let sounds be themselves rather than vehicles for man-made theories or expressions of human sentiments."[18]

"Chance" and "silence" were Cage's transports into this domain. "Chance" allowed the composer to bypass his subjective preferences and habits in order to make way for sonic conjunctions and assemblages that were not his own. And "silence," for Cage, names not the absence of sound (an impossibility, he repeatedly pointed out), but the absence of *intentional* sound, an attention to the sonic life of what he variously called the world, nature, and the real.[19] *4′33″* remains Cage's most elegant attempt along these lines. But so

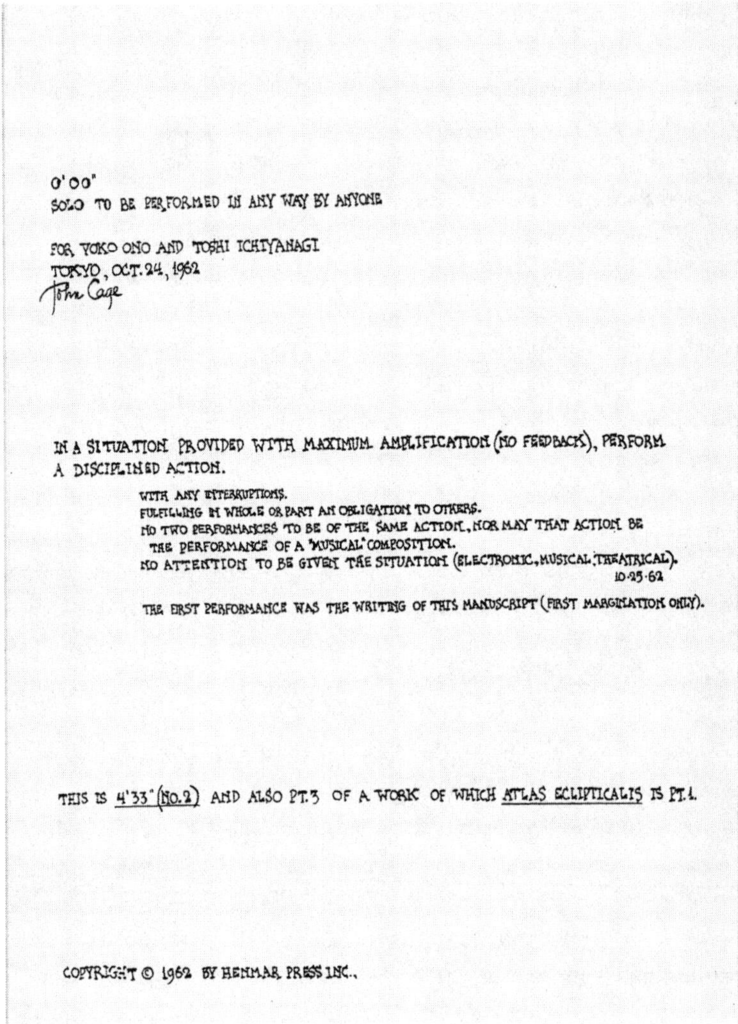
0'00"
SOLO TO BE PERFORMED IN ANY WAY BY ANYONE

FOR YOKO ONO AND TOSHI ICHIYANAGI
TOKYO, OCT. 24, 1962
John Cage

IN A SITUATION PROVIDED WITH MAXIMUM AMPLIFICATION (NO FEEDBACK), PERFORM A DISCIPLINED ACTION.

WITH ANY INTERRUPTIONS.
FULFILLING IN WHOLE OR PART AN OBLIGATION TO OTHERS.
NO TWO PERFORMANCES TO BE OF THE SAME ACTION, NOR MAY THAT ACTION BE THE PERFORMANCE OF A "MUSICAL" COMPOSITION.
NO ATTENTION TO BE GIVEN THE SITUATION (ELECTRONIC, MUSICAL, THEATRICAL).
10·25·62

THE FIRST PERFORMANCE WAS THE WRITING OF THIS MANUSCRIPT (FIRST MARGINATION ONLY).

THIS IS 4'33" (NO. 2) AND ALSO PT. 3 OF A WORK OF WHICH ATLAS ECLIPTICALIS IS PT. 1.

COPYRIGHT © 1962 BY HENMAR PRESS INC.,

Fig. 5.2 John Cage, *0'00" (4'33" No. 2)*, 1962. © 1962 by Henmar Press, Inc. Used by permission of C. F. Peters Corporation.

much of his work reveals that Cage conceived of sound (natural and cultural alike) as a ceaseless flow, and composition as the act of drawing attention to or accessing it.

Cage's conception of open, purposeless process is an affirmation of Bergsonian duration, the affirmation of a post-theological, nonanthropocentric, ateleological universe that is without origin, end, or purpose. Musical minimalism affirmed a similar conception of time. Composers such as La

Monte Young, Tony Conrad, Steve Reich, Philip Glass, Pauline Oliveros, Charlemagne Palestine, and Éliane Radigue explored what Gilles Deleuze calls "non-pulsed time," as opposed to the "pulsed time" of classical composition. "Pulsed time" has nothing to do with regular, repetitive pulses (often a key feature of musical minimalism). Rather, it is the time of narrative development that organizes the musical piece into identifiable sections and landmarks, allowing listeners to know where they are and where they are going. It sets up conflicts to be resolved that actively solicit the listener's sense of narrative time. Hence, Deleuze remarks, pulsed time is the time of the *Bildungsroman*, the novel of education, which "measures, or scans, the formation of a subject."[20]

The "non-pulsed time" of the minimalists is something else entirely. Minimalist compositions typically dispense with narrative and teleology, and are uninterested in charting the progress of a hero, whether it be the composer, the solo instrument, or the listening subject. Rather, as the Belgian minimalist composer Wim Mertens notes, "the music exists for itself and has nothing to do with the subjectivity of the listener . . . ; the subject no longer determines the music, as it did in the past, but the music now determines the subject."[21] Steve Reich notes that his early minimalist compositions "participate in a particular liberating and impersonal kind of ritual. Focusing in on the musical process makes possible that shift of attention away from *he* and *she* and *you* and *me* outwards towards *it*."[22] That is, the non-pulsed time of minimalist composition places composer, performer, and listener on a wave of becoming that flows, shifts, and changes, but very gradually, so that one loses any clear sense of chronological time (what Deleuze calls "Chronos") and instead is immersed in a floating, indefinite time, a pure process (Deleuze's "Aion").[23]

Installing Duration: Postminimalism in the Visual Arts

Cage was content to call this sonic flux "music" and remained more or less satisfied with the role of "composer," even as he vastly expanded music to include all sound and relinquished a great deal of compositional authority. Yet Cage's work had a profound effect on artists interested in exploring sound beyond the musical context. Max Neuhaus's first foray into nonmusical sound work, *LISTEN* (1966; fig. 5.3), carried Cage's *4′33″* beyond the concert hall and neatly figured his own exit from the world of music. Neuhaus invited friends and acquaintances to gather at a musical venue, stamped

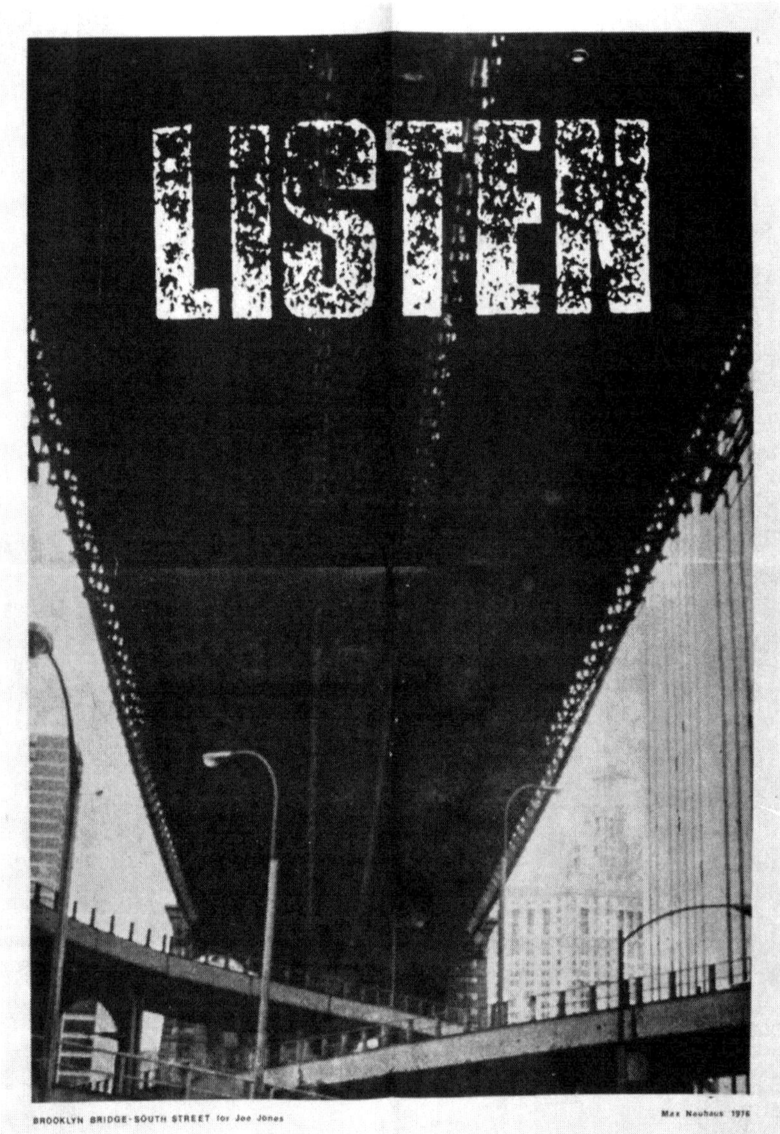

Fig. 5.3 Max Neuhaus, *LISTEN*, 1966. Poster of the Brooklyn Bridge taken from South Street, 1976. © Estate of Max Neuhaus.

their hands with the word "LISTEN," and promptly led them outside on a tour of local power plants, highway underpasses, and neighborhoods that were to be experienced aesthetically as sound environments. At the same time, Neuhaus extended Cage's work with radios and simultaneity. *Public Supply I* (1966) used WBAI's radio studio as a kind of proto-Internet to stage a massive participatory sound clash, inviting listeners to call in to the station with their sonic contributions—chatter, yelps, saxophone squonks, power-tool noises, car-horn honks, TV dialogue, and so on—which Neuhaus mixed live on the air.

Drive-In Music (1967) marks Neuhaus's final break with music and his first foray into "sound installation." The installation of sound allowed him to dispense with live performance and thus to remove what he called "the onus of entertainment" that burdened music but of which, Neuhaus felt, the visual arts were largely free.[24] Indeed, for Neuhaus, the concerns of sound installation are shared more fully by the visual arts than by music. "In terms of classification," he told William Duckworth in 1982,

> I'd move the installations into the purview of the visual arts even though they have no visual component, because the visual arts, in the plastic sense, have dealt with space. Sculptors define and transform spaces. I create, transform, and change spaces by adding sound. This spatial concept is one which music doesn't include; music is supposed to be completely transportable.[25]

This interest in site specificity was just one of the concerns Neuhaus shared with visual artists of the time. Indeed, while the impetus for Neuhaus's sound installations came, in part, from the Cagean tradition of experimental music, it was equally affected by the emergence, at the same time, of installation practices in the visual arts. Not coincidentally, these practices shared Cage's dismissal of clock time and discrete artistic objects in favor of works that engaged the temporality of process, becoming, and duration.

Michael Fried's enormously influential 1967 essay "Art and Objecthood" took aim at these installation practices, drawing a fundamental distinction between, on the one hand, autonomous works of art that suspend time and absorb the spectator's attention, and, on the other, "theatrical" or "literalist" works that engage the spectator's physical presence in space and time and thereby short-circuit the achievement of an aesthetic epiphany.[26] Much has been written about Fried's essay, and I don't wish to rehearse those critical polemics here. I simply want to show that, despite its utter silence about sound, "Art and Objecthood" helpfully illuminates the importance and radicalness of the sound art that emerged concomitantly with minimalism and "expanded field" practices in the visual arts, and to show that it does so precisely via an examination of aesthetic temporality.

In that essay, Fried espouses a formalist modernism according to which art is essentially self-sufficient and self-aware, concerned with its own nature and medium. The modernist paintings and sculptures Fried champions have, he argues, an interior, syntactical unity. They are whole and complete, and, as such, possess a magisterial presence that absorbs the spectator in a peculiarly aesthetic experience transcending the banality of everyday life. By contrast, the "theatrical" works Fried decries are heteronomous. They offer not self-sufficient unities but essentially incomplete or open situations that solicit the spectator's presence and draw attention to the material conditions of their exhibition. As Fried's major target, Robert Morris, famously put it, sculptural installations such as his own "take . . . relationships out of the work and make . . . them a function of space, light, and the viewer's field of vision."[27] That is, such works do not absorb the viewer in contemplation of the work's interior formal relationships, but rather explore the temporal and spatial relationships that obtain *between* the work and the viewer's mobile body. This betweenness, these relationships, and this distance between beholder and artwork, Fried writes, "make . . . the beholder a subject and the piece in question . . . an object."[28] "Literalist" or "theatrical" work, then, threatens to collapse the distinction between artworks and ordinary objects, in all their dumb obstinacy. "Whereas literalist work aimed to project and hypostatize objecthood," Fried wrote in a retrospective essay, "the abstract painting and sculpture I admired sought to undo or neutralize objecthood in one way or another."[29]

Yet, despite the title of the essay and the attention it gives to the topic, objecthood plays a secondary role in Fried's analysis, for his true concern lies elsewhere.[30] That concern emerges in Fried's discussion of the sculptor Tony Smith's revelatory night drive on the unfinished New Jersey Turnpike. Fried quotes Smith's retrospective account of this defining event:

> When I was teaching at Cooper Union in the first year or two of the fifties, someone told me how I could get onto the unfinished New Jersey Turnpike. I took three students and drove from somewhere in the Meadows to New Brunswick. It was a dark night and there were no lights or shoulder markers, lines, railings, or anything at all except the dark pavement moving through

> the landscape of the flats, rimmed by hills in the distance, punctuated by stacks, towers, fumes, and colored lights. This drive was a revealing experience. The road and much of the landscape was artificial, and yet it couldn't be called a work of art. On the other hand, it did something for me that art had never done. At first I didn't know what it was, but its effect was to liberate me from many of the views I had had about art. It seemed that there had been a reality there that had not had any expression in art. The experience on the road was something mapped out but not socially recognized. I thought to myself, it ought to be clear that's the end of art. Most painting looks pretty pictorial after that. There's no way you can frame it, you just have to experience it.[31]

Smith's experience is not one of objects, but, as Fried notes, of "empty, or 'abandoned,' *situations*." "What replaces the object," Fried continues, "—what does the same job of distancing or isolating the beholder, of making him a subject, that the object did in a closed room—is above all the endlessness, or objectlessness, of the approach or onrush of perspective."[32] Indeed, what vexes Fried about minimalism and installation practices generally is not really "objecthood" at all, since such works may be void of objects. What vexes him is something else, namely, the conception of *time* affirmed in such work. Fried writes:

> I want to emphasize something that may already have become clear: the experience in question *persists in time*, and the presentment of endlessness that, I have been claiming, is central to literalist art and theory is essentially a presentment of endless or indefinite *duration*. . . . The literalist preoccupation with time—more precisely with the *duration of the experience*—is, I suggest, paradigmatically theatrical, as though theater confronts the beholder, and thereby isolates him, with the endlessness not just of objecthood but of *time*; or as though the sense which, at bottom, theater addresses is a sense of temporality, of time both passing and to come, *simultaneously approaching and receding*, as if apprehended in an infinite perspective.[33]

Minimalism and installation, then, affirm a conception of time in its unlimited flow, its interminable fluid duration. And this Fried finds intolerable, for, in line with a modernist lineage that extends back to Roger Fry and, ultimately, to Kant's aesthetics, Fried enlists art in the project of escaping this temporal flux. For Fried, art offers (or ought to offer) a metaphysical, theological experience. With "modernist painting and sculpture," he remarks,

> it is as though one's experience . . . *has no* duration . . . because *at every moment the work itself is wholly manifest*. . . . It is this continuous and entire *presentness*, amounting, as it were, to the perpetual creation of itself, that one experiences as a kind of *instantaneousness*, as though if one were infinitely more acute, a single infinitely brief instant would be long enough to see everything, to experience the work in all its depth and fullness, to be forever convinced by it.[34]

Fried recapitulates Bergson's two conceptions of time and emphatically decides against duration in favor of a temporality of discrete moments in which only the present truly exists. This "abstract time," Bergson noted six decades before Fried's essay, "is always speaking of a given moment—a static moment, that is—and not of flowing time."[35] It "implies a metaphysic in which the totality of the real is postulated complete in eternity, and in which the apparent duration of things expresses merely the infirmity of the mind that cannot know everything at once."[36] It thus accords with "*the world of the mathematician*," "*a world that dies and is reborn at every instant—the world which Descartes was thinking of when he spoke of continued creation*."[37] "But," Bergson replies, "duration is something very different from this," something deeper from which mathematical temporality is derived as an intellectual abstraction.[38] "Real duration is that duration which gnaws on things and leaves on them the mark of its tooth. If everything is in time, everything changes inwardly, and the same concrete reality never recurs."[39] Thus, Bergson concludes:

> We perceive duration as a stream against which we cannot go. It is the foundation of our being, and, as we feel, the very substance of the world in which we live. It is no use to hold up before our eyes the dazzling prospect of a universal mathematic; we cannot sacrifice experience to the requirements of a system.[40]

Of course, Fried frames his argument not in mathematical but in "overtly theological" terms.[41] After all, his essay opens with a quotation from the Puritan theologian Jonathan Edwards and famously concludes with a salvific couplet: "We are all literalists most or all of our lives. Presentness is grace."[42] As such, he recapitulates the dream of metaphysics and theology from Plato through Kant, Hegel, and Laplace, the dream of transcending time altogether, the fantasy of a God's-eye view to which all of time and history would be present at once and in which becoming would be annulled by pure, simple, present being.[43] Nietzsche relentlessly criticized such metaphysical and theological fantasies, revealing them to be symptoms of a profound contempt for nature, life, and the sensuousness that is at the heart of aesthetic experience.

As Fried rightly noted, the new generation of artists in the 1960s rejected this conception of time and its underlying theology, asserting instead an antimetaphysical and often deeply Bergsonian notion of time as duration. In a text published in *Artforum* a year after the appearance of Fried's essay in that same magazine, Robert Smithson explicitly countered Fried with a celebration of the artist's immersion in the Dionysian flux of time and matter that dissolves all objects and subjects. Art critics and the art market, Smithson noted, fasten on "art objects" and assign them "commodity values." Yet such objects are merely souvenirs from the artist's plunge into the "dedifferentiated," "oceanic" flux that constitutes the real aesthetic experience. "When a *thing* is seen through the consciousness of temporality, it is changed into something that is nothing," Smithson wrote. "Separate 'things,' 'forms,' 'objects,' 'shapes,' etc. with beginnings and endings are mere convenient fictions: there is only an uncertain disintegrating order that transcends the limits of rational separations. The fictions erected in the eroding time stream are apt to be swamped at any moment."[44]

A year later, and once again in *Artforum*, Robert Morris concurred with Smithson, celebrating "the detachment of art's energy from the craft of tedious object production" in favor of an art composed of "mutable stuff which need not arrive at the point of being finalized with respect to either time or space."[45] In this fourth and final installment of his "Notes on Sculpture," subtitled "Beyond Objects," Morris criticized early minimalist three-dimensional work (his own included) as still too objectlike and instead championed installations (for example, those of Barry Le Va, Richard Serra, Smithson, and Morris himself) composed of "fields of stuff which have no central contained focus and extend into or beyond the peripheral vision." Such installations, Morris argued, shift the viewer's focus from "figure" to "ground," affirming a "dedifferentiated" mode of vision that implies "constant change" and encounters "chance, contingency, indeterminacy—in short, the entire area of process."[46] Morris's words echo those of Cage, who deeply influenced him and, as we have seen, had called for a shift from musical objects to sonic processes by means of chance, contingency, and indeterminacy.[47]

Sound art grew out of this artistic milieu, emerging via a radicalization of musical minimalism, on the one hand, and postminimalist sculptural installation, on the other. Sound was better suited than other media to satisfy Smithson's and Morris's desire for artworks that resist reification and model the Dionysian flux. The temporality and ephemerality of sound allow it to bypass objecthood and the instantaneity of opticality. Combined with the often site-specific setting of sound installation, these qualities make sound art resistant to commodification and, instead, encourage experience and participation. Made of ephemeral movements of air, sound is at once thoroughly material and yet intangible. A sound installation can at once be empty and full: void of objects, but replete with sensory material. Sound is the most immersive of sensory phenomena and at low frequencies is nondirectional. As such, it draws attention to the total field or situation rather than directing it to a thing or set of things. Much in the way that Morris, Le Va, and others sought a dedifferentiated form of installation that shifted focus from figure to ground, sound art shifted perception from the rarefied cultural domain of music, with its selection of discrete tones and timbres, to the engulfing field of environmental sound.

Time's Square

Both the Cagean tradition in experimental music and postminimalist installation practices in the visual arts, then, offered profound refigurations of aesthetic temporality. Though not identical, these refigurations were directed toward a notion of time that has held sway in European culture, a conception of time that accords with the metaphysical and theological privilege of being over becoming and for which the only genuine temporal modality is the present. The ideal, autonomous musical work of European modernity attempts to master time's elusive flow by making it a measured, closed, integral totality—an entity or time-object. Likewise, the ideal work of visual art is an integral, autonomous whole that, at each moment, is fully present. In both cases, the auditor or spectator is ideally placed at the center of this aesthetic experience—or rather, like Laplace's God, is placed at its transcendent apex, able to survey the whole and encompass the temporal field. Against this conception of time, Cage and the postminimalists affirmed a notion of time as duration—an infinite, open process in which presence and completeness are forever deferred, a boundless flow that engulfs the auditor or spectator in a field that cannot be totalized.

Neuhaus's recurrent rejections of musical time in favor of sonic space must be read in this context. For, via sound installation, Neuhaus did not escape or reject time itself (surely an impossibility, particularly given the irreducibly temporal medium of sound). Rather, he rejected a particular conception of time: the measured, bounded temporality of the musical time-object. By the same token, Neuhaus's sound installations affirm duration. They are, in his words, "sound continuums," "sound works without a beginning or an end."[48] Indeed, from early to late, Neuhaus's "permanent" installations have taken time as their explicit subject. In the earliest of these, *Times Square* (1977), the titular reference to time is not incidental, not merely a designation of the work's location. Rather, the piece is a profound invitation to duration. Twenty-four hours a day, for decades now, the installation has broadcast a stream of rich metallic drones from deep inside a subway vent on a pedestrian island in New York's busiest district. Audible but unobtrusive, the drones blend with and subtly alter the bustling sonic environment. This sonic stream is continuous; but it is experienced by visitors and passers-by at particular moments within this temporal continuum. Such moments of conscious or unconscious apprehension serve as openings onto a flow of duration of which we are a part but that also surpasses us.

To some degree, of course, this is true of any work of art, which, though durable, is experienced in temporal slices. But, as Nietzsche and Schopenhauer pointed out, sound is fundamentally durational in a deeper sense. It pulls us out of the *principium individuationis* affirmed by the plastic arts and, instead, plunges us into the flux of time.[49] It is not a thing that undergoes change; rather, it is change, flow, itself. As Bergson puts it, describing both becoming and sound: "*There are changes, but there are underneath the change no things which change: change has no need of a support. There are movements, but there is no inert or invariable object which moves: movement does not imply a mobile.*"[50] Whereas clock time (and the musical time-object) is a "discrete" or "quantitative multiplicity," Bergson describes duration as a "continuous" or "qualitative multiplicity," a temporal flow that is heterogeneous and continuous, composed of different elements or states that are inextricably fused.[51] One could hardly find a better description of the drone: a complex, fluid torrent composed of myriad tones, microtones, overtones, and combination tones that interpenetrate one another. Indeed, in a rich passage on sound, Bergson seems to point to the drone as the ideal sensuous presentation of duration. "A melody to which we listen with our eyes closed, heeding it alone," he writes,

> comes close to coinciding with this time, which is the very fluidity of our inner life; but it still has too many qualities, too much definition, and we must first efface the difference among the sounds, then do away with the distinctive features of sound itself, retaining of it only the continuation of what precedes into what follows and the uninterrupted transition, multiplicity without divisibility and succession without separation, in order to rediscover basic time. Such is immediately perceived duration, without which we would have no idea of time.[52]

A musical melody—a series of overlapping pitches that we draw together in memory—provides a fine first approximation of duration. Yet these pitches are still too discrete, distinct, and defined; and the whole composed by these pitches—the musical melody or phrase—is itself too bounded. So Bergson suggests that we melt these pitches together into a continuous, fluid mass—in short, a rich drone. To grasp duration, perhaps we need to go a step further, generalizing this flux beyond sound. Even so, the drone provides the richest sensuous manifestation of duration.

The drone has always been a figure of temporal continuity and endlessness.[53] To emphasize this aspect, the Theatre of Eternal Music often began its drone performances before the arrival of the audience and continued to play for hours, reaching the point where, as Feldman noted, form gives way to scale.[54] Regardless, a musical performance is always temporally bounded. And so, in pursuit of duration, La Monte Young eventually turned to continuous electronic sound generation and long-term installation. Young's installations remain carefully controlled environments, refuges from their sonic and temporal surroundings. By contrast, Neuhaus's *Times Square* (fig. 5.4) is an open system composed not only of the tones broadcast by the artist, but also of the ever-changing sonic environment that they color and with which they blend. It thus richly figures the open-ended, differential flow of duration.

Just as the title of Cage's *4′33″* implicates both space and time, so, too, does Neuhaus's title, *Times Square*. Indeed, the two works are fundamentally akin, though the latter performs a sort of spatiotemporal inversion of the former. As I noted above, *4′33″* explicitly engages two conceptions of

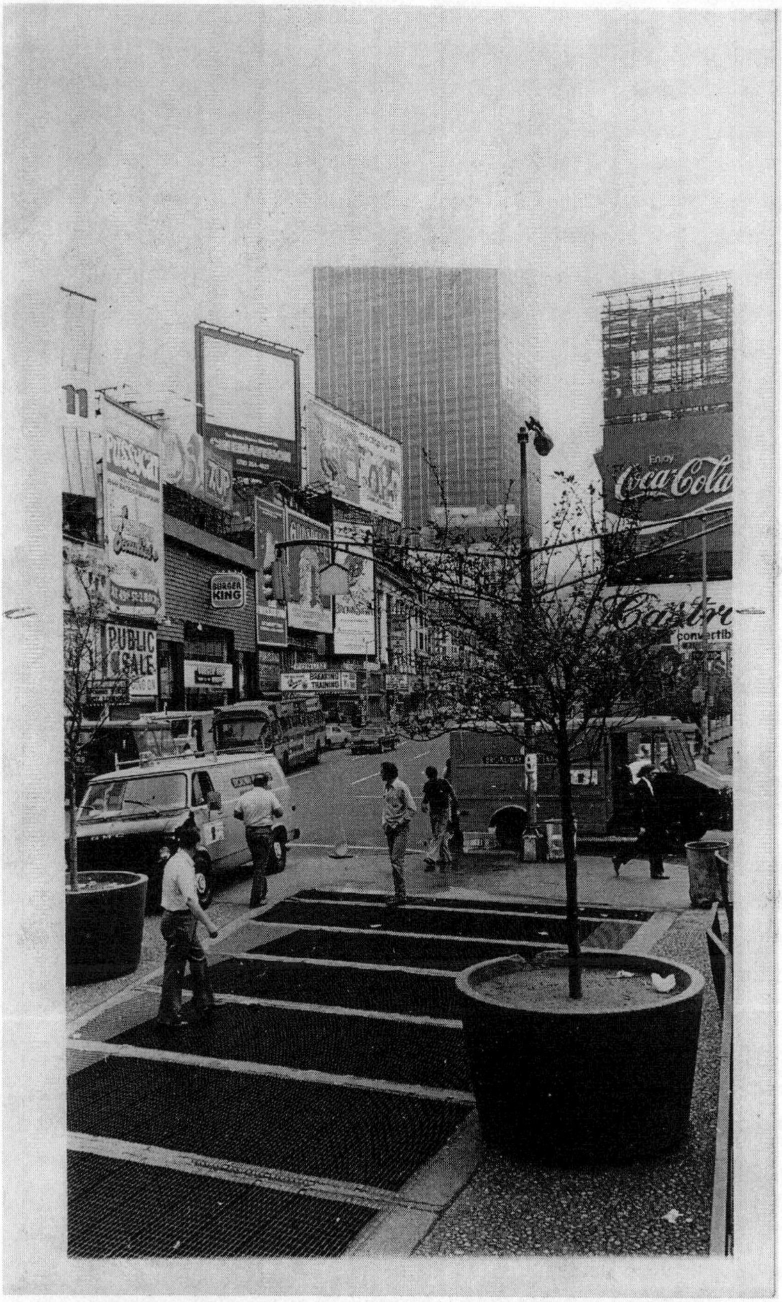

Fig. 5.4 Max Neuhaus at his installation *Times Square*, ca. 1977. Digital sound signal in a ventilation chamber, 20 × 40 feet, Broadway between Forty-fifth and Forty-sixth Streets, New York City. Proposed in 1973, extant 1977–92, 2002–present. ©Estate of Max Neuhaus.

time: the chronometric time of its title, which provides a determinate temporal opening, and the indeterminate durational flux of sound onto which it opens. For the temporal marker in Cage's title, *Times Square* substitutes a spatial, geographical reference. This is apt, for what is fixed in Neuhaus's piece is not the temporal window but the spatial region. *Times Square* (which we can read as "time's square") also offers an opening onto duration: a kind of spatial chasm through which a temporal flux emerges. In Cage's piece what performs this opening is a period of silence; in Neuhaus's, it is a zone of continuous sound. Through Cage's silence we hear the particular sonic field that fills the space and time of the performance—a synecdoche for the vast flux of time and sound that stretches beyond us. Neuhaus's unobtrusive drone draws the ambient flux into it, implicating the vibrational field of Times Square, and, by extension, the vibrational flux of the world.

Time Pieces

The relationship between sound and time is even more explicitly an issue in the series of "Moment Works" or "Time Pieces" that Neuhaus has installed in various public contexts over the past twenty-five years. In each of these works, a regular temporal interval is marked by a slow sonic crescendo that abruptly ceases, leaving what Neuhaus describes as an "aural afterimage."[55] The first of these, Neuhaus's contribution to the 1983 Whitney Biennial, was a sort of prototype. It deployed a live electronic processing system that collected street sounds from the stretch of Madison Avenue outside the museum, sent these through a computer program, and then broadcast the result into the Whitney's courtyard sculpture garden. Over the course of fifteen minutes, the computer program increasingly altered the pitch and timbre of the sampled sounds and layered this over the live material. Every quarter hour, the cumulative coloration of the street sounds was suddenly wiped away, leaving an undistorted sonic reflection.

For subsequent realizations of this idea, Neuhaus abandoned live processing for the electronic drones that have become his signature, a sound that Neuhaus describes as "resembling the after-ring of large bells."[56] These "Time Pieces" retained the form of a gradual increase in sonic material culminating in an abrupt break; but they settled on a five-minute crescendo that disappears at regular temporal intervals—on the half hour in the installation at Kunsthalle Bern (1989–91), five minutes before the hour in the version at Graz (2003–), on the hour in the installation at Beacon (2006–), and on the halachic hours of the Jewish ritual day in the version at Stommeln-Pulheim (2007–).

These "Time Pieces," then, would seem to be just that: timepieces or clocks; and Neuhaus would seem to have acceded to the circumscription of sound by measured time. Yet, in fact, these installations resonate with a different practice of marking time: the liturgical, ceremonial, and civic practice of bell ringing that preceded the mechanical clock by centuries.[57] In his magnificent history of this practice, the cultural historian Alain Corbin notes that bell ringing not only preceded the quantitative, homogeneous time ushered in by the mechanical clock but was in many respects at odds with clock time and with the scientific and economic rationalism that mandated it.[58] Whereas the clock marks out a sequence of equidistant, equivalent, indifferent, and interchangeable instants, village bells announced privileged moments: births, baptisms, marriages, funerals, festivals, liturgical hours, holidays, and so forth. In the ordinary flow of time, such events were singularities, remarkable moments of change where what followed differed fundamentally from what preceded. Peals of bells thus referred not to the abstract, indifferent time of scientific measure, but to the concrete life of the community and to its collective rhythms.

Neuhaus's "Time Pieces" engage both conceptions of time at once. Their regular sonic signals accommodate the time of the clock. Yet, they simultaneously force an opening within clock time that resonates with the very different, qualitative time of the bell. This opening is achieved by reversing the natural envelope of the bell stroke, which begins with an abrupt, loud attack followed by a slow, steady decay. By contrast, Neuhaus's installations build amplitude over the course of five minutes; and their abrupt disappearance heightens the listener's awareness of the ambient sound that, until the break, mixed with the harmonic drone. The effect is similar to that generated by dub reggae producers, whose remixes of reggae singles suddenly drop out vocal or guitar tracks to open cavernous, ghostly spaces and provoke vertiginous, hallucinatory experiences. Rather than music, Neuhaus dubs environmental sound. Precisely tuned to their sonic sites, Neuhaus's drones slowly insinuate themselves into the environment, drawing ambient sounds into their flow. They then suddenly withdraw the leading sound, effectively amplifying the ambient elements in the mix while producing a psychoacoustic after-ring, a symmetrical sound envelope that doubles (dubs) the sounding drone and colors the ensuing "silence."

In the courtyard at Dia:Beacon, for example, the low rumble of institutional HVAC units is overlaid with the clatter of silverware and bits of conversation from the museum café, punctuated by the occasional rattle and howl of a passing train, the flutter and chirp of birds, or the low moan of a distant airplane. Invisibly and inconspicuously, a low, dense chord emerges from within this sonic field—a wavering drone in which various tones and partials seem to quiver and bounce, emerge and withdraw. Present but unobtrusive, the drone could easily escape conscious awareness—except at its peak, when the courtyard is bathed in a rich, consonant sonority. No sooner is it fully audible than it disappears. Suddenly, voices and birdsong seem louder and crisper, and the hush of air vents more aesthetically appealing. Neither present nor fully absent, the sonic after-ring recedes slowly from auditory memory. As it does, ambient sound is gradually drawn down to its ordinary amplitude.

Like Neuhaus's other "moment pieces," *Time Piece Beacon* marks time. But it also marks a temporary rift in time akin to the spatial breach encountered in *Times Square*. It presents a sort of temporal and sonic singularity that signals an alteration of ordinary experience: the opening onto a different time, a nonchronological time. I noted above that chronological time subordinates time to space such that time becomes what Bergson calls "the fourth dimension of space."[59] Discrete moments are laid out side by side, and time is conceived as the quantitative measure of movement or change. Yet what chronology cannot account for is the most crucial aspect of time: that it passes. For, if each moment is a discrete unit, how can the present pass? To do so, it would somehow have to jump the interval between two moments. The problem is not solved by making the interval infinitely divisible, for, rather than eliminating it, this only makes the interval smaller. It is this purely quantitative and spatial thinking about time that led Zeno the Eleatic to conclude that motion is impossible—that the runner can never traverse the stadium, that Achilles can never overtake the tortoise, and that the flying arrow is forever at rest.[60] But to eliminate motion and change is to eliminate nature and matter, to retreat into a meta-physical pseudo-world of thought unsullied by natural becoming.

Chronological time also engenders perplexities about the existence of the past. It raises not only the question of how one moment can dislodge another and send it into the past, but also the question of whether the past comes into being only after the present has passed. If so, *into what* does the present pass, and what sort of existence does that dimension then have?

Bergson and Deleuze solve these puzzles by positing a deeper, nonchronological, nonspatial conception of time: what Bergson calls duration and Deleuze, nonpulsed time or Aion. In order for the present to pass, they argue, it must be not a discrete entity, but a continuity inextricably bound with moments past and to come. Moreover, in order for the present to pass, there must exist a domain of the past into which it can pass. That is, the past must coexist with the present whose past it is. It must exist (or subsist) as a (virtual) field into which the (actual) present can pass. Memory shows us that this is the case, for when I am prompted to remember some event or idea, I do so by drawing it from a reservoir of the past that coexists with my actual, present experience but that remains for the most part latent or virtual. What this argument reveals, Deleuze notes,

> is the most fundamental operation of time: since the past is constituted not after the present that it was but at the same time, time has to split itself in two at each moment as present and past, which differ from each other in nature, or, what amounts to the same thing, it has to split the present in two heterogeneous directions, one of which is launched toward the future while the other falls into the past. Time has to split at the same time as it sets itself out or unrolls itself: it splits into two dissymmetrical jets, one of which makes all the present pass on, while the other preserves all the past. Time consists of this split [. . . which reveals] the perpetual foundation of time, non-chronological time.[61]

For Deleuze, this conception of time flashes forth in the "crystal-images" of postwar cinema. It equally emerges in Neuhaus's *Time Pieces*. In place of the bell stroke that marks chronological time, the sudden disappearance of the drone creates a caesura, a gap or break in chronological time. In this gap, the drone lingers, but virtually, in memory. This virtual domain of the past, ignored or suppressed by ordinary experience, becomes suddenly sensuous and evident. At the same time, the ambient flux amplified by the drone presses into the future. Though the drone will return once again an hour later, this ambient flux will not be the same but ever new. We witness here the splitting of time that is the condition of time's passage, the division of the present into a simultaneous past and future. Rather than marking the instants of the clock, then, Neuhaus highlights temporal passage, becoming itself. Here, time does not measure anything. It is not external to movement and change. It is itself that movement and change, the fluid element in which all entities are borne along, from which they emerge and into which they recede.

Against Becoming and Duration? The Sound of Hyper-Chaos

From *Times Square* to the *Time Pieces*, Neuhaus's installations set sound into space, not to circumvent time but to reveal its most fundamental dimension. This connection between sound and time is not incidental, for, as we have seen, sound is the primary means by which duration is sensuously revealed. It's not surprising, then, that time is so often the subject of sound art, from Christina Kubisch's *Clocktower Project* (1997), which rewired a nineteenth-century bell tower to respond to varying conditions of light rather than clock time, and David Grubbs's *Between a Raven and a Writing Desk* (1999), a looped, hourlong musical composition that at once marks and slackens clock time, to Jem Finer's *Longplayer* (1999), a thousand-year-long composition broadcast from a London lighthouse, and R. Luke Dubois's *SSB* (2008), which digitally stretches *The Star-Spangled Banner* across the four-year span of the American electoral cycle.

Another recent project, the German sound artist Florian Hecker's *Speculative Solution* (2011), explicitly investigates the metaphysics of time, aiming to provoke by means of sound a conception of temporality rigorously opposed to the becoming and duration theorized by Bergson and manifested in the work of Cage and Neuhaus.[62] Hecker's project is rooted in the philosophy of Quentin Meillassoux, who argues that that the absolute—the ground of all being—is time, "*but a very special time*" that Meillassoux terms "hyper-chaos."[63] Before turning to Hecker's project, then, I must briefly rehearse Meillassoux's argument for this novel conception of time, a complicated argument that proceeds dialectically by revealing the deficiencies in several competing positions.[64]

Meillassoux arrives at "hyper-chaos" through an attack on "correlationism," which, as we have seen, names any philosophical position that denies access to reality in itself on the grounds that we can only ever apprehend the real as correlated to and mediated by thought or discourse, never as it exists independently. Correlationism founders on what Meillassoux calls "ancestral" claims, that is, scientific claims concerning the world as it existed prior to the emergence of life or any human subjects to whom it could be correlated (e.g., the claim, based on radiometric dating, that the Earth formed roughly 4.56 billion years ago). Such claims pose a dilemma for the correlationist, who must either accept that they describe the world anterior to and independent of thought and discourse, and thus renounce correlationism; or assert the radically idealist, absurdly anthropocentric, and scientifically insupportable position that the prehuman past did not precede the correlation but is a retrojection of it. For Meillassoux, the former is the only viable conclusion. Nonetheless, he does not dismiss correlationism on these empirical grounds. Rather, he offers an immanent critique, attacking it from the inside.

Correlationism is staunchly antirealist; but it goes further, rejecting every form of absolutism, every claim to know the absolute or the in-itself. It thus rejects not only realist but also idealist absolutism. Against the direct realist, who insists that the world really is more or less as it appears to be, the correlationist points out that every apprehension of the real is always the apprehension *of* a human subject, and hence that what the realist takes to be the world in itself is merely a correlate of thought. Accepting this argument, the idealist acknowledges that we cannot escape the correlationist circle—that it is impossible *to think* a world *independent of thought*. Indeed, the idealist transforms the circle into a metaphysical principle, rejecting the very notion of an independently existing world and maintaining instead that the world fundamentally is the world-for-thought. This line of argument, Meillassoux claims, leads not only to Hegelian idealism but also to a broader position he calls "subjectalism," which encompasses panpsychism and every other position that attributes to nature the perceptive, affective, or volitional capacities of the human subject.[65]

Correlationism cannot tolerate this idealist absolutism any more than it can tolerate the absolutism of the realist; but it must combat it with a different argument, since the idealist fully accepts the circularity of thought and being. Against idealism and "subjectalism," the correlationist insists on the *facticity* of the correlation, its status as a contingent fact. Being is correlated with thought; but this correlation is not a necessary feature of reality. Rather, it is simply a contingent feature of the subject's relationship to the real. It is true that the thinker cannot conceive a world independent of thought, acknowledges the correlationist, but this does not mean that there is no such thing, just as my inability to conceive what it is like to be dead does not prove that death is impossible. Any claim to necessity is dogmatic, claims the correlationist; everything is contingent.

The idealist radicalized the correlationist's argument against realism to establish an absolute principle: the absolute co-implication of thought and being. In a structurally similar move, Meillassoux radicalizes the correlationist's argument against idealism to establish his own conception of the absolute: time as hyper-chaos. How does he arrive at this conclusion? In its refutation of idealist absolutism, correlationism implicitly acknowledges an alternative to the correlation, its possible nonbeing, and thus the existence of a world beyond the correlation. Moreover, correlationism does not merely posit the *existence* of such a domain (as did Kant); it offers a *positive characterization* of it. Asserting the nonnecessity of the correlation between thought and being, the correlationist unwittingly erects contingency (or, as Meillassoux calls it, "factiality" [*factualité*]) as an absolute principle. Every particular fact, occurrence, or entity is contingent, the correlationist maintains, but not the principle of contingency itself that establishes this to be universally the case. In this way, correlationism itself breaks out of the vicious circle that it asserted against realism and is led to a new absolutism, a new "speculative realism." No longer claiming ignorance of the real beyond the correlation, it is now led to assert that we *do* know this reality and that the real is fundamentally contingent, admitting no necessity.

This has far-reaching consequences. The absolutization of contingency is not the mere affirmation of *empirical* contingency, the banal assertion that all things are precarious and perishable. If contingency is *absolute*, it applies not only to things and facts but also to laws, which, in this conception, simply become facts without any necessity. In other words, the argument from contingency or factiality amounts to a rejection of the principle of sufficient reason, according to which everything must of necessity have a reason or a cause. As Meillassoux puts it:

> Everything and every world *is* without reason, and is thereby *capable of actually becoming otherwise without reason*. . . . "Unreason" . . . is an absolute ontological property, and not the mark of the finitude of our knowledge. . . . The truth is that there is no reason for anything to be or to remain thus and so rather than otherwise, and this applies as much to the laws that govern the world as to the things of the world. Everything could actually collapse: from trees to stars, from stars to laws, from physical laws to logical laws; and this not by virtue of some superior law whereby everything is destined to perish, but by virtue of the absence of any superior law capable of preserving anything, no matter what, from perishing.[66]

This absolute principle of unreason is *time* and, specifically, time as hyper-chaos, a conception of time fundamentally at odds with the time of becoming or duration we have seen affirmed in the work of Neuhaus, Cage, and others. After all, Meillassoux points out, the time of becoming and duration implicitly depends on laws of succession and transformation that ensure continual passage and ceaseless change. But, if contingency is absolute, it would undermine such laws. "This hyperchaotic time," Meillassoux writes, "is able to create and destroy even becoming, producing without reason fixity or movement, repetition or creation."[67] Hyper-chaos can just as readily support persistent order as frenetic disorder, determination as randomness, stasis as change. As hyper-chaos, time does not *necessarily* pass; things do not *necessarily* change from this to that. There is no *necessary* continuity from one moment to the next. At any moment anything can happen, which is why Meillassoux calls it the time of "the possible" or "the may-be" [*peut-être*], rather than the time of being [*être*] or of becoming [*devenir*].[68] In short, hyper-chaos not only permits but is defined by the miracle, the sudden irruption *ex nihilo* that undermines the so-called laws of nature, though Meillassoux is quick to note that such miraculous occurrences testify not to the existence but to the inexistence of God, the impossibility of a necessary being who could control contingency from without.[69]

It is this conception of time that Hecker aims to engage in *Speculative Solution*, a set of four compositions commissioned by the philosopher Robin Mackay's publishing house Urbanomic in discussion with Meillassoux, who contributed an essay to the accompanying CD booklet and discussed the project with Hecker and Mackay along the way.[70] As Mackay notes, Hecker's project was "to create a work in which the sensible is employed to make felt the facticity not just of things, but of laws."[71] Meillassoux, Hecker, and Mackay acknowledge that this project is fraught with difficulties. In the first place, hyper-chaos is the conclusion of a purely deductive argument that does not draw on any empirical evidence or require any sensory support. As Meillasssoux himself replies to Hecker and Mackay: "you cannot illustrate this special object of philosophy, because any illustration will always fall within the domain of facts."[72] Moreover, hyper-chaos is consistent with *any* eventuality whatsoever—with perfect order, utter randomness, fluid becoming, total stasis, and so on. Mozart provides as much evidence for it as does Merzbow. Indeed, Meillassoux worries that a sonic presentation of hyper-chaos could take the form of a postmodern collage of random quotations.[73] Finally, the bounded, finite nature of the recording and the potential for repetition inherent in any such document are sufficient to transform even the most random, abrupt, or spontaneous event into a seemingly necessary one.[74]

Despite these perils, Mackay, Meillassoux, and Hecker suggest a number of possible artistic and sonic strategies. Perhaps the best sensible to hyper-chaos, Meillassoux proposes, "is the world where you have this continuity, and inside it you have this pure break, a break that is too harsh for classical probability."[75] Similarly, Mackay proposes that an audible microcosm of hyper-chaos might set up various modes of sonic organization analogous to natural laws and then violate them. The aim, then, would be

> to create a piece in which "control systems" (i.e. the laws which define and govern objects) are subject to the same dynamic, stochastic, etc. treatments as the "facts" or "objects" that take place within them . . . to create an exaggerated sense of staticness; to emphasize the impact of an order's abrupt end; to present the same elements interacting under extremely different control regimes; to become accustomed to a subtle set of laws, only for those laws to then disappear into something obtusely obvious.[76]

Finally, Mackay proposes that, even if it is not possible to offer an adequate sensual presentation of hyper-chaos, Hecker's sound work could function as a rational prosthesis, a *memento cogito* aimed at sensually habituating the mind to hyper-chaos so as to prepare its leap from the sensible to the more purely rational.[77] This empirical supplement to cognition—the equivalent of a geometrical diagram—would itself require supplements that facilitate this leap. Hence Mackay and Hecker conclude that the entire *Speculative Solution* package—a box containing the CD, a booklet of theoretical texts, and five loose ball bearings (fig. 5.5)—should be considered a sort of "toolbox for conceiving of hyper-chaos rather than trying to present it."[78]

Hecker's contribution to this package consists of four electronic compositions: a thirty-two-minute piece and a nineteen-minute piece bracketing two three-minute, identically titled tracks that are close variants of one another. Each of the longer pieces is a sequence of brief sections (rarely lasting more than a minute or two) that are abruptly juxtaposed with sections exhibiting contrasting textures, timbres, and rhythms, making each composition seem like a sampler or catalog. While occasionally employing bits of broadband noise, Hecker prefers relatively pure, crisp tones in the middle and high registers, fashioning them into off-kilter hocketing pulses and alea-

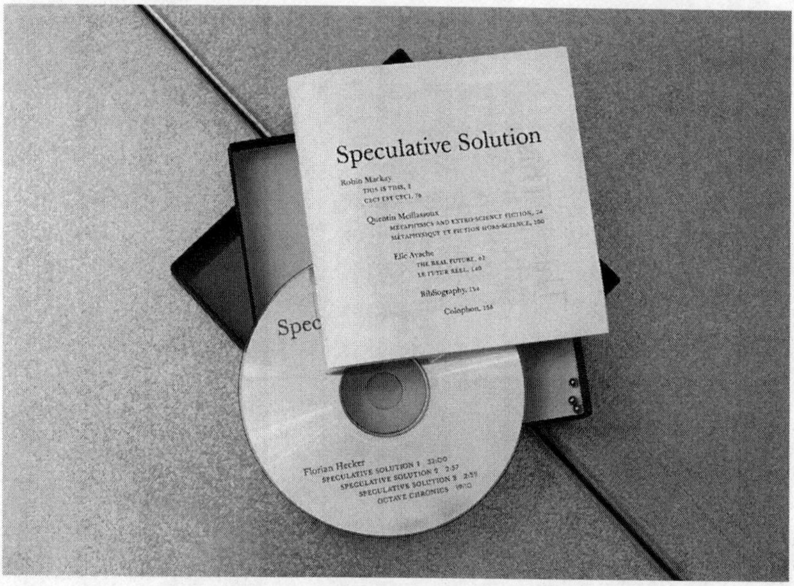

Fig. 5.5 Florian Hecker, *Speculative Solution*, 2011, Editions Mego eMEGO 118. Box with 160-page booklet, CD, and five ball bearings. Designed by Tina Frank, Florian Hecker, and Elvira Stein. Courtesy of Tina Frank.

toric polyrhythms that, given their dizzying complexity, lead the listener to attend to their more graspable component rhythms. For example, in one three-minute stretch of "Speculative Solution 1," a melody that randomly bounces among a small set of raspy, chirping pitches generating vertiginous psychoacoustic effects suddenly gives way to a calm organ drone that fades to a brief silence, from which burst overlapping patterns of glassy tones forming short, repetitive figures that accelerate and decelerate and are then overlaid with sirenlike organ intervals that rise in pitch like a slow, reversed Doppler effect. The shorter pieces consist entirely of one slowly chugging rhythm built from clipped and echoing digital drum beats. The tracks are repetitive but imprecisely so, their elements never falling in exactly the same place, their subtly shifting layers both engaging and frustrating the desire for a clear and stable meter.

For all its shifts and changes, however, Hecker's sound world is remarkably consistent. His timbral palette and rhythmic choices are fully characteristic of the experimental electronica fostered from the mid-1990s through the 2000s by the German record labels Raster-Noton and Mille Plateaux, and by the Austrian label Mego, which released *Speculative Solution* and more than a dozen other recordings by Hecker. The structure of Hecker's pieces is certainly more paratactical than the fluid and minimalist productions favored by most artists on those labels, but not much more so than that of classic electronic compositions such as Stockhausen's *Kontakte* (1959–60) or Györgi Ligeti's *Artikulation* (1958), which *Speculative Solution* resembles in several respects. Moreover, Hecker's abrupt shifts are so regular as to be predictable. Rarely do we hear long stretches of the same material; and when we do—as in the second half of the final piece, "Octave Chronics"—it sits so well within the sound world Hecker has established that it does not violate our expectations. Hecker's compositions do not descend into long stretches of silence or suddenly burst into samples from Brahms, Beyoncé, or documentary audio. Rather, they obey a clear set of material and structural rules and fall well within established traditions of electronic music. One never really feels, as Meillassoux says of hyper-chaos, that "everything is possible, anything can happen."[79] Rather, one feels only that a relatively small set of things could happen, and that they consistently do.

Indeed, the radical discontinuities Hecker seeks have been a basic feature of artistic practice at least since the advent of cinematic montage, which operates through the cut, the sharp break in continuity juxtaposing two incommensurable images. This aesthetic of the break was sonically developed by the practitioners of musique concrète, by Stockhausen's "moment form" compositions, and by Burroughs's audio cut-ups, entering popular culture through hip-hop sampling with its principle of "cut 'n' mix." These cultural forms may manifest nonchronological time (a clash of different temporal and spatial frames, for example) and allow almost anything to happen (for objects to disappear, for cars to fly, for the material base of film or sound recording suddenly to dissolve, etc.); but this is not the time of hyper-chaos—not only because hyper-chaos resists sensuous presentation, but also because it is an untenable theory of time.

Like Parmenides and Zeno, his ancient rationalist predecessors, Meillassoux privileges the discrete instant and severs all connections between instants.[80] If "everything is possible" and "anything can happen," that is because there is no necessary relationship between one instant and any other. Each instant is as causally and logically disconnected from those that precede or succeed it as it is from more remote instants. Given this conception of the discrete instant, however, it is difficult to understand how there could ever be more than one instant, how any instant could pass or give way to another. Elucidating his account of time, Meillassoux writes: "Things must be this, *then* other than this; they are, *then* they are not."[81] But what accounts for this "*then*"—that is, for the passage from "this" to "other than this," from being to nonbeing? Meillassoux will reply that nothing accounts for it—or, rather, that what accounts for it is radical contingency, according to which one instant or state of affairs replaces another *without reason*. If this is so, then the principle of succession is not immanent to the instants themselves but instead requires a force that transcends them—namely hyper-chaos. Indeed, despite Meillassoux's rejection of necessary entities (such as God) and insistence that radical contingency affirms the immanence of time,[82] hyper-chaos plays a distinctly theological and transcendent role in his philosophy. Unconstrained by any material force, it is necessary and omnipotent, as capable of generating miracles as of recreating the world anew at every moment such that it appears to be orderly and regular. That is, Meillassoux does not think time itself but rather posits a force outside time, a deus ex machina that constantly rolls the Cantorian dice and thereby brings new instants into existence.[83]

As such, Meillassoux confuses time with states of affairs *in* time, temporal passage with situations of longer or shorter duration. After all, even states of "stasis," "fixity," and "perdurance" are always subject to time as becoming. As Bergson puts it, "there is no essential difference between passing from one state to another and persisting in the same state," because "the state itself is nothing but change."[84] Time is perpetual difference, a becoming-other that permits neither identity nor identical repetition. Hence, Meillassoux's idea of "little static worlds—worlds with absolutely no becoming" is nonsensical.[85] The world can never be put on pause, not even by a transcendent being or process. If, miraculously, such a being could produce a state of affairs in which all activity were paused, such a state of affairs would nevertheless persist in time, the relentless succession of which would render it different from one moment to the next. "Fixity" and "change," "stasis and "movement," then, simply name differences of degree not of kind, different speeds of becoming rather than differences between becoming and some "time without becoming."

Radical contingency or hyper-chaos is premised on the principle of noncontradiction, which, for Meillassoux, is not only a condition of rational thought but "an absolute ontological truth."[86] A contradictory entity, he notes, could never change because it would already *be* what it *is not*. "It could never become other than it is, since it already *is* this other": *a* and not-*a*; *b* and not-*b*; and so on for every other property.[87] As such, a contradictory entity would be not *contingent* but *necessary*, an entity that would "preclude any dimension of alterity through which the entity could be subjected to change."[88] Yet, by the same token, a noncontradictory entity could never change because it would already be fully present to itself, without any impetus to become other than it is.[89] While it is different from other entities, a noncontradictory entity of the Meillassouxian sort is also utterly disconnected from all others and not impelled by or toward them in any way. Just as Zeno took the infinite divisibility of space to prove the impossibility of movement, Meillassoux's radically disconnected instants reveal the impossibility of temporal passage, the sine qua non of time. Both arguments are unwitting *reductios*. Zeno's logic is as powerless to deny movement as Meillassoux's is powerless to deny time's continuous succession. Time cannot be turned into a numerical and discrete multiplicity without ceasing to be time. In truth, however, neither time nor being consists of discrete instants or entities that are present to themselves. Rather, each consists solely of becomings, physical processes differentiated by their relative speeds and the materials through which they flow.

Meillassoux declares himself a materialist, defining this position as affirming both the irreducibility of matter to thought and the ontological priority of the former over the latter.[90] And, as we have seen, he begins *After Finitude* by countering correlationism with evidence from empirical science, which describes an "ancestral" time prior to human thought. Yet the central argument of the book—the argument for hyper-chaos—vitiates this materialism and undermines the temporal and causal continuity that provide the very foundations of science and scientific evidence. Meillassoux arrives at hyper-chaos through thought alone, showing not only that this thesis requires no empirical confirmation, but also that it is impervious to falsification by empirical evidence. Attempting to overcome correlationism from the inside, Meillassoux succumbs to it, subsuming empirical reality within thought and thereby reversing the priority of matter to thought characteristic of every materialism.[91] Hyper-chaos is thus nothing more than what a more compelling theorist of time and contingency, the theoretical physicist Lee Smolin, calls "a Harry Potter story about things that might be true" rather than a theory that has any purchase in material reality.[92]

As Hume showed, the contingency of the world is revealed not by logical laws (which, for him, are never more than tautologies) but by empirical facts, which disclose an open-ended and changeable world in which the future need not conform to the past, and in which no event or being is ever necessary. À la Meillassoux, we can extend this radical contingency to encompass not only empirical facts but also the so-called laws of nature, which could have been (and still could be) otherwise. Yet the evidence for this claim would come not from rational deduction but from verifiable and testable hypotheses—hypotheses of the sort advanced by Smolin, who argues that natural "laws" evolved by a process of "cosmological natural selection" and are thus subject to the same contingency or non-necessity as biological organisms.[93]

Ever since Parmenides and Plato, rationalists have been antagonistic to becoming (which confounds the category of being and the distinction between being and nonbeing) and to the natural, empirical world that relentlessly manifests it. While sharing little of his predecessors' urge toward fixity and permanence, Meillassoux nonetheless treats time as the result of logical deduction instead of a material fact and ignores all empirical evidence of becoming. But time is inseparable from natural change. Apart from this material support, it is nothing. It does not reside outside of matter as some transcendent force that directs eventualities. Rather, it is the immanent register of change, to which all natural, material entities (the only entities that exist) are inexorably subject. Meillassoux is right to assert that time is subject to no necessity except the necessity of contingency; but this contingency is guaranteed not by the inviolability of noncontradiction but by the universality of material becoming, difference, and change.

Though all things are subject to becoming, sound plays a special role in making time audible. It manifests this natural flux more richly and more palpably than any other phenomena and reveals time in all its heterogeneous becoming. No matter how structurally fractured they might be, sonic compositions and sound installations bear witness to and chart these flows, which are always riven by cuts that intercept and articulate them, dam them up, slow them down, filter them, unleash new flows, and so on, the way a synthesizer shapes and articulates a flow of electrons. The art of sound is precisely the art of unleashing, cutting, and shaping these flows, which are temporal or nothing at all, always manifesting the passage, the relentless becoming-other that is time.

PART III

The Optical and the Sonic

6 AUDIO/VISUAL

AGAINST SYNAESTHETICS

In the summer of 2005 the New York City media art center Eyebeam hosted an exhibition titled *What Sound Does a Color Make?*, described by the curators as presenting work by contemporary artists "who conflate sound and vision," using digital technology "to explore the sense of synesthesia."[1] Alongside video projections, installations, and interactive play stations by a new generation of artists, the exhibition featured a selection of classic video artworks from the 1970s that used image to manipulate sound and vice versa. The Eyebeam show joined a spate of exhibitions that drew analogies between artistic practices and synaesthesia, the neurological condition in which stimulation of one sensory modality triggers involuntary sensation in another, such that, for example, one sees sounds or hears odors. A few months prior, the Museum of Contemporary Art, Los Angeles and the Centre Pompidou in Paris mounted different but overlapping large-scale surveys that situated contemporary audiovisual crossovers within the history of synaesthetic art experiments since 1900. Both MOCA's *Visual Music* and the Pompidou's *Sons & lumières* drew parallels between the concerns of early twentieth-century painters such as Wassily Kandinsky and Hans Richter, who attempted to render sound as image, and early twenty-first-century media artists such as Jim Hodges and Christian Marclay, whose visual art is often prompted by musical concerns.

Such efforts to conjoin sound and image have become common in the post-millennium art world, evident in more recent exhibitions such as *See This Sound* at the Lentos Kunstmuseum Linz (2009), *Art & Music: Search for New Synesthesia* at the Museum of Contemporary Art Tokyo (2012), *Art or Sound* at the Fondazione Prada Venice (2014), and *Soundscapes* at the National Gallery in London (2015). All these exhibitions represent attempts by visual arts institutions to come to terms with the emergence of sound art as a distinct field and with audio as an increasingly prominent medium for artists since the late 1990s. In nearly all cases, the reception of sound has been ambivalent. While officially opening their doors to sound, galleries and museums have at the same time manifested considerable anxiety about this new guest. This is tellingly manifested in exhibitions organized under the banner of synaesthesia, which ensures that sound is admitted only under the condition that it be chaperoned by the visual and, more often than not, has served as a mechanism by which to silence rather than amplify the sonic.

In this final chapter, I want to explore these conjunctions of sound and image in twentieth- and twenty-first-century art, examining the promises of sensory unity, the anxious appropriation of sound within the visual arts, and the potential for productive confrontations and collaborations between the audio and the visual. Operating between and beyond traditional aesthetic categories, sound art has rekindled promises and anxieties rooted deep in the history of visual modernism, which, far from welcoming sound, reveals a series of vexed encounters with it.

From *Gesamtkunstwerk* to Synaesthesia

We humans are endowed with five senses, five different channels through which we gather information about our ever-changing environment. Communicating between inside and outside, four of these sensory channels originate in facial orifices—eyes, ears, nose, and mouth—that open our bodies onto the world. The remaining sense, touch, is dispersed across the entire surface of the skin, an enveloping membrane that registers the minutest of stimuli.

The division of the arts largely accords with this sensory distribution and fragmentation, and also with the traditional hierarchy that separates the two "noble senses" (seeing and hearing) from their more vulgar associates (taste, touch, and smell). Painting and sculpture address the eyes, music the ears. The former belong in the museum or gallery, the latter in the concert hall. Each has its own history, which only rarely overlaps with the other. And while there are surely mixed arts—theater and cinema, for example—we still unproblematically speak of "the visual arts" and distinguish them from music as apples to oranges.

However, despite this sensory fragmentation, physiological dispersal, and aesthetic hierarchy, we experience the world as a unity. We don't feel ourselves to be constantly coordinating and translating between heterogeneous streams of sensory data. Rather, the world seems to come to us undivided and complete. Acknowledging this mysterious emergence of unity from plurality, Aristotle posited a sort of shared sense—a *koinē aisthēsis, sensus communis,* or common sense—whose role was to connect the five sensory streams and ensure their agreement with one another.[2] Aristotle's hypothesis profoundly influenced his successors; and variants of it continue to inform current scientific research.[3]

If we experience the world as a sensory unity, shouldn't the arts affirm this union? On this question, modernism was deeply divided. One of its most powerful and influential theorists, Clement Greenberg, argued that the distinctiveness of the modern consisted precisely in the segregation of the arts from one another and the autonomous development of each. In particular, Greenberg was concerned to purge the visual arts of every extravisual sensation (tactility, for example) in order to render them "purely optical."[4] The Russian filmmaker Dziga Vertov agreed, celebrating the "kino-eye." "We protest against the mixing of the arts which many call synthesis," he wrote in a 1922 manifesto. "The mixture of bad colors, even those ideally selected from the spectrum, produces not white, but mud. . . . WE are cleansing *kinochestvo* of foreign matter—of music, literature, and theater; we seek our own rhythm, one lifted from nowhere else."[5] Nonetheless, from the outset, prominent modern artists pressed an alternative position, advocating for sensory and aesthetic unity. This call was boldly sounded by the composer and dramatist Richard Wagner in his 1849 essay "The Artwork of the Future," which insisted that only a true synthesis of all the arts—a *Gesamtkunstwerk* or "total work of art"—could realize art's true purpose. Wagner wrote:

> Each separate faculty of man is limited by bounds; but his united, agreed, and reciprocally helping faculties—and thus his faculties in *mutual love* of one another—combine to form the self-completing, unbounded, universal faculty of men. Thus too has every *artistic* faculty of man its natural bounds, since man has not *one only Sense* but separate *Senses;* while every faculty springs from its special sense, and therefore each single faculty must find its bounds in the confines of its correlated sense. But the boundaries of the separate senses are also their joint meeting-points, those points at which

> they melt in one another and each agrees with each: and exactly so do the faculties that are derived from them touch one another and agree. Their confines, therefore, are removed by this agreement; but only those that love each other can agree, and "to love" means: to acknowledge the other, and at like time to know one's self. Thus Knowledge through Love is Freedom; and the freedom of man's faculties is—*All-faculty*.
>
> Only the Art which answers to this "all-faculty" of man is, therefore, *free*; and not the Art-*variety*, which only issues from a single human faculty. The Arts of Dance, of Tone, of Poetry, are each confined within their several bounds; in contact with these bounds each feels herself unfree, be it not that, across their common boundary, she reaches out her hand to her neighbouring art in unrestrained acknowledgment of love. The very grasping of this hand lifts her above the barrier; her full embrace, her full absorption in her sister—i.e., her own complete ascension beyond the set-up barrier—casts down the fence itself. And when every barrier has thus fallen, then are there no more *arts* and no more boundaries, but only *Art*, the universal, undivided.[6]

In the decades that followed this proclamation, Wagner's call for a union of the senses was bolstered by a burst of interest—artistic *and* scientific—in the related but distinct phenomenon of synaesthesia. The *Gesamtkunstwerk* promised to conjoin all the arts and stimulate all the senses at once. Synaesthesia is also characterized by a union of the senses but generally only of two, and in an asymmetrical configuration: a primary, inducing sensation—for example, sound—that activates a secondary, concurrent sensation—for example, color. This neurological condition had fascinated philosophers and scientists at least since 1690, when John Locke reported the case of a blind man who claimed to understand the color scarlet as the sound of a trumpet.[7] But it wasn't until the late nineteenth and early twentieth centuries that synaesthesia became a hot topic for scientific research.[8] It also sparked the interest of painters, composers, and poets, who were drawn to the imaginative possibilities and spiritual resonances of sensory union. In his celebrated poem "Correspondences" (1857), Charles Baudelaire wrote of "odors . . . sweet as flutes, and green as any grass."[9] Baudelaire's Symbolist compatriot Arthur Rimbaud drew equivalences between vowels, colors, textures and odors: the letter "A" invoked a "black hairy corset of shining flies / Which buzz around cruel stench"; "E," the "whiteness of vapors and tents"; and so on.[10] As visual artists began to abandon figuration

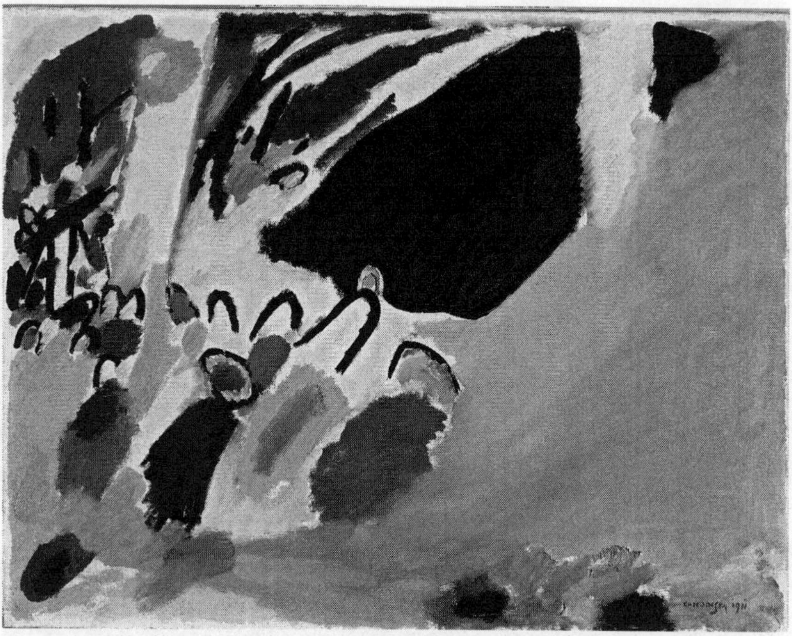

Fig. 6.1 Wassily Kandinsky, *Impression III (Concert)*, 1911. Oil on canvas, 30⅞ × 39 9/16 inches. Städtische Galerie im Lenbachhaus und Kunstbau München.

and approach abstraction, they often looked for inspiration to music, conceived as the purest and least mimetic of the arts. "All art constantly aspires towards the condition of music," declared the critic Walter Pater in 1877, a remark echoed by many pioneers of pictorial abstraction.[11] Kandinsky's proto-abstract painting *Impression III (Concert)* (1911; fig. 6.1) was directly inspired by the thrill of hearing Arnold Schoenberg's first atonal works at a concert in Munich. Others such as Paul Klee, Marsden Hartley, and František Kupka took inspiration from Bach, attempting visual counterpoint akin to the rhythmic structure of the fugue.

The late nineteenth-century craze for synaesthetic cross-wirings prompted inventors to abandon traditional artistic media and musical instruments and instead to build new machines that attempted to connect sound with color. In the late 1860s the Alsatian chemist and musician Frédéric Kastner developed an instrument he called the Pyrophone, in which a small keyboard produced both sound and colored light by igniting gas jets that lit thirteen crystal pipes protruding from a console. The invention struck Wagner as a promising facilitation of the *Gesamtkunstwerk*; and the composer made a failed attempt to finance its use in his operatic productions.[12] Two and a half decades later the British inventor and art professor Alexander Rimington built what he was the first to call a "color organ," an instrument that made no sound but used a standard organ keyboard to illuminate fourteen arc lamps that glowed with different shades and intensities of color.

Kastner's and Rimington's inventions sparked widespread fascination with "visual music," provoking artists and inventors to construct numerous variants on the color organ. In the first few decades of the twentieth century, the artistic avant-garde was drawn to these inventions not so much as musical instruments, but as mechanisms capable of animating abstract forms through a sort of cinematic projection. The Russian Futurist painter Wladimir Baranoff-Rossiné developed his *piano optophonique* (1920–23), a complex keyboard-controlled contraption that made sounds while projecting light through an array of mirrors, filters, lenses, and hand-painted discs. At the Weimar Bauhaus, Ludwig Hirschfeld-Mack constructed a machine that translated music into projections of mobile forms and colored light. The Danish-American artist Thomas Wilfred upgraded the color organ with his Clavilux (1922), which employed a bank of dials and sliding keys to rotate bulbs and mirrors that displayed ethereal, flamelike wisps of dancing color he called "Lumia."

These live projections of visual music were paralleled by the exploration of musically inspired (but primarily silent) abstraction on film. As in the work of Baranoff-Rossiné and Hirschfeld-Mack, the "absolute film" of Hans Richter and Viking Eggeling (modeled on the purely instrumental "absolute music" of the nineteenth century) aimed to animate the rhythmic and harmonic relationships inherent in nonrepresentational painting, endowing them with the temporal dimension characteristic of music. The pulsing, growing, shrinking, and overlapping rectangles in Richter's *Rhythmus 21* (1921; fig. 6.2) are meant to evoke the musical experience of volume, pitch, harmony and, above all, rhythm. In Eggeling's *Symphonie diagonale* (1924), a series of comblike forms alternate and succeed one another like chords, while curved and angled lines are drawn on the screen like silent melodies.

True to Pater's formulation, all these art forms—abstract canvases, color organs, and absolute cinema—aspired not so much to music as to its "condition," that is, to its nonrepresentationality, temporality, rhythm, and, often, its perceived "spirituality." No *Gesamtkunstwerke*, these generally silent artistic forms made little attempt to conjoin the visual with the sonic. Some

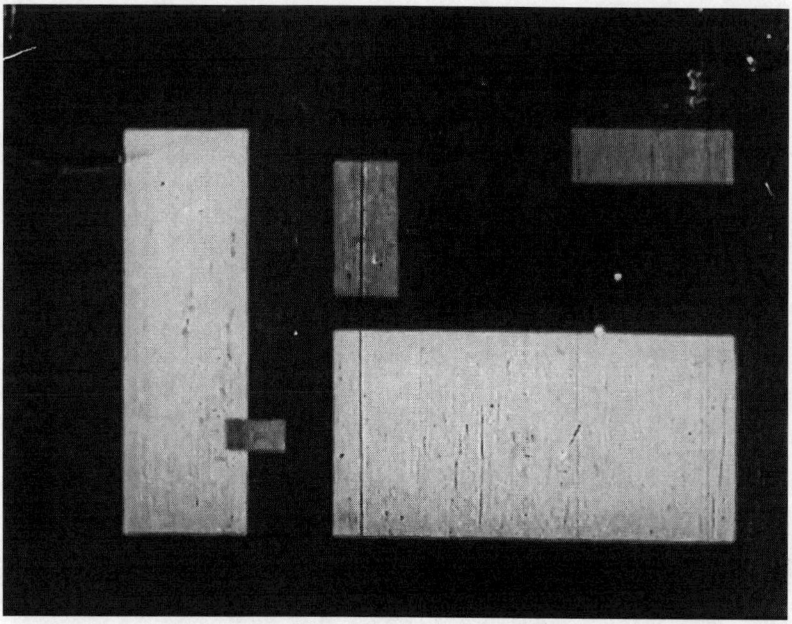

Fig. 6.2 Hans Richter, *Rhythmus 21*, 1921–24, 35mm film, 5 minutes, b&w, silent.

artists may have hoped synaesthetically to evoke the experience of sound by means of image. Yet, for the most part, music was called upon as an artistic precedent or existing model to validate visual art's perilous move toward abstraction, enabling painters and filmmakers to thwart the criticism that nonrepresentational art was arbitrary, childish, or merely decorative.[13] "One can compare Coloured Rhythm to music," wrote Guillaume Apollinaire in 1914, discussing the visual music experiments of Léopold Survage, "but the analogies are superficial, and it really is an independent art having infinitely varied resources of its own."[14] As Greenberg put it, the visual avant-garde appropriated music as method rather than as sensual effect.[15] Paradoxically, then, music and sound enabled the visual arts to pursue their own purely optical aims.

Sound/Image

With the advent of sound cinema in the late 1920s, the dream of the *Gesamtkunstwerk* and of a synaesthetic art would seem to have been realized. Artists such as Mary Ellen Bute enthusiastically embraced this idea, producing

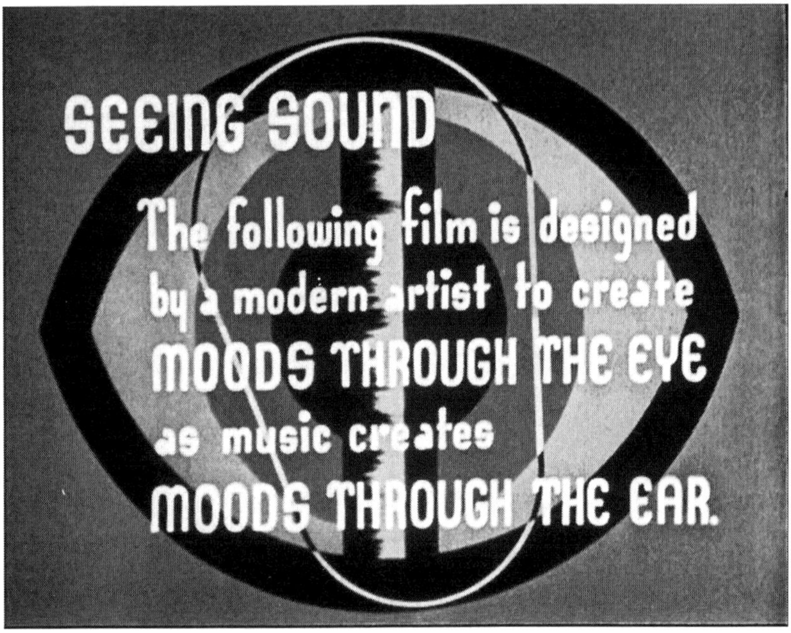

Fig. 6.3 Introductory title, Mary Ellen Bute, *Synchromy No. 2*, 1936, 16mm film, 5 minutes, b&w, sound.

a series of "Seeing Sound" films in the 1930s that attempted "to create moods through the eye as music creates moods through the ear" by providing "a pictorial accompaniment in abstract forms" to music by Wagner, Edvard Grieg, Camille Saint-Saëns, and J. S. Bach (fig. 6.3).[16] Bute described her film *Rhythm in Light* (1934) as "a modern artist's impression of what goes on in the mind when listening to music."[17] Likewise, Oskar Fischinger introduced his 1938 film *An Optical Poem* with a title that read: "To most of us music suggests definite mental images of form and color. The picture you are about to see is a novel scientific experiment. Its object is to convey these mental images in visual form."[18]

Yet the development of sound film was not universally celebrated by filmmakers and other artists. In 1928 three of the most prominent representatives of Soviet cinema, Sergei Eisenstein, Vsevolod Pudovkin, and Grigori Alexandrov, issued a statement warning that sync sound would surely be used merely to bolster cinematic illusion and favor the visual. "Sound used in this way," they noted, "will destroy the culture of montage." Instead, the trio advocated the nonsynchronization of sound and image, a contrapuntal relationship between the two that would resist the subordination of sound to image, encouraging a tension that could thwart naturalistic illusion. To this end, the trio concluded, "*the first experiments in sound must aim at a sharp discord with the visual images.*"[19] The playwright, theorist, and film actor Antonin Artaud also objected to the arrival of "talking pictures," but primarily because they favored speech and other articulate sounds at the expense of the rich and vast domain of noises that, like Luigi Russolo, Artaud felt would form the sonic art of the future.[20]

A few years later Walter Ruttmann took up and pushed to the extreme these calls for the exploration of noise and the nonsynchronous relationship between sound and image. One of the founders of absolute film, Ruttmann inverted his early experiments in "visual music." His 1930 film *Weekend* consists solely of a soundtrack without images: an eleven-minute collage of concrete noises—hammers, cash registers, sirens, voices, incidental music, and so on—that denies the viewer any visual accompaniment. The film might be understood as a complement to the silent visual music of Richter's *Rhythmus 21*, Eggeling's *Symphonie Diagonale*, or Ruttmann's own *Opus* series; yet the prevailing cinematic hierarchy of the visual over the sonic prevents this complementarity, ensuring that the absence of the visual is experienced not so much as an invitation to synaesthesia than as a lack and disjunction between sound and image.[21] Ruttmann himself referred to *Weekend* as "a blind film," remarking that it "employed sound as an end in itself" rather than as a provocation for the visual imagination.[22]

Such resistance to the seamless merging of sound and image, of hearing and seeing, is as prevalent in modern and contemporary art as is the desire for synaesthetic union or the *Gesamtkunstwerk*. It comes in part from the suspicion that any convergence of the senses is likely to retain the hierarchy that subordinates all other modalities to the visual. It is equally born of the desire not to eliminate the unique differences between the senses and the rich aesthetic tensions these differences generate.

While Kandinsky, Klee, and many other early modernists pursued the dream of *synaesthesia*, Marcel Duchamp instead championed *anaesthesia*. The selection of the "readymades," he noted, "was based on a reaction of visual indifference with at the same time a total absence of good or bad taste . . . in fact a complete anesthesia."[23] Indeed, Duchamp consistently resisted the notion that art should be primarily "retinal," aiming instead to push it toward the conceptual and the verbal. Likewise, in several works he aimed at a noncochlear sonic art, or what one critic calls "music for the deaf," "silent noise."[24] With his sisters Yvonne and Magdeleine, Duchamp composed *Erratum Musical* (1913), a score generated by a chance technique (picking notes out of a hat) accompanied by a readymade lyric (the dictionary definition of a randomly chosen word, *imprimer*: "To make an imprint mark with lines a figure on a surface impress a seal on wax").[25] Both the text and the title allude to printing: the text to the phono-graphic impression of lines or figures on a wax surface, the title to a misprint in written signs (words or musical symbols). Indeed, the title suggests that the piece itself is an error—perhaps the error of conceiving the silent wax cylinder or printed visual score as "musical." The "assisted readymade" *With Hidden Noise* (1916) also presents the visual object as faulty and sound as purely conceptual. Though the work is in principle a sound-making toy, when elevated to the status of an art object displayed inertly in a museum it loses this auditory character, the trace of which remains only in the title, its sonic source now "hidden" or "secret," suggested by language alone. Finally, Duchamp's rotary works—*Disks Bearing Spirals* (1923), *Rotary Demisphere (Precision Optics)* (1925), *Anemic Cinema* (1926), and *Rotoreliefs* (1935)—blend phonography with cinema while undercutting both. Flipping the turntable on its side, Duchamp replaces the coiled grooves of the phonograph record with spiraling textual puns and vortices of visual lines. Music becomes silent cinema, but an anemic cinema of hypnotic repetition.

A whole lineage of Duchamp-inspired art followed suit. Joseph Beuys's *The Silence* (1973), for example, is a sculptural object consisting simply of the five reels of Ingmar Bergman's 1962 film *The Silence*, the film's celluloid drenched in copper and zinc and sealed in galvanized canisters. Eliminating both sound and image from Bergman's film, Beuys's stack of canisters draws attention to film not as "talking pictures" but as mute material. This line of attack is furthered in Christian Marclay's *The Sound of Silence* (fig. 2.4), a photograph of Simon & Garfunkel's 1964 single "The Sound of Silence" that displays the record as a mute visual object. Marclay's piece references Beuys and Duchamp but also René Magritte, whose famous 1929 painting *The Treachery of Images* presents the bluntly scribbled text *Ceci n'est pas un pipe* ("This is not a pipe") below a stylized image of a pipe. Magritte's painting highlights the disjunctions between word, image, and object. Marclay's photograph extends this disjunction to sound, noting, like Beuys, that this mute image and object capture the silence to which Simon & Garfunkel's song and Bergman's film could only paradoxically allude. Marclay's piece is a joke, but an epistemologically and ontologically profound one, the humor of which consists in an evident confusion of categories: photograph, object, and text are absurd because they cannot be what they claim they are. Sound is thereby shown to be of another order, one inadequately represented or even foreclosed by the imaginary domain of the visual and the symbolic domain of the written word.

In the late 1940s the radio-engineer-turned-composer Pierre Schaeffer celebrated a defining property of audio recording and radio transmission: the ability to separate sounds from their visible sources. This affirmation cut against the grain of modern thought, for influential theorists such as Martin Heidegger, Theodor Adorno, and Max Horkheimer had assailed these technologies for dulling our auditory sensibility.[26] Schaeffer, however, argued that records and radio triumphantly subvert the hegemony of vision and make possible the experience of "sound as such." In doing so, Schaeffer reasoned, they revive a neglected form of listening he termed "acousmatic," in deference to the ancient *akousmatikoi,* disciples of Pythagoras who were made to listen to their master's voice while he was hidden behind a curtain.[27] Bruce Nauman's *Concrete Tape Recorder Piece* (1968) is a Duchampian pun on Schaeffer, and also an homage to *With Hidden Noise* and a response to Robert Morris's *Box with the Sound of Its Own Making* (1961). A 650-pound concrete block with a power cord protruding from it, this piece was described by Nauman as a "tape recorder with a tape loop of a scream wrapped in a plastic bag and cast into the center of a block of concrete." Here, too, the noise is hidden, silent—or rather silenced, for Nauman's piece is more ominous than Duchamp's or Morris's. Its sound is entombed—repeated infinitely but inaudible, buried by the sculptural form that negates it. As such, the piece is perhaps an analog to Edvard Munch's *Scream* (1893) but more confounding, its sonic source denied all expression, auditory or visual.

Schaeffer's position remains a significant one within the practice of sound art today, manifested most dramatically in the work of the Spanish artist Francisco López, who, in live performance, distributes blindfolds to his listeners, seats them facing away from him, and delivers sonic abstractions that generally thwart recognition of the concrete sounds from which they are generated. Any sound art worthy of the name affirms something of this effort to restore to sound its ontological and aesthetic value. Yet for the most part, contemporary sound artists and their curators have been interested in *negotiating* the visual, rather than *rejecting* it wholesale. In fact, the very tension of such negotiation is often central to this uncertain art form operating between music and visual art, medium specificity and a postmedium condition. Without rejecting multimedia and multimodal work, sound art reminds us that seeing is not hearing and aims to thwart the imperial aspirations of the visual.

Synaesthetics 2.0

As with the synaesthesia craze of a century ago, the contemporary art world's attraction to sensory cross-wirings is part of a more general cultural formation. In current scientific research, for example, freak occurrences of colored hearing or tactile smell have become the objects of a booming industry within the flourishing field of cognitive neuroscience. Though synaesthesia affects at most 4 percent of the population and is considered a benign condition rather than an illness,[28] scientific research on the phenomenon has grown steadily since the 1980s, with a particular burst of interest since 2000.[29] Much of this new interest can be attributed to the development of brain-imaging technologies—notably fMRI (functional magnetic resonance imaging) and PET (positron emission tomography)—that, not coincidentally, are themselves "synaesthetic" in their psychedelic visual representation of nonvisual sensory phenomena.[30] This fascination with imaging, the desire and ability to present all information visually, and the epistemological priority of the visual are intensified in digital culture, in which the image has become currency and seeing ("eyeballs," in Internet advertising parlance) is pervasively monetized.[31]

But calling brain-imaging technologies "synaesthetic" is linguistically and conceptually sloppy. Such technologies do not conjoin different senses, allowing them to be experienced together; rather, they translate one kind of data into another. Indeed, more generally, digital technologies do not facilitate a union of the senses but make possible something quite different: the intertranslatability of media—for example, the ability to render sound as image or (in principle) image as sound. As Friedrich Kittler foresaw back in the mid-1980s,

> The general digitization of channels and information erases the differences among individual media. Sound and image, voice and text are reduced to surface effects, known to consumers as interface. Sense and the senses turn into eyewash. . . . Inside the computers themselves everything becomes a number: quantity without image, sound, or voice. And once optical fiber

> networks turn formerly distinct data flows into a standardized series of digitized numbers, any medium can be translated into any other.[32]

Such facile translations are too often called "synaesthetic" in art today. Moreover, they are almost invariably unidirectional: everything is rendered in the dominant language of the image.[33] "It is always the screen that radiates power and spectacle," writes the composer and film theorist Michel Chion, "and it is always the image, the gathering place and magnet for auditory impressions, that sound decorates with its unbridled splendor."[34] Early abstraction summoned music in the service of its own purely visual ends. In audiovisual work today, visuality is the supplement that comes to the aid of the sonic and thereby testifies to its poverty. Music videos, YouTube clips, and all the monitors, screens, and projection surfaces that populate galleries and museums today reveal the need for sound to be made whole through the image, and the need to secure its fugitive, diffuse, and permeable material within the bounds of a rectangular frame. Bute's "seeing sound" films already manifested both these attitudes—sound as an alibi for the abstract image and the visual as a necessary supplement for the sonic. The latter prevails in "visual music" projects today. Take, for example, *Optofonica*, a 2009 collection curated by the Italian artist Tez, who presents twenty-two visualizations created by or in collaboration with prominent electronica producers such as Scanner, Kim Cascone, Richard Chartier, Kaffe Matthews, and Kurt Hentschläger. Introducing the compilation, the Dutch synaesthesia researcher Cretien van Campen promises "synesthetic experiences of colored sounds or musical images."[35] Yet, though many are elegant and inventive, the videos arbitrarily conjoin electronic music often deemed "abstract" with image tracks that, though for the most part nonrepresentational, serve to concretize and ground the music. No neurological or aesthetic necessity conjoins these registers—no synaesthesia but only synchresis, the habit of associating anything one hears with anything one sees.[36]

Nonetheless, this imbalance of media and sensory modalities in contemporary art is true to the neurological experience of synaesthesia. Just as sound-image correlations in "synaesthetic" art projects are largely arbitrary, so too are cross-modal correlations neurologically idiosyncratic: within the population of synaesthetes, there is no regularity at all in, for example, sound-color pairings. Moreover, while this condition (and the aesthetic analogy to it) may suggest the ideal of sensuous plenitude and sensory cross-mixing, by far its most common expression is the unidirectional visual experience of sound. (Sound induced by sight is extremely rare.)[37] In the aesthetic domain, even when generated to enhance aural experience—for example, the 1960s light shows featured in several recent exhibitions; music videos; or the iTunes Visualizer—the visual is almost never a mere accompaniment to the auditory. As the film theorist Christian Metz points out, our syntax and entrenched sensual hierarchy hold us in thrall to a metaphysics according to which sight and touch signify being and presence, while sound—spatially vague, materially elusive, and temporally ephemeral—signifies absence and can only have the status of a secondary "attribute" in relation to a primary visual and tactile "substance."[38] Cinema might in principle be a synaesthetic art, an intersensorial conjunction of sound and image. In practice, however, cinematic sound is almost invariably subservient to the image.[39] So it is with synaesthetic art more generally. Indeed, the dominance of the visual in synaesthetic art corresponds with the prevailing idea that sound-in-itself is unnatural or inadequate, in need of an anchor in the visible.

Sound Figures

Another line of inquiry and experimentation, however, promises more direct and non-arbitrary correlations between sound and image. In 1787 Ernst Chladni, known today as the father of modern acoustics, drew a violin bow along the edge of a brass plate sprinkled with a thin layer of sand. The vibrating surface bounced the granules into symmetrical forms: stars, waves, grids, and labyrinths he termed "sound figures" (*Klangfiguren*; fig. 6.4). Chladni's demonstration seemed to make visible and palpable the hitherto elusive and fleeting materiality of sound; and his lecture-performances dazzled crowds throughout Europe. Napoleon was so impressed that he invited Chladni for a private performance at the Tuileries Palace and financed a French translation of the scientist's magnum opus that, in gratitude, was humbly dedicated to the emperor.[40]

Chladni's experiments (and their elaboration in the late 1960s by Hans Jenny) have proven to be a consistent inspiration for sound artists. Carsten Nicolai's *Wellenwanne* (2001), Douglas Henderson's *Untitled 2004* (2004), Seth Cluett's *cloud-to-air* (2013), and other recent projects have used subsonic sound to generate rippling interference patterns in trays of liquid, while Aura Satz's film *Onomatopoeic Alphabet* (2010) elegantly explores such "sound figures" in all their volatile vibration. Alvin Lucier anticipated

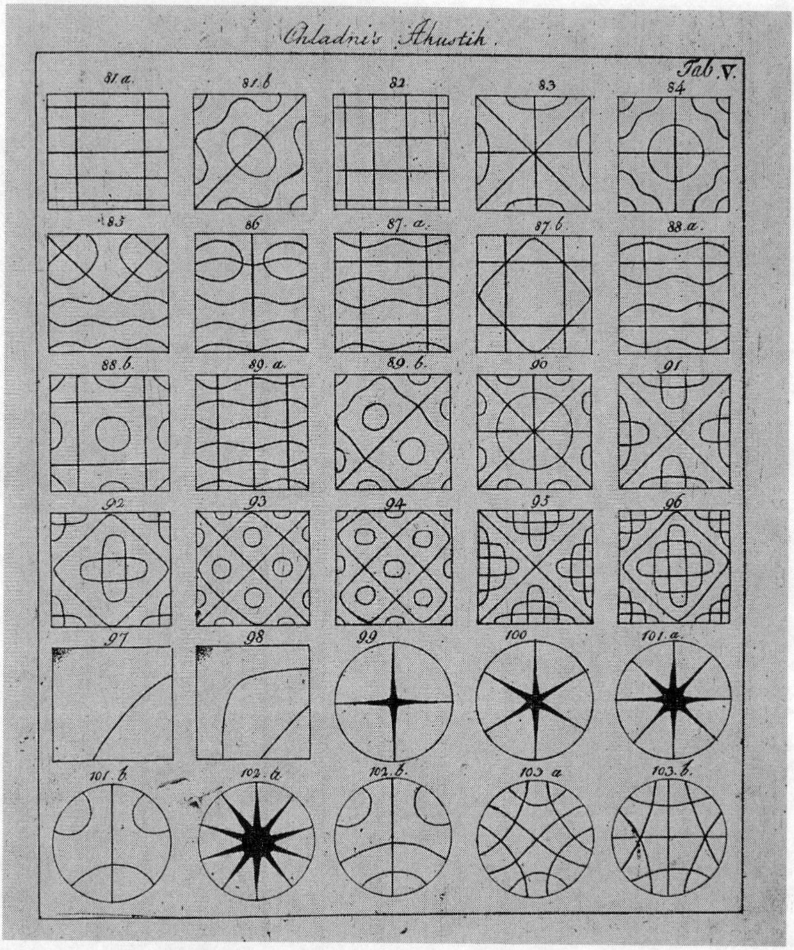

Fig. 6.4 Plate from Ernst Chladni's *Die Akustik*, 1802, showing various *Klangfiguren* (sound figures).

all these projects in the early 1970s with his performance installation *The Queen of the South* (1972), which calls for acoustic and electronic instruments to activate any sort of granular material strewn across a responsive surface, and for the results to be made visible to the audience through a video projection (fig. 6.5). Anxious to avoid *son et lumière*, that is, the mere visual accompaniment to existing music, Lucier instead aimed to explore the powerful materiality of sonic vibration, the capacity of sound to move physical bodies. As such, he encouraged performers to adopt an experimental rather than an illustrative attitude, to draw or sculpt with sound in real

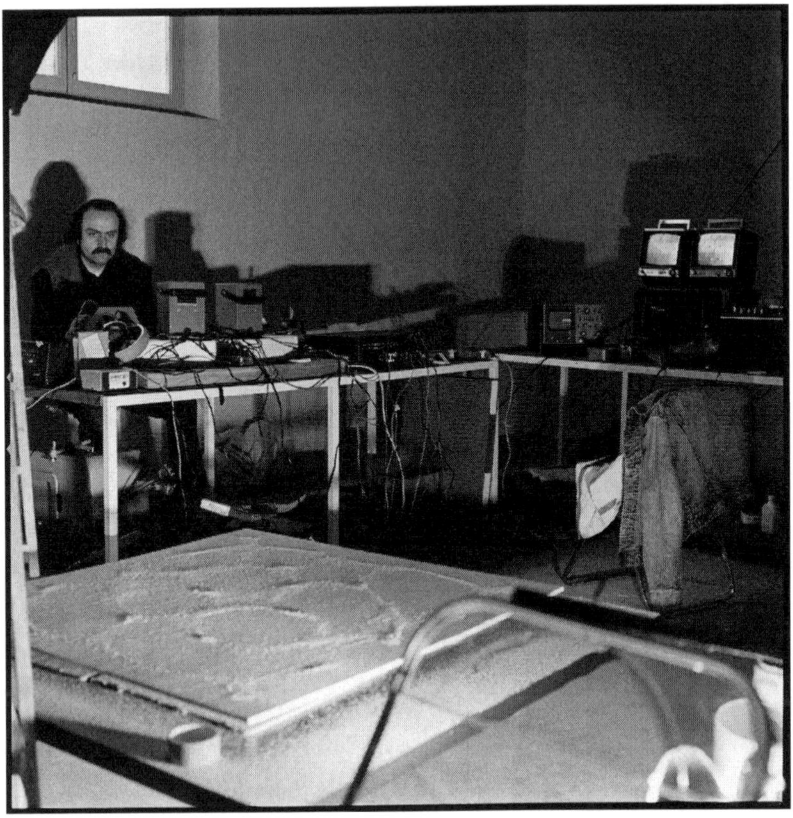

Fig. 6.5 Alvin Lucier performing *The Queen of the South*, 1972, at art/tapes/22, Florence, Italy, 1974. Photo © Gianni Melotti, Gianni Melotti Archives, Florence.

time, "to put sounds into a material and experience the modes of vibration of the sound in that material."[41]

This materialist emphasis on frequency and vibration characterizes the more recent Chladni-inspired projects as well, distinguishing them from earlier efforts at "visual music" that merely drew speculative analogies between music and visual form. Edison's invention of the phonograph played a key intermediary role here. Unlike the musical score, which offers a purely conventional and symbolic depiction of music, the phonograph needle directly carved acoustic vibrations into a pliable material, producing grooves that the needle could retrace and render as sound. In the early 1920s, fully aware of the early "visual music" films of Richter, Eggeling, and Ruttmann, László Moholy-Nagy proposed experimenting with the direct relationship between the visible grooves carved into a phonograph record and the sounds they produce. Transforming the phonograph record from an instrument of recording and reproduction into an instrument for creative production, Moholy-Nagy urged artists to cut designs directly into the record surface, generating "sound effects"—not only human and animal but "mechanical, metallic, and mineral sounds"—that no longer obeyed the established musical scale but instead established "a new graphic and mechanical scale." Such a tangible, visual object would indeed be a kind of score, Moholy-Nagy noted, but a "groove-manuscript score," a score of frequency and vibration instead of symbolic notation.[42]

Given the microscopic size of the phonograph record's grooves, Moholy-Nagy's project proved difficult to realize. But a few years later he discovered a more feasible means of conjoining the visible and the audible: creative use of the optical soundtrack in the sound film. The newly developed "Tri-Ergon" system (employed by Ruttmann for *Weekend*) recorded sound waves on a thin strip alongside the image track as graphic patterns that, during projection, were converted back into sound by a photoelectric cell. Moholy-Nagy saw in this new technology the possibility of "a true opto-acoustic synthesis," "not merely montage of the optical and acoustic sections, but a mutually integrated montage of both." "We ought to begin with a series of experiments in the sound element," he wrote, suggesting that "sound units" be "traced directly on to the sound track."[43]

Soon a number of artists and scientists—notably Oskar Fischinger, Rudolph Pfenninger, Arseny Avraamov, Evgeny Sholpo, Boris Yankovsky, and Moholy-Nagy himself—began directly intervening at the level of the soundtrack, producing films in which the same graphic material appeared on celluloid as both image and sound. Fischinger had been inspired by Ruttmann to begin making "visual music" films in the early 1920s and at the end of the decade followed Ruttmann in seizing on the sonic possibilities of optical sound.[44] In his Berlin studio he painted sawtooth patterns, stars, dots, ovals, undulating waves, and other designs on paper, then photographed them onto the left side of the filmstrip to produce what he called "sounding ornaments" (*tönende* or *klingende Ornamente*) (adopting the design term "ornament" in order to circumvent the Nazi's ban on "abstract" art; fig. 6.6).[45] Fischinger thus took the optical soundtrack as a device for experimental sonic composition, imagining a "music-painting artist" who goes beyond "mere notes" and instead "bases everything on the primary fundamental of music, namely the wave-vibration or oscillation in and of

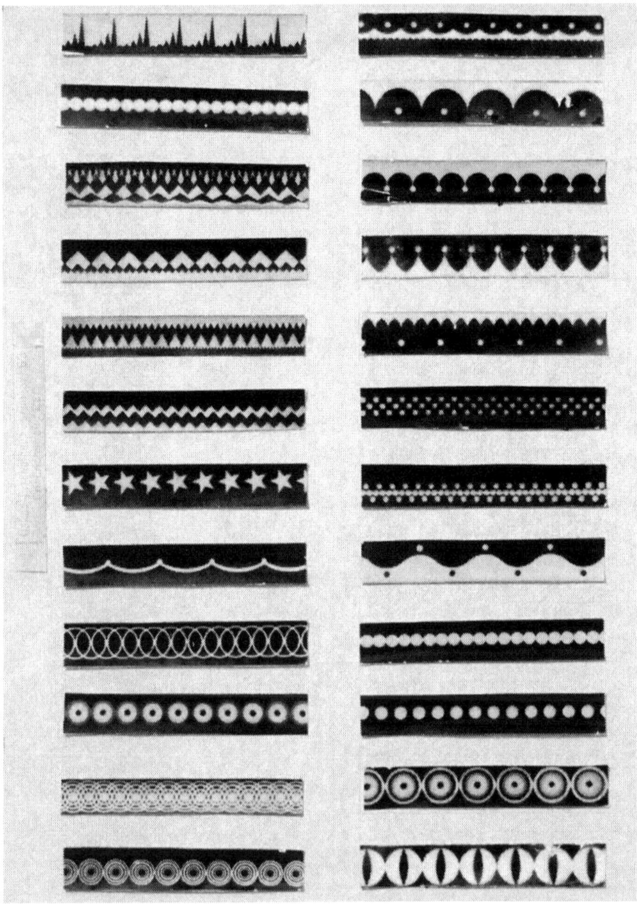

Fig. 6.6 Detail from a display card made by Oskar Fischinger for his *Ornament Sound* experiments, ca. 1931. © Center for Visual Music, www.centerforvisualmusic.org.

itself." Such designs, he remarked, not only "produce refined, intricate musical sounds but also they appear unexpectedly as attractive visual images." Indeed, the filmmaker felt that this mechanical, indexical union of sound and image finally achieved the synaesthetic *Gesamtkunstwerk* he had been striving for. "Between ornament and music persist direct connections," he declared, "which means that ornaments are music. . . . These ornaments are drawn music—they are sound." Given the "combination of sounding ornaments with visible, filmic, spatial forms and movements," he concluded, "the unity of all the arts is definitively, finally achieved, is become unquestionable fact."[46]

Such direct, indexical correlations between image and sound inspired generations of experimental artists. From the 1930s on, the Scottish-born Canadian filmmaker Norman McLaren produced soundtracks by scratching or painting directly on the optical sound strip. Around 1950, following Pfenninger's technique, McLaren and his collaborator Evelyn Lambart built up a catalog of striated cards and photographed them onto the sound strip frame-by-frame, enabling precise control of pitch, volume, and timbre.[47] This process culminated in *Synchromy* (1971), a fugue consisting of three electronic musical parts, the graphic sources of which were choreographed onscreen as animated, multicolored columns. Two years prior, inspired by John Cage and McLaren's earlier work, the American painter and musician Barry Spinello made a film titled *Soundtrack* in which ink-drawn figures and dry-transfer decals occupied both the sound and image portions of clear film leader. Spinello compared the film to the experience of driving on a highway while watching "fences, trees, posts, and the dots and lines of the highway divider" cross one's field of vision. "One imagines what they would sound like if they were passed through the photo-electric cell of the projector," he mused.[48] In the late 1970s the English filmmaker Guy Sherwin began doing just that, filming railway lines, lights, and passing scenery from a moving train (*Soundtrack* [1977], *Night Train* [1979]), tilting the camera up and down in front of a grated metal staircase (*Musical Stairs* [1977]), tracking along an iron railing (*Railings* [1977]), and then printing this visual material on the optical soundtrack to produce sputtering rhythmic oscillations and mechanical tones. Sherwin's London Film-makers Co-op compatriot Lis Rhodes also made direct connections between sound and image. For *Dresden Dynamo* (1971–72) she affixed Letraset and Letratone decals to clear celluloid, creating layered patterns of dots and lines that, extended into the soundtrack field, became audible as a collage of pitched noise and static. Rhodes's film installation *Light Music* (1975; fig. 6.7) employed two projectors facing one another to radiate an assortment of vertical and horizontal bars that generated rumbling pulses and fluttering glissandi.

At the same time, the composer and architect Iannis Xenakis was developing UPIC,[49] a computerized system that could instantaneously render graphic figures as electronic sound. Using an electromagnetic pen and a conductive tablet attached to a mainframe computer, even a noncomposer could produce music by drawing and thus forgo both the graphical limitations of conventional musical notation and the literacy required to interpret it. Today, countless tablet apps and visual programming languages do much

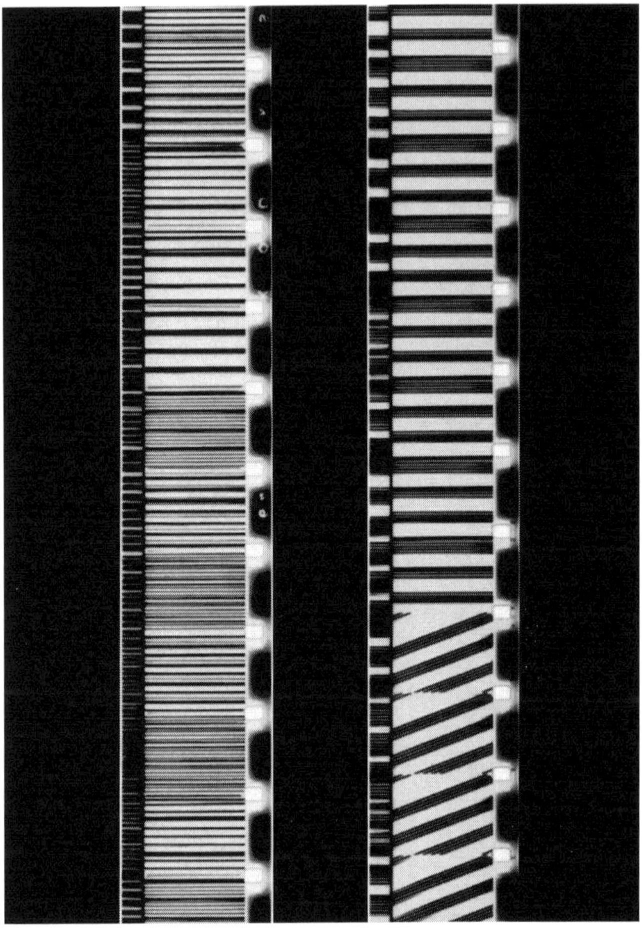

Fig. 6.7 Lis Rhodes, film strips from *Light Music*, 1975, two-channel 16mm film installation, 25 minutes, b&w, sound. Courtesy of the artist.

the same thing. Nonetheless, the retro UPIC has attracted contemporary sound artists such as Russell Haswell and Florian Hecker, who fed the system a variety of images (pornography, disaster photos, scientific images) and produced dense drawings of their own to generate intense noise compositions.[50]

Registering both sound and image as modulations of electronic signals, video promised a relationship between the auditory and the visual that was more direct than that of film. This purely electronic conjunction enabled video art pioneers such as Nam June Paik and Steina and Woody Vasulka to use sound to alter image and vice versa in real time. Documenting a series of experiments, *Video Power* (1978) employs Steina's amplified violin to warp the video image and change its scan rate. In the Vasulkas's *Noisefields* (1974), the frenetically squelchy electronic soundtrack is controlled by the energy of a pulsing video image. A generation later, the visual artist and electronic music producer Carsten Nicolai drew on these early video experiments to update Chladni for the age of television. Attributed to Nicolai's alias, Noto, *telefunken* (2000; fig. 6.8) was issued as a standard audio CD containing thirty short tracks that, even for lovers of minimalist electronica, are not much to listen to: a collection of impulse frequencies and test tones ranging from a few seconds to a minute long.[51] Yet this is not stand-alone audio. A disc insert instructs the listener to plug the outputs of the CD player into the video and audio inputs of a TV monitor. Played in this configuration, the tracks generate raster patterns that call to mind Ruttmann's *Opus IV* (1925) and Rhodes's *Light Music* while also laying bare the electronic conditions of the video medium. The first twenty pieces produce a spellbinding array of white horizontal bars that rise and fall, merge and part, expand and contract on the television's black ground. The final ten trigger blocks of light that pulse, throb, bend, waver, and hold for a moment before vanishing, as though from an unbearable strain.

Such audio-visual crossovers have become common in contemporary art and music. The projects led by the Austrian video artist Billy Roisz, for example, generate continuous live feedback loops between electronic image and sound. In the duo NotTheSameColor, the turntablist Dieb13 (Dieter Kovačič) sends audio fragments (including video signals recorded onto vinyl) to Roisz, who transforms them into light shards and painterly washes and then returns them to Kovačič for further transformation. AVVA, her collaboration with Toshimaru Nakamura, involves another layer of feedback. Nakamura connects the output of a mixing board to the board's own input, generating a palette of feedback tones that provide the source material for Roisz's video images, which provoke further responses from Nakamura, thus continuing the generative loop.

Whether film, video, music, sculpture, or installation, nearly all this work is presented as "synaesthetic." Echoing Fischinger, Rhodes notes that, in *Dresden Dynamo*, "what you see is what you hear." Likewise, Spinello conceives sound and image as "a single entity"; Sherwin describes his optical sound films as "technological 'synaesthesia'"; Roisz calls her projects "electric synaesthesia"; and Haswell and Hecker maintain that their UPIC compositions

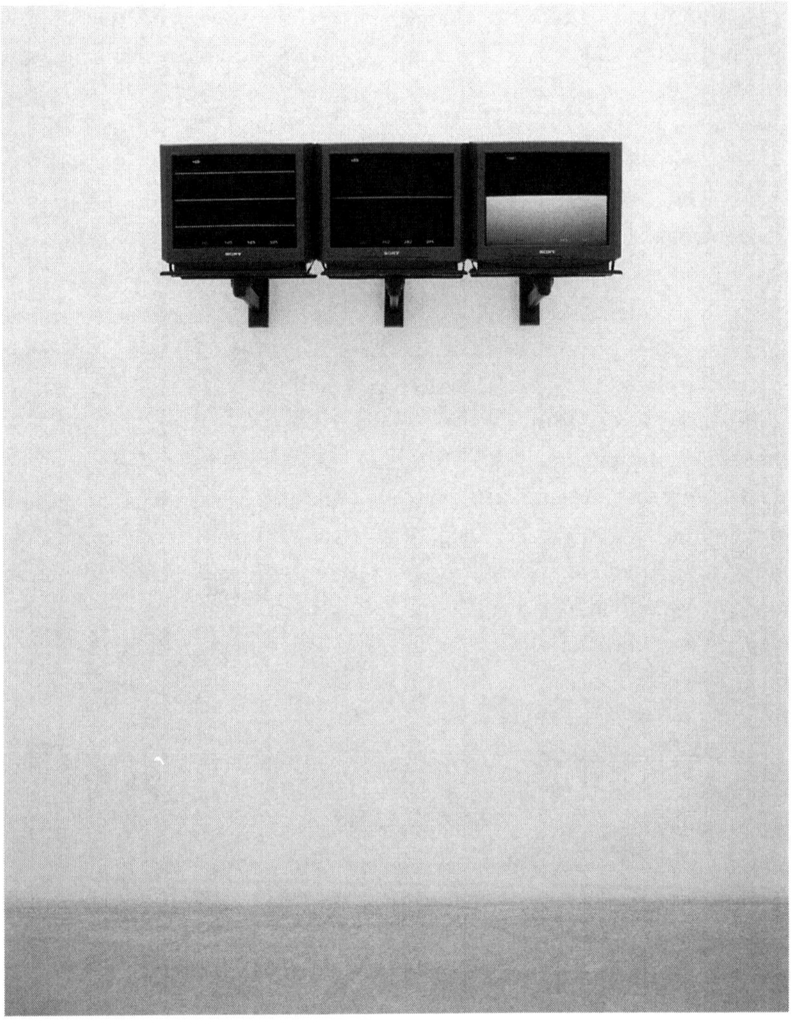

Fig. 6.8 Carsten Nicolai, *telefunken*, 2000, CD player, CD, HiBlack Trinitron TV, dimensions variable. Photo: Atsushi Nakamichi/Nacása & Partners. © 2017 courtesy Galerie EIGEN + ART Leipzig/Berlin, Pace Gallery, and 21st Century Museum of Contemporary Art, Kanazawa, Artist Rights Society (ARS), New York/VG Bild-Kunst, Bonn.

"assist the experience of synaesthesia."[52] The correlations between sound and image at the heart of these projects are surely more direct and less arbitrary than those in so much of the "visual music" tradition. Yet these sound-image correspondences are technological rather than neurological. That is, they happen in the black box of the machine rather than in the brain; and we merely observe external conjunction rather than experience internal unity. As such, the conjunction differs little from the more speculative analogies of Bute or the iTunes Visualizer. Taken on their own, the graphic ornaments, striations, and Letraset transfers that constitute the soundtracks of these films hardly provoke the spontaneous experience of specific sounds—or, if they do, it is only through prolonged training and practice akin to lip reading or even musical literacy. Those peculiar individuals who can identify particular pieces of music by the sight or touch of phonograph grooves are guests on late-night talk shows and the subjects of amazed news reports rather than ordinary, untrained subjects.[53] And though wave forms abound in the iconography of contemporary visual culture—from GarageBand and SoundCloud graphics to gallery installations by sound artists such as Lawrence Abu Hamdan, Christina Kubisch, and Carsten Nicolai—few of us discern in these forms anything more than a generic symbol of the auditory, a symbol that, in the cultural shift from music to sound, has now supplanted the eighth note in the graphic imagination.

Here we ought to recall Friedrich Nietzsche's remark about Chladni's discovery. Intrigued with the scientist's experiments but wary of their misinterpretation, Nietzsche wrote in an early essay: "One can imagine a man who is totally deaf and has never had a sensation of sound," he wrote. "Perhaps such a person will gaze with astonishment at Chladni's sound figures; perhaps he will discover their causes in the vibrations of the string and will now swear that he must know what men mean by 'sound.'"[54] Wary of the attempt to reduce sound to sight, Nietzsche insists that the visual and the auditory constitute distinct domains and that the relationship between the two can only ever be a matter of translation or metaphor (in the etymological sense of "carrying over") that leaves an unassimilable remainder. For Nietzsche, the distinction between the metaphorical and the literal is simply that the latter no longer acknowledges the difference that constitutes it, taking itself to *be* what it *represents.* Such literalness is a chief characteristic of the aesthetic discourse of synaesthesia today, one that, as Kittler notes, is encouraged by the ready translatability of digital media. The fact that all digital material shares a common base—binary code—supports the illusion that sound, image, word, and movement can be made identical and interchangeable. What is forgotten is that they can be made so only via the intermediary of arbitrary mapping formulae decided in advance. Instead of teaching us something aesthetically or neurologically salient about the operation of the senses, the discourse of synaesthesia blurs their boundaries, obscuring the specificity of hearing and seeing in order then to submit the auditory to the rule of the visual.

Dubs and Versions

After her forays into optical sound as image, Rhodes turned her attention to language, attempting to discover "the 'sound pictures' of words." Doing so shook her confidence in the unity of sound and image. "These filmic experiments demonstrated the impossibility of making a connection between 'what is said to be seen' and 'what is seen to be said,' she concluded. "Seeing is never believing, or lip sync a confirmation of authenticity."[55] In films such as *Light Reading* (1978), Rhodes verbally interrogated the image and visually dissolved language into fragments, clips, and stills incapable of coalescing into a genuine or meaningful unity. A few years earlier her LFMC colleague Mike Dunford offered a simpler but equally revealing demonstration of Rhodes's conclusion about the visual voice. In Dunford's 1974 film *SYNC.SND.* (fig. 6.9), a male voice offscreen asks a series of questions about the early history of sound cinema over the noisy whir of a film camera or projector.[56] Onscreen, in extreme close-up, a pair of lips are synced with the voice of a woman who responds matter-of-factly to the interviewer's questions. Question and answer proceed for five minutes, covering developments in film sound from the 1890s through the 1940s, until the screen goes black and the same round of questions begins again. This time, however, the synchronization is several seconds off. For the remainder of the film, sound and image attract and repel one another, occasionally returning to sync but only for a few fleeting instants. The desire for sync sound supersedes the desire for meaning, as the viewer watches and listens not for semantic content but for those consummating moments when sound and image coincide. The materiality of vocal articulation—evident from the beginning in the focus on lips, tongue, teeth, and saliva—is heightened by the nonsynchronized image, which renders the mouth and its movements strange, fleshy, and viscous. Sound and image are revealed as distinct yet equal partners the correlation of which is a technological feat rather than a natural, inexorable occurrence.

For decades now experimental film and video have explored these tensions between sound and image, countering the desire (both commercial and synaesthetic) to draw them together. In different ways, Louise Lawler and Christian Marclay unsettle what in cinematic parlance is called the

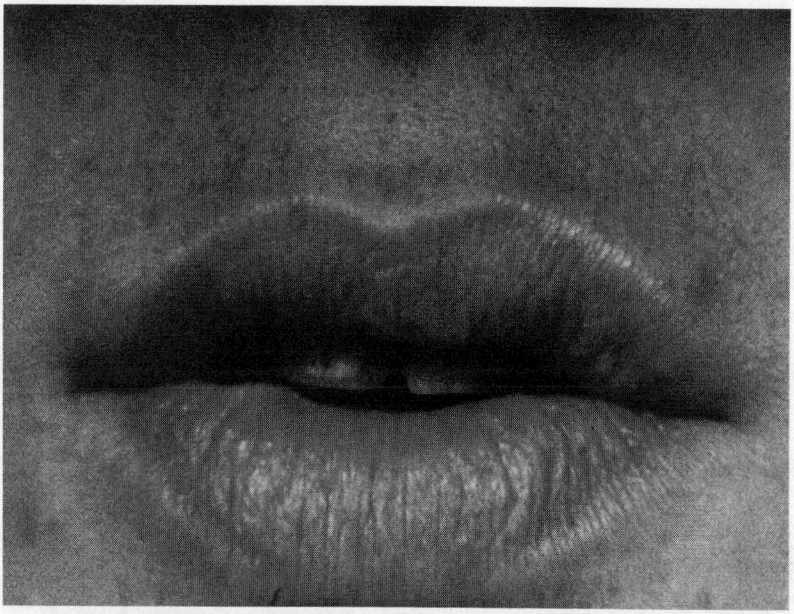

Fig. 6.9 Mike Dunford, *SYNC.SND.*, 1974, 16mm film, 6 minutes, color, sound. Courtesy of the artist.

"marriage" between sound and image demanded by Hollywood film. Recalling Ruttmann's *Weekend,* Lawler's *A Movie Will Be Shown Without the Picture* (1979; fig. 6.10) presents a well-known Hollywood film (*The Misfits* or *Saturday Night Fever*, for example) in an ordinary movie theater but without the image track, thus drawing attention to the soundtrack and the reactions of the audience to it. Marclay's *Up and Out* (1998) pairs the image track of Michelangelo Antonioni's 1966 film *Blow-Up* (which investigates the veracity of the photographic image) with the soundtrack of Brian DePalma's 1981 remake *Blow Out* (which probes the authenticity of recorded sound). Like Dunford's film, Marclay's reveals both the power of cinematic synchresis and the intractable difference and parallelism of these streams, which refuse to converge.

Several other recent projects probe this duality between synchresis and autonomy, the attraction and repulsion between sound and image. Mathias Poledna's silent black-and-white dance film *Version* (2004; fig. 6.11) might be viewed as a latter-day instance of "visual music."[57] Instead, however, the film disarticulates the two terms of that phrase and offers a retrospective critique of the visual music tradition. In what appears to be a single long take, the

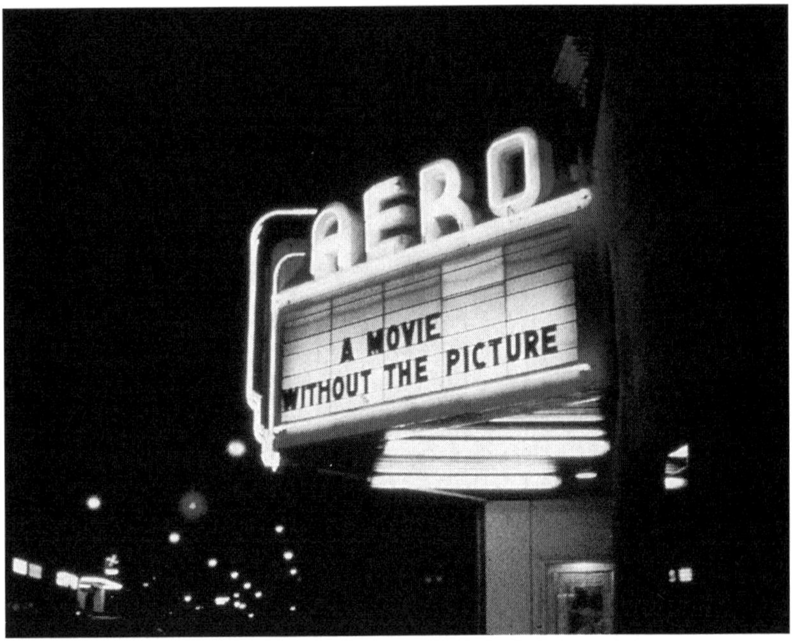

Fig. 6.10 Marquee for Louise Lawler, *A Movie Will Be Shown Without the Picture*, 1979, film, variable length, no image, sound. Courtesy of the artist and Metro Pictures, New York.

camera wanders slowly across a group of young men and women dressed in casual clothes and dancing impassively on a partially lit soundstage. The film consists entirely of close-ups and extreme close-ups, capturing only fragments in motion—a hand, a skirt, a torso, a pair of knees or feet. Forgoing any establishing shot and generally avoiding faces, it is difficult to tell just how many dancers there are; and the camera often finds itself in the spaces between bodies, leaving the screen fully black. The film's silence is experienced as a lack, an absence that the viewer struggles to fill. The prevalence of close-ups thwarts even visual rhythm and synchronization. Without any sound to guide the eye and draw the fragments together into a whole, it is not clear that all the dancers are moving to the same music. Occasionally the camera alights briefly on movements that appear to be choreographed—two figures turn and snap fingers in tandem, for example. For the most part, however, the dancers appear as solitary figures absorbed in their own activity.

The film's title gives a clue to its absent musical content while at the same time highlighting the withdrawal of the sonic. In Jamaican DJ culture, a "ver-

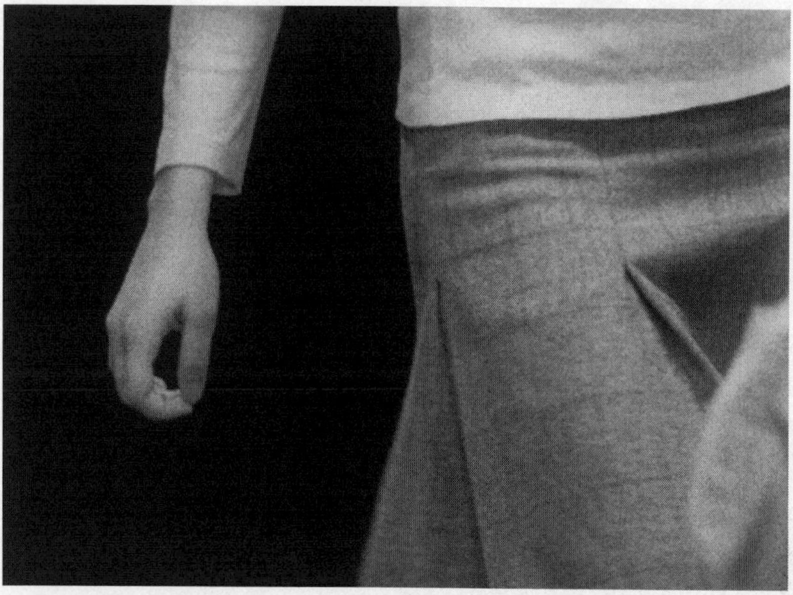

Fig. 6.11 Mathias Poledna, *Version*, 2004, 16mm film installation, 10 minutes, b&w, silent. Courtesy of the artist and Richard Telles Fine Art.

sion" is a reggae single with the vocal track removed. Initially, in the late 1960s, such "versions" were issued as instrumental B sides, intended for MCs ("deejays") to improvise ("toast") over at dance-hall events or sound-system parties. Eventually producers such as King Tubby, Errol Thompson, and Lee "Scratch" Perry began to treat the "version" (or "dub") as a musical work in its own right. These versions drastically altered the original tracks, fragmenting the vocals or dropping them out entirely, eliminating the melody instruments in order to foreground a bass line or a hi-hat rhythm, splicing in portions of other tracks, and highlighting studio effects such as echo, delay, and reverb. In short, the version or dub strips away a song's melodic attractions in order to reveal its rhythmic and technological infrastructure. More broadly, a version or dub is a double, a doppelgänger, or a *duppy*, Jamaican patois for a spirit or ghost, a shadowy other that haunts the living.[58]

Poledna's film is a visual version, a flip side or in-version that withdraws sound entirely, leaving only an image that testifies to the indispensability of the soundtrack. Like the forlorn image track itself, the silent dancers appear ghostly, insubstantial, mere apparitions of projected light; and the film itself is but a version or *duppy* in search of the sonic force that animates it. True to its title, *Version* is itself a version. From the same shoot, Poledna produced another film, *Sufferer's Version* (2004), this time accompanied by the missing soundtrack, which turns out to be "Working Hard for the Rent Man," a reggae single recorded in the late 1970s by Junior Delahaye for the Bronx-based label Wackie's and rereleased in 2003 by the German dub-house imprint Basic Channel. Whereas *Version* is made to run as a loop in a gallery setting, *Sufferer's Version* is for cinematic presentation only and was initially screened by Poledna in a program alongside two other classic black-and-white experimental dance films, Maya Deren's *Meditation on Violence* (1948) and Peter Kubelka's *Adebar* (1957), of which Poledna's two films are clearly versions.[59] Both Deren's and Kubelka's films feature music from ethnographic recordings—Chinese flute and Haitian drumming in Deren's, pygmy flute in Kubelka's—added to the image after the fact, suggesting the detachability and independence of image and sound, the status of both as versions without origin or unity.

In film terminology, "dubbing" names the postproduction process of recording additional sound to supplement, clarify, enliven, or replace sync sound. A key source of such sound is provided by Foley artists, the subject of Julian Rosefeldt's three-channel film installation *The Soundmaker (Trilogy of Failure, Part 1)* (2004; fig. 6.12).[60] In the center screen a man enters an apartment, tosses his keys to the side, takes off his hat and jacket, walks to the bathroom to urinate, sits at a table to eat, reads a magazine on a couch, stares at a TV, and then, for no apparent reason, begins to assemble all his furniture into a makeshift sculptural installation in the center of the room. The camera follows the man's activities, framing him in a medium long shot while tracking left and right in a slow, pendular motion across the space of the apartment. Shot from above and from the front, respectively, the left and right screens display a narrow, cluttered Foley studio, in which the same man dressed in the same clothes calmly attempts to generate in real time all the sounds that ought to accompany the action in the center. Several times during this looped, thirty-five-minute piece, these scenes shift places: the Foley artist appears in the center screen, while on the left and right the camera tracks across the interior walls of the apartment; or the two shots of the Foley studio appear side by side, as the apartment is seen from above by a camera that slowly rotates clockwise. After returning the pieces of furniture to their original locations, the man puts on his hat and coat, grabs his keys, and walks out the door, the camera following him onto a bustling soundstage. On the middle screen a rotating camera cranes up to reveal that the set of the Foley studio shares a wall with the apartment set. On the

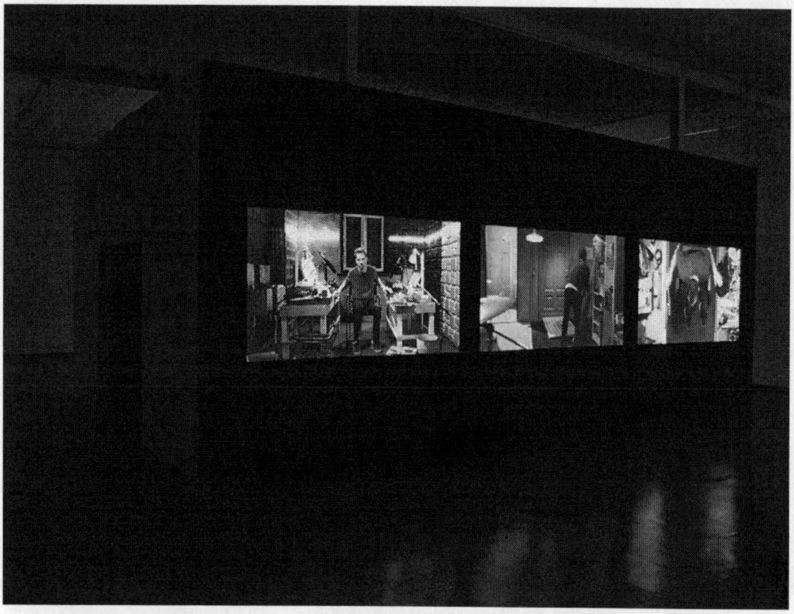

Fig. 6.12 Julian Rosefeldt, *The Soundmaker (Trilogy of Failure, Part 1)*, 2004, 35 minutes, three-screen film installation, Super 16mm transferred to DVD, color, sound. Installation at the Royal Academy of Arts, London, 2008. Courtesy of the artist.

left and right screens the camera circles the exterior of the apartment set, passing studio carpenters, lighting technicians, and prop masters along the way, until it arrives once again where it began at the beginning of the film, and the loop starts over again.

The plot of the film is minimal, the activities of the actor by turns ordinary and absurd. Yet, formally, the three screens demand considerable attention and scrutiny on the part of the audience. The Foley artist does a remarkably good job of providing effects for each of the actor's movements but occasionally slips up: footsteps are not quite synced; the sound of a coffee cup placed on a table is delayed; items fall in the Foley studio and make a clatter not matched in the apartment scene; and so on. Images fall out of sync as well, the same scene appearing temporally or spatially staggered on two of the screens. Sometimes the image and sound in the apartment scene are synced, but not with the Foley artist's movements. Only one sound in the film is tightly linked with image—the abrupt shift from the ambient noise of the soundstage to the relative silence of the set (and vice versa), at the beginning and the end of the loop—and that shift is implausible, given what we see: that the set is fully open to its noisy exterior. Throughout the loop, we struggle to match sound with image, sound with sound, and image with image. True to the installation's title and focus on Foley, sound plays a central role. But it is the image of the soundmaker that gives us the first clues to all the mismatches of sounds and images. Image informs sound and sound image, but in ways that thwart the seamless coincidence celebrated by synaesthesia discourse. Relentlessly striving in Sisyphean cycles and circles, sound and image invariably fail to cohere or coincide.

Like Poledna's, Manon de Boer's film installations frequently center on music, exploring disjunctions between sound and image that amplify the differences between these registers and reveal their respective ontologies. *Presto, Perfect Sound* (2006) produces a seamless audio rendition of the final movement from Bartók's Sonata for Solo Violin by splicing multiple takes made evident by jump cuts in the image track. In *Dissonant* (2010) a dancer carefully listens to a piece of music and then dances to it from memory. Her eight-minute choreography is captured on standard one-hundred-foot rolls of 16mm film that record for less than three minutes. Between rolls of film, the screen goes black, though the dancer's expressive movements are audible throughout. The tour de force in this series is de Boer's 2008 film installation *Two Times 4'33"* (fig. 6.13), the best and most revealing recording of Cage's classic. A camera pans across of the interior of a grand piano, then settles on a pianist who sits down, opens a score on the music rack, presses the button of a timer, and then stares intently at the sheet music without playing. Ambient sound fills the soundtrack. The rumble of accelerating trucks and staccato shriek of car horns are audible from offscreen, as are the rustling trees and the rain visible through the large windows behind the pianist, who taps the timer on and off twice more, marking the beginning and ending of the composition's three movements. When the piece is complete, the pianist stands up and bows to offscreen applause that continues as he leaves the frame and the screen fades to black. As the sounds of applause diminish, the image reappears, the camera once again panning across the piano. But this time it does not come to rest on the pianist, who, as in the first version, sits down and taps the timer. Instead, it continues to pan in a slow circle across the attentive faces of the few dozen young men and women who make up the audience. Leaving the audience, the camera tracks outside the small concert studio, revealing bushes, power lines, and tram cables shaken by strong gusts of wind. Yet no sounds accompany these blustery images or *any* images at all in this second half of the film. The soundtrack is silent,

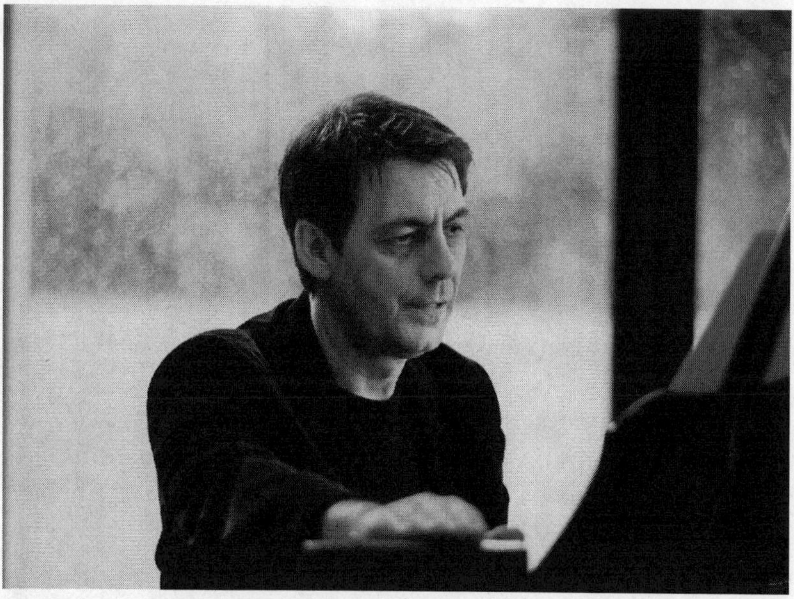

Fig. 6.13 Manon de Boer, *Two Times 4'33"*, 2008, 35mm film installation, 10 minutes, color, surround sound. © Manon de Boer. Courtesy of Auguste Orts, Brussels

except for the clicks of the timer. In this way, de Boer effectively shifts sonic focus from the ambient sound internal to the film to the ambient sound of the external viewing environment, from the concert studio onscreen to the cinema or gallery in which we watch the film, providing a soundtrack that is new each time the film is shown. The first version is a *recording* of the piece, the second stages a *live performance* of it. The first invites sounds from outside the frame and concert hall, but contains this sound within the space of the film. The second opens out not only beyond the frame and the concert hall, but also beyond the film itself, offering a rigorously Cagean take on "silent" cinema and a deconstruction of "visual music."

Sound Cinema: Film and Video as Sonic Art

Such disjunctions between the auditory and the visual are not the only alternatives to the classic subordination of sound to image or to "synaesthetic" projects that amount to the same thing. Several recent collaborations between filmmakers and sound artists fundamentally affirm the sonic and reveal the capacities of cinema as a form of sonic art. The work of the

Scottish artist Luke Fowler is exemplary here. Since 2001 Fowler has made a series of beguiling films that combine the concerns of structural-materialist cinema with documentary and archival practices. These films often present what the artist calls "portraits" of maverick artists, intellectuals, and ordinary people. Musicians and composers are prominent among his subjects—for example, the elusive post-punk musician Xentos Jones (*The Way Out* [2003]); the experimental composers Cornelius Cardew (*Pilgrimage from Scattered Points* [2006]) and Christian Wolff (*For Christian* [2016]); and the electronic music pioneer Martin Bartlett (*Electro-Pythagoras* [2016])—and Fowler has collaborated with sonic artists such as Richard Youngs, Charles Curtis, Taku Unami, Mark Fell, and Ernst Karel. Fowler's most explicit and sustained engagement with sound is *A Grammar for Listening* (2009), a trilogy of films each made in collaboration with a different sound artist: Lee Patterson, Eric La Casa, and Toshiya Tsunoda. All three artists are prominent practitioners of "field recording," a form of sonic art that, like Fowler's visual practice, combines a documentary impulse with an impulse to employ found material toward more aesthetic and compositional ends. As such, these artists operate between the two poles set out within classic debates around musique concrète: on the one hand, the referentiality and site specificity of recorded sound, and, on the other, the detachability of sound from source and site that enables an engagement with sonic matter itself.

The musique concrète pioneer Pierre Schaeffer was the most vociferous advocate of this latter position, calling for an "acousmatic" or "reduced listening" that would bracket the circumstances of sonic production in order to attend to the "sonorous objects" themselves. Perhaps paradoxically, given Schaeffer's efforts to preclude the visual from sonic apprehension, Fowler's project (initially titled *Ontology of Sound*) was inspired by Schaeffer.[61] From the outset, the filmmaker was guided by a set of central questions:

> To what degree could Schaeffer's "reduced listening" (a concept that seems to be one of the central tenets of field recording) be achieved when "accompanied" by the moving image; would the moving image become superfluous, a mere banality, or could it give sound more depth; could there then be a "reduced viewing," a viewing which renounces the usual secondary status of sound in film, in order to establish an equal footing with that of the image; is there an underlying political and social reality repressed by the field recorder in the act of gathering their exotic sound souvenirs; can the union between sound and image cast light on the fraught ecology of our

present condition? Such inquiries hint at the complex realities underneath the surface of Schaeffer's "pure listening."[62]

In pursuit of these inquiries, Fowler worked to foster a genuinely equal collaboration, inviting each of the sound artists to sites near Glasgow that he thought would engage their sonic sensibilities and following them to locations in their home cities that they believed would excite him. Fowler studied the work of these audio artists and observed them in action, seeking to adapt his image production to the technical, compositional, and aesthetic modalities of his collaborators.[63] At the same time, he was keenly aware of the differences between the capacities of the camera and those of the microphone. "Sound recording and filming often work with phenomena that are quite distinct," Fowler acknowledged,

> the camera being limited to documenting light across surfaces, whilst a microphone could record something that was miles away or a contact mic could transduce the vibrations deep within a surface or object, sounds that would often be imperceptible to the senses. So, though we collaborated, we also trusted one another to find something of equivalent importance . . . which at times was very difficult. But it was also in those times that I found that I was really struggling to "see" something that my interaction with the camera, the place, and the situation would just seem to coalesce.[64]

If portraiture figures prominently in Fowler's work, so does landscape, and his films often shift between the two to explore the material environment in which his subjects live and work.[65] Fowler's collaborators make only the briefest of cameo appearances in the *Grammar* trilogy. Nonetheless, he has described these films as "meta-portraits" of the three artists, all of whom, as field recordists, are dedicated to exploring sonic landscapes or soundscapes.[66] Each film, then, is distinct in its style, form, and content, determined not only by the working methods of its subject but also by the visual and acoustic environment in which he works.

Part 1 (with Lee Patterson) is organized as a sort of primer in elementary acoustics, divided into seven numbered sections with didactic titles such as "Emissions and reflections with structure-borne vibrations" (fig. 6.14). Yet the sounds and images are poetic and mysterious rather than dryly instructive. "Eavesdropping upon events that are both alien yet utterly quotidian," Patterson uses hydrophones, contact mics, and air mics to amplify sound

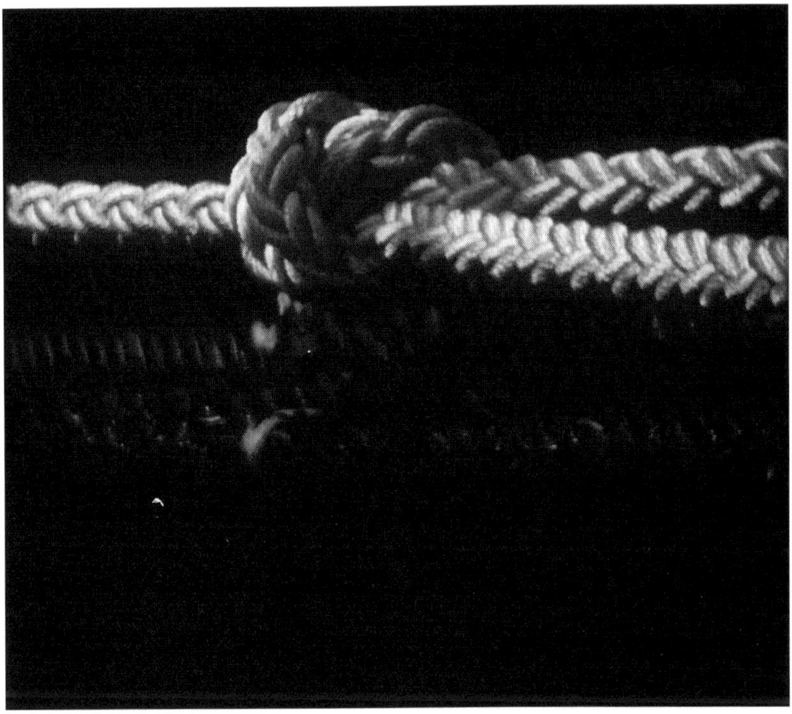

Fig. 6.14 Luke Fowler, *A Grammar for Listening, Part 2*, 2009, 16mm film, 21 minutes, color, mono optical sound. In collaboration with Eric La Casa. © Luke Fowler and Eric La Casa. Courtesy of the artist and the Modern Institute/Toby Webster, Ltd., Glasgow.

worlds inaudible to the unassisted ear and to capture vibrations traveling through water, metal, concrete, air, and other materials.[67] His soundscape for *Grammar 1* is full of richly textured and exotic sounds drawn from pools of water, metal fence posts and wires, burning walnuts, and vibrating springs. To match Patterson's sonic micro-phony, Fowler filmed predominantly in close-up, lingering on the visible textures of objects and producing a flow of vivid color images, the sources of which are often not evident. In several sequences the camera pulls focus in and out, switching background and foreground in a way that matches Patterson's shifts from, for example, the microphonic domain of underwater creatures to the macroscopic drones of the marshland field. In-camera dissolves and double exposures provide a visual analog to the crossfades and dense layering in the soundtrack. Indeed, throughout the film, Fowler visibly foregrounds the technical intervention that makes possible the film's sound and image worlds, incorporating fast-motion sequences, light flares, and other such effects. At the same time, the film acknowledges the profound differences between camera and tape recorder—the surface of image and the depth of sound; the sequential cuts in the image track and the layered flow of the audio; the three-minute length of the 16mm film roll and the long durational capacity of the digital recorder. Image and sound adhere loosely to one another not only phenomenologically but also technically. Instead of optically printing Patterson's soundtrack, *Grammar 1* presents it as a separate .wav file that enables a stereo mix and better sound quality. The result is a film composed of two streams that run in parallel, resonant with one another but only loosely synced and resolutely distinct.

In contrast to the measured delicacy of Patterson's soundtrack, with its fluid crossfades, Eric La Casa's sonic composition for *Grammar 2* is dynamic and dramatic, full of sharp attacks that punctuate tense and volatile sonic passages. It too is divided into seven sections or movements marked not with titles but with lushly colored monochrome screens accompanied by silence. Within each movement, these monochromes flash briefly between images, drawing attention to Fowler's edits and amplifying the drama of the soundtrack. The sources of La Casa's sounds are often either identifiable or revealed on screen. Yet he abjures *vérité*-style field recording in favor of auteur composition that affirms the artificiality and artistry of his mix. A bassy rumble with reverberant clatter, voices, and clacking footsteps is abruptly filtered to become a thin rushing drone interrupted by spongy percussive plunks. An incongruous collection of horns and bell sounds (back-up beepers, clanging alarms, and fog horns) play off of one another in the soundtrack as the image cuts between a busy food warehouse and an ominously rippling seascape. Tied tightly to the optical soundtrack, Fowler's editing largely follows La Casa's, producing a montage that accentuates the rhythm of the sound composition, sometimes displaying the (likely) sources of the sounds, other times turning away from them in contrapuntal fashion. Again, Fowler works to densify his images via multiple exposures and to highlight their artificiality with in-camera edits, light flares, fast motion and other techniques. Playing with the modalities of their collaboration, one sequence shows La Casa recording in a dark tunnel to the sound of Fowler's Bolex, which shuts off to end the section. The rattle of the Bolex reemerges in the film's coda, starting and stopping several times as in-camera fades and a final light flare abruptly bring *Part 2* of *A Grammar for Listening* to a close.

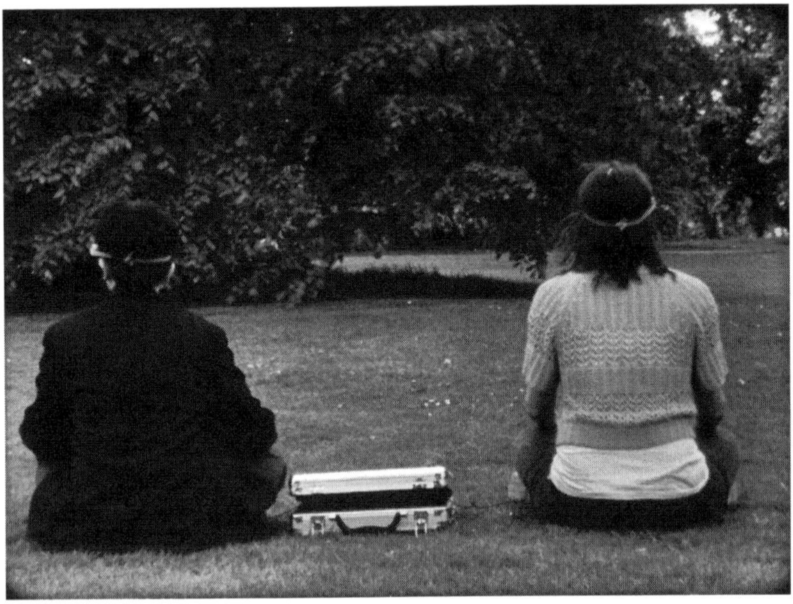

Fig. 6.15 Luke Fowler, *A Grammar for Listening Part 3*, 2009, 16mm film, 13 minutes, color, stereo digital sound. In collaboration with Toshiya Tsunoda © Luke Fowler and Toshiya Tsunoda. Courtesy of the artist and the Modern Institute/Toby Webster, Ltd., Glasgow.

The final film in the trilogy is markedly different from its predecessors. Half the length of the others, *Part 3* is a series of long takes centering on two human figures—Fowler's collaborator Toshiya Tsunoda and a woman, Hattie Spires—filmed from behind as they sit motionless beside each other at three locations in London's Hyde Park and Kensington Gardens (fig. 6.15). Attached by a headband to one side of each figure's head is a recording contraption that we later learn, through an onscreen text, is a stethoscope with a built-in air mic. The stethoscope, the text notes, records the vibrations of muscles and the flow of blood through the body, while the air mic gathers sounds from the environment. The right and left channels of the soundtrack are distinctly different. In the right, we hear the muffled drone of city ambience—traffic noise, wind, and distant voices. The left channel is significantly quieter, making audible the faint sounds of breathing and, occasionally, a sloshy gurgle. The film is simple, even banal; but it presses a set of paradoxes: How can one film listening—the titular subject of the trilogy?[68] More specifically, how can the single eye of the camera lens correspond to binaural listening by two different people who produce what Tsunoda calls "a stereo image"?[69] How can the camera image, a mere surface, capture the interior depths of the subject, the vibrations of which can be registered by the microphone? And, finally, how can either image or sound capture an intentional state—the focus of a subject's attention on a particular object—and, moreover, a double intentionality? The film poses these questions without resolving them. Indeed, its inability or failure to resolve them constitutes the film's success, provoking further inquiries into sound, image, and the possible relationships between the two. Taken as a whole, *A Grammar for Listening* offers a set of experiments that point both to the resonances between sound and image and the limits each encounters in its approach to the other.

An alternative strategy for sound-image interaction has been advanced by artists associated with the Sensory Ethnography Lab (SEL), an audiovisual collaborative at Harvard University managed by the sound artist Ernst Karel, the sound designer for many of the lab's projects and a leading figure in the field recording movement. Since 2007 the SEL has produced a series of extraordinary films, installations, and sound pieces that explode the conventions of documentary form. The most astonishing and radical of these projects is the feature-length avant-documentary *Leviathan* (2012), directed by Lucien Castaing-Taylor and Véréna Paravel and filmed entirely aboard a groundfish trawler off the coast of New Bedford, Massachusetts, a hub of the nineteenth-century whaling industry and still America's most lucrative fishing port. Aptly described as "immersive," the film achieves this effect largely through sonic means. This is due in no small part to Karel's remarkable 5.1 surround-sound mix, which, in contrast to the flat and stationary rectangle of the image, truly engulfs the listener in three dimensions and constantly moves sound among its six channels. Yet even the image track conforms more closely to what Marshall McLuhan has called "acoustic space" than to the "visual space" that typically dominates film and video.[70] Seeing is frontal, requiring distance and light, which enable the subject to perceive the world perspectivally as a bounded field organized by a vanishing point and containing discrete objects set side by side. By contrast, hearing is more proximal, multidirectional, and unbounded. As McLuhan puts it, acoustic space is "multicentered and reverberating," "gyroscopic," "like being inside a sphere, 360 degrees without margins; like swimming underwater; or balancing on a bicycle."[71] *Leviathan* propels the image into this sort of acoustic space. Shot largely at night on a lurching ship via small, low-resolution GoPro cameras attached to the heads, chests, and wrists of the fishermen and mounted onto extension poles, the image is profoundly

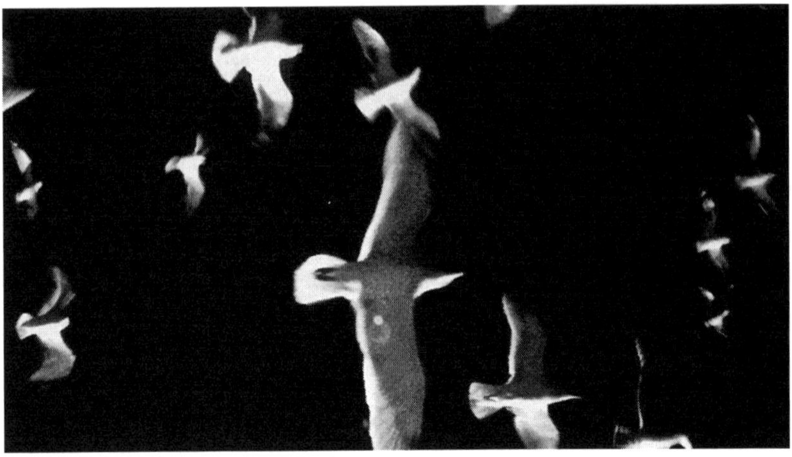

Fig. 6.16 Lucien Castaing-Taylor and Véréna Paravel, *Leviathan*, 2012, 35mm and DCP, 87 minutes, color, surround sound.

disorienting.[72] The film opens with the rush of wind and the roar of the ocean over a black screen into which a flare of orange light gradually intrudes in the lower right-hand corner. For the next five minutes shards of color flit across the screen like experimental animation. When this chiaroscuro occasionally reveals an object—a gloved hand, a chain, a hoisted vat—it offers the viewer no clear position or perspective. The middle portion of the film focuses on human subjects in the less turbulent and better-lit cabin of the ship. Even there, however, it tends to presents them in extreme close-up, fixing on a forearm, an eye, or a boot, and providing little bearing in visual space. The camera frequently plunges underwater, jetting through marine debris as through stars in outer space; or it dips above and below the water's frothy surface, tossing with the boat and throwing the horizon into confusion. Detached from the human eye, the camera's mechanical eye spins and twists through an uncertain space. In a marvelous sequence toward the end of film, an inverted camera on a boom pole reveals a flock of gulls flying upside down, the white spray of the ocean appearing above and behind them like clouds, producing an Escher-like visual paradox (fig. 6.16). The white birds blend into the tossing surface of the ocean, becoming abstract flashes of light on a black ground.

The indistinctness of this acoustic space is accentuated by the soundtrack, dominated throughout by a droning amalgam of broadband noises: predominantly, the steady rumble of the ship's engine modulated by howling

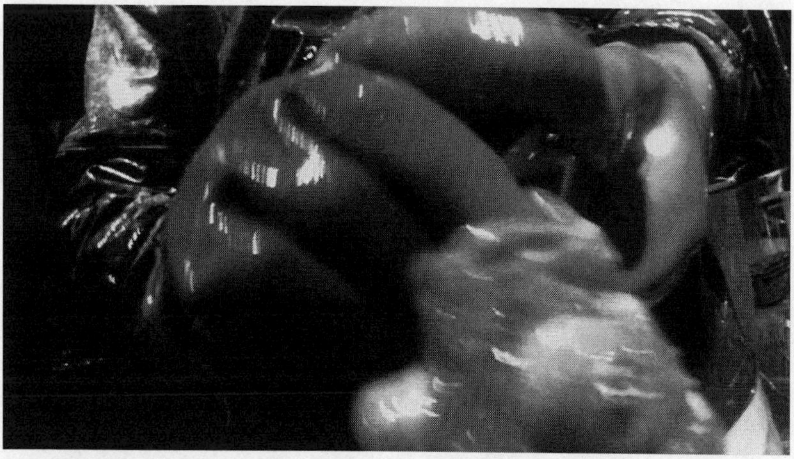

Fig. 6.17 Lucien Castaing-Taylor and Véréna Paravel, *Leviathan*, 2012, 35mm and DCP, 87 minutes, color, surround sound.

wind and clamorous surf. Amidst this incessant but heterogeneous and shifting flow, crisply tactile sounds ripple at the surface: aqueous glugs and burbles, clanging chains, the hiss of surf spray, the squeal of a winch. Human speech is scarce and all but drowned in the mix. Rarely intelligible, it always emerges as though piped through a distant radio or intercom, offering affect and intensity rather than meaning.

Indeed, though it documents our technological plunder of the sea, *Leviathan* subsumes human beings within material nature, emphasizing the continuities between the human and the animal, the animate and the inanimate world.[73] The glistening weather gear worn by the fisherman obscures human form, transforming arms and legs into tentacles, hands into claws, and feet into flippers or fins (fig. 6.17). Like the bulging eyes and bloated bodies of the fish that slosh around the ship's hold, the fishermen appear in close-up as hunks of exhausted and sea-soaked flesh, meaty stuff relentlessly under threat of being engulfed by the howling elements that surround them, kin to the slabs of definned flatfish they toss overboard. The soundtrack's drone heightens this foreboding of overwhelming immersion—the noise of wind, sea, and rain reminding us of that immemorial sonic flux that precedes and exceeds the human and indeed all life. "Noise," "nautical," and "nausea," we know, are not only etymologically but sensually related, connections *Leviathan* affirms to the fullest.[74] In the sound of the sea, Leibniz heard this sonic flux, the clear-confused, distinct-obscure roar that allows us dimly to perceive the connection between our limited perception and the cosmic totality that stretches around us in every spatial and temporal direction, a totality in which we float but that we can never master.[75]

Sound amplifies image, and image illuminates sound. But this is not synaesthesia, not some quirky neurological or arbitrary technological triggering of one sense by another. *Leviathan* relies on and clarifies the distinction between visual and acoustic space, the capacities of the eye and ear, revealing what the image can and cannot do. The film's visual abstraction exposes the flatness of the screen, its image distortions and anomalous camerawork emphasizing the apparatuses of image production. *Leviathan* equally draws attention to the soundtrack and, in doing so, breaks the unitary illusion fostered by ocularcentric cinema, which denies sound any autonomy, requiring instead that it dutifully support the image. If the film reverses this subordination, pulling image into the immersive field of sound, it does so against the tide of dominant cinematic practice, in relationship to which it can only be seen and heard as aberrant.

A Transcendental Exercise of the Faculties

Appealing to the authority of neuroscience and thus, it would seem, to a materialist account of sensation, synaesthetics revives the Wagnerian dream of sensory and aesthetic fusion and the Aristotelian supposition of a common sense that would explain how five distinct sensory channels can result in a unified experience. But, as the ordinary meaning of the phrase suggests, such a "common sense" can only ever apprehend the *doxa*, what "everybody knows" and experiences every day. This is exactly what the Soviet filmmakers worried about at the advent of sync sound: that cinema would recapitulate ordinary perception, generating the naturalistic "'illusion' of talking people, of audible objects, etc."[76] And it is why Nietzsche warned against a facile reading of Chladni's *Klangfiguren*. Common sense enjoins what Gilles Deleuze calls an "empirical exercise of the faculties" that apprehends *what is sensed* but not the *being of the sensible* itself.[77] The latter is revealed only when common sense is confounded and sensation comes up against its limits, when the unity of the subject and the unity of the object are no longer given. Such experiences provoke a "transcendental exercise of the faculties," revealing the limits of each sense and the differences and disparities that provide the very conditions of possibility for ordinary empirical experience. A rigorous materialism, then, would operate not on the empirical level of common sense, but on this transcendental level, where the faculties are unhinged and one witnesses the differential processes that constitute the world of our everyday experience. Eisenstein and Nietzsche knew that art is the privileged domain in which this sensory experimentation takes place and thus that its metaphysical value is enormous. The films and installations of Poledna, Rosefeldt, the Sensory Ethnography Lab, and others show how much cinema can contribute to this metaphysical project, resisting both the assimilation and the segregation of the senses, instead fostering a collaboration between sound and image that acknowledges the irreducible differences between these media and their sensory modalities while exploring the intensities that these differences can generate.

NOTES

INTRODUCTION

1. *New Sound, New York: 25 Years beyond New Music, New York* [festival brochure] (New York: The Kitchen, 2005).

2. A sampling of such work can be found in Mark M. Smith, ed., *Hearing History: A Reader* (Athens: University of Georgia Press, 2004); Michael Bull and Les Back, eds., *The Auditory Culture Reader*, 2nd ed. (New York: Bloomsbury, 2016); Jonathan Sterne, ed., *The Sound Studies Reader* (New York: Routledge, 2012); and Trevor Pinch and Karin Bijsterveld, eds., *The Oxford Handbook of Sound Studies* (Oxford: Oxford University Press, 2012).

3. Manuel DeLanda, *A Thousand Years of Nonlinear History* (New York: Zone, 1997).

4. Seth Kim-Cohen, *In the Blink of an Ear: Toward a Non-Cochlear Sonic Art* (New York: Continuum, 2009).

5. Friedrich Kittler, *Gramophone, Film, Typewriter*, trans. Geoffrey Winthrop-Young and Michael Wutz (Stanford, CA: Stanford University Press, 1999), 15–17, 22, and 24.

6. Quentin Meillassoux, *After Finitude*, trans. Ray Brassier (New York: Continuum, 2008), 5 and passim.

7. See Michel Foucault, *The Order of Things*, trans. Alan Sheridan (New York: Routledge, 2002), 371–422; Jacques Derrida, "The Ends of Man," in *Margins of Philosophy*, trans. Alan Bass (Chicago: University of Chicago Press, 1982), 109–36; and Louis Althusser, "Marxism and Humanism," in *For Marx*, trans. Ben Brewster (London: Verso, 2005), 219–47.

8. Meillassoux, *After Finitude*, 5ff., 50ff.

9. Friedrich Nietzsche, *Beyond Good and Evil*, trans. Walter Kaufmann (New York: Vintage, 1966), 161 (§230), translation modified.

10. John Cage, "Experimental Music," *Silence: Lectures and Writings* (Hanover, NH: Wesleyan University Press, 1961), 10.

11. See, for example, Max Neuhaus, "Sound Art?," wall text for "Volume: Bed of Sound," P.S. 1 Contemporary Art Center (July 2–September 30, 2000), http://www.max-neuhaus.info/soundworks/soundart/SoundArt.htm; Alan Licht, *Sound Art: Beyond Music, Between Categories* (New York: Rizzoli, 2007), chap. 1; the conversation between Stephen Vitiello and Marina Rosenfeld in *NewMusicBox*, March 1, 2004, http://www.newmusicbox.org/articles/Stephen-Vitiello-and-Marina-Rosenfeld; Douglas Kahn, "Sound Art, Art, Music," *Iowa Review Web* 8, no. 1, special issue on sound art, ed. Ben Basan (February–March 2006), http://thestudio.uiowa.edu/tirw/TIRW_Archive/feb06/kahn2.html; and David Toop, "Cross-Platform: Haroon Mirza," *Wire*, March 2012, 20.

12. On the origins of the term "sound art," see Kahn, "Sound Art, Art, Music," and Licht, *Sound Art*, 11.

13. Hilary Putnam, "Why Is a Philosopher?" in *Realism with a Human Face*, ed. James Conant (Cambridge, MA: Harvard University Press, 1990), 118. For a comparison of analytic and Continental antirealisms, see Lee Braver, *A Thing of This World: A History of Continental Anti-Realism* (Evanston, IL: Northwestern University Press, 2007).

14. See Arnaud Villani, "The Problem of an Immanent Metaphysics," in *Gilles Deleuze and Metaphysics*, ed. Alain Beaulieu, Edward Kazarian, and Julia Sushytska (Lanham, MD: Lexington Books, 2014), vii–x. In an interview with Villani, Deleuze notably remarked: "I am a pure metaphysician. . . . Bergson says that modern science has not found its metaphysics, the metaphysics it needs. It is that metaphysics that interests me." Deleuze, "Responses to a Series of Questions," *Collapse* III (2007): 41–42. Cf. Deleuze, *Negotiations*, trans. Martin Joughin (New York: Columbia University Press, 1995), 88–89, 136; and Deleuze and Guattari, *What Is Philosophy?*, trans. Hugh Tomlinson and Graham Burchell (New York: Columbia University Press, 1994), 9. DeLanda describes his own position and Deleuze's as "materialist metaphysics" in *Deleuze: History and Science* (New York: Atropos, 2010), 81ff. Nietzsche is a trickier case. A relentless critic of metaphysics and realism, Nietzsche himself offers an account of the real as "becoming" and "will to power." In *Nietzsche: Naturalism and Interpretation* (Berkeley and Los Angeles: University of California Press, 1999), I try to show that his realism and antirealism are compatible. Here I emphasize Nietzsche's contribution to an "immanent metaphysics."

15. DeLanda quips that "for decades, admitting that one was a realist was the equivalent of acknowledging [that] one was a child molester." Quoted in Graham Harman, "DeLanda's Ontology: Assemblage and Realism," *Continental Philosophy Review* 41, no. 3 (2008): 368.

16. See, for example, Andrew Cole, "Those Obscure Objects of Desire," *Artforum*, Summer 2015, 318–23, and Ben Kafka, "Braving the Elements: On Jussi Parikka's Geology of Media," *Artforum*, November 2015, 89–90. Object-oriented ontology's founder, Graham Harman, bluntly declares, "I do not think matter exists . . . only form exists" and thus "emphatically reject[s] materialism" in favor of what he calls "immaterialism." See Harman and Manuel DeLanda, *The Rise of Realism* (Cambridge: Polity, 2017), 24, and Harman's contribution to "A Questionnaire on Materialisms," *October* 155 (Winter 2016): 51. The originator of actor-network theory, Bruno Latour, reveals his distaste for "materialism" in "Can We Get Our Materialism Back, Please?," *Isis* 98 (2007): 138–42.

17. See, for example, Slavoj Žižek and Glyn Daly, *Conversations with Žižek* (Cambridge: Polity, 2004), 97, and Karen Barad, *Meeting the Universe Half-Way: Quantum Physics and the Entanglement of Matter and Meaning* (Durham, NC: Duke University Press, 2007).

18. See Michele Hilmes, "Is There a Field Called Sound Culture Studies? And Does It Matter?," *American Quarterly* 57, no. 1 (March 2005): 249–59, and Veit Erlmann and Michael Bull's editorial introduction to the inaugural issue of the journal *Sound Studies* (2015). On the explosive increase in sound-art exhibitions since the late 1990s, see Seth Cluett, "Ephemeral, Immersive, Invasive: Sound as Curatorial Theme, 1966–2013," in *The Multisensory Museum: Cross-Disciplinary Perspectives on Touch, Sound, Smell, Memory, and Space*, ed. Nina Levent and Alvaro Pascual-Leone (Lanham, MD: Rowman & Littlefield, 2014).

19. Brian Kane, "Sound Studies without Auditory Culture: A Critique of the Ontological Turn," *Sound Studies* 1, no. 1 (2015): 3.

CHAPTER ONE

1. Maryanne Amacher, "Synaptic Island: A Psybertonal Topology," in *Architecture as a Translation of Music*, ed. Elizabeth Martin (New York: Princeton Architectural Press, 1994), 32. For further description of the "Music for Sound-Joined Rooms" series, see Jeff Bartone and Gordon Monahan, "God's Big Noise: Interview with Maryanne Amacher," *Musicworks* 41, Summer 1988; Eliot Handelman, "Interview with Maryanne Amacher," *RaRa Speaks* (blog), January 4, 2010, http://raraspeaks.tumblr.com/post/316070088; Amacher's liner notes to her *Sound Characters (making the third ear)* (Tzadik TZ 7043); and "Extremities: Maryanne Amacher in Conversation with Frank J. Oteri," *NewMusicBox*, May 1, 2004, http://www.newmusicbox.org/articles/extremities-maryanne-amacher-in-conversation-with-frank-j-oteri.

2. For examples, see Peter Watrous, "Maryanne Amacher," *New York Times*, February 28, 1988, http://www.nytimes.com/1988/02/28/arts/music-maryanne-amacher.html; and Brian Reinbolt, "18th Annual Electronic Music Plus Festival," *Computer Music Journal* 15, no. 4 (Winter 1991): 91.

3. Amacher, "Perceptual Geography: Third Ear Music and Structure Borne Sound," in *Audio Culture: Readings in Modern Music*, ed. Christoph Cox and Daniel Warner, rev. ed. (New York: Bloomsbury, 2017), 123. See also Amacher's liner notes to *Sound Characters*, and Bartone and Monahan, "God's Big Noise," 4.

4. Joanna Demers subtly examines the tensions between materiality and signification in experimental electronic music and sound art, though her philosophical account of materialism and materiality differs from my own. See her *Listening through the Noise: The Aesthetics of Experimental Electronic Music* (Oxford: Oxford University Press, 2010), particularly Part I, and "Materialism, Ontology, and Experimental Music Aesthetics," in *Tomorrow Is the Question: New Directions in Experimental Music Studies*, ed. Benjamin Piekut (Ann Arbor: University of Michigan Press, 2014), 254–74.

5. See Derrida, "Structure, Sign, and Play in the Discourse of the Human Sciences," in *Writing and Difference*, trans. Alan Bass (Chicago: University of Chicago Press, 1978), 278–93, and his interview with Julia Kristeva in *Positions*, trans. Alan Bass (Chicago: University of Chicago Press, 1981), 19–20 and 64–65.

6. Ferdinand de Saussure, *Course in General Linguistics*, trans. Roy Harris (New York: Bloomsbury, 2013), 138–40; Jacques Lacan, *The Seminar of Jacques Lacan, Book I: Freud's Papers on Technique, 1953–1954*, ed. Jacques-Alain Miller, trans. John Forrester (New York: W. W. Norton, 1988), 66; Lacan, *The Seminar of Jacques Lacan, Book XX: Encore 1972–1973*, ed. Jacques-Alain Miller, trans. Bruce Fink (New York: W. W. Norton, 1998), 32; Lacan, "The Function and Field of Speech and Language in Psychoanalysis," in *Écrits*, trans. Bruce Fink (New York: W. W. Norton, 2006), 229; Jacques Derrida, *Of Grammatology*, trans. Gayatri Chakravorty Spivak (Baltimore, MD: Johns Hopkins University Press, 1976), 158, 163; Roland Barthes, "The Death of the Author," in *Image, Music, Text*, ed. and trans. Stephen Heath (London: Fontana, 1977), 147; Stuart Hall, *Representation & the Media*, dir. Sut Jhally (Northampton, MA: Media Education Foundation, 2002), DVD transcript, http://www.mediaed.org/transcripts/Stuart-Hall-Representation-and-the-Media-Transcript.pdf; and Slavoj Žižek, *The Ticklish Subject* (London: Verso, 2009), 33. On several occasions Derrida has sought to clarify his infamous claim "there is nothing outside the text," maintaining that what he calls "the text"

extends beyond "the book" to encompass power relations and political contexts. See, for example, "But Beyond . . . (Open Letter to Anne McClintock and Rob Nixon)," trans. Peggy Kamuf, *Critical Inquiry* 131, no. 1 (Autumn 1986): 155–70. Nevertheless, Derrida remains resolutely antirealist, committed to the view that, "from the moment that the sign appears, that is to say, from the very beginning, there is no chance of encountering anywhere the purity of 'reality'" (Derrida, *Of Grammatology*, 91). This pervasive antirealism or correlationism is prevalent in Anglo-American philosophy as well. For a broad survey of antirealism in contemporary Anglo-American and European philosophy, see Lee Braver, *A Thing of This World* (Evanston, IL: Northwestern University Press, 2007).

7. See Quentin Meillassoux, *After Finitude*, trans. Ray Brassier (New York: Continuum, 2008), 5 and passim. For an historical overview of correlationism and recent critiques of the position, see the introduction to *Realism Materialism Art*, ed. Christoph Cox, Jenny Jaskey, and Suhail Malik (Berlin: Sternberg Press, 2015), 15–31.

8. For a related critique, see Karen Barad, "Posthumanist Performativity: Toward an Understanding of How Matter Comes to Matter," *Signs: Journal of Women in Culture and Society* 28, no. 3 (Spring 2003): 801–31.

9. Seth Kim-Cohen, *In the Blink of an Ear: Toward a Non-Cochlear Sonic Art* (New York: Continuum, 2009). Brandon LaBelle, *Background Noise: Perspectives on Sound Art* (New York: Continuum, 2006), also attempts to shift sound art discourse away from the naturalistic interpretation toward a discussion of the embodied, relational, contextual, social, and political nature of sound.

10. Kim-Cohen, *In the Blink of an Ear*, 112.

11. See Piekut, "Chance and Certainty: John Cage's Politics of Nature," *Cultural Critique* 84 (Spring 2013): 134–63, and "Sound's Modest Witness: Notes on Cage and Modernism," *Contemporary Music Review* 31, no. 1 (February 2012): 3–18. Piekut's conception of modernity is drawn from Bruno Latour, *We Have Never Been Modern*, trans. Catherine Porter (Cambridge, MA: Harvard University Press, 1993).

12. Piekut, "Chance and Certainty," 147–48, and "Sound's Modest Witness," 15.

13. The philosopher Nelson Goodman offers a particularly bald endorsement of this claim, maintaining that we make the stars, for example, "by making a space and time that contains those stars." Goodman, "On Starmaking," in *Starmaking: Realism, Anti-Realism, and Irrealism*, ed. Peter J. McCormick (Cambridge, MA: MIT Press, 1996), 145. For a critique of this strategy, see Meillassoux, *After Finitude*, 1–27.

14. For a more extended analysis of these concepts, see my *Nietzsche: Naturalism and Interpretation* (Berkeley and Los Angeles: University of California Press, 1999).

15. Since the 1970s Anglo-American philosophers have debated whether or not, and to what degree, music can be considered a "representational" art. For overviews of this debate, see Stephen Davies, *Musical Meaning and Expression* (Ithaca, NY: Cornell University Press, 1994), and Aaron Ridley, *The Philosophy of Music: Theme and Variations* (Edinburgh: Edinburgh University Press, 2004), chapter 2.

16. Eduard Hanslick, *On the Musically Beautiful*, trans. Geoffrey Payzant (Indianapolis, IN: Hackett, 1986), 28.

17. R. Murray Schafer, *The Soundscape: Our Sonic Environment and the Tuning of the World* (Rochester, VT: Destiny Books, 1994), 6.

18. René Descartes, *Compendium of Music*, trans. Walter Robert (Rome: American Institute of Musicology, 1961), 11; and G. W. Leibniz, "Principles of Nature and Grace, Based on Reason," in *Philosophical Essays*, ed. Roger Ariew and Daniel Garber (Indianapolis: Hackett, 1989), 212. See also Leibniz's April 17, 1712 letter to Christian Gold-

bach and 1714 letter to Prince Eugen, both quoted in Friedrich Kittler, "Lightning and Series—Event and Thunder," *Theory, Culture, and Society* 23, nos. 7–8 (2006): 68. For more on the 1712 letter, see Daniel Heller-Roazen, *The Fifth Hammer: Pythagoras and the Disharmony of the World* (New York: Zone, 2011), 83–84. Amy Cimini offers a helpful reading of the Cartesian account of music, as well as a discussion of Amacher's sonic materialism. See Cimini, "The Secret History of Musical Spinozism," in *Spinoza beyond Philosophy*, ed. Beth Lord (Edinburgh: Edinburgh University Press, 2012), 94–97, 102–4, and the related essay "Gilles Deleuze and the Musical Spinoza," in *Sounding the Virtual: Gilles Deleuze and the Theory and Philosophy of Music*, ed. Brian Hulse and Nick Nesbitt (London: Ashgate, 2010), 129–44.

19. Arthur Schopenhauer, *The World as Will and Representation*, Vol. 1, trans. E. F. J. Payne (New York: Dover, 1969). While Kant uses the Greek philosophical term *phenomena* more or less interchangeably with the German *Erscheinung* (appearance), and *noumena* more or less interchangeably with the German *Ding an sich* (thing in itself), Schopenhauer rejects the Greek pair in favor of the German pair, though Payne persisted in rendering *Erscheinung* as "phenomena." My quotations from Payne's translation are altered accordingly.

20. In this and many other respects, Schopenhauer's distinction between representation and will anticipates Henri Bergson's distinction between analysis and intuition. See Bergson, "Introduction to Metaphysics," in *The Creative Mind: An Introduction to Metaphysics*, trans. Mabelle L. Andison (Mineola, NY: Dover, 2007), 133–69.

21. See Schopenhauer, *World as Will and Representation*, Vol. 1, 104–5.

22. Schopenhauer, *World as Will and Representation*, Vol. 1, 179.

23. Schopenhauer, *World as Will and Representation*, Vol. 1, 257.

24. Schopenhauer, *World as Will and Representation*, Vol. 1, 262–63; cf. 257.

25. Schopenhauer grants that "music is the language of feeling and passion" and, at the same time, that it "is in the highest degree a universal language . . . like geometrical figures and numbers," *World as Will and Representation*, Vol. 1, 259, 262.

26. Friedrich Nietzsche, *Ecce Homo*, "Why I Write Such Good Books: *The Birth of Tragedy*," §1 in *On the Genealogy of Morals and Ecce Homo*, trans. Walter Kaufmann and R. J. Hollingdale (New York: Vintage Books, 1969), 270.

27. Nietzsche, *The Birth of Tragedy*, §8, in *The Birth of Tragedy and The Case of Wagner*, trans. Walter Kaufmann (New York: Vintage Books, 1967), 64–65. Further references to *The Birth of Tragedy* are cited parenthetically in the text by section number.

28. For a more sustained anti-Hegelian reading of *The Birth of Tragedy*, see Gilles Deleuze, *Nietzsche and Philosophy*, trans. Hugh Tomlinson (New York: Columbia University Press, 1983), 8ff.

29. Arthur Schopenhauer, *The World as Will and Representation*, Vol. 1, trans. E. F. J. Payne (New York: Dover, 1969), 19. Cf. §18.

30. Immanuel Kant, *Critique of Pure Reason*, trans. Paul Guyer and Allan W. Wood (Cambridge: Cambridge University Press, 1998), 117 (Bxxx); cf. 700 (A849/B877). For more on Nietzsche's critique of Kant's distinctions between noumena and phenomena, and between thing in itself and appearance, see my *Nietzsche: Naturalism and Interpretation*, 176–84.

31. See Schopenhauer, *On the Basis of Morality*, trans. E. F. J. Payne (Indianapolis: Bobbs-Merrill, 1965), chap. 2.

32. Unless otherwise indicated, italics in quoted passages are in the source.

33. As we will see, John Cage will affirm this conception of art as "the imitation of

nature in her manner of operation." See Cage, *Silence: Lectures and Writings* (Hanover, NH: Wesleyan University Press, 1961), 9, 100, 155, 173, 194; and *A Year from Monday: New Lectures and Writings* (Middletown, CT: Wesleyan University Press, 1969), 18, 31, and 75.

34. Nietzsche's 1886 preface (particularly §5) confirms this reading of *The Birth of Tragedy*, as does "Why I Write Such Good Books." See also *Birth of Tragedy*, §17.

35. Nietzsche, *The Will To Power*, trans. Walter Kaufmann and R. J. Hollingdale (New York: Vintage, 1968), §853.

36. Cf. *Birth of Tragedy*, §8, and *Will to Power*, §1050.

37. For Nietzsche, "being" has two related meanings. On the one hand, it names distinct and subsistent empirical particulars, individual entities. On the other, it names transcendent entities that are immune from becoming or change. As a naturalist, Nietzsche holds that there is only becoming and change and hence that, strictly speaking, there are no autonomous, subsistent empirical particulars. The illusion of empirical beings, Nietzsche holds, is due in part to the Platonist projection of transcendent being onto the empirical. For this account, see, e.g., *Twilight of the Idols*, "Reason in Philosophy," §1, in *The Portable Nietzsche*, ed. and trans. Walter Kaufmann (New York: Penguin, 1976), 279–80.

38. This notion of "unity" or "unithood" (*Einheit*) is surely different from that of the "primordial unity" (*Ur-Eine*) spoken of in *The Birth of Tragedy*. The former clearly refers to the (Apollonian) illusion of identity and individuation characteristic of empirical beings, while the latter refers to the fundamental set of forces that constitute the realm of becoming or the Dionysian. Aware of this potential confusion, the later Nietzsche qualifies his talk of becoming and the Dionysian, describing them instead as continuums or multiplicities instead of unities. I discuss this issue more fully below.

39. Nietzsche, *Twilight of the Idols*, "Reason in Philosophy," §5, in *The Portable Nietzsche*, 482. Cf. Nietzsche, *The Gay Science*, trans. Walter Kaufmann (New York: Vintage, 1974), §§110, 112, 121.

40. Nietzsche, *Twilight of the Idols*, "Reason in Philosophy," §2.

41. Nietzsche, "Why I Write Such Good Books," §3.

42. See Nietzsche, *The Gay Science*, §§108–9, 343–44.

43. See Gilbert Simondon, "The Genesis of the Individual," trans. Mark Cohen and Sanford Kwinter, in *Incorporations*, ed. Jonathan Crary (New York: Zone, 1992), 296–319; Ilya Prigogine and Isabelle Stengers, *Order out of Chaos* (New York: Bantam Books, 1984), 7, 9, and passim; Gilles Deleuze and Félix Guattari, *A Thousand Plateaus*, trans. Brian Massumi (Minneapolis: University of Minnesota Press, 1987), 329, 408ff.; and Manuel DeLanda, "Immanence and Transcendence in the Genesis of Form," *South Atlantic Quarterly* 96, no. (Summer 1997): 499–514, and *A Thousand Years of Nonlinear History* (New York: Zone, 1997).

44. Nietzsche, *On the Genealogy of Morals*, First Essay, 45 (§13).

45. For an extended examination and interpretation of will to power, see my *Nietzsche: Naturalism and Interpretation*, chap. 5.

46. Nietzsche, *Writings from the Late Notebooks*, ed. Rüdiger Bittner, trans. Kate Sturge (Cambridge: Cambridge University Press, 2003), 247 (§14 [79]). For examples, see *Nietzsche: Naturalism and Interpretation*, 239ff. Compare Deleuze's extension of the term "contemplation" to describe the activities of "not only people and animals, but plants, the earth, and rocks." Deleuze and Guattari, *What Is Philosophy?*, trans. Hugh Tomlinson and Graham Burchell (New York: Columbia University Press, 1994),

212, and Deleuze, *Difference and Repetition*, trans. Paul Patton (New York: Columbia University Press, 1994), 74–75.

47. Deleuze writes: "Having liberated himself from Schopenhauer and Wagner, [Nietzsche] explored a world of impersonal and pre-individual singularities, a world he then called Dionysian or of the will to power, a free and unbound energy . . . which traverses men as well as plants and animals independently of the matter of their individuation and the forms of their personality." Gilles Deleuze, *The Logic of Sense*, ed. Constantin V. Boundas, trans. Mark Lester with Charles Stivale (New York: Columbia University Press, 1990), 107. Cf. Deleuze, *Difference and Repetition*, 258.

48. Nietzsche, *Writings from the Late Notebooks*, 38–39 (§38 [12]).

49. Nietzsche, *Beyond Good and Evil*, 39 (§36), translation modified.

50. The passage invites comparison with Gilles Deleuze's conception of being as both "univocal" and "multiple." See Deleuze, *Difference and Repetition*, 35ff., and *The Logic of Sense*, 177–80.

51. "Transcendental" should not be confused with "transcendent." For Kant, the "transcendental" designates the conditions for the possibility of empirical experience, whereas the "transcendent" names what lies entirely outside such experience.

52. "Transcendental empiricism" is not only an epistemological theory (an account of what and how we know) but also an ontological theory (an account of what there is, independent of our knowledge). Thus it can also be termed "transcendental realism" or "transcendental materialism." On "transcendental empiricism," see, e.g., Gilles Deleuze, *Bergsonism*, trans. Hugh Tomlinson and Barbara Habberjam (New York: Zone, 1988), 23, 30; and Deleuze, *Difference and Repetition*, 56–69, 222.

53. See Deleuze, *Difference and Repetition*, 208ff., 213–14, 279, and "The Actual and the Virtual," trans. Eliot Ross Albert, in Gilles Deleuze and Claire Parnet, *Dialogues II* (New York: Columbia University Press, 2007), 148–52. On the relationships among the virtual, the intensive, and the actual, see DeLanda, *Intensive Science and Virtual Philosophy* (London: Continuum, 2002). I discuss virtuality more fully in chap. 2.

54. Deleuze maintains that, while morphogenetic processes are ordinarily hidden and intensive differences tend to be canceled in the actual entities of empirical experience, exceptional physical and mental states caused by vertigo, delirium, and psychedelic drugs allow these processes to be perceived and felt. Moreover, he argues that modern and contemporary art, cinema, and music explore these intensive processes and bring them to sensory awareness, as do the "minor sciences" of metallurgy, hydrodynamics, and nonequilibrium thermodynamics. See, e.g., Deleuze, *Difference and Repetition*, 237, 193; *Francis Bacon: The Logic of Sensation*, trans. Daniel W. Smith (Minneapolis: University of Minnesota Press, 2003), 39–54; *What Is Philosophy*, chap. 7; *A Thousand Plateaus*, 411; and DeLanda, *Intensive Science and Virtual Philosophy*, 64ff. I discuss this issue more fully in chap. 4.

55. Deleuze, *Difference and Repetition*, 222.

56. Deleuze, *Difference and Repetition*, 222–23.

57. See, e.g., Deleuze, *Difference and Repetition*, 213–14, and "The Method of Dramatization," in *Desert Islands and Other Texts, 1953–1974*, ed. David Lapoujade, trans. Michael Taormina (New York: Semiotext(e), 2004), 101–3.

58. In its first edition, the full title of book was *The Birth of Tragedy out of the Spirit of Music*.

59. Deleuze, *Francis Bacon*, 48. Variations on this phrase appear throughout Deleuze's later work. See, for example, "Making Inaudible Forces Inaudible," in *Two*

Regimes of Madness: Texts and Interviews 1975–1995, ed. David Lapoujade, trans. Ames Hodges and Mike Taormina (New York: Semiotext[e], 2006), 156–60; *A Thousand Plateaus*, 95–96, 248, 265–66, 342–43; and *What Is Philosophy?*, 182.

60. See Deleuze and Guattari, *A Thousand Plateaus*, 39–74, 502ff.

61. See DeLanda, *A Thousand Years of Nonlinear History*.

62. For helpful examinations of the flows of images in contemporary culture, see David Joselit, *After Art* (Princeton, NJ: Princeton University Press, 2013); and Hito Steyerl, "In Defense of the Poor Image," *e-flux journal* 10 (November 2009): http://www.e-flux.com/journal/in-defense-of-the-poor-image, and "The Spam of the Earth: Withdrawal from Representation," *e-flux journal* 32 (February 2012): http://www.e-flux.com/journal/32/68260/the-spam-of-the-earth-withdrawal-from-representation.

63. Gilles Deleuze, "Vincennes Session of April 15, 1980, Leibniz Seminar," trans. Charles J. Stivale, *Discourse* 20, no. 3 (Fall 1998): 78; also at https://www.webdeleuze.com/textes/50. I return to this passage and elaborate on it more fully in chap. 4.

64. Carl Kerényi, *Dionysos: Archetypal Image of Indestructible Life*, trans. Ralph Manheim (Princeton, NJ: Princeton University Press, 1976), xxxii–xxxv. Kerényi remarks that *zoë* is "the life with which modern biology concerns itself." Thus, for example, the *bios/zoë* distinction is taken up by Richard Dawkins as the distinction between "individual bodies" and "independent DNA replicators, skipping like chamois, free and untrammelled down the generations . . . , immortal coils shuffling off an endless succession of mortal ones." *The Selfish Gene*, 30th anniversary ed. (Oxford: Oxford University Press, 2006), 234.

65. Casey O'Callaghan, *Sounds: A Philosophical Theory* (Oxford: Oxford University Press, 2007).

66. Pierre Schaeffer, "Acousmatics," in Cox and Warner, *Audio Culture*, 95–101. For a more orthodox phenomenological reading of Schaeffer, see Brian Kane, "*L'objet sonore maintenant*: Pierre Schaeffer, Sound Objects, and the Phenomenological Reduction," *Organised Sound* 12, no. 1 (2007): 15–24, and *Sound Unseen: Acousmatic Sound in Theory and Practice* (Oxford: Oxford University Press, 2014), chap. 1.

67. Francisco López, "Profound Listening and Environmental Sound Matter," in Cox and Warner, *Audio Culture*, 107.

68. López, "Profound Listening," 105.

69. For this reason, López rejects Schaeffer's phrase "sound object" in favor of "sound matter," which he feels "better reflects the continuity of the sonic material one finds in sound environments." See López, "Profound Listening," 107.

70. See O'Callaghan, *Sounds*, 11, 26–27, 57–71.

71. This notion of the incorporeal event or effect can be found throughout Deleuze's corpus. For some key instances, see *The Logic of Sense*, 4 and passim; *Dialogues II*, 63–66; *A Thousand Plateaus*, 86ff.; and *What Is Philosophy?*, 21, 126–27, 156ff.

72. Bergson, "The Perception of Change," in *The Creative Mind*, 122; italics in the original.

73. For Deleuze's discussion of the ontology of the verb, see *The Logic of Sense*, 182–85. The priority of the infinitive as an expression of pure events and pure becomings is a theme that runs throughout Deleuze's work.

74. See Deleuze, *The Logic of Sense*, 7, 70, 181–82.

75. Deleuze and Guattari, *A Thousand Plateaus*, 261; cf. *Dialogues II*, 92ff., 151–52. Deleuze draws the term from the medieval philosopher Duns Scotus, but also from Charles Sanders Peirce and Gilbert Simondon.

76. Jean-François Augoyard and Henry Torgue, eds., *Sonic Experience: A Guide to Everyday Sounds*, trans. Andra McCartney and David Paquette (Montreal: McGill-Queens University Press, 2005). On Deleuze's notions of event and effect, see 10, 154n16. Deleuze briefly discusses "sound effects" as instances of incorporeal events in *The Logic of Sense*, 7, 70, 181–82.

77. See Chris Kubick and Anne Walsh, "Sound Library: A Motion Picture Event," *Leonardo Music Journal* 16 (December 2006): 54–55, and "F is for Foley," *Cabinet* 23 (Fall 2006): 18–19.

78. In addition to the work of Chris Kubick and Anne Walsh, discussed below, see/hear Brian Conley's *War! Serbia vs. the United States* (1999), a live radio performance in which two teams, one in Belgrade, the other in New York, staged an auditory battle fought solely with cartoon sound effects (documented on *BitStreams: Sound Works from the Exhibition at the Whitney Museum of American Art*, JDK 06 CD, 2001); and Julian Rosefeldt's *The Soundmaker* (2006), examined in chap. 6.

79. The project is documented at http://www.doublearchive.com/projects/full_metal_jackets.php.

80. An excerpt is available at http://socalledsound.com.

81. "In art, and in painting as in music, it is not a matter of reproducing or inventing forms, but of capturing forces. For this reason no art is figurative"; *Francis Bacon: The Logic of Sensation*, 48. This rejection of representation and signification in favor of a materialist analysis of expression and force runs throughout Deleuze's work.

82. Deleuze and Guattari, *What Is Philosophy?*, 164.

83. Deleuze, *Negotiations: 1972–1990*, trans. Martin Joughin (New York: Columbia University Press, 1995), 137. I have adopted the translation suggested by Daniel Smith in his introduction to Deleuze, *Essays Critical and Clinical*, trans. Daniel W. Smith and Michael A. Greco (Minneapolis: University of Minnesota Press, 1997), xxx–xxxi.

84. Deleuze and Guattari, *What Is Philosophy?*, 168.

85. Deleuze, *Cinema 1: The Movement-Image*, trans. Hugh Tomlinson and Barbara Habberjam (Minneapolis: University of Minnesota Press, 1986), 102, 91–103 in general.

86. See Roger Fry, "An Essay in Aesthetics," *Vision and Design* (New York: Brentano's, 1924), 11–25.

87. Fry, "Essay in Aesthetics," 12, 19.

88. Fry, "Essay in Aesthetics," 23.

89. See Deleuze and Guattari, *What Is Philosophy?*, 173–74. "*Affects are precisely these non-human becomings of man*, just as percepts . . . are *nonhuman landscapes of nature*" (169).

90. See Deleuze and Guattari, *A Thousand Plateaus*, 160–61, 270.

91. Deleuze, *Difference and Repetition*, 68.

92. Amacher, in Bartone and Monahan, "God's Big Noise," 5. Amacher's description resonates with the writings of a composer who greatly inspired her, Edgard Varèse. Relinquishing the term "music" in favor of "organized sound," Varèse proposed compositions featuring "moving masses," "shifting planes," and "zones of intensities" that would attract or repulse one another, expand or dilate, collide or combine. See Varèse, "The Liberation of Sound," in Cox and Warner, *Audio Culture*, 17–21.

93. Denis Hollier offers a reading of Antonin Artaud's theatrical and cinematic work along similar lines. See "The Death of Paper, Part Two: Artaud's Sound System," *October* 80 (Spring 1997): 27–37.

94. See Kim-Cohen, *In the Blink of an Ear*, 12–13 and chapter 5.

95. In some rare passages, Derrida suggests just this; and, in those passages, he does so with reference to Deleuze and Nietzsche. See, for example, "Différance," *Margins of Philosophy*, trans. Alan Bass (Chicago: University of Chicago Press, 1982), 17, and *Of Grammatology*, trans. Gayatri Chakravorti Spivak (Baltimore, MD: Johns Hopkins University Press, 1974), 70. Derrida's analysis of performative utterances in "Signature Event Context" also suggests that language might be subsumed under a broader theory of force. For the most part, however, Derrida and Derrideans have remained within the analysis of textuality more narrowly defined and of linguistic and conceptual difference. For materialist readings of Derrida that take his account to be compatible with scientific and philosophical naturalism, see Henry Staten, "Derrida, Dennett, and the Ethico-Political Project of Naturalism," *Derrida Today* 1, no. 1 (January 2008): 19–41, and Martin Hägglund, "Radical Atheist Materialism: A Critique of Meillassoux," in *The Speculative Turn: Continental Materialism and Realism*, ed. Levi Bryant, Nick Srnicek, and Graham Harman (Melbourne: Re-Press, 2011), 114–29.

CHAPTER TWO

1. As Deleuze puts it: "There is never a flow first and then a code that imposes itself upon it. The two are coexistent." Seminar, November 16, 1971, trans. Rojan Josh, https://www.webdeleuze.com/textes/116. Cf. Deleuze and Guattari, *Anti-Oedipus: Capitalism and Schizophrenia*, trans. Robert Hurley et al. (Minneapolis: University of Minnesota Press, 1983), 1–2, 36–37.

2. This project would draw from and synthesize, for example, the soundscape studies of R. Murray Schafer, Bernie Krause, Jean-François Augoyard, Emily Thompson, and Bryan Pijanowski; Gary Tomlinson's evolutionary prehistory of music; the work of auditory historians Richard Cullen Rath, Bruce R. Smith, Mark M. Smith, John Picker, Alain Corbin, and Karin Bijsterveld; the sonic anthropology of Steven Feld, Stefan Helmreich, and Veit Erlmann; Henri Lefebvre's "rhythmanalysis"; Steve Goodman's history of sonic warfare; Barry Blesser, Linda-Ruth Salter, and Brandon LaBelle's studies of architectural acoustics; the work of David Toop; Hillel Schwartz's history of noise; Jonathan Sterne's history of sound reproduction technologies; and much more.

3. Here, and in what follows, "decoding" means uncoding or decodifying rather than decipherment.

4. Jacques Attali, *Noise: The Political Economy of Music*, trans. Brian Massumi (Minneapolis: University of Minnesota Press, 1985), 26. Subsequent references are given in the text in parentheses.

5. Here Attali cites Henri Atlan, the Spinozist biophysicist who challenged the purely entropic conception of information theory, showing instead that noise contains a principle of self-organization that generates order. See, for example, "Noise as a Principle of Self-Organization," in *Henri Atlan: Selected Writings*, ed. Stefanos Geroulanos and Todd Meyers (New York: Fordham University Press, 2011), 95–113. Atlan is also a crucial figure for Michel Serres, whose books *The Parasite*, trans. Lawrence R. Schehr (Minneapolis: University of Minnesota Press, 1982), and *Genesis*, trans. Geneviève James and James Nielson (Ann Arbor: University of Michigan Press, 1995), extend Atlan's arguments about the generative capacity of noise. The recent scientific literature on this topic is summarized in Bart Kosko, *Noise* (New York: Viking, 2006).

6. See Deleuze, *Difference and Repetition*, trans. Paul Patton (New York: Columbia University Press, 1994), 209ff.; and "How Do We Recognize Structuralism?," in *Des-*

ert Islands and Other Texts, 1953–1974, ed. David Lapoujade, trans. Michael Taormina (New York: Semiotext[e], 2004), 179.

7. Deleuze, "The Method of Dramatization," 101.

8. Attali uses the term as it is employed in "catastrophe theory," the theory of bifurcations and singularities in the mathematical study of nonlinear dynamics.

9. Bergsonian, Spinozist, and Nietzschean in inspiration, Deleuze and Guattari develop this conception of history in *A Thousand Plateaus*, trans. Brian Massumi (Minneapolis: University of Minnesota Press, 1987), where they write: "Everything coexists, in perpetual interaction. . . . All history does is to translate a coexistence of becomings into a succession," 430. On the distinction between becoming and history, see Deleuze, *Negotiations*, trans. Martin Joughin (New York: Columbia University Press, 1995), 170–71, and Deleuze and Guattari, *What Is Philosophy?*, trans. Hugh Tomlinson and Graham Burchell (New York: Columbia University Press, 1994), 59, 96, 110–13. Raymond Williams's characterization of different forms as "residual," "dominant," or "emergent" captures an aspect of this coexistence but still grasps it within a schema of dialectical progression. See Williams, *Marxism and Literature* (Oxford: Oxford University Press, 1977), 121–27.

10. In support of this notion of coexistence, Attali quotes Deleuze and Guattari's *A Thousand Plateaus*. See *Noise*, 44.

11. See Chris Cutler, "Necessity and Choice in Musical Forms," *File under Popular: Theoretical and Critical Writings on Music* (New York: Autonomedia, 1992), 20–38; "Plunderphonia," in *Audio Culture: Readings in Modern Music*, rev. ed., ed. Christoph Cox and Daniel Warner (New York: Bloomsbury), 197–216; and "The Road to Plunderphonia," *Quaderns d'àudio* 4 (2011), http://rwm.macba.cat/uploads/20110104/QA_04_Cutler.pdf. Cutler developed his account independently of Attali, to whom he never refers. In "Plunderphonia" (199), originally published in 1994, Cutler remarks that "Necessity and Choice" was written in 1980, though a note in *File under Popular* (20) maintains that it was written for a conference held in 1982. In addition to his work as a theorist, Cutler has been a key figure in experimental and improvised music since the early 1970s, performing with seminal avant-rock bands such as Henry Cow and Pere Ubu, improvising with Fred Frith, Zeena Parkins, Otomo Yoshihide, and many others, and collaborating with Iancu Dumitrescu and the Hyperion Ensemble. In addition to Cutler and Attali, see Alfred W. Crosby, *The Measure of Reality: Quantification in Western Society, 1250–1600* (Cambridge: Cambridge University Press, 1997), chap. 8, and Hope Strayer, "From Neumes to Notes: The Evolution of Music Notation," *Musical Offerings* 4, no. 1 (2013): 1–14.

12. On these devices, see Albert Lord, *The Singer of Tales* (Cambridge, MA: Harvard University Press, 1988), chap. 3, which develops the work of Lord's mentor Milman Parry, "the Darwin of oral literature."

13. As we will see, this folk mode comes to be aided and accelerated by audio recording, the third of Cutler's memory systems.

14. Such divergent replication is not unique to biological systems. It is also manifested by inorganic forms such as crystals and in the cultural transmission of languages and memes. On the divergent replication of crystals, see Richard Dawkins, *The Blind Watchmaker* (New York: W. W. Norton, 1996), 213ff. On linguistic and memetic replication, see Dawkins, *The Selfish Gene*, 30th anniversary ed. (Oxford: Oxford University Press, 2006), chap. 11, and Daniel Dennett, *Darwin's Dangerous Idea* (New York: Simon & Schuster, 1995), chap. 12.

15. On natural selection and the evolution of the folk song, see Cecil Sharp, *English Folk Song: Some Conclusions*, 4th ed. (Belmont, CA: Wadsworth, 1965), chap. 3, and Ralph Vaughan Williams, "National Music," chap. 4 in *National Music and Other Essays*, 2nd ed. (Oxford: Oxford University Press, 1987). Also see the work of Parry and Lord, cited above.

16. Pierre Lévy, *Becoming Virtual: Reality in the Digital Age*, trans. Robert Bononno (New York: Plenum, 1998). In many ways Lévy's conception of virtualization helpfully explicates and extends Deleuze's conception of the virtual in ways that Deleuze himself acknowledged. (See "The Actual and the Virtual," trans. Eliot Ross Albert, in Gilles Deleuze and Claire Parnet, *Dialogues II* [New York: Columbia University Press, 2007], 171n4.) Yet, unlike Deleuze's and DeLanda's accounts, Lévy's is anthropocentric and progressive, firmly separating human beings from the rest of nature and taking human history to be a story of progressive virtualization. I do not follow Lévy in this respect.

17. My use of the term "subsist" here follows Deleuze, not Lévy, who distributes the terms "subsist" and "exist" differently. On virtual "subsistence," see Deleuze, *The Logic of Sense*, trans. Mark Lester (New York: Columbia University Press, 1990), 5, 19, 21, 111.

18. See Lévy, *Becoming Virtual*, 110ff. The notion of "arche-writing," "general writing," or "writing in general" runs throughout Derrida's early books (*Speech and Phenomena, Writing and Difference, Writing and Difference, Of Grammatology, Dissemination*). See, for example, "Signature Event Context," *Margins of Philosophy*, trans. Alan Bass (Chicago: University of Chicago Press, 1982), 308–30.

19. On habit and contraction as basic forms of memory, see Deleuze, *Difference and Repetition*, 70ff. Deleuze's account is inspired in part by the philosopher and heterodox evolutionist Samuel Butler, whose theory of "unconscious memory" has also influenced contemporary evolutionary biologists such as Lynn Margulis. See Margulis and Dorion Sagan, *What Is Life?* (Berkeley and Los Angeles: University of California Press, 1995), 221ff.

20. Cutler, "Necessity and Choice," 26.

21. Cutler, "Necessity and Choice," 26.

22. Christopher Small notes that the function of notation in other cultural traditions is similar. "Many cultures, it is true, have developed ways of notating their music, but these notations have functioned mostly as mnemonics, *after* the creative fact, to help the musician remember what he did; only in western music has the written score become the medium through which the act of composition takes place, and this long *before* the actual sounds are heard." *Music, Society, Education* (Hanover, NH: Wesleyan University Press, 1996), 30.

23. On the emergence of the musical work, see Lydia Goehr, *The Imaginary Museum of Musical Works* (Oxford: Oxford University Press, 1992).

24. Karl Marx, *Capital*, Vol. 1, in *The Marx-Engels Reader*, 2nd ed., ed. Robert C. Tucker (New York: W. W. Norton, 1978), 319ff.; and Georg Lukács, "Reification and the Consciousness of the Proletariat," in *History and Class Consciousness: Studies in Marxist Dialectics*, trans. Rodney Livingstone (Cambridge, MA: MIT Press, 1971), 83ff.

25. On this, see Jacques Charpentier, quoted in Derek Bailey, *Improvisation: Its Nature and Practice in Music* (New York: Da Capo, 1992), 59; Christopher Small, *Music of the Common Tongue* (London: J. Calder, 1987), 231ff., 281ff.; and Michael Chanan, *Musica Practica* (London: Verso, 1994), 54ff.

26. See Nietzsche, "On Truth and Lies in a Nonmoral Sense," in *Philosophy and Truth: Selections from Nietzsche's Notebooks of the 1870s*, ed. and trans. Daniel Breazeale

(New Jersey: Humanities Press International, 1979), 83, and Ludwig Wittgenstein, *The Blue and Brown Books* (New York: Harper & Row, 1958), 17–18.

27. The tradition of musical Platonism was arguably inaugurated in the mid-nineteenth century by the German musical formalist Eduard Hanslick, who maintained that, "philosophically speaking, the composed piece, regardless of whether it is performed or not, is the completed artwork." *On the Musically Beautiful*, trans. Geoffrey Payzant (Indianapolis: Hackett, 1986), 48. More recent proponents of musical Platonism include Jerrold Levinson, *Music, Art, and Metaphysics* (Ithaca, NY: Cornell University Press, 1990), chaps. 4 and 10; Peter Kivy, *The Fine Art of Repetition: Essays in the Philosophy of Music* (Cambridge: Cambridge University Press, 1993), chaps. 2–5; and Julian Dodd, *Works of Music: An Essay in Ontology* (Oxford: Oxford University Press, 2007). Kivy and Dodd maintain that musical works are eternal types; Levinson does not.

28. This insight spurred the recording career of the great classical pianist Glenn Gould, discussed below.

29. What Derrida notes about writing in general applies fully to the musical score: "My 'written communication' must, if you will, remain legible despite the absolute disappearance of every determined addressee in general for it to function as writing, that is, for it to be legible. It must be repeatable—iterable—in the absolute absence of the addressee or of the empirically determinable set of addressees." "Signature Event Context," 315.

30. Plato, *Phaedrus*, 574b ff., in *Plato: Complete Works*, ed. John M. Cooper (Indianapolis: Hackett, 1997), 551ff. See also Derrida's reading of these passages in "Plato's Pharmacy," *Dissemination*, trans. Barbara Johnson (Chicago: University of Chicago Press, 1981), 61–171. In the context of contemporary music, the composer John Zorn has reiterated these Socratic/Platonic worries, "deliberately [choosing] not to publish (or even write down) the rules [to his 'game pieces'], preferring to explain them [himself] in rehearsal as part of an oral tradition." See Zorn, "The Game Pieces," in Cox and Warner, *Audio Culture*, 275–80.

31. Derrida, "Signature Event Context," 316.

32. The song of the Kauai 'ō'ō can be heard via the Macaulay Library at Cornell Lab of Ornithology, http://macaulaylibrary.org/audio/6049. Listen also to the World Soundscape Project's *Vancouver Soundscape 1973*, Cambridge Street CSR-2CD 9701, 1997.

33. Of course, this is not to deny that sound recording involves translation (selection, coding, decoding), as do biological and written systems of recording as well. Biological memory filters sound through the ear, the neurology of memory, and the structure of language in a circuit that flows through the body alone. Written memory translates phonemes or tones into alphabetic or musical symbols in a circuit that passes through the intermediary of the written page and is read by the human eye, mouth, and hand. Analog sound recording renders sound waves as grooves or configurations of metal oxide particles, and digital recording as sequences of zeros and ones that are encoded in a physical medium and decoded by a machine. Nonetheless, the *outputs* of these translation systems are very different. Both biological and written memory produce new performances in the present, while sound recording actualizes past sonic events.

34. Cutler, "Necessity and Choice," 33.

35. Thomas Alva Edison, "The Phonograph and Its Future," *North American Review* 126 (June 1878): 527–36, available at http://www.phonozoic.net/n0020.htm.

36. Cutler, "Plunderphonia," 142.

37. The distinction between Chronos (actual, chronometric time) and Aion (virtual, nonchronometric time) is central to Deleuze's book *The Logic of Sense* (see, for example, 5, 61ff., 162ff). Though Deleuze does not always retain the terms, the distinction persists throughout his work. See, for example, *A Thousand Plateaus*, 262ff.; *Cinema 2: The Time-Image*, trans. Hugh Tomlinson and Robert Galeta (Minneapolis: University of Minnesota Press, 1989), 78–83, 98ff.; *What Is Philosophy?*, 96, 111, 156ff.; and *Negotiations*, 141, 170–71. In *Difference and Repetition* (86ff.), "Aion" is called "the pure and empty form of time," which Deleuze relates to Nietzsche's notion of "eternal recurrence." See also Deleuze's "On Four Poetic Formulas That Might Summarize the Kantian Philosophy," *Essays Critical and Clinical*, trans. Daniel W. Smith and Michael A. Greco (Minneapolis: University of Minnesota Press, 1997), 27–29.

38. For example, the track "Wind," originally released on the record *HMV Weather Effects* in 1935 and included on the 2011 compilation *. . . i listen to the wind that obliterates my traces*, disc 1, Dust to Digital DTD-20, a collection of archival recordings curated by the sound artist Steve Roden.

39. See Bergson, "Memory of the Present and False Recognition," in *Mind-Energy*, trans. H. Wildon Carr (Westport, CT: Greenwood Press, 1975), 156–68, and *Matter and Memory*, trans. Nancy Margaret Paul and W. Scott Palmer (New York: Zone Books, 1988), 133–34.

40. Attali, *Noise*, 125–26.

41. Writing in the mid-1970s, Attali was surely unaware of hip-hop, which was just emerging at the time. Yet he was certainly aware of the musique concrète founder Pierre Schaeffer, whom he quotes, and John Cage, whose *Imaginary Landscape No. 4* (1951), *Williams Mix* (1952), and *Imaginary Landscape No. 5* (1955) are pioneering instances of creative sampling and collage. Attali might also have been acquainted with dub reggae, which, in the early 1970s, began to use recording technology to alter existing reggae tracks and produce myriad different versions of them. In a few passages, Attali suggests that developments such as these indicate "musicians' anxious questioning of repetition" and rather vaguely mentions "new instruments," offering the peculiar example of the "image recorder," which presumably refers to the videocassette recorder (*Noise*, 136, 144). Yet, for the most part, Attali is so allergic to audio recording that his discussion of "composition" ignores it entirely, instead celebrating live and unmediated amateur music making. The heavily revised and abridged second edition of *Noise* (*Bruits*, nouvelle éd. [Paris: Fayard, 2001]) champions the MP3 format as signaling the death of audio recording as a commodity, but continues to celebrate live, amateur, and private music making as the only genuine instances of "composition." The discussions of reggae, rap, and techno in the revised edition are brief, superficial, and full of errors, and there is virtually no mention of sampling as creative appropriation. Lack of attention to these creative practices leads Attali to construe sound recording as simply the production of closed, dead objects, signaling a failure to acknowledge that creative appropriation, virtuality, futurity, and difference are at the very heart of audio recording.

42. Cutler, "Necessity and Choice," 33, 35.

43. See Glenn Gould, "The Prospects of Recording," in Cox and Warner, *Audio Culture*, 180ff. For readings of Gould as a sort of musical Platonist, see Kathleen M. Higgins, *The Music of Our Lives* (Philadelphia: Temple University Press, 1991), 29–30, and Andy Hamilton, "The Art of Improvisation and the Aesthetics of Imperfection," in

Teaching Music in Secondary Schools: A Reader, ed. Gary Spruce (London: Routledge, 2002), 212–13.

44. Gould, "The Prospects of Recording," 121ff.

45. László Moholy-Nagy, "Production–Reproduction" (1922) and "New Form in Music: Potentialities of the Phonograph" (1923), which appear together as "Production–Reproduction: Potentialities of the Phonograph" in Cox and Warner, *Audio Culture*, 481–84.

46. The history of these experiments is helpfully chronicled in Cutler's "Plunderphonia."

47. Listen, for example, to James Tenney, *Collage #1 (Blue Suede)* (1961) and *Viet Flakes* (1966); Terry Riley, *Music for the Gift* (1963) and *Poppy Nogood and the Phantom Band "All Night Flight"* (1968); Steve Reich, *It's Gonna Rain* (1965) and *Come Out* (1966); Pauline Oliveros, *Bye Bye Butterfly* (1965) and *I of IV* (1966); Brian Eno, *Discreet Music* (1975) and (with Robert Fripp) *No Pussyfooting* (1973); Frank Zappa, *Absolutely Free, Lumpy Gravy*, and *We're Only In It for the Money* (all 1967); the Beatles, "Tomorrow Never Knows" (1966) and "Revolution 9" (1968); Miles Davis, *In a Silent Way* (1969), *Bitches Brew* (1970), and *On the Corner* (1972); and Lee "Scratch" Perry, *Blackboard Jungle Dub* (1973).

48. Martin, quoted in Simon Reynolds, *Generation Ecstasy: Into the World of Techno and Rave Culture* (Boston: Little, Brown, 1998), 280.

49. Kevin Kelly, "Gossip is Philosophy: Brian Eno Interview," *Wired*, May 1995, https://www.wired.com/1995/05/eno-2/.

50. See Ted Gioia, *The Imperfect Art: Reflections on Jazz and Modern Culture* (New York: Oxford University Press, 1988), 63–66; James Lincoln Collier, *The Making of Jazz* (Boston: Houghton Mifflin, 1978), 72; Evan Eisenberg, *The Recording Angel: Music, Records, and Culture from Aristotle to Zappa*, 2nd ed. (New Haven, CT: Yale University Press, 2005), 117–18; and Eno, "The Studio as Compositional Tool," in Cox and Warner, *Audio Culture*, 185–86.

51. While all traditional scores are "graphic" in the sense that they are consist of black symbols on a page, the terms "graphic score" and "graphic notation" designate musical scores that employ idiosyncratic or nontraditional symbols and systems of notation that tend to be unique to each piece.

52. Earle Brown, prefatory note to *Folio and Four Systems* (New York: Associated Music Publishers, 1954), http://www.earle-brown.org/images/file/media/Folio%20and%20Four%20Systems%20Prefatory%20Note.pdf.

53. Earle Brown, liner notes to *Earle Brown: Music for Piano(s) 1951–1995*, David Arden, piano, New Albion NA082 CD, 1996.

54. See the collection of passages (by Braxton, Anthony Davis, and others) on composition and improvisation in Cox and Warner, *Audio Culture*, 353–54.

55. For example, John Zorn, *The Parachute Years, 1977–1980: Lacrosse, Hockey, Pool, Archery*, Tzadik TZ 7316, 7 CDs, 1997; and *Cobra*, Tzadik TZ 7335 CD, 2002.

56. John Cage, foreword to *A Year from Monday* (Middletown, CT: Wesleyan University Press, 1969), ix–x.

57. Roman Haubenstock-Ramati, "Music and Abstract Art: Remarks on 'Constellations,' A Suite of 25 Etchings" (1971), *Konstellationen* (Vienna: Galerie Ariadne, n.d.).

58. Quoted in John Holzaepfel, liner notes to *David Tudor and Gordon Mumma*, New World Records NWR80651 CD, 2006 http://www.newworldrecords.org/uploads/fileAdomv.pdf.

59. On Marclay's early work, see Douglas Kahn, "Christian Marclay's Early Years: An Interview," *Leonardo Music Journal* 13 (2003): 17–21; Marclay's liner notes to *Records '81–'89*, Atavistic ALP62CD, 1997; Jason Gross, "Christian Marclay Interview," *Perfect Sound Forever* (March 1998) http://www.furious.com/perfect/christianmarclay.html; and Marclay's conversation with Yasunao Tone, *Music* 1 (1997), 39–45.

60. Marclay, liner notes to *Records '81–'89*.

61. "Recorded sound is dead sound, in the sense that it's not 'live' anymore," Marclay once told an interviewer. "The music is embalmed. I'm trying to bring it back to life through my art." Quoted in Cox and Warner, *Audio Culture*, 477.

62. See John Cage, *Silence: Lectures and Writings by John Cage* (Hanover, NH: Wesleyan University Press, 1961), 13, 39, 69.

63. For an exhibition at Exit Art in 2001, Marclay produced a visual companion piece to *Record Without a Cover*: a wall grid of two hundred record covers, all copies of Herb Alpert's *Whipped Cream and Other Delights*. A variation on Warhol, the display revealed not only production differences among the various copies but also differences in wear and tear owing to each copy's unique history of circulation. See Christian Marclay, "The Inner Sleeve," *Wire*, October 2009, 77.

64. Christian Marclay, introduction to a performance of *Graffiti Piece* at the Museum of Modern Art, New York, September 13, 2006 http://www.moma.org/explore/multimedia/audios/75/102.

65. Eco, "Poetics of the Open Work," in Cox and Warner, *Audio Culture*, 243.

66. See "Conversation between Christian Marclay and David Toop," in *Arcana III: Musicians on Music*, ed. John Zorn (New York: Hip's Road, 2008), 144.

67. See Jace Clayton, "How Music Travels," in *Uproot: Travels in Twenty-First-Century Music and Digital Culture* (New York: Farrar, Straus & Giroux, 2016), 58–86.

68. Not only is it always dependent on physical objects (brains, stone tablets, paper, vinyl, computers, server farms, etc.) for storage and transmission, but information (along with matter and energy) is now generally considered by physicists and materialist philosophers to be a fundamental constituent of the physical world. The classic paper on the subject is Rolf Landauer, "Information Is Physical," *Physics Today* 44 (May 1991): 23–29, discussed in Tom Siegfried, *The Bit and the Pendulum: From Quantum Computing to M Theory; The New Physics of Information* (New York: John Wiley & Sons, 2000), 57–76. For philosophical accounts, see Daniel Dennett, "Real Patterns," *Journal of Philosophy* 88, no. 1 (1991): 27–51, and James Ladyman, "Things Aren't What They Used to Be: On the Immateriality of Matter and the Reality of Relations," in *Realism Materialism Art*, ed. Christoph Cox et al. (Berlin: Sternberg, 2015), 35–40.

69. Jonathan Sterne, "The MP3 as Cultural Artifact," *New Media & Society* 8, no. 5 (2006): 831. Cf. Diedrich Diederichsen, "Music—Immateriality—Value," *e-flux journal* 16 (May 2010), http://www.e-flux.com/journal/16/61276/music-immateriality-value, and Kenneth Goldsmith, "Six File-Sharing Epiphanies," in Cox and Warner, *Audio Culture*, 221–23. On the property status of digital music, see also Jacques Attali, "Ether Talk," *Wire*, July 2001, 70–73, and Mark Katz, *Capturing Sound: How Technology Has Changed Music* (Berkeley and Los Angeles: University of California Press, 2004), chap. 8.

70. See Attali, *Bruits*, nouvelle éd., 241ff., "Ether Talk," 73, and Angus Carlyle, "The Prophecy of Noise: An Interview with Jacques Attali," http://www.vibrofiles.com/essays_attali.php; Marcus Boon, "Collateral Damages," *Wire*, November 2011, 16; and Richard Barbrook, "The Hi-Tech Gift Economy," *First Monday* 3, no. 12 (December 7, 1998), http://www.firstmonday.org/htbin/cgiwrap/bin/ojs/index.php/fm/article/view/631/552.

71. See Diedrich Diederichsen, *On (Surplus) Value in Art* (New York: Sternberg, 2008), 46–50, and "Music—Immateriality—Value." Nearly two decades ago John Perry Barlow forecast a postdigital renaissance of live performance in "The Economy of Ideas," *Wired*, March 1994, http://www.wired.com/wired/archive/2.03/economy.ideas_pr.html. Attali underscores this idea in "Ether Talk," 73.

72. See Karl Marx and Friedrich Engels, *Manifesto of the Communist Party*, in *The Marx-Engels Reader*, 475ff., and Marx, *Capital*, Vol. 3, trans. David Fernbach (London: Penguin, 1981), 358. Deleuze and Guattari develop this conception of capitalism in *Anti-Oedipus*, 139ff., 222ff. See also Deleuze's seminars from 1971, particularly the seminar of November 16, 1971, https://www.webdeleuze.com/textes/116, and the seminar of December 14, 1971, https://www.webdeleuze.com/textes/119.

CHAPTER THREE

1. Quoted in Kittler, *Gramophone, Film, Typewriter*, trans. Geoffrey Winthrop-Young and Michael Wutz (Stanford, CA: Stanford University Press, 1999), 22.

2. Edison, "The Perfected Phonograph," *North American Review* 146 (June 1888): 646, which refers back to "The Phonograph and Its Future," *North American Review* 126 (June 1878): 531ff. Both essays are available at http://www.phonozoic.net/library.html. On the early history of the phonograph and its relationship to speech and writing, see Lisa Gitelman, "New Media Publics," in *Always Already New: Media, History, and the Data of Culture* (Cambridge, MA: MIT Press, 2006), 25–57.

3. See Plato, *Phaedrus*, 276a. My account here borrows, of course, from Derrida's early work on speech and writing, presented in texts such as *Speech and Phenomena*, trans. David B. Allison (Evanston, IL: Northwestern University Press, 1973); "Plato's Pharmacy," in *Dissemination*, trans. Barbara Johnson (Chicago: University of Chicago Press, 1981); and "Signature Event Context," in *Margins of Philosophy*, trans. Alan Bass (Chicago: University of Chicago Press, 1982)

4. Jacques Derrida, "Signature Event Context," 316; my italics. This conception of the "machine" runs throughout Derrida's work, notably his discussions of Freud's "mystic writing pad" in "Freud and the Scene of Writing," in *Writing and Difference*, trans. Alan Bass (Chicago: University of Chicago Press, 1978), 196–231, and *Archive Fever: A Freudian Impression*, trans. Eric Prenowitz (Chicago: University of Chicago Press, 1996). In all these texts, Derrida argues, with and against Freud, that consciousness and memory operate in the manner of a mechanical prosthesis. I discuss these issues more fully below.

5. Edison, "The Man Who Invents," *Washington Post*, April 19, 1878, http://www.phonozoic.net/n0031.htm.

6. For more on this, see Douglas Kahn, "Histories of Sound Once Removed," in *Wireless Imagination: Sound, Radio, and the Avant-Garde*, ed. Douglas Kahn and Gregory Whitehead (Cambridge, MA: MIT Press, 1992), 14–26. Of course, phonography also inspired, and was inspired by, interest in the occult and spiritualism. See Erik Davis, "Recording Angels: The Esoteric Origins of the Phonograph," in *Undercurrents: The Hidden Wiring of Modern Music*, ed. Rob Young (New York: Continuum, 2002), 15–24.

7. For discussions of the ear phonautograph, see Jonathan Sterne, *The Audible Past: Cultural Origins of Sound Reproduction* (Durham, NC: Duke University Press, 2003), chap. 1, and Steven Connor, *Dumbstruck: A Cultural History of Ventriloquism* (Oxford: Oxford University Press, 2000), 356–61.

8. Sterne, *The Audible Past*, 33, 71, and "The MP3 as Cultural Artifact," *New Media and Society* 8, no. 5 (2006): 837.

9. Roland Barthes, "Listening," in *The Responsibility of Forms*, trans. Richard Howard (New York: Hill & Wang, 1985), 245–60.

10. Barthes, "Listening," 245, 247.

11. Barthes, "Listening," 245. Compare Igor Stravinsky's remark: "To listen is an effort, and just to hear is no merit. A duck hears also"; quoted in Stravinsky and Robert Craft, *Memories and Commentaries* (London: Faber & Faber, 2001), xvii.

12. Barthes, "Listening," 245, 249.

13. Barthes, "Listening," 245.

14. David Hume, *A Treatise on Human Nature*, ed. L. A. Selby-Bigge (Oxford: Oxford University Press, 1978), 252.

15. See Hume: "The whole of this doctrine leads us to a conclusion, which is of great importance to the present affair, *viz.* that all the nice and subtle questions concerning personal identity . . . are to be regarded rather as grammatical than as philosophical difficulties" (*Treatise*, 262). Hume's rejection of the self is supported by more recent neurophilosophical accounts such as Thomas Metzinger, *Being No One: The Self-Model Theory of Subjectivity* (Cambridge, MA: MIT Press, 2003), and Derek Parfit, "Divided Minds and the Nature of Persons," in *Mindwaves: Thoughts on Intelligence, Identity, and Consciousness*, ed. Colin Blakemore and Susan Greenfield (Oxford: Basil Blackwell, 1987), 19–26.

16. *On the Genealogy of Morals*, Essay I, §13, in *On the Genealogy of Morals and Ecce Homo*, trans. Walter Kaufmann and R. J. Hollingdale (New York: Vintage Books, 1969), 45. In *Twilight of the Idols*, Nietzsche writes: "Everywhere [language] sees a doer and a doing; it believes in will as the cause; it believes in the 'I,' in the I as being, in the I as substance, and it *projects* this faith in the I-substance upon all things." *The Portable Nietzsche*, ed. and trans. Walter Kaufmann (New York: Viking, 1968); translation modified. For more on Nietzsche's critique of the self, see my *Nietzsche: Naturalism and Interpretation* (Berkeley and Los Angeles: University of California Press, 1999), 118–39.

17. Nietzsche, *Writings from the Late Notebooks*, ed. Rüdiger Bittner, trans. Kate Sturge (Cambridge: Cambridge University Press, 2003), 139.

18. Nietzsche, "Reason in Philosophy," in *Twilight of the Idols*.

19. Hume, *Treatise*, 253.

20. See, for example, *Writings from the Late Notebooks*, 115, 165, 264.

21. Nietzsche, *Genealogy of Morals*, 77, 151.

22. See, for example, *Beyond Good and Evil*, trans. Walter Kaufmann (New York: Vintage, 1966), §§6, 12, 19, and *Writings from the Late Notebooks*, §§40 [21], 40 [46], 2 [151–52], 14 [79].

23. Nietzsche, *Writings from the Late Notebooks*, §14 [98].

24. See Nietzsche, *The Gay Science*, trans. Walter Kaufmann (New York: Vintage, 1974), §§333, 354, and the early essay "On Truth and Lies in a Nonmoral Sense," in *Philosophy and Truth: Selections from Nietzsche's Notebooks of the 1870s*, ed. and trans. Daniel Breazeale (Atlantic Highlands, NJ: Humanities Press International, 1979).

25. For Butler on life, habit, and consciousness, see his *Life and Habit* (London: Trübner, 1878), *The Notebooks of Samuel Butler*, ed. Henry Festing Jones (London: Hogarth Press, 1985), esp. 39–92, and *Erewhon* (London: Penguin, 1985), 198–226. For a related account, see William James, *The Principles of Psychology*, Vol. 1 (New York: Henry Holt, 1890), chap. IV.

26. Deleuze first develops the notion of "habit" and "passive synthesis" in *Difference and Repetition*, trans. Paul Patton (New York: Columbia University Press, 1994), 70–79. He returns to this idea in the second chapter of *Anti-Oedipus*, trans. Robert Hurley et al. (Minneapolis: University of Minnesota Press, 1983), and again in *What Is Philosophy?*, trans. Hugh Tomlinson and Graham Burchell (New York: Columbia University Press, 1994), 104–6, 210–18.

27. See, for example, Gilles Deleuze and Félix Guattari, *A Thousand Plateaus*, trans. Brian Massumi (Minneapolis: University of Minnesota Press, 1987), 371, 408ff.

28. Prigogine and Isabelle Stengers, *Order out of Chaos* (New York: Bantam Books, 1984), 14 (and cf. 165). See also Prigogine, "Order out of Chaos," in *Disorder and Order*, ed. Paisley Livingston (Saratoga, CA: Anma Libri, 1984), 46.

29. Whitehead invents the term "prehension" for this generalized perception: "The word *perceive* is, in our common usage, shot through and through with the notion of cognitive apprehension. So is the word *apprehension*, even with the adjective *cognitive* omitted. I will use the word *prehension* for *uncognitive apprehension*: by this I mean *apprehension* which may or may not be cognitive." *Science in the Modern World* (New York: Macmillan, 1925), 69. For prehension as "taking account," see 41–42, where Whitehead quotes the materialist philosopher Francis Bacon, who writes: "It is certain that all bodies whatsoever, though they have no sense, yet they have perception; for when one body is applied to another, there is a kind of election to embrace that which is agreeable, and to exclude that which is ingrate; and whether the body be alterant or altered, evermore a perception precedeth operation; for else all bodies would be like one to another. And sometimes this perception, in some kind of bodies, is far more subtile than sense; so that sense is but a dull thing in comparison of it: we see a weather-glass will find the least difference of the weather in heat or cold, when we find it not. And this perception is sometimes at a distance, as well as upon the touch; as when the loadstone draweth iron; or flame naphtha of Babylon, a great distance off. It is therefore a subject of a very noble inquiry, to enquire of the more subtile perceptions; for it is another key to open nature, as well as the sense; and sometimes better."

30. Brian Massumi, *Semblance and Event: Activist Philosophy and the Occurrent Arts* (Cambridge, MA: MIT Press, 2011), 26.

31. Deleuze, *Difference and Repetition*, 73.

32. See Deleuze and Guattari, *What Is Philosophy?*, 212–13, and *Difference and Repetition*, 75.

33. Deleuze, *Difference and Repetition*, 75, 78.

34. Deleuze, *Difference and Repetition*, 74.

35. Deleuze, *Difference and Repetition*, 74; italics mine.

36. See Deleuze and Guattari, *What Is Philosophy?*, 211, 212, 215. The term "superject" is from Whitehead, who writes: "For Kant, the world emerges from the subject; for the philosophy of organism [Whitehead's own position], the subject emerges from the world—a 'superject' rather than a 'subject.'" *Process and Reality* (New York: Free Press, 1978), 88.

37. "Everything I've written is vitalistic, at least I hope it is," remarked Deleuze in a 1988 interview. "On Philosophy," *Negotiations*, trans. Martin Joughin (New York: Columbia University Press, 1995), 143. Elsewhere, however, his relationship to vitalism—and to the supposed opposition between vitalism and mechanism—is more complex. See, for example, *Anti-Oedipus*, 283ff., and *What Is Philosophy?*, 213. Deleuze's "vitalism" has been recently criticized by Quentin Meillassoux, Ray Brassier, and others,

who see it as fundamentally idealist or "subjectalist," that is, as projecting traits of the human subject (thought, sentience, will, life, etc.) into inanimate nature. See Meillassoux, "Iteration, Reiteration, Repetition: A Speculative Analysis of the Sign Devoid of Meaning," in *Genealogies of Speculation: Materialism and Subjectivity Since Structuralism*, ed. Armen Avanessian (London: Continuum, 2016), 121–22, 124, 132; and Brassier, *Nihil Unbound: Enlightenment and Extinction* (Basingstoke: Palgrave Macmillan, 2007), 196ff., 227ff. While this critique may apply to traditional vitalisms, it does not apply to Deleuze's, which, I argue, undermines both sides of the opposition life/inert matter and accounts for the nature of life in a manner fully consonant with contemporary evolutionary biology. By contrast, Meillassoux's remarks on the emergence of life are oddly pre-Darwinian. See Meillassoux, "Potentiality and Virtuality," trans. Robin Mackay, in *The Speculative Turn: Continental Realism and Materialism*, ed. Levi Bryant et al. (Melbourne: Re-Press, 2011), 235, and the critique of Meillassoux in Martin Hägglund, "Radical Atheist Materialism: A Critique of Meillassoux," in *The Speculative Turn*, 121–22.

38. On this feature of Darwinism, see Daniel Dennett, *Darwin's Dangerous Idea: Evolution and the Meanings of Life* (New York: Simon & Schuster, 1995), chaps. 2–3.

39. On "desiring-machines," see *Anti-Oedipus*, passim. On the "machinic phylum," see *A Thousand Plateaus*, 406ff., and Manuel DeLanda, "Nonorganic Life," in *Incorporations*, ed. Jonathan Crary and Sanford Kwinter (New York: Zone, 1992), 129–67.

40. See *Anti-Oedipus*, 2, 36, 41. Also see Manuel DeLanda's discussion of hurricanes as, literally, steam motors in *A Thousand Years of Nonlinear History*, 58–59.

41. See Deleuze, *Desert Islands*, 219.

42. An amateur philosopher, Edison sketched a related theory of the organism and of matter as a collection of machines. See *The Diary and Sundry Observations of Thomas Alva Edison*, ed. Dagobert D. Runes (New York: Philosophical Library, 1948), 215ff., 241ff.

43. On sensation, see Deleuze and Guattari, *What Is Philosophy?*, 211ff., and Deleuze, *Francis Bacon: The Logic of Sensation*, trans. Daniel W. Smith (New York: Continuum, 2003).

44. Aden Evens offers a helpful account of hearing in *Sound Ideas* (Minneapolis: University of Minnesota Press, 2005), 1ff.

45. This example occurs throughout Henri Bergson's discussions of duration.

46. Butler, *Erewhon*, chap. 24, and "Darwin among the Machines," in *Notebooks*, 46.

47. Kittler, *Gramophone, Film, Typewriter*, 23.

48. Cage, "Future of Music: Credo," *Silence*, 4.

49. I allude to Iannis Xenakis's *Concret PH* on *Xenakis: Electronic Music*, Electronic Music Foundation EMF CD 003, 1997; Luc Ferrari's *Presque Rien*, INA-GRM 245172 CD, 1995; and Alvin Lucier's *I Am Sitting in a Room*, Lovely CD 1013, 1993.

50. Paul DeMarinis, "On Sonic Spaces," in *Sound*, ed. Caleb Kelly (London: Whitechapel Gallery, 2011), 74.

51. Kittler, *Gramophone, Film, Typewriter*, 23; my italics. For Lacan's discussion of the materiality of language in relationship to telecommunications technology, see *The Seminar of Jacques Lacan, Book II: The Ego in Freud's Theory and in the Technique of Psychoanalysis, 1954–1955*, ed. Jacques-Alain Miller, trans. Sylvana Tomaselli (New York: W. W. Norton, 1988), 82–83.

52. Sterne, *The Audible Past*, 33, 43, 71.

53. Kittler, *Gramophone, Film, Typewriter*, 22, 24. Elsewhere, Kittler writes: "It is

Edison's phonograph that first allows for the possibility of a methodical, distinct separation between the real and the symbolic." "The World of the Symbolic: A World of the Machine," in *Literature, Media, Information Systems*, ed. John Johnson (Amsterdam: G+B Arts International, 1997), 139–40. My use of the terms "symbolic" and "Real" follows Friedrich Kittler's Nietzschean, materialist reading of Lacan rather than the Kantian, idealist reading favored by Slavoj Žižek, Alain Badiou, and others.

54. Freud, "A Note upon the 'Mystic Writing Pad,'" in *General Psychological Theory: Papers on Metapsychology*, ed. Philip Rieff (New York: Simon & Schuster, 1991), 213.

55. Freud, "A Note upon the 'Mystic Writing Pad,'" 215.

56. On this issue see Derrida, "Freud and the Scene of Writing," 226ff.

57. The literary-theoretical texts are primarily *The Ticket That Exploded* (New York: Grove, 1962), particularly the appendix, titled "The Invisible Generation"; "Playback from Eden to Watergate" and "Electronic Revolution," in Burroughs and Daniel Odier, *The Job: Topical Writings and Interviews* (London: John Calder, 1984); and "Ten Years and a Billion Dollars" and "It Belongs to the Cucumbers" in *The Adding Machine: Selected Essays* (New York: Seaver Books, 1986). Recordings of Burroughs's literary and tape cut-up experiments are collected on *Break Through in Grey Room*, Sub Rosa SR 08 CD, 2001, and *Nothing Here Now but the Recordings*, disc 4 of *The Best of William Burroughs from Giorno Poetry Systems*, Mercury 314 536 700–2, 4 CDs, 1998.

58. Burroughs, "Invisible Generation," 213.

59. Deleuze calls this the "universal thought flow," which, for the most part, is characterized by stupidity, cliché, and conformity. To think or to create, for Deleuze, is to cut into this flow and extract something from it. See Deleuze, "Vincennes Session of April 15, 1980, Leibniz Seminar," trans. Charles J. Stivale. *Discourse* 20, no. 3 (Fall 1998): 78. For a helpful discussion of this idea, see Daniel W. Smith, "On the Becoming of Concepts," in *Essays on Deleuze* (Edinburgh: Edinburgh University Press, 2012), 140–45.

60. See *The Job*, 12, 187.

61. See Luis P. Villareal, "Are Viruses Alive?" *Scientific American* 291, no. 6 (December 2004): 100–105. The debate about whether or not viruses are alive continues to rage. See, for example, David Moreira and Purificación López-Garcia, "Ten Reasons to Exclude Viruses from the Tree of Life," *Nature Reviews Microbiology* 7 (April 2009): 306–11; Jean-Michel Claverie and Hiroyuki Ogata, "Ten Good Reasons Not to Exclude Giruses from the Evolutionary Picture," *Nature Reviews Microbiology* 7 (August 2009): 615; and Siobhan Gallagher, "New Study Shows Viruses Can Have Immune Systems," *TuftsNow* (February 27, 2013) http://now.tufts.edu/news-releases/new-study-shows-viruses-can-have-immune-syste.

62. Butler, *Erewhon*, chap. 24, and "Darwin among the Machines," in *Notebooks*, 46.

63. Cf. Dawkins: "When you plant a fertile meme in my mind you literally parasitize my brain, turning it into a vehicle for the meme's propagation in just the way that a virus can parasitize the genetic mechanism of a host cell. And this isn't just a way of talking—the meme for, say, 'belief in life after death' is actually realized physically, millions of times over, as a structure in the nervous systems of individual men the world over." *The Selfish Gene*, 30th anniversary ed. (Oxford: Oxford University Press, 2006), 192. Dawkins's conception of memes has been developed by Daniel Dennett, who regards language itself as a viral meme. See his *Consciousness Explained* (New York: Little, Brown, 1991), 199–252, and *From Bacteria to Bach and Back: The Evolution of Minds* (New York: W. W. Norton, 2017), 173, 189, 205–47. Douglas Kahn notes that Burroughs's concept of memetics derives from the work of Richard Semon, an

early twentieth-century biologist whose concept of the "mneme" anticipates Dawkins's "meme." See Kahn, *Noise, Water, Meat: A History of Sound in the Arts* (Cambridge, MA: MIT Press, 1999), 314ff.

64. Burroughs, "Invisible Generation," 213. A nearly identical passage appears earlier in *The Ticket That Exploded*, 163.

65. Burroughs, "Invisible Generation," 217.

66. "Inching . . ." and "The Saints Go Marching . . ." appear on *Nothing Here Now but the Recordings*. The other pieces appear on *Break Through in Grey Room*.

67. Burroughs, "Invisible Generation," 206.

68. Burroughs, "Invisible Generation," 207–8.

69. Burroughs, "Electronic Revolution," 185.

70. Burroughs, "Electronic Revolution," 185–86. See also *The Adding Machine*, 53, 59.

71. Burroughs, "Electronic Revolution," 185. A more recent essay from the same journal makes just this point about déjà vu: "If the brain's memory system is like a tape recorder, it is as if the recording head has got muddled with the playback head." Helen Phillips, "Déjà Vu: Where Fact Meets Fantasy," *New Scientist* 2701 (March 25, 2009): 28, cited in Steven Connor, "Looping the Loop: Tape-Time in Burroughs and Beckett" (2010), http://www.stevenconnor.com/looping/.

72. Burroughs, "Invisible Generation," 205, 208.

73. *The Job*, 28. Elsewhere Burroughs puts it slightly differently: "Perhaps when you cut into the present the future leaks out." "Origin and Theory of the Tape Cut-Ups," on *Break Through in Grey Room*.

74. Barthes, "Listening," 245, 258.

75. Freud, "Recommendations to Physicians Practicing Psycho-Analysis," quoted in Barthes, "Listening," 252. Barthes's translator, Richard Howard, quotes Joan Rivière's translation, which I find less clear than the original Strachey translation, quoted here from *The Freud Reader*, ed. Peter Gay (New York: W. W. Norton, 1989), 360.

76. Freud, "Recommendations," quoted in Barthes, "Listening," translation from *The Freud Reader*, 357.

77. Kittler, *Gramophone, Film, Typewriter*, 87ff. In the "Dora" case, Freud remarks that his account is "not absolutely—phonographically—exact, but it can claim to possess a high degree of trustworthiness." *The Freud Reader*, 175, partially quoted by Kittler in *Gramophone, Film, Typewriter*, 90.

78. See Barthes, "Listening," 252; my italics.

79. Barthes, "Listening," 255. Barthes famously developed this idea in an essay published a few years earlier, "The Grain of the Voice," in *The Responsibility of Forms*, 267–77.

80. Ferdinand de Saussure, *Course in General Linguistics*, trans. Roy Harris (New York: Bloomsbury, 2013), 139. For a critique of Saussure and Barthes on this issue, see Mladen Dolar, *A Voice and Nothing More* (Cambridge, MA: MIT Press, 2006), 14ff., 197n10.

81. Hugo Ball, *Flight Out of Time: A Dada Diary*, ed. John Elderfield, trans. Ann Raimes (Berkeley and Los Angeles: University of California Press, 1996), 57. Boris Groys reads Ball's *Lautgedichte* "as the self-destruction of the traditional poem; as the exposure of the downfall and disappearance of the individual voice; the descent of the human form into the totality of the material flow." Groys continues: "[Ball] experienced and described the reading of his work as an exhausting exposure of the human voice to

the demonic forces of noise. . . . allowing them to reduce his own voice to pure noise, to senseless, purely material process." Groys, "Entering the Flow," in *In the Flow* (London: Verso, 2016), 15–16.

82. See Steve McCaffery, "From Phonic to Sonic: The Emergence of the Audio-Poem," in *Sound States: Innovative Poetics and Acoustical Technologies*, ed. Adalaide Morris (Chapel Hill: University of North Carolina Press, 1997). Much of this history can be heard on *Revue OU: An Anthology of Sound Poetry 1958–1974*, Alga Marghen 15vocsono45.1, 4 CDs, 2002.

83. Barthes, "Listening," 259.

84. Though he wrote chamber and orchestral pieces throughout the 1950s and early 1960s, Lucier counts his 1965 piece *Music for Solo Performer* as the proper beginning of his compositional career. See "Discovery is Part of the Experience," in Alvin Lucier, *Reflections: Interviews, Scores, Writings* (Köln: MusikTexte, 1995), 26. *North American Time Capsule* was initially issued in 1968 on an LP titled *Extended Voices*, Odyssey 32 16 0156 LP, 1967, a collection of experimental vocal pieces by Lucier, John Cage, Pauline Oliveros and others performed by the Brandeis University Chamber Chorus under Lucier's direction. *NATC* was reissued on Lucier's *Vespers and Other Early Works*, New World Records, 80604–2 CD, 2002.

85. For more on this contrast, see Georgina Born, *Rationalizing Culture: IRCAM, Boulez, and the Institutionalization of the Musical Avant-Garde* (Berkeley and Los Angeles: University of California Press, 1995), 40–65. Along similar lines, Michael Nyman's seminal text *Experimental Music: Cage and Beyond* (Cambridge: Cambridge University Press, 1999; originally published in 1974) sharply contrasts "avant-garde" musical practice with "experimental music." See also my "The Jerrybuilt Future: The Sonic Arts Union, ONCE Group and MEV's Live Electronics," in *Undercurrents*, 35–44.

86. Cage, "Experimental Music: Doctrine," in *Silence: Lectures and Writings by John Cage* (Hanover, NH: University Press of New England/Wesleyan University Press, 1961), 13. Cf. 39, 69.

87. Lucier, "*North American Time Capsule*," in *Reflections*, 408.

88. Lucier, telephone interview with Christoph Cox, July 19, 2006.

89. On the cultural history of the vocoder, see Mara Mills, "Media and Prosthesis: The Vocoder, the Artificial Larynx, and the History of Signal Processing," *Qui Parle* 21, no. 1 (Fall–Winter 2012): 107–49; Jacob Smith, "Tearing Speech to Pieces: Voice Technologies of the 1940s," *Music, Sound, and the Moving Image* 2, no. 2 (Autumn 2008): 183–206; Alexander G. Weheliye, "'Feenin': Posthuman Voices in Contemporary Black Popular Music," *Social Text* 71 (Summer 2002): 21–47; and Dave Tomkins, *How To Wreck a Nice Beach: The Vocoder from World War II to Hip Hop* (Brooklyn: Melville House, 2010).

90. See Manfred R. Schroeder, "Speech Processing," in *Signal Processing for Multimedia*, ed. J. S. Bynes (Amsterdam: IOS Press, 1999), 129.

91. See Peter Manning, *Electronic and Computer Music*, rev. and expanded ed. (Oxford: Oxford University Press, 2004), 39ff., and Joel Chadabe, *Electric Sound: The Past and Promise of Electronic Music* (Upper Saddle River, NJ: Prentice Hall, 1997), 35ff.

92. See Manning, *Electronic and Computer Music*, 187ff.; Chadabe, *Electric Sound*, 108ff.; and "Recollections by John Pierce," *Music with Computers: The Historical CD of Digital Sound Synthesis (Computer Music Currents 13)*, Wergo WER 2033–2 CD, 1995, liner notes, 9.

93. Many of these early computer pieces were released in 1962 on the Decca LP

Music from Mathematics, Decca DL 79103 LP. They are currently available on the CD *Music with Computers*.

94. See Lucier, "Origins of a Form: Acoustical Exploration, Science, and Incessancy," *Leonardo Music Journal* 8 (1998): 5.

95. Lucier, interview with Cox.

96. Lucier, prose score for *The Only Talking Machine of Its Kind in the World*, in *Reflections*, 308.

97. Lucier, prose score for *The Duke of York*, in *Reflections*, 324.

98. The piece appears on Lucier, *Bird and Person Dyning*, Cramps/Get Back GET 420 LP, 2002.

99. Lucier, *I Am Sitting in a Room*, Lovely CD 1013, 1993. The prose score appears in *Reflections*, 312–14.

100. See Kittler, *Gramophone, Film, Typewriter*, 49–50.

101. See Dolar, *A Voice and Nothing More*, chap. 1.

102. On the relationship between "music" and "sound art" in Lucier's work, see his interview with N. B. Aldrich, "What Is Sound Art?," EMF Institute, 2003, http://www.nbaldrich.com/media/pdfs/what_is_sound_art.pdf.

103. Cage, "Future of Music: Credo," in *Silence*, 4.

104. In his liner notes to *I Am Sitting in a Room*, Nicolas Collins also objects to this characterization, though on somewhat different grounds. Lucier describes himself as a "phenomenologist" in an interview with Douglas Simon, though his characterization of this stance is more in line with a sort of scientific materialism. "The Poetry of Science: *Music on a Long Thin Wire* (1977): Interview with Douglas Simon," in *Reflections*, 194.

105. Lucier, "Origins of a Form," 8. Lucier refers to his *Queen of the South* (1972), which presents the eighteenth-century German physicist E. F. P. Chladni's experiments in the visualization of sound; *Tyndall Orchestrations* (1976), which, in the manner of the nineteenth-century Irish physicist John Tyndall, investigates the effects of sound on gas flames; *Music for Pure Waves, Bass Drums and Acoustic Pendulums* (1980), which, Lucier notes, "is simply an orchestration of an experiment I discovered in a British college textbook on the physics of sound" ("Origins of a Form," 9); and *Spira Mirabilis* (1994), based on the biologist D'Arcy Thompson's drawings of insect movements. One might also include *Music for Solo Performer* (1965), based on the research of the physicist Edmond Dewan; *Vespers* (1969), inspired by the cognitive ethologist Donald R. Griffin's work on acoustic orientation and sensory biophysics; *Quasimodo the Great Lover* (1971), inspired by the biologist Roger S. Payne's research on whale communication; and *Music on a Long Thin Wire* (1977), which began as a collaboration with the physicist John Trefny.

106. Initially conceived as a piece to be played by one or more performers, Lucier soon altered his conception. "I was not happy with any of these performances," he wrote in 1992. "The music never went beyond a kind of poetic improvisation. I finally decided to remove my hand from the musical process." The available recording consists of four realizations from 1979 in which "no alteration of the tuning or manipulation of the wire was made in any way. The wire played itself." Liner notes to *Music on a Long Thin Wire*, Lovely Music LCD 1011, 1992.

107. See Lucier's interview with Douglas Simon, "Composite Identities of Real or Imagined Persons: *The Duke of York* (1971)," in *Reflections*, 120–24.

108. Lucier, "Imitating One Set of Sounds with Another: *(Hartford) Memory Space (1970)*: Interview with Douglas Simon," in *Reflections*, 100–102.

109. Lucier, "Every Room Has Its Own Melody: *'I Am Sitting in a Room'* (1970): Interview with Douglas Simon," in *Reflections*, 88.

110. Lucier, "Composite Identities," 118; my italics.

111. "Alvin Lucier in Conversation with Thomas Moore," Marymount Manhattan College, New York City, January 12, 1983, http://thomasmoore.info/interview-alvin-lucier.

112. In a commentary on Bergson, Deleuze writes: "Memory is not in us; it is we who move in a Being-memory, a world-memory"; *Cinema 2: The Time Image*, trans. Hugh Tomlinson and Robert Galeta (Minneapolis: University of Minnesota Press, 1989), 98. On the notion of "ontological memory," see Deleuze, *Bergsonism*, trans. Hugh Tomlinson and Barbara Habberjam (New York: Zone Books, 1988), chap. III.

113. See Lucier's description of his process of composition in "Composite Identities," 116ff.

114. Lucier, prose score for *The Duke of York*, 324.

115. Lucier, "Composite Identities," 126.

116. Lucier, "Composite Identities," 124.

CHAPTER FOUR

1. For a history of sound art exhibitions, see Seth Cluett, "Ephemeral, Immersive, Invasive: Sound as Curatorial Theme, 1966–2013," in *The Multisensory Museum: Cross-Disciplinary Perspectives on Touch, Sound, Smell, Memory, and Space*, ed. Nina Levent and Alvaro Pascual-Leone (Lanham, MD: Rowman & Littlefield, 2014).

2. Max Neuhaus, "Sound Art?," http://www.max-neuhaus.info/soundworks/soundart/SoundArt.htm. For a compilation of responses by artists and critics, see "Sound Art? An Archive," *Ear Room* (blog), 2009–http://earroom.wordpress.com/sound-art.

3. See, for example, Alan Licht, *Sound Art: Beyond Music, Between Categories* (New York: Rizzoli, 2007), 210–11; Joanna Demers, *Listening through the Noise: The Aesthetics of Experimental Electronic Music* (Oxford: Oxford University Press, 2010), 124, 129; and Chris Mann, "What Is Sound Art? An Interview with N. B. Aldrich," EMF Institute, 2003, http://www.nbaldrich.com/media/pdfs/what_is_sound_art.pdf.

4. See, e.g., "Audio Files: Sound Art Now: An Online Symposium," moderated by Christoph Cox, Artforum.com, April–May 2004, http://artforum.com/symposium/id=6682.

5. See Brian Kane, "Musicophobia, or Sound Art and the Demands of Art Theory," *nonsite.org* 8 (January 20, 2013): http://nonsite.org/article/musicophobia-or-sound-art-and-the-demands-of-art-theory. The term "musicomania" is my own but is suggested by Luigi Russolo's rebuke of "musicomaniacs" in "The Art of Noises: Futurist Manifesto," in *The Art of Noises*, trans. Barclay Brown (New York: Pendragon Press, 1986), 25.

6. See Ultra-red, *Five Protocols for Organized Listening* (2012), http://www.ultrared.org/uploads/2012-Five_Protocols.pdf.

7. See, e.g., Licht, *Sound Art*, 14, 16–17; Brandon LaBelle, *Background Noise: Perspectives on Sound Art* (New York: Continuum, 2006), 151; and Nick Collins, Margaret Schedel, and Scott Wilson, "Sound Art," in *Electronic Music* (Cambridge: Cambridge University Press, 2013), 151.

8. See, e.g., Carsten Seiffarth, "About Installation Art," *Kunstjournalen B-post* (2012), http://www.kunstjournalen.no/12_eng/carsten-seiffarth-about-sound-installation-art; Bernd Schulz, introduction to *Resonances: Aspects of Sound Art*, ed. Bernd Schulz (Heidelberg: Kehrer Verlag, 2002), 14; Sabine Sanio, "Aspekte der Klangkunst," quoted in

Andreas Engström and Åsa Stjerna, "Sound Art or *Klangkunst*: A Reading of the German and English Literature on Sound Art," *Organised Sound* 14, no. 1 (2009): 12; Stephen Vitiello, "What Is Sound Art? An Interview with N. B. Aldrich," EMF Institute, 2003, http://www.nbaldrich.com/media/pdfs/what_is_sound_art.pdf; Demers, *Listening through the Noise*, 6, 175; and Gascia Ouzounian, "Sound Art," in *Encyclopedia of Aesthetics*, ed. Michael Kelly, 2nd ed. (Oxford: Oxford University Press, 2014), 27–31, which provides a helpful overview. For an objection to this view, see Douglas Kahn, "Sound Art, Art, Music," *Iowa Review Web* 7, no. 1 (August 2005), http://thestudio.uiowa.edu/tirw/TIRW_Archive/feb06/Kahn_Sound_Art.pdf.

9. Michel Serres, *Genesis*, trans. Geneviève James and James Nielson (Ann Arbor: University of Michigan Press, 1995), 7, 13

10. As the father of information theory, Claude Shannon, put it: "The fundamental problem of communication is that of reproducing at one point either exactly or approximately a message selected at another point." "A Mathematical Theory of Communication," *Bell System Technical Journal* 27, no. 3 (July 1948): 379.

11. Varèse, "The Liberation of Sound," in *Audio Culture: Readings in Modern Music*, ed. Christoph Cox and Daniel Warner, rev. ed. (New York: Bloomsbury, 2017), 20.

12. Abraham Moles, *Information Theory and Esthetic Perception*, trans. Joel E. Coen (Urbana: University of Illinois Press, 1966), 78.

13. Serres wrote his doctoral thesis on Leibniz, who has remained crucial to his philosophy.

14. Leibniz's differential theory of the unconscious has been revived by Gilles Deleuze, who finds in it a compelling alternative to Freud's conflictual model. See, for example, Deleuze, *Difference and Repetition*, trans. Paul Patton (New York: Columbia University Press, 1994), 107–8, and Seminar April 29, 1980, https://www.webdeleuze.com/textes/55.

15. G. W. Leibniz, *Philosophical Essays*, ed. and trans. Roger Ariew and Daniel Garber (Indianapolis: Hackett, 1989), 211. This example (and the associated examples of the mill and waterfall) are recurrent in Leibniz's corpus. They appear in the *Discourse on Metaphysics*, the letters to Arnauld, the *New Essays on Human Understanding*, and elsewhere.

16. This theory receives its fullest elaboration in Leibniz, *New Essays on Human Understanding*, ed. and trans. Peter Remnant and Jonathan Bennett (Cambridge: Cambridge University Press, 1996), 52ff., 115ff. "Apperception" is Leibniz's technical term for conscious perception, while unconscious perceptions are generally termed "perceptions" or "minute perceptions."

17. In their translation of Leibniz's *New Essays on Human Understanding* (e.g., 52), Remnant and Bennett translate as "potentialities" and "implicit" what, in Leibniz's French, are *virtualités* and *virtuel*, respectively.

18. Henri Bergson explores this issue in great detail. And, indeed, it is from Bergson that Gilles Deleuze derives his distinction between the virtual and the actual. We see, however, that this distinction can be traced back beyond Bergson to Leibniz.

19. See, for example, Leibniz, *New Essays*, 54–55, 113, and also *Discourse on Metaphysics*, §8–9, *Principles of Nature and Grace* §13, and *Monadology* §61, the latter three included in *Philosophical Essays*.

20. Aden Evens, *Sound Ideas: Music, Machines, and Experience* (Minneapolis: University of Minnesota Press, 2005), 14.

21. See also *Discourse on Metaphysics*, §§8–9, in *Philosophical Essays*, 40–42.

22. Bart Kosko, *Noise* (New York: Viking, 2006), 65.

23. On the two interpretations of Leibniz's theory of perception, see Deleuze, *Difference and Repetition*, 213–14; *The Fold: Leibniz and the Baroque*, trans. Tom Conley (Minneapolis: University of Minnesota Press, 1988), 87ff.; and Deleuze, Seminar April 29, 1980.

24. Leibniz, *New Essays*, 134.

25. Gilles Deleuze, "Vincennes Session of April 15, 1980, Leibniz Seminar," trans. Charles J. Stivale. *Discourse* 20, no. 3 (Fall 1998): 78, translation modified.

26. See Leibniz, *New Essays*, 113, and, *The Monadology*, in *Philosophical Essays*, 215–16. Serres discusses this theory in *Genesis*, 20.

27. Serres, *Genesis*, 13.

28. Serres, *Genesis*, 37. Balzac's story is the subject of this book's first chapter and an important touchstone in subsequent chapters. See Honoré de Balzac, *The Unknown Masterpiece and Gambara*, trans. Richard Howard (New York: New York Review of Books, 2001).

29. See chap. 1. In a brief remark, Deleuze suggests this rich connection between Leibniz and Nietzsche: "Leibniz very nearly encountered Dionysus at the sea shore or near the water mill. Perhaps Apollo, the clear-confused thinker, is needed in order to think the Ideas of Dionysus"; *Difference and Repetition*, 214.

30. See Kittler, *Gramophone, Film, Typewriter*, trans. Geoffrey Winthrop-Young and Michael Wutz (Stanford, CA: Stanford University Press, 1999), 23, and the discussion of Kittler in chap. 3.

31. Kittler, *Gramophone, Film, Typewriter*, 23.

32. Luigi Russolo, "The Art of Noises," 25.

33. Russolo, "The Art of Noises," 24, 25.

34. Russolo, "The Art of Noises," 27, 25.

35. For a rich discussion of the theme of continuity in Russolo and Futurism, see Luciano Chessa, *Luigi Russolo, Futurist: Noise, Visual Arts, and the Occult* (Berkeley and Los Angeles: University of California Press, 2012), 143ff.

36. F. T. Marinetti, "The Variety Theater," and Carlo Carrà, "The Painting of Sounds, Noises, and Smells" in Lawrence Rainey, Christine Poggi, and Laura Wittman, eds., *Futurism: An Anthology* (New Haven, CT: Yale University Press, 2009), 159, 157. In the same volume see also Marinetti, "Technical Manifesto of Futurist Literature," 120, "Destruction of Syntax—Radio Imagination—Words-in-Freedom," 146–47, and "Dynamic and Synoptic Declamation," 221, in which Marinetti calls for the Futurist to "metallize, liquefy, vegetalize, petrify, and electrify his voice, merging it with the vibrations of matter itself."

37. Russolo, "The Art of Noises: Futurist Manifesto," 25–26. See also Russolo's essays "The Noises of Nature and Life (Timbres and Rhythms)," "The Noises of War," and "The Noises of Language (Consonants)," in *The Art of Noises*, 41–60.

38. Russolo, "The Conquest of Enharmonicism," in *The Art of Noises*, 62. On Russolo's theory of enharmony, see Chessa, *Luigi Russolo*, 141–50.

39. Russolo, "The Conquest of Enharmonicism," 63.

40. Russolo, "The Conquest of Enharmonicism," 62.

41. Pierre Schaeffer, *In Search of a Concrete Music*, trans. Christine North and John Dack (Berkeley and Los Angeles: University of California Press, 2012), 14.

42. Schaeffer, *In Search of a Concrete Music*, 13, 25, 65–66.

43. See Schaeffer, *In Search of a Concrete Music*, 14.

44. See Pierre Schaeffer, "Acousmatics," in Cox and Warner, *Audio Culture*, 95–101.

45. John Cage, "Future of Music: Credo," in *Silence: Lectures and Writings* (Hanover, NH: Wesleyan University Press, 1961), 3. Reprinted in Cox and Warner, *Audio Culture*, 27–30.

46. Cage, "Future of Music," 6.

47. Cage remarked in a 1948 lecture: "[I have the desire] to compose a piece of uninterrupted silence and sell it to the Muzak Co. It will be 3 or 4½ minutes long—those being the standard lengths of 'canned' music, and its title will be *Silent Prayer*. It will open with a single idea which I will attempt to make as seductive as the color and shape and fragrance of a flower. The ending will approach imperceptibility." "A Composer's Confessions," in *John Cage: Writer*, ed. Richard Kostelanetz (New York: Limelight Editions, 1993), 43.

48. This aspect of radio transmission was crucial for Maryanne Amacher, who collaborated with Cage on "Lecture on the Weather" (1975). Indeed, Amacher likened broadcasting to the weather as something "always available," "a non-discreet, continuous presence in the city—there like the weather—whether we open or shut our windows, look or do not look, it is there." Describing *City-Links #1 (Buffalo)* (1967), broadcast on public radio, Amacher wrote: "Tuning-in to WBFO [is] like tuning-in the weather, seeing what it's doing now—seeing slight and bigger changes as its forming its course." From a WBFO brochure in "Maryanne Amacher: City-Links (Documents from the Amacher Archive)," http://www.ludlow38.org/files/oei54-542011p845-865.pdf.

49. For instances of this phrase, see Cage, "Introduction to *Themes and Variations*," in Cox and Warner, *Audio Culture*, 312; *Conversing with Cage*, ed. Richard Kostelanetz, 2nd ed. (New York: Routledge, 2003), 44; "Anything I Say Will Be Misunderstood: An Interview with William Duckworth," in *John Cage at Seventy-Five*, ed. Richard Fleming and William Duckworth (Lewisburg, PA: Bucknell University Press, 1989), 22; and Cage, "Preface to 'Lecture on the Weather,'" in *Empty Words: Writings '73–'78* (Middletown, CT: Wesleyan University Press, 1979), 3. On Cage's subversive musicomania, see Stephen Davies, "John Cage's *4'33"*: Is It Music?," in *Themes in the Philosophy of Music* (Oxford: Oxford University Press, 2003).

50. "There is no such thing as an empty space or an empty time. There is always something to see, something to hear. In fact, try as we may to make a silence, we cannot." Cage, "Experimental Music," in *Silence*, 8.

51. Serres calls the first, empirical level that of "phenomenon" and "phenomenology," and the second, transcendental level the level of ontology, "of being itself."

52. I use "noumenal" here not in the Kantian sense of that which is inaccessible to experience but in the Deleuzian sense of the intensive, differential forces that produce empirical entities. See, e.g., Deleuze, *Difference and Repetition*, 222.

53. See Kostelanetz, *Conversing with Cage*, 65.

54. R. Murray Schafer, "The Music of the Environment," in Cox and Warner, *Audio Culture*, 31–32. This 1973 pamphlet was expanded to become the 1977 book *The Tuning of the World*, reprinted as *The Soundscape: Our Sonic Environment and the Tuning of the World* (Rochester, VT: Destiny Books, 1994). Schafer began to develop these ideas in an earlier text, *The New Soundscape: A Handbook for the Modern Music Teacher* (Scarborough, Ontario: Berandol Music, 1969).

55. Schafer, *The Soundscape*, 271.

56. Listen, for example, to the two-disc set *The Vancouver Soundscape 1973/Soundscape Vancouver 1996*, Cambridge Street Records, CSR-2CD 9701, 1997.

57. Schafer, *The Soundscape*, 43, and "The Music of the Environment," 32.

58. This distinction is made evident in the work of the sound artist and theorist Francisco López, who allies himself with Schaeffer against Schafer. See, for example, his essays "Schizophonia vs. *l'objet sonore*: Soundscapes and Artistic Freedom" (1997) and "Environmental Sound Matter" (1998), both available at http://www.franciscolopez.net/essays.html. The tensions between these approaches were already evident in *Presque rien no. 1, "la lever du jour au bord de la mer,"* a 1970 piece by Schaeffer's protégé Luc Ferrari that distills into a twenty-one-minute composition hours of field recordings of morning sounds in a Dalmatian island fishing village (*Presque Rien*, INA-GRM 245172 CD, 1995). Prominent soundscape composers today include Francisco López, Chris Watson, Jana Winderen, Lee Patterson, Toshiya Tsunoda, Jacob Kirkegaard, Andreas Bick, and Ernst Karel.

59. Thus, the Māndūkya Upanishad begins: "OM—this whole world is that syllable!" *The Early Upanishads*, trans. Patrick Olivelle (Oxford: Oxford University Press, 1998), 475. On Indian sonic metaphysics, see Guy L. Beck, *Sonic Theology: Hinduism and Sacred Sound* (Columbia: University of South Carolina Press, 1993), and "Hinduism and Music," in *Sacred Sound: Experiencing Music in World Religions*, ed. Guy L. Beck (Waterloo, Ontario: Wilfrid Laurier University Press, 2006).

60. See Beck, *Sonic Theology*, 212, which quotes Joachim-Ernst Berendt, *Nada Brahma: The World Is Sound*, trans. Helmut Bredigkeit (Rochester, VT: Destiny Books, 1987), 15–16. Both scholars implicitly refer to Monier Monier-Williams's *Sanskrit-English Dictionary* (Oxford: Clarendon Press, 1899), which confirms these definitions and etymologies. See also Ravi Shankar, *My Music, My Life* (New York: Simon & Schuster, 1968), 17.

61. See Alain Daniélou, *The Ragas of Northern Indian Music* (London: Barrie & Rockliff, 1968), 20–21, which quotes and discusses the *Sangīta-makaranda*. See also Schafer, *The Soundscape*, 260.

62. Leibniz, "Principles of Nature and Grace," 206.

63. La Monte Young and Marian Zazeela, "In Conversation with Frank J. Oteri," *New Music Box*, October 1, 2003, http://www.newmusicbox.org/articles/la-monte-young-and-marian-zazeela-at-the-dream-house/. See also La Monte Young and Marian Zazeela's interview with Gabriella Zuckerman, *American Mavericks*, American Public Media, July 2002, http://musicmavericks.publicradio.org/features/interview_young.html. In these passages, Young draws from Daniélou's *Ragas of Northern Indian Music*, a key resource for him. On this, see Jeremy Grimshaw, *Draw a Straight Line and Follow It: The Music and Mysticism of La Monte Young* (Oxford: Oxford University Press, 2011), 170.

64. From the 1990s on, the titles of Young's compositions and installations have primarily been simply lists of the frequencies that compose them. On the Pythagorean tradition and its discontents, see Daniel Heller-Roazen, *The Fifth Hammer: Pythagoras and the Disharmony of the World* (New York: Zone, 2011).

65. In a similar vein, the composer and music historian Kyle Gann writes: "In Cage's aesthetic, individual musical works are metaphorically excerpts from the cacophonous roar of all sounds heard or imagined. Young's archetype, equally fundamental, attempts to make audible the opposite pole: the basic tone from which all possible sounds emanate as overtones. If Cage stood for Zen, multiplicity, and becoming, Young stands for yoga, singularity, and being. Together they are the Heraclitus and Parmenides of twentieth-century music." "The Outer Edge of Consonance: Snapshots from the

Evolution of La Monte Young's Tuning Installations," in *Sound and Light: La Monte Young and Marian Zazeela*, ed. William Duckworth and Richard Fleming (Lewisburg, PA: Bucknell University Press, 1996), 153.

66. On Radigue's early work, see Emmanuel Holterbach, "Éliane Radigue: Feedback Works, 1969–1970," and Radigue's interview with Holterbach about the feedback works, April 5, 2011, both in the liner notes to Éliane Radigue, *Feedback Works: 1969–1970*, Algha Marghen, plan-R Algha040 LP, 2013. See also Julien Bécourt, "Éliane Radigue: The Mysterious Power of the Infinitesimal," *Red Bull Music Academy* (blog), 2015, http://daily.redbullmusicacademy.com/specials/2015-eliane-radigue-feature/.

67. See Radigue's 1996 interview with Kalvos and Damian, *eContact* 10, no. 2 (August 2008), http://econtact.ca/10_2/RadigueEl_KD.html, and Holterbach, "Radigue: Feedback Works."

68. Emmanuel Holterbach's reconstruction of the installation's audio component appears on *Feedback Works: 1969–1970*.

69. See Holterbach, "Éliane Radigue: Feedback Works."

70. Kubick and Walsh's installation was first presented in the group show *On Being an Exhibition*, Artists Space, New York, October 12–December 7, 2007. For more on the project, see http://www.doublearchive.com/projects/room_tone.php.

71. The piece is documented at http://www.brandonlabelle.net/room_tone.html, in *Brandon LaBelle: Room Tone* (Berlin: Errrant Bodies, 2015), and in Labelle's essay "Room Tone," in the digital exhibition catalog *Soundtracks*, ed. Rudolf Frieling and Tanya Zimbardo (San Francisco: San Francisco Museum of Modern Art, 2017), https://www.sfmoma.org/publication/soundtracks/brandon-labelle-room-tone.

72. The installation *Chora for Three* was shown in the group exhibition *Displacement* (2008) at Greenbelt in Brooklyn, NY. *Chora for* was presented in 2008 at Issue Project Room, also in Brooklyn. The hard-of-hearing sound artist Alison O'Daniel offered another take on audible silence in her multimedia exhibition *Room Tone* at the Knockdown Center, Queens, NY, in 2016.

73. This piece is examined more fully in chap. 3. Other such homages to Lucier are Lucy Raven's instruction piece *Room Tone* (2012) and Nicolas Collins's site-specific, computer-generated composition *Roomtone Variations* (2013–14).

74. Kirkegaard, *4 Rooms*, Touch Tone 26 CD, 2006.

75. Francisco López, *Wind [Patagonia]*, and/OAR and/27 CD, 2007.

76. Of course any choice and framing of material is a form of editing; and the choice of microphones and recorders involves a degree of processing. Through passages of audible distortion, López makes us aware of these choices, while also highlighting the degree to which they are involved in any form of listening. For to listen is to edit; and, fabricated by millennia of natural selection, ears, too, are mechanical devices that contract sound. On this issue, see chap. 3.

77. See Pierre Lévy, *Becoming Virtual*, trans. Robert Bononno (New York: Plenum, 1998) and my discussion of sonic virtualization and actualization in chap. 2.

78. Kane, "Sound Studies without Auditory Culture: A Critique of the Ontological Turn," *Sound Studies* 1, no. 1 (2015): 2–21.

79. For a helpful overview of metaontology, see Francesco Berto and Matteo Plebani, *Ontology and Metaontology: A Contemporary Guide* (New York: Bloomsbury, 2015).

80. DeLanda, *A Thousand Years of Nonlinear History* (New York: Zone, 1997), 21.

81. See Karl Marx, "The Fetishism of Commodities and the Secret Thereof," in

Capital, Vol. 1, excerpted in *The Marx-Engels Reader*, 2nd ed., ed. Robert C. Tucker (New York: W. W. Norton, 1978), 319–29, and Georg Lukács, "Reification and the Consciousness of the Proletariat," in *History and Class Consciousness*, trans. Rodney Livingstone (Cambridge, MA: MIT Press, 1971), 83–222.

82. See *On the Camera Arts and Other Consecutive Matters: The Writings of Hollis Frampton*, ed. Bruce Jenkins (Cambridge, MA: MIT Press 2009), 125–30.

83. Goodman's aesthetics is part of a radical antirealist project he calls "irrealism," according to which the world is entirely constructed through the use of symbols. See his *Ways of Worldmaking* (Indianapolis: Hackett, 1978).

84. My example is drawn from Britta Voss, "Of the River and Time," *Oceanus Magazine* 51, no. 2 (Winter 2016): 4–7, http://www.whoi.edu/cms/files/14G0694-Oceanus_v51n2-p4-7_225687.pdf.

85. Lockwood began assembling her "River Archive" in the late 1960s and mounted her first installation, *Play the Ganges Backwards One More Time, Sam*, at The Kitchen in 1974. This was followed by a series of "sound maps" of the Hudson River (1982), the Danube (2005), and the Housatonic River (2010). On the distinction between "music" and "sound art" in Lockwood's work, see her interview with N. B. Aldrich, "What Is Sound Art?," EMF Institute, 2003, http://www.nbaldrich.com/media/pdfs/what_is_sound_art.pdf.

86. Annea Lockwood, liner notes to *A Sound Map of the Danube*, Lovely Music LCD 2083, 2008.

87. Lockwood, liner notes to *A Sound Map of the Housatonic River*, 3Leaves 3L018 CD, 2013.

88. *Sound Map of the Hudson River* began as an installation at the Hudson River Museum in Yonkers, NY, and later appeared as a recording on Lovely Music, LCD 2081. *Sound Map of the Danube* (2005) and *Sound Map of the Housatonic River* (2010) also began as installations that were later documented on CD.

89. See Yngvar W. Isachsen, "The Adirondacks: Still Rising after All These Years," *Natural History Magazine*, May 1992, 30–34. Isachsen's "hotspot" thesis is controversial but remains the standard account.

90. J. L. Austin, *Sense and Sensibilia* (Oxford: Clarendon Press, 1962), 8.

91. See Ilya Prigogine and Isabelle Stengers, *Order out of Chaos* (New York: Bantam, 1984), 111; Prigogine and Gregoire Nicolis, *Exploring Complexity* (New York: W. H. Freeman, 1989), 56–60; and Manuel DeLanda, *Intensive Science and Virtual Philosophy* (London: Continuum, 2002), 64–68.

92. John Cage, "Composition as Process II: Indeterminacy," in *Silence* (Hanover, NH: Wesleyan University Press, 1961). I discuss this issue further in chap. 5.

93. See Joan La Barbara, "Voice Is the Original Instrument," *Contemporary Music Review* 21, no. 1 (March 2002): 35–48.

94. Recordings of this and the other pieces discussed here are archived on Joan La Barbara, *Voice Is the Original Instrument: Early Works*, Lovely Music LCD 3003. See the verbal score for "Voice Piece" in Walter Zimmerman, *Desert Plants: Conversations with Twenty-Three American Musicians* (Vancouver: A.R.C. Publications, 1976), 157–62, and at http://home.snafu.de/walterz/biblio/10_joan_labarbara.pdf.

95. Tom Johnson, "Research and Development: Joan La Barbara (January 27, 1975)," in *The Voice of New Music: New York City, 1972–82* (Eindhoven: Het Apollohuis, 1989), 164–66, and at http://tvonm.editions75.com/articles/1975/research-and-development-joan-la-barbara.html.

CHAPTER FIVE

1. Max Neuhaus, "Program Notes," in *Sound Works*, Vol. 1, *Inscription* (Ostfildern: Cantz, 1994), 34. In interviews from the 1980s and '90s, Neuhaus repeated this claim. See, for example, his 1982 interview with William Duckworth (*Sound Works*, Vol. 1, 42–49 and http://www.max-neuhaus.info/bibliography/Duckworth.pdf), the 1990 conversation with Ulrich Loock (*Sound Works*, Vol. I, 122–35), and the interview excerpts in Michael Tarantino's "Two Passages" (1998) http://www.max-neuhaus.info/soundworks/vectors/passage/twopassages/Two_Passages.pdf.

2. Max Neuhaus, introduction to *Sound Works*, Vol. III, *Place* (Ostfildern: Cantz, 1994), 5, www.max-neuhaus.info/soundworks/vectors/place/.

3. Max Neuhaus quoted in Alicia Zuckerman, "Max Neuhaus's 'Times Square,'" *Arts Electric*, May 30, 2002, http://www.emf.org/artselectric/stories/2002/020530_neuhaus.html. Jeremy Grimshaw discusses La Monte Young's tuning installations in much the same way, as "spatialized sound" that involves "a dimension not ruled by time." See Grimshaw, *Draw a Straight Line and Follow It: The Music and Mysticism of La Monte Young* (Oxford: Oxford University Press, 2011), 114–15. Young himself distinguishes between "the artificiality of measured time" and "real time," a distinction similar to the one I draw here. See Young and Zazeela, "Dream House," in *Selected Writings* (Munich: Heiner Friedrich Gallery, 1969), reissued ubuclassics, 2004, http://www.ubu.com/historical/young/young_selected.pdf.

4. See the conversation between Vitiello and Marina Rosenfeld in *NewMusicBox*, March 1, 2004, http://www.newmusicbox.org/article.nmbx?id=2414, and "Audio Files: Sound Art Now: An Online Symposium," Artforum.com, April–May 2004, http://artforum.com/index.php?pn=symposium&id=6682. See also Alan Licht, *Sound Art: Beyond Music, Between Categories* (New York: Rizzoli, 2007), 16; Brandon LaBelle, *Background Noise: Perspectives on Sound Art* (New York: Continuum, 2006), 151; and Carsten Seiffarth, "About Installation Art," *Kunstjournalen B-post* (2012), http://www.kunstjournalen.no/12_eng/carsten-seiffarth-about-sound-installation-art.

5. John Cage, "Composition as Process II: Indeterminacy," in *Silence*, 36, reprinted in *Audio Culture: Readings in Modern Music*, ed. Christoph Cox and Daniel Warner, rev. ed. (New York: Bloomsbury), 253.

6. *For the Birds: John Cage in Conversation with Daniel Charles* (London: Marion Boyers, 2009), 80.

7. For example, see *Silence*, 9, 100, 155, 173, 194, and *A Year from Monday: New Lectures and Writings* (Middletown, CT: Wesleyan University Press, 1967), 18, 31, 75.

8. Cage, "Composition as Process II," 38. Cf. Cage, *For the Birds*, 150.

9. For a discussion of Bergson's influence on Cage, see Branden W. Joseph, *Experimentations: John Cage in Music, Art, and Architecture* (New York: Bloomsbury, 2016), 146ff.; and *Random Order: Robert Rauschenberg and the Neo-Avant-Garde* (Cambridge, MA: MIT Press, 2003), 47–56.

10. On this, see Henri Bergson, *Time and Free Will*, trans. F. L. Pogson (New York: Harper & Row, 1960), 75ff. Bergson's initial training was in mathematics, which he abandoned to become a philosopher. Gilles Deleuze argues that Bergson's distinction between clock time and duration reworks the mathematician G. B. R. Riemann's distinction between "discrete multiplicities" and "continuous multiplicities." See Deleuze, *Bergsonism*, trans. Hugh Tomlinson and Barbara Habberjam (New York: Zone, 1988), 39ff.

11. These arguments run throughout Bergson's work but receive their most sus-

tained formulation in *Time and Free Will* (1888), "Memory of the Present and False Recognition" (1908), and *Duration and Simultaneity* (1922). See the selections from these texts in *Henri Bergson: Key Writings*, ed. Keith Ansell Pearson and John Mullarkey (New York: Continuum, 2002). I return to these arguments in the final section of this chapter.

12. Morton Feldman, "Between Categories," in *Give My Regards to Eighth Street: Collected Writings of Morton Feldman*, ed. B. H. Friedman (Cambridge, MA: Exact Change, 2000), 86–87.

13. Feldman, quoted in B. H. Friedman, "Morton Feldman: Painting Sounds," in *Give My Regards to Eighth Street*, xxvi.

14. Cage in *Conversing with Cage*, ed. Richard Kostelanetz, 2nd ed. (New York: Routledge, 2003), 65.

15. In the text version of the score published by C. F. Peters/Henmar Press in 1960, Cage notes that "the work . . . may last any length of time."

16. Kostelanetz, *Conversing with Cage*, 69.

17. Kostelanetz, *Conversing with Cage*, 65.

18. Cage, "Experimental Music," in *Silence*, 10.

19. See, for example, *Silence*, 191, and *Conversing with Cage*, 65, 110, 127, 186–87, 220, 233–34.

20. See Deleuze, "Vincennes Seminar Session, May 3, 1977: On Music," trans. Timothy S. Murphy, *Discourse* 20, no. 3 (Fall 1998), 209ff., https://www.webdeleuze.com/textes/5.

21. Mertens, *American Minimal Music* (London: Kahn & Averill, 1983), 90. The relevant portion of this text is reprinted in Cox and Warner, *Audio Culture*, 425–30.

22. Steve Reich, "Music as a Gradual Process," in *Writings about Music* (New York: New York University Press, 1974), reprinted in Cox and Warner, *Audio Culture*, 431–33.

23. On Chronos and Aion and their relationship to music, see the "Vincennes Seminar, May 3, 1977," and *A Thousand Plateaus*, 262. Deleuze first presents the Stoic distinction between Chronos and Aion in *The Logic of Sense*, ed. Constantin Boundas, trans. Mark Lester and Charles Stivale (New York: Columbia University Press, 1990). The difference between Goethe's *Bildungsroman* and Kleist's "pure 'stationary process'" is discussed in Deleuze and Guattari, *A Thousand Plateaus*, 268–69. Jonathan D. Kramer calls this Cagean, minimalist conception of time "vertical." See Kramer, *The Time of Music: New Meanings, New Temporalities, New Listening Strategies* (New York: Schirmer Books, 1988), 54–58, 375–97.

24. Neuhaus, "Modus Operandi," in *Sound Works*, Vol. I, 18–19, http://www.max-neuhaus.info/soundworks/vectors/passage/modusoperandi.

25. Interview with Duckworth.

26. See Michael Fried, "Art and Objecthood," in *Art and Objecthood: Essays and Reviews* (Chicago: University of Chicago Press, 1998), 148–72.

27. Robert Morris, quoted in Fried, "Art and Objecthood," 153.

28. Fried, "Art and Objecthood," 154.

29. Fried, "An Introduction to My Art Criticism," in *Art and Objecthood*, 41.

30. This concern is discussed in detail in Pamela M. Lee, *Chronophobia: On Time in the Art of the 1960s* (Cambridge, MA: MIT Press, 2004), 36–81.

31. Smith, quoted in Fried, "Art and Objecthood," 157–58.

32. Fried, "Art and Objecthood," 159.

33. Fried, "Art and Objecthood," 166–67.

34. Fried, "Art and Objecthood," 167.

35. Henri Bergson, *Creative Evolution*, trans. Arthur Mitchell (New York: Modern Library, 1944), 25, 26.

36. Bergson, *Creative Evolution*, 45.

37. Bergson, *Creative Evolution*, 26–27.

38. Bergson, *Creative Evolution*, 45.

39. Bergson, *Creative Evolution*, 52.

40. Bergson, *Creative Evolution*, 45.

41. Fried, "An Introduction to My Art Criticism," 46.

42. Fried, "Art and Objecthood," 168.

43. Cf. Laplace: "We ought then to regard the present state of the universe as the effect of its anterior state and the cause of the one which is to follow. Given for one instant an intelligence which could comprehend all the forces by which nature is animated and the respective situation of the beings who compose it—an intelligence sufficiently vast to submit this data to analysis—it would embrace in the same formula the movements of the greatest bodies of the universe and those of the lightest atom; for it, nothing would be uncertain and the future, as the past, would be present in its eyes." Pierre-Simon, Marquis de Laplace, *A Philosophical Essay on Probabilities* (1814), trans. Frederick Wilson Truscott and Frederick Lincoln Emery (New York: Dover, 1951), 4.

44. Robert Smithson, "A Sedimentation of the Mind: Earth Projects," in *Robert Smithson: The Collected Writings*, ed. Jack Flam (Berkeley and Los Angeles: University of California Press, 1996), 102–4, 111–13.

45. Robert Morris, "Notes on Sculpture, Part 4: Beyond Objects," in *Continuous Project Altered Daily: The Writings of Robert Morris* (Cambridge, MA: MIT Press, 1993), 68.

46. Morris, "Notes on Sculpture, Part 4," 57, 61, 67.

47. On the relationship between Cage and Morris, see Branden W. Joseph, "Robert Morris and John Cage: Reconstructing a Dialogue," *October* 81 (Summer 1997): 59–69. Joseph discusses Cage's reception by Fried in "The Tower and the Line: Toward a Genealogy of Minimalism," *Grey Room* 27 (Spring 2007): 58–81, a version of which appears in Joseph's *Beyond the Dream Syndicate: Tony Conrad and the Arts after Cage* (New York: Zone, 2008).

48. Neuhaus, cited in Tarantino, "Two Passages"; interview with Duckworth.

49. For more on this, see chap. 1.

50. Bergson, "The Perception of Change," in *The Creative Mind: An Introduction to Metaphysics*, trans. Mabelle L. Andison (Mineola, NY: Dover, 2007), 122.

51. See, for example, *Time and Free Will*, chap. II, and the opening section of *Creative Evolution*.

52. Bergson, *Duration and Simultaneity*, in *Key Writings*, 205. Bergson goes on to extend the interior, psychological intuition of duration, this "inner time," to "the time of things," "the duration of the universe." This passage is clearly a revision of Bergson's earlier view, according to which musical melody is presented as the best figure of duration. See *Time and Free Will*, 100ff.

53. La Monte Young writes: "The drone is the first sound. It lasts forever and cannot have begun but is taken up again from time to time." "Dream House," in *Selected Writings*. For more on the drone, see chap. 4.

54. The Theatre of Eternal Music member Tony Conrad discusses this temporal experience in his unpublished essay "Duration" (2004), which draws a distinction between time and duration that is different from but resonates with Bergson's.

55. See the text panel in Neuhaus's drawing for *Time Piece Beacon*, http://www.max-neuhaus.info/images/TimePieceBeacon.gif; cf. the introduction to his "Moment Works," http://www.max-neuhaus.info/soundworks/vectors/moment/intro, and "Notes on Place and Moment," in *Sound Works*, Vol. I, 97–101, http://www.max-neuhaus.info/soundworks/vectors/moment/notes.

56. See the text panel in Neuhaus's drawing for *Times Square*, http://www.max-neuhaus.info/images/TimesSquare.gif.

57. Neuhaus himself associates his "Time Pieces" with the history of bell ringing. See his introduction to the "Moment Works" and his "Notes on Place and Moment."

58. See Alain Corbin, *Village Bells: Sound and Meaning in the Nineteenth-Century French Countryside*, trans. Martin Thom (New York: Columbia University Press, 1998), 110 ff.

59. See *Time and Free Will*, 109, and *Duration and Simultaneity*, in *Key Writings*, 214.

60. On these paradoxes, see G. S. Kirk and J. E. Raven, *The Presocratic Philosophers: A Critical History with a Selection of Texts* (Cambridge: Cambridge University Press, 1957), 291ff. Bergson examines Zeno's "confusion between motion and the space traversed" in *Time and Free Will*, 112ff., and "The Perception of Change," 117–18, 120–21.

61. Deleuze, *Cinema 2: The Time-Image*, trans. Hugh Tomlinson and Robert Galeta (Minneapolis: University of Minnesota Press, 1989), 81. This passage largely summarizes the conclusions of Bergson's 1908 essay "Memory of the Present and False Recognition," in *Mind-Energy*, trans. H. Wilden Carr (London: Macmillan, 1920), 127ff., to which Deleuze alludes throughout his corpus. See, for example, Deleuze's *Nietzsche and Philosophy*, trans. Hugh Tomlinson (New York: Columbia University Press, 1983), 47–49, *Bergsonism*, 54ff., and *Difference and Repetition*, trans. Paul Patton (New York: Columbia University Press, 1994), 79ff.

62. Hecker, *Speculative Solution*, Editions Mego eMEGO 118/Urbanomic UF13, CD, 2011.

63. Quentin Meillassoux, "Time without Becoming," *Spike* 35 (Spring 2013): 100, 102. Meillassoux has vacillated between the terms "hyper-chaos" (*hyper-Chaos*) and "superchaos" (*Surchaos*) but seems to have settled on the former. See Meillassoux, "Iteration, Reiteration, Repetition: A Speculative Analysis of the Sign Devoid of Meaning," trans. Robin Mackay, in *Genealogies of Speculation: Materialism and Subjectivity since Structuralism*, ed. Armen Avanessian and Suhail Malik (London: Bloomsbury, 2016), 193n26.

64. Meillassoux presents this argument in *After Finitude: An Essay on the Necessity of Contingency*, trans. Ray Brassier (London: Continuum, 2008), and helpfully summarizes it in "Time without Becoming."

65. See Meillassoux, "Iteration, Reiteration, Repetition."

66. Meillassoux, *After Finitude*, 53.

67. Meillassoux, "Time without Becoming," 102.

68. Meillassoux, "Time without Becoming," 102.

69. See Meillassoux, "Potentiality and Virtuality," in *The Speculative Turn: Continental Materialism and Realism*, ed. Levi Bryant, Nick Srnicek, and Graham Harman (Melbourne: Re-Press, 2011), 232–33, 235. Meillassoux's commitment to the notion of irruptions *ex nihilo* is evident throughout his work, from his 1997 doctoral thesis "L'inexistence divine" (selections from which were translated by Graham Harman in *Quentin Meillassoux: Philosophy in the Making* [Edinburgh: University of Edinburgh

Press, 2011], 175–238) to the essay "Iteration, Reiteration, Repetition," published in its complete form in 2016. For Meillassoux, such miraculous events do not have their origin in some transcendent God. After all, the notion of God as a necessary being is forbidden by the radical contingency the philosopher espouses. Nonetheless, Meillassoux identifies neither with the believer (for whom God exists) nor with the atheist (for whom God does not exist). Rather, he asserts that "God does *not yet* exist"—in other words, that radical contingency and the intelligibility of irruptions ex nihilo allow for the possibility of God's future advent. Moreover, this possibility seems to be more than one among many. Indeed, in a strangely Kantian turn, Meillassoux declares that the possibility of God's future existence—and with it the possibility of immortality and cosmic justice—is what gives meaning to all ethical thought and political action, and staves off nihilism and despair. See "The Immanence of the World Beyond," trans. Peter M. Candler Jr., Adrian Pabst, and Aaron Riches, in *The Grandeur of Reason: Religion, Tradition, and Universalism*, ed. Connor Cunningham and Peter Candler (London: SCM Press, 2010), 444–78.

70. See "Speculative Solution: Quentin Meillassoux and Florian Hecker Talk Hyperchaos," Urbanomic Document UFD001 (2010), https://www.urbanomic.com/wp-content/uploads/2015/06/Urbanomic_Document_UFD001.pdf.

71. "Speculative Solution," 8.

72. "Speculative Solution," 6.

73. See "Speculative Solution," 3, 5–6.

74. As Brian Eno notes in relationship to recordings of improvised music: "Almost any arbitrary collision of events listened to enough times comes to seem very meaningful." "The Studio as Compositional Tool," in Cox and Warner, *Audio Culture*, 186. Alluding to Leibniz, Meillassoux makes a similar point, noting "that any sequence, however disordered, can always be conceived as an example of a more elaborate law." "Speculative Solution," 2. The reference is presumably to Leibniz, *Discourse on Metaphysics*, §§6–7.

75. "Speculative Solution," 3.

76. "Speculative Solution," 8, 9. See also Mackay, "This Is This," *Speculative Solution* CD booklet, 21.

77. See Mackay in "Speculative Solution," 9, and "This Is This," 3–7.

78. Mackay in "Speculative Solution," 3. Cf. Hecker in the same text, 1.

79. Meillassoux, *After Finitude*, 65.

80. My critique of Meillassoux has benefited from a number of other critiques, particularly Ray Brassier, *Nihil Unbound: Enlightenment and Extinction* (Basingstoke: Palgrave Macmillan, 2007), 85–94, and a group of essays collected in *The Speculative Turn*, particularly Martin Hägglund, "Radical Atheist Materialism: A Critique of Meillassoux"; Peter Hallward, "Anything Is Possible: A Reading of Quentin Meillassoux's *After Finitude*"; Alberto Toscano, "Against Speculation, or A Critique of the Critique of Critique: A Remark on Quentin Meillassoux's *After Finitude* (After Colletti)"; and Adrian Johnston, "Hume's Revenge: À Dieu, Meillassoux?"

81. Meillassoux, *After Finitude*, 70.

82. See Meillassoux, "Potentiality and Virtuality," 232.

83. Martin Hägglund makes a similar point, arguing that to posit hyper-chaos "is not to think the implications of time but to posit an instance that has power *over* time, since it may stop and start succession at will." "Radical Atheist Materialism," 121.

84. Bergson, *Creative Evolution*, 4.

85. Meillassoux, "Speculative Solution," 3.

86. Meillassoux, *After Finitude*, 71.

87. Meillassoux, *After Finitude*, 69–70. Cf. "Time and Becoming," 103.

88. Meillassoux, *After Finitude*, 70.

89. See Hägglund," "Radical Atheist Materialism," 117–18.

90. See Meillassoux, "Time without Becoming," 96, 100, and *After Finitude*, 36. See also Meillassoux's interview with Harman in Harman, *Quentin Meillassoux*, 165.

91. For a critique along these lines, see Brassier, who concludes: "Far from reconciling rationalism with materialism, the principle of factiality . . . continues to subordinate extra-conceptual reality to a *concept* of absolute contingency." *Nihil Unbound*, 93.

92. See "Think about Nature: A Conversation with Lee Smolin," *Edge.org* (blog), May 14, 2013, http://edge.org/conversation/think-about-nature.

93. See Smolin, "Think about Nature," and *Time Reborn: From the Crisis in Physics to the Future of the Universe* (Boston: Houghton Mifflin Harcourt, 2013).

CHAPTER SIX

1. Kathleen Forde, "What Sound Does a Color Make?," and Judith Olch Richards, foreword to *What Sound Does a Color Make?* (New York: Independent Curators International, 2005), 8, 19.

2. See Aristotle, *On the Soul*, III.1–2, in *A New Aristotle Reader*, ed. J. L. Ackrill (Princeton, NJ: Princeton University Press, 1987), 187–91. For a helpful discussion of this and other passages in Aristotle on common sense, see Daniel Heller-Roazen, *The Inner Touch: Archaeology of a Sensation* (New York: Zone, 2007), chap. III.

3. See Richard Cytowic, *Synesthesia: A Union of the Senses*, 2nd ed. (Cambridge, MA: MIT Press, 2002), 75.

4. See Clement Greenberg, "Modernist Painting," in *Clement Greenberg: The Collected Essays and Criticism*, Vol. 4, *Modernism with a Vengeance* (Chicago: University of Chicago Press, 1993).

5. Dziga Vertov, "We: Variant of a Manifesto," in *Kino-Eye: The Writings of Dziga Vertov*, ed. Annette Michelson, trans. Kevin O'Brien (Berkeley and Los Angeles: University of California Press, 1984), 7. The translator notes that *kinochestvo* is a Vertovian neologism meaning the abstract quality of the cinematic eye.

6. Richard Wagner, "The Art-Work of the Future," in *Richard Wagner's Prose Works*, Vol. I, trans. W. Ashton Ellis (London: Kegan Paul, Trench, Trübner, 1892), 97–98. While more fluid, Emma Warner's recent translation of this text is imprecise, losing Wagner's repetitions and emphases. See Richard Wagner, "The Artwork of the Future," trans. Emma Warner, in "The Artwork of the Future," special issue, *Wagner Journal* (2012): 28.

7. John Locke, *Essay Concerning Human Understanding*, ed. Roger Woolhouse (London: Penguin, 1997), Book IV, §11.

8. See the historical table of publication statistics in Crétien van Campen, "Artistic and Psychological Experiments with Synesthesia," *Leonardo* 32, no. 1 (1999): 11.

9. Charles Baudelaire, "Correspondences," in *Les fleurs du mal*, trans. Richard Howard (Jaffrey, NH: David R. Godine, 1982), 15.

10. Arthur Rimbaud, "Vowels," in *Rimbaud: Complete Works, Selected Letters*, trans. Wallace Fowlie and Seth Whidden (Chicago: University of Chicago Press, 2005), 141.

11. Walter Pater, *The Renaissance* (New York: Modern Library, 1919), 111.

12. Dieter Daniels, "Hybrids of Art, Science, Technology, Perception, Entertain-

ment, and Commerce at the Interface of Sound and Vision," in *See This Sound: Audiovisuology 2, Essays: Histories and Theories of Audiovisual Media and Art*, ed. Dieter Daniels and Sandra Naumann (Cologne: Walther König, 2011), 18.

13. See Peter Vergo, *The Music of Painting* (London: Phaidon, 2010); Standish Lawder, *The Cubist Cinema* (New York: New York University Press, 1975), chap. 3; and Malcolm Cook, "Visual Music in Film, 1921–1924: Richter, Eggeling, Ruttmann," in *Music and Modernism, 1849–1950*, ed. Charlotte de Mille (Newcastle upon Tyne: Cambridge Scholars, 2011), 206–28. See also my "Music, Noise, and Abstraction," in *Inventing Abstraction, 1910–1925*, ed. Leah Dickerman (New York: Museum of Modern Art, 2012), 144–47.

14. Guillaume Apollinaire, quoted in Cook, "Visual Music in Film," 208.

15. Clement Greenberg, "Towards a Newer Laocoon," in *The Collected Essays and Criticism*, Vol. 1, *Perceptions and Judgments, 1939–1944*, ed. John O'Brian (Chicago: University of Chicago Press, 1986), 31.

16. Title texts from Mary Ellen Bute and Ted Nemeth's *Synchromy No. 2* (1936), and Bute, Nemeth, and Melville Webber's *Rhythm in Light* (1934), collected in *Unseen Cinema: Early American Avant-Garde Film, 1894–1941*, Vol. 3, *Light Rhythms, Music and Abstraction* (New York: Anthology Film Archives, 2005), DVD.

17. Title text from Bute, Nemeth, and Webber, *Rhythm in Light*.

18. Fischinger, *An Optical Poem* (1938), collected in *Unseen Cinema: Early American Avant-Garde Film, 1894–1941*, Vol. 7, *Viva la Dance: The Beginnings of Ciné-Dance* (New York: Anthology Film Archives, 2005), DVD.

19. Sergei Eisenstein, Vsevolod Pudovkin, and Grigori Alexandrov, "Statement on Sound," in Eisenstein, *Selected Works*, Vol. 1, *Writings, 1922–1924*, ed. Richard Taylor (Bloomington: Indiana University Press, 1988), 114. In a text begun the same year, László Moholy-Nagy offered a more optimistic assessment of the sound film. Yet, while celebrating its possibilities, he too warned against the naturalistic use of sound and the subordination of sound to image. See "Problems of the Modern Film," in *Moholy-Nagy*, ed. Krisztina Passuth (London: Thames & Hudson, 1985), 314. Revisiting the relationship between image and sound in a 1935 essay, Moholy-Nagy ceded to Eisenstein and his colleagues that "the development of the talking picture has unfortunately verified the gloomiest predictions of the defenders of silent films." "Supplementary Remarks on the Sound and Color Film," in *Moholy-Nagy*, ed. Richard Kostelanetz (New York: Praeger, 1970), 139. In the 1930s Eisenstein turned toward a Symbolist fascination with synaesthesia and the *Gesamtkunstwerk*. (See, for example, "The Synchronization of the Senses," in *The Film Sense*, ed. Jay Leyda [New York: Meridian, 1957], 69–109.) Understanding this turn as provoked by the pressures of Stalinism and the official aesthetic of socialist realism, the American experimental filmmaker Hollis Frampton noted the continued importance of the "Statement," which, he remarked in 1981, "has met with no direct critique or reply in more than a half century." Lamenting "the stagnation of the sound track as an independent and coeval information channel," Frampton suggested that "the deferred dream of the sound film presents itself to be dreamed again." "Film in the House of the Word," in *On the Camera Arts and Consecutive Matters: The Writings of Hollis Frampton*, ed. Bruce Jenkins (Cambridge, MA: MIT Press, 2009), 169.

20. See Denis Hollier, "The Death of Paper, Part Two: Artaud's Sound System," *October* 80 (Spring 1997): 27–37.

21. See Michel Chion, *Audio-Vision: Sound on Screen*, trans. Claudia Gorbman (New York: Columbia University Press, 1994), 143–44.

22. Walter Ruttmann, "Compilation of Excerpts from Interviews and Articles, 1927–1937," booklet insert, *Walther Ruttmann: "Berlin, die Sinfonie der Großstadt"& "Melodie der Welt"* (Munich, Berlin, and Mainz: Edition Filmmuseum, 2008), DVD.

23. Marcel Duchamp, "Apropos of 'Readymades,'" in *Salt Seller: The Writings of Marcel Duchamp*, ed. Michael Sanouillet and Elmer Peterson (Oxford: Oxford University Press, 1973), 141.

24. Carol P. James, "Duchamp's Silent Noise/Music for the Deaf," in *Marcel Duchamp: Artist of the Century*, ed. Rudolf Kuenzli and Francis M. Naumann (Cambridge, MA: MIT Press, 1989), 106–26. See also Seth Kim-Cohen, *In the Blink of an Ear: Toward a Non-Cochlear Sonic Art* (New York: Continuum, 2009).

25. Marcel Duchamp, "Musical Erratum," in *Salt Seller: The Writings of Marcel Duchamp*, ed. Michael Sanouillet and Elmer Peterson (New York: Oxford University Press, 1973), 34.

26. See Martin Heidegger, "The Turning," in *The Question Concerning Technology and Other Essays*, trans. William Lovitt (New York: Harper & Row, 1977), 48; Theodor Adorno, "A Social Critique of Radio Music," in *Radiotext(e)*, ed. Neil Strauss (New York: Semiotext(e), 1993), 272–79; and Max Horkheimer, *Dawn and Decline: Notes 1926–1931 and 1950–1969*, trans. Michael Shaw (New York: Seabury Press, 1978), 162.

27. Pierre Schaeffer, "Acousmatics," in *Audio Culture: Readings in Modern Music*, ed. Christoph Cox and Daniel Warner, rev. ed. (New York: Bloomsbury, 2017), 95–101.

28. See Julia Simner, Catherine Mulvenna , Noam Sagiv, Elias Tsakanikos, Sarah A. Witherby, Christine Fraser, Kirsten Scott, and Jamie Ward, "Synaesthesia: The Prevalence of Atypical Cross-Modal Experiences," *Perception* 35, no. 8 (2006): 1024–33.

29. See Christopher T. Lovelace, "Synesthesia in the Twenty-First Century: Synesthesia's Ascent," in *The Oxford Handbook of Synesthesia*, ed. Julia Simner and Edward Hubbard (Oxford: Oxford University Press, 2013), 409–12, and van Campen, "Artistic and Psychological Experiments with Synesthesia," 11.

30. See Hinderk M. Emrich, Janina Neufeld, and Christopher Sinke, "Synesthesia: A Neurological Phenomenon," in *Audiovisuology I: See This Sound*, ed. Dieter Daniels and Sandra Naumann (Cologne: Walter König, 2010), 418 and the website of the American Synesthesia Association, http://www.synesthesia.info/aboutus.html.

31. For a helpful analysis of the image economy in contemporary culture, see David Joselit, *After Art* (Princeton, NJ: Princeton University Press, 2013).

32. Friedrich Kittler, *Gramophone, Film, Typewriter*, trans. Geoffrey Winthrop-Young and Michael Wutz (Stanford, CA: Stanford University Press, 1999), 1–2.

33. See Sean Day, "Some Demographic and Socio-Cultural Aspects of Synesthesia," in *Synesthesia: Perspectives from Cognitive Neuroscience*, ed. Lynn C. Robertson and Noam Sagiv (Oxford: Oxford University Press, 2005), 11–33, and "Demographic Aspects of Synesthesia," http://www.daysyn.com/Types-of-Syn.html, which reveal that by far the highest incidences of synaesthesia are those in which the concurrent sensation is visual.

34. Chion, *Audio-Vision*, 143.

35. Cretien van Campen, "Reorganizing the Brain," booklet insert, *Optofonica*, LINE 041, 2009, DVD.

36. "Synchresis" (synchronism + synthesis) is a neologism coined by Chion in *Audio-Vision*, 63–64, and *passim*.

37. See Cytowic, *Synesthesia*, 16–17. See also Steven Connor, "Intersensoriality" (2004), http://www.stevenconnor.com/intersensoriality, and Sean A. Day, "Demo-

graphic Aspects of Synesthesia." Though by far the most common type of synaesthesia is colored graphemes (numbers or letters), colored hearing (chromesthesia) is the most common pairing of two senses.

38. Christian Metz, "Aural Objects," in *Film Sound: Theory and Practice*, ed. Elisabeth Weis and John Belton (New York: Columbia University Press, 1985), 154–61.

39. See Chion, *Audio-Vision*, 143ff.

40. See H.-J. Stöckmann, "Chladni Meets Napoleon," *European Physical Journal Special Topics* 145, no. 1 (June 2007): 15–23.

41. Alvin Lucier, "Seeing Sound: *The Queen of the South* (1972) and *Tyndall Orchestrations* (1976)," in *Reflections: Interviews, Scores, Writings, 1965–1994* (Cologne: Musik-Texte, 1995), 138–39.

42. László Moholy-Nagy, "Production–Reproduction: Potentialities of the Phonograph," in Cox and Warner, *Audio Culture*, 481–84. My account here draws from Thomas Y. Levin's history of sound-image relations in early twentieth-century media, "'Tones from Out of Nowhere': Rudolph Pfenninger and the Archaeology of Synthetic Sound," *Grey Room* 12 (Summer 2003): 32–79. Yet in Derridean fashion, Levin advances the thesis that synthetic sound has its origins in writing or the graphic, showing it to be an instance of the arbitrary rather than the indexical sign. This conclusion is strikingly at odds with that of a key source for Levin, Friedrich Kittler, who shows, on the contrary, that synthetic sound (the origins of which lie in phonography) is of the order of the real rather than the symbolic—that phonographic inscription is not that of arbitrary signs but of mathematical-physical frequencies and vibrations. See Kittler, *Gramophone, Film, Typewriter*, 13–17, 22–25, 46ff.

43. Moholy-Nagy, "Problems of the Modern Film," in Passuth, *Moholy-Nagy*, 314. In her discussion of the history of sound film, Vivian Sobchack remarks that "optical sound, or sound-on-film, literally achieved synaesthetic cooperation and bodily union with the film's primary and expressive organs." *The Address of the Eye: A Phenomenology of Film Experience* (Princeton, NJ: Princeton University Press, 1992), 254.

44. See William Moritz, "Non-Objective Film: The Second Generation," in *Film as Film: Formal Experiment in Film, 1910–1975* (London: Arts Council of Great Britain, 1979), 61.

45. See Richard Russett and Cecile Starr, *Experimental Animation: Origins of a New Art*, rev. ed. (New York: Da Capo Press, 1988), 58.

46. Oskar Fischinger, "Sounding Ornaments" (1932), in William Moritz, *Optical Poetry: The Life and Work of Oskar Fischinger* (Bloomington: Indiana University Press, 2004), 179–81. In the early 1970s Moritz compiled Fischinger's fragments into a film titled *Ornament Sound Experiments*, which has been shown at synaesthesia-based exhibitions such as *Sons & lumières* (2004), *Visual Music* (2005), and *See This Sound* (2009). Levin tries to drive a wedge between Fischinger and Pfenninger, arguing that, while the former treated sound as secondary to and a representation of the graphic ornament, the latter reversed this hierarchy and "*destroyed the logic of acoustic indexicality*" ("'Tones from out of Nowhere,'" 57–59). Fischinger's film and writings, partially quoted above, do not support this view; and, in the work of both artists, sound is indexically tied to graphic marks.

47. See Norman McLaren, *Technical Notes* (Montreal: National Film Board of Canada, 2006), 57–58, 61–71.

48. Barry Spinello, "Notes on 'Soundtrack,'" in Russett and Starr, *Experimental Animation*, 176. An earlier version of this text appeared in *Canyon Cinemanews* 69, no. 3

(1969): 11–12, and was reprinted as "Letter from Oakland, California" in Scott MacDonald, *Canyon Cinema: The Life and Times of an Independent Film Distributor* (Berkeley and Los Angeles: University of California Press, 2008), 123–25.

49. The acronym stands for Unité Polyagogique Informatique du CEMAMu, itself an acronym for the Centre d'Études de Mathèmatique et Automatiques Musicales, the research center founded by Xenakis to undertake interdisciplinary research in the arts and sciences.

50. Haswell and Hecker, *Blackest Ever Black*, Warner Classics 2564 64321–2 CD, 2007.

51. Noto, *telefunken*, raster-noton n-r032 CD, 2000.

52. Rhodes in "The Tanks at Tate Modern: Lis Rhodes," a video documentary produced to accompany the installation of *Light Music* at Tate Modern, July 18, 2012–January 20, 2013, http://www.tate.org.uk/whats-on/tate-modern-tanks/display/lis-rhodes-light-music; Barry Spinello, "On Sound and Image as a Single Entity," *Offscreen* 11, nos. 8–9 (September 2007), http://offscreen.com/view/soundforum_3; Sherwin, introduction to the booklet accompanying *Optical Sound Films, 1971–2007*, London: LUX, 2008, DVD; Roisz, notes to "elesyn 15.625," https://vimeo.com/16960417; and Haswell, quoted in Curtis Roads, "Blackest Ever UPIC," liner notes to Haswell and Hecker, *Blackest Ever Black*.

53. Levin describes a few such cases in "'Tones out of Nowhere,'" 70n15.

54. Friedrich Nietzsche, "On Truth and Lies in a Nonmoral Sense," in *Philosophy and Truth: Selections from Nietzsche's Notebooks of the Early 1870s*, ed. and trans. Daniel Breazeale (Atlantic Highlands, NJ: Humanities Press, 1979), 82.

55. Lis Rhodes, "Flashback from a Partisan Filmmaker," *Filmwaves* 6 (Winter 1998–99), reprinted at http://www.luxonline.org.uk/articles/partisan(1).html and cited in Aura Satz's helpful essay "Shapes with the Sound of Their own Making," *Cabinet* 44 (Winter 2011–12): 33–39.

56. Dunford's film bears some similarity to Bruce Nauman's *Lip Sync* (1969), which focuses on the artist's mouth, upside down, repeatedly reciting the title phrase as the sound goes in and out of sync with the image. Nauman's piece owes much to the phasing technique of the composer Steve Reich, whom he had met the year prior and with whom he performed the same year.

57. In an essay on Poledna, Nora M. Alter compares *Version* to Richter's *Rhythmus* series. "Transformations of the Archive," in *After the Digital Divide: German Aesthetic Theory in the Age of New Media*, ed. Lutz Koepnick and Erin McGlothlin (Rochester, NY: Camden House, 2009), 160.

58. On the etymological connection between "dub" and "duppy," see John Corbett, "Brothers from Another Planet: The Space Madness of Lee 'Scratch' Perry, Sun Ra, and George Clinton," in *Extended Play: Sounding Off from John Cage to Dr. Funkenstein* (Durham, NC: Duke University Press, 1994), 20–21.

59. In 2004–6 Poledna screened *Sufferer's Version* alongside Deren's film in programs held at Galerie Meyer Kainer in Vienna, Richard Telles Fine Art in Los Angeles, and the 2006 Whitney Biennial in New York. In 2006 Kubelka's film was added to the program, which was screened at Witte de With in Rotterdam and Galerie Daniel Buchholz in Köln.

60. The three-channel film can be viewed at: http://www.julianrosefeldt.com/film-and-video-works/the-soundmaker-2004.

61. See Schaeffer, "Acousmatics," in Cox and Warner, *Audio Culture*, 97, and Luke

Fowler, "Transitional Words," in *8 Metaphors (Because the Moving Image Is Not a Book)*, ed. Isla Leaver-Yap (London: LUX, 2011), 17–18. On the initial title of the film, see Lee Patterson, "Cross-Collaborations," also in Leaver-Yap, *8 Metaphors*, 18.

62. Fowler, "Transitional Words," 17–18.

63. See Patterson, "Cross-Collaborations," and Fowler, "Sound Cinema: Luke Fowler in Conversation with Christoph Cox," *Ear Room* (September 4, 2011), https://earroom.wordpress.com/2011/09/04/sound-cinema-luke-fowler-in-conversation-with-christoph-cox/.

64. Fowler, in "Sound Cinema."

65. See Ed Halter, "Portrait, Landscape," in *Luke Fowler: "The Poor Stockinger" and Extracts from the Two-Frame Film Archive* [exhibition catalog], Jaffe-Friede Gallery, Hopkins Center for the Arts, Dartmouth College, April 2–May 5, 2013.

66. Fowler, in "Sound Cinema." In *Grammar*, part 3, Tsunoda is on screen for much of the film, though always shot from behind.

67. Lee Patterson, interviewed by Christoph Cox in *8 Metaphors*, 29, and quoted in *framework: afield* (blog) #293, July 18, 2010, http://www.frameworkradio.net/2010/07/293–2010–07–18/.

68. As Marcel Duchamp famously remarked in a note from *The 1914 Box*: "One can look at seeing; one can't hear hearing." Sanouillet and Peterson, *Salt Seller*, 23.

69. Toshiya Tsunoda, interviewed by Christoph Cox in *8 Metaphors*, 34, 35.

70. See Marshall McLuhan, "Visual and Acoustic Space," in McLuhan and Bruce R. Powers, *The Global Village: Transformations in World Life and Media in the Twenty-First Century* (Oxford: Oxford University Press, 1989), 35–47, reprinted in Cox and Warner, *Audio Culture*, 89–94.

71. McLuhan, "Visual and Acoustic Space," 90.

72. Castaing-Taylor and Paravel discuss the equipment and procedures used for *Leviathan* in Scott MacDonald, *Avant-Doc: Intersections of Documentary and Avant-Garde Cinema* (Oxford: Oxford University Press, 2015), 404–10.

73. Castaing-Taylor and Paravel make remarks along these lines in MacDonald, *Avant-Doc*, 408. The cast credits aptly mix the names of the fisherman with the Latin names of the fish species.

74. See Michel Serres, *Genesis*, trans. Geneviève James and James Neilson (Ann Arbor: University of Michigan Press, 1995), 13.

75. On these themes, see chap. 4.

76. Eisenstein et al., "Statement," 258.

77. See Deleuze, *Difference and Repetition*, trans. Paul Patton (New York: Columbia University Press, 1994), 56–57, 139–41, 236. For a helpful explication of this idea, see Daniel W. Smith, "Deleuze's Theory of Sensation: Overcoming the Kantian Duality," in *Essays on Deleuze* (Edinburgh: Edinburgh University Press, 2012), 89–105.

INDEX

Page numbers in italics refer to figures.